Thinking on the Edge

Thinking on the Edge

Essays by Members of the International Society for
Philosophical Enquiry

Edited by
Richard A. Kapnick
and
Aidan A. Kelly, Ph.D.

Agamemnon Press
Burbank, California
1993

About the Cover

I am that which I have been; that which I have not been, I will become.

This cover represents the mind operating on the edge of consciousness, on the edge of knowledge; always working to that transition point where everything comes together. The unknown is on one side, the doubtful is on the other, and the only certainty you have is where you are at the moment.

—Kelly Freas,
Artist

Conception, realization, and execution by Richard A. Kapnick.
Physics consultant, Kip S. Thorne, California Institute of Technology.
Data input by Alison Collier.
Technical editing by Aidan A. Kelly.
Production direction by Julie O'Ryan.
Book design by Robert Ishi.
Jacket design by Susan Shankin.
Jacket art by Frank Kelly Freas.
Line art by John Choi, Stanford University.
Typesetting by Andresen Graphic Services, Tucson, AZ.
Printing and binding by Jostens, Visalia, CA.

DEDICATION

This book is dedicated to Betty Hansen, tireless and
dedicated President of the International Society for
Philosophical Enquiry.

READ

CHAPTERS

CONTENTS

Section V. The Future of Technology.

Section VI. "There's a Method in My Madness."

HOW THIS BOOK CAME TO BE

Richard A. Kapnick, ISPE Senior Fellow,
Member of the ISPE Board of Elected Officers,
and Editor of *Telicom,* the ISPE Monthly Journal.

In 1946, Mensa came into being. A Britisher named Dr. Lance Ware was its founder. The whole idea was to found an organization that would make it easier for persons of high intelligence to find one another. There was a lot of discussion about the entrance requirements for Mensa. Dr. Ware finally settled on only one requirement: to join Mensa, one had to demonstrate an intelligence quotient (IQ) at or above the 98th percentile. That is to say, the applicant had to be in the top 2 percent of the population in terms of general intellectual functioning. If, for example, there were 200 people in your high-school graduating class, only the four smartest people might qualify for Mensa—a select group, for sure.

Over the years, the Mensa concept has spread over the entire planet. Mensa has become a worldwide phenomenon, with more than 100,000 members. It has evolved principally as a social organization, thereby fulfilling its initial objective. Most of the folks in Mensa are warm, friendly, and outgoing. About 10 percent actively participate in most of the Mensa social functions. Most of the rest seem to join as an "ego trip," to prove something to themselves or others, to learn their own intellectual level, or for a myriad of other reasons. These folks are the great "silent majority" of Mensa.

The success of Mensa has spawned more than a dozen other high-IQ organizations. Most have more stringent requirements than Mensa (although there have been several attempts to start high-IQ clubs for "the top 5 percent"). The most significant of these organizations include Intertel, The International Society for Philosophical Enquiry (ISPE), Triple 9, The Prometheus Society, and Mega.

Intertel was formed as "the legion of intelligence" for those at or above the 99th percentile of general intellectual functioning. Intertel has between 1,500 and 2,700 members worldwide (mostly in the United States). This group seems to lack strong vision and purpose. The principal focus of Intertel is the monthly newsletter, *Integra*, produced by a couple of dedicated volunteers from Ohio. There are too few members to conveniently stage regular meetings. This is mostly a problem of geography rather than of a lack of desire on the part of members to socialize.

In 1974, Chev. Dr. Christopher Harding of Queensland, Australia, founded an even higher-IQ group which he called "The Thousand." This name represented the fact that only one person in a thousand qualified. The entrance requirement was set at or above the 99.9th percentile of general intellectual functioning. Initially, 19 persons passed the test he constructed for entrance. Later this organization became known as The International Society for Philosophical Enquiry (ISPE).

The focus of the ISPE has not been on the entrance requirement, but rather on achievement of the members and on peer support for the type of accomplishments that benefit civilization. The greatest achievement of the ISPE to date is the unveiling of latent talent in a number of members who otherwise would never have recognized and developed their own abilities. The development of these gifts has allowed individual members to make meaningful contributions to mankind.

Shadowing ISPE with the same entrance requirement is the Triple 9 Society. This is strictly a "high-IQ club" with its monthly newsletter as its principal benefit to members.

The Prometheus Society sets its entrance requirement at the 99.997th percentile of general intellectual functioning. There are just over 100 members around the world. Many are also members of Mensa and the ISPE. They communicate by a monthly newsletter called *Gift of Fire*, which is produced by Monty Walker of Glendale, California.

The Mega Society takes its name from the fact that only one person in a million can qualify. The entrance requirement is set at the 99.9999th percentile. This group has 20 members, and is run by Jeff Ward of San Diego, California.

Mr. Palmer McCurdy, historian of the ISPE, provides this chart summarizing the various high-IQ groups of significance:

Society	Equivalent Percentile	Equivalent Minimum IQ	Standard Deviations
Mensa	98.0000	132	2
Intertel	99.0000	138	2.375
ISPE	99.9000	150	3.125
Triple 9	99.9000	150	3.125
Prometheus	99.9970	164	4
Mega	99.9999	170	4.375

Advancement within the ISPE is the characteristic unique to this organization. There are seven levels of membership: Associate, Member, Fellow, Senior Fellow, Senior Research Fellow, Diplomate, and Philosopher. Everyone begins at the Associate level, having provided evidence of the minimum IQ requirements to the ISPE Director of Admissions. There are seven types of accomplishments mandated by the ISPE Charter which allows members to advance. These range from written communications among members to original discoveries that benefit mankind.

To advance from Associate to full Member, one must submit evidence of three accomplishments to the ISPE Personnel Director. Once accepted, the Associate is moved to a full Membership position with suffrage. After a tenure of at least one year as Member, application can be made to upgrade to the level of Fellow. Evidence of three more accomplishments within the past year must be shown for this upgrade.

Continued advancements are then earned with at least a year of tenure at each level until the level of Diplomate is reached. Diplomate is the highest level of membership that may be earned by a member of the ISPE.

There is, however, another level of membership: Philosopher. This level cannot be earned. Rather, this highest level of membership may be spontaneously awarded without application through nomination by the Awards Committee and a vote of the enfranchised members. It is bestowed only on individuals who have achieved at least the level of "Fellow," and who, in the opinion of the Awards Committee, have made significant and outstanding contributions to civilization. Even though more than 1,000 people have joined and/or passed through the ranks of the ISPE since its founding in 1974, the level of Philosopher has been awarded only about a dozen times. The ISPE is one of the few places in the world where one can actually get credentials as a philosopher.

In March 1992, I was contemplating what I could do to advance from the level of Fellow to the level of Senior Fellow in the Society. It occurred to me that high-IQ groups are mostly vanity clubs, loaded with underachievers who validate themselves, not with accomplishments, but with a wall plaque from one or more of the high-IQ groups. These trophies tell the individual and the world how smart he really is.

It seemed to me that the real achievers of the world were out there achieving, not sitting and admiring a wall plaque. These real achievers belonged not to the high-IQ groups, but to such organizations as the American Association for the Advancement of Science, the American Academy of Science, the American Philosophical Association, and similar prestigious organizations.

How could I help motivate our ISPE membership to such lofty levels of accomplishment? Here's all this latent talent languishing for a plethora of reasons. It needed a shove to get it started. The ISPE certainly has the leadership and the structure to encourage the habit of high achievement. Yet even in this organization, most of the membership suffers from lethargy and underachievement. Most join at the Associate level and never advance beyond that stage. Very few actually take advantage of the advancement ladder and begin achieving anywhere near their potential.

The obvious answer soon struck me. All those highly respected groups that are loaded with achievers hold symposia and seminars in which the membership (and certain outsiders who are luminaries in their field) submit papers for presentation to the group. The best of these papers are subsequently published. That's how discoveries of importance to science and philosophy are made public. That's how civilization advances.

If the ISPE was to motivate its members to similar high achievement, we, too, must hold symposia in which the members presented papers which contained their discoveries and new thinking of merit. In April 1992, I mailed a call for papers to all 500 ISPE Associates and Members, as well as to 300 lapsed Members. This call proposed a symposium to be held over the July 4th weekend near San Francisco, California. This was a convenient location, since American Mensa holds an Annual Gathering (AG) of its membership at various locations around the country. The ISPE Symposium would be concurrent with the 1992 Mensa AG.

Normally, 1,000 to 1,500 Mensa members attend the AG. About six to eight of these Mensans also belong to ISPE. For several years, ISPE members who attend the Mensa AG have met informally while attending the AG. This year, I would formalize that meeting, and hold the first ISPE Symposium at which members' papers would be presented. These papers would then be published in book form for sale to the public. Voila! The ISPE would transition to a position of high esteem in the world community. At last, the ISPE could join the ranks of the most professional and respected of the world's philosophic/scientific research organizations; a lofty goal, for sure.

I thought that perhaps 10 or 15 members might submit papers for presentation. What a surprise when nearly 70 ISPE members submitted 109 papers, totaling nearly 700 pages! Fifteen ISPE members actually attended the San Francisco AG and the first ISPE Symposium. I wheeled in enough sets of all the papers submitted to give each attendee a full set. In addition, copies were made for some of the non-attending ISPE leadership. In all, this project required more than 12,000 photocopied pages. Attending members were asked to read and jury the submissions. Five members completed this project.

Subsequently, Aidan Kelly of Agamemnon Press in Burbank, California, joined the project. Dr. Kelly is one of the most respected editors of college textbooks, scientific publications, and other erudite periodicals in the world. He read and helped jury all the papers. Certain of the papers were also reviewed by Dr. Kip S. Thorne, who is head of the Magellan Space Probe project at the Jet Propulsion Laboratory in Pasadena, California, and one of the world's most respected theoretical astrophysicists. He is well-known as a person who is on the cutting edge of new thinking—the perfect person to help jury some of the more technical papers.

Here, now, for your enjoyment is the fruit of considerable labor. The papers in this book represent the best recent thinking of the members of the ISPE: the best of the papers presented at the 1992 ISPE Symposium. *Thinking on the Edge* is the first anthology of thought from any of the high-IQ societies ever to be widely published. It is a monumental achievement for our organization, and it signals the beginning of our transition to becoming one of the great philosophic / scientific research organizations in the world.

I hope that you will enjoy reading these essays, and that you will look forward to our publication of papers from the Second Annual ISPE Symposium, to be held at the 1993 Mensa AG in Orlando, Florida.

I am also happy to thank Alkis Doucakis, ISPE Special Projects Coordinator, for his help and support on this project. I am also grateful to the Trustees, officers, and members of the ISPE for their help and contributions that have made this book possible. I especially thank all those who came to the first ISPE Symposium in July 1992, those who contributed articles for this project, and those who helped jury the articles and winnow them down to our final selection. To you all, I say, live long and prosper.

RAK
London, England
January 1993

THE ISPE: SOME REFLECTIONS ON ITS EVOLVING STRUCTURE AND LEADERSHIP STYLE

Laura J. van Arragon,
Member, ISPE Board of Trustees

Most of our members are not politically inclined or even regularly active contributors. This I do not bemoan; indeed, I accept it as an important reality when we design charters (yawn) and organization charts (glaze). For many of us, our main involvement with the ISPE from one year to the next consists of reading *Telicom*. For me, living in an isolated bush town, although I subscribe to over forty publications, *Telicom* is a feast, as are, in their own inimitable way, the *Economist* and the *National Review*. It is our steadily improving forum for the exchange of ideas and discoveries, for reflection and enlightenment. The autobiographies are more than a fascinating kaleidoscope of idiosyncratic personalities and unusual accomplishments. In them, by contrast or comparison, we see reflected our own life stories, struggles, and vicissitudes. Incrementally, the thoughtful perusal of the autobiographies permits us, nay, compels us, to reflect philosophically on the significance of our lives.

The more active (and reactive) members take advantage of the opportunities to contribute to the intellectual and philosophic interchange and to serve in the various leadership roles. Our system of graded membership levels earned by achievements and contributions acts as an incentive to become active participants. The leadership roles are essentially nonpolitical: officers exist to provide structure and to facilitate; otherwise they are nonintrusive. Consequently, and also as a result of sensible editorial policies, such as refusing to provide a forum for character assassins, fomenters of trouble, and solipsist bores, the society is mercifully free from the perennial political infighting and turbulence that afflicts other groups.

Nonetheless, the ISPE has had its teething problems, its dissenters and detractors. Every three years or so, some disgruntled ego whose high intellect merely adds power to irresponsibility seizes on some minor spark of grievance, and seeks by huffing and puffing to kindle it into a major conflagration to burn down our house. Such eruptions have a wearisome predictability of tactics, duration, and outcome. Now that the dust has settled over the latest distasteful disruption, it is profitable to re-examine our goals, structure, and policies to derive or reinforce insights and conclusions.

In a typical case, the dissenter fails to persuade the Officers by reasoned argument of the justice of his cause and so resorts to pressure tactics: threats to resign, which are subsequently and disappointingly withdrawn, *ad hominem* attacks, scurrilous articles submitted to *Telicom,* limited mailings, followed by mass mailings, containing a barrage of bizarre charges and allegations, pages, nay reams, of advanced nitpicking claiming heinous malfeasance by the leadership, threats of litigation, and dire predictions that the fate of our beloved Society, if not of civilization itself, is at stake. Typically, in the later stages of the contretemps, the Officers, heedful of the sage advice of Solomon and LBJ respectively, answer not a fool according to his folly, lest he be wise in his own conceit, and don't get involved in a spraying contest with a skunk. The rest of us, amusedly, irritatedly, or resignedly, file the furious fables appropriately.

However, mud and manure, even those emanating from the fever swamps, have clinging properties, and it is beneficial to address some of the concerns and doubts that naturally arise in the minds of even discerning, judicious, and nonpartisan members.

Our society began in late 1974, when Chris Harding sent a newsletter to 19 individuals who had scored at the 99.9th percentile on his Skyscraper test. Harding soon relinquished his leadership role by nominating Steve Whiting for President and entrusting the organization to him by mid-1975. In Harding's own words:

> It was Steve Whiting who made the ISPE what it is today. What I wished for was simply to gather together people capable of doing the highest-level research work. It was Steve who organized the Society through the 'grade system,' and through his personal persistence it became highly organized. I owe him an immense debt of gratitude. I feel he expressed what most of the early members wanted. We were all tired of rag-tag groups.

Whiting drafted the first Charter, designed the structure of the Society, and articulated its goals.

Steve Whiting was a striking figure: war hero, creative and prolific inventor, business executive, long-distance motorcycle record holder, project engineer for the DEW line in Alaska, author and lecturer, and holder of numerous patents. He was a dynamic organizer and forceful leader. He was an elitist who was passionately dedicated to the ideal of service for the betterment of mankind. As a realist, he recognized that in any society, most of the work is done by a small minority of dedicated achievers who are often plagued by obstructionists and footdraggers. Despite his somewhat commandeering, take-charge style, I found him to be a charming, responsive, flexible, and communicative individual.

Soon after joining the ISPE in the spring of 1976, I suggested to Steve that membership growth would be facilitated by accepting high scores on tests other than the Skyscraper. He immediately pursued this idea, had it researched, and drafted a Charter amendment which passed in October 1976. A year later he wrote me that our three-fold membership increase was due largely to this measure. Another selection issue was the IQ versus AQ debate. Harding and Whiting rejected testing for intelligence alone in favor of testing for a broader level of ability, creativity, and condivergent thinking skills, which the Skyscraper, and its successor, the W87, did. Steve wished to "avoid the brilliant illiterates," and for a number of years the prospective members were required to score high on Harding's vocabulary tests as well as on the standardized intelligence tests. Steve wanted a membership of demonstrated outstanding intellectual and linguistic ability. I agreed with Wittgenstein's dictum that "the limits of my language are the limits of my mind," and still regret that later, in spite of strong protests, the vocabulary requirement was dropped for reasons I thought insufficiently cogent.

The democracy issue is a perennial red herring and needs some illumination or clarification. In the ISPE, new members do not have a vote. As Steve wrote in June 1980, "All of our officers agree that the ISPE is not a 'democracy' in which new and uninformed Associate Members may vote, but more nearly resembles a professional society, in which a period of internship is required before enfranchisement. That was the key to the late rebellion." The reference was to a dissident group of five who insisted that Associates be enfranchised immediately, and when they could not prevail by fair means, turned to foul (as outlined above). Steve struck an Ethics Committee of impeccable credentials to adjudicate, and the troublemakers were expelled. Forceful but effective. Soft doctors make stinking wounds. He was quite amenable to constructive disagreement and, in fact, welcomed it:

> The democratic process, as typified by parliamentary procedure, is incorporated into our Charter and its amendments, which allow for

reasonable, nonpersonal debate according to parliamentary procedure, rather than the destructive forensic debate in which character assassination is accepted.

But he was well aware of the perils of hyper-democracy:

If we did not have some screening process to inhibit the membership in general from proposing uncontrolled numbers of amendments and issues, and if we permitted discussion and debate on all issues, we should soon become a debating society, and the use of *Telicom* as a forum for the exchange of thoughts, ideas, and discoveries for the edification of all, would not be possible for lack of space.

In planning his own succession, Steve took pains to create a structure whereby the most able (as measured by tests) and the most productive (as indicated by past performance and service) of the membership would continue to hold the reins of power, and to direct the affairs of the Society, without being hampered by the unproductive squabbling, infighting, and purposelessness that often characterize similar groups. I approved of his intent, but strongly registered my concerns about possible uproar and mischief over perceptions of secretive and cabalistic individuals manipulating the Society. He fully agreed with my objections, and then set about creating a formal, constitutionally valid Board of Trustees.

We repeatedly sought to involve Harding in the decisionmaking structure and selected him as a Philosopher and Trustee. Afflicted with a debilitating illness which resulted in permanent disability status, he eventually gave the Chairman of the Board of Trustees his proxy vote on all ISPE matters, and repeatedly sent his resignation as Trustee, which at last we regretfully accepted. Some aspects of administration are by nature confidential and tactful, rather than secretive or manipulative. If, for example, as a result of a stroke, I were to lose a goodly portion of my mental faculties, and become incapable of rational decisionmaking, I have full confidence that the leadership would discreetly list me as Trustee Emeritus, rather than blazon the sad facts in a *Telicom* headline. Few members, I trust, would assume that I was the victim of a conspiracy or a palace coup.

Each of our Presidents has been competent, assertive, and forceful, has had to be, and has had the approval and support of the vast majority of members. In summary, after almost 16 years as a member, including nine as Trustee, I am satisfied that our Society is flourishing because of the inspiration of its Founder, Chris Harding, the dynamism, vision, and organization of its first President, Steve Whiting, and some exceptionally able and diligent officers and editors, including the present incumbent. Effectively to develop from a few dozen to over five hundred members has required gradual evolution of structure and style, rather than political squabbles and sudden upheavals. Such development is reflected in the revised Charter, the product of a great deal of input, experience, and energetic work over the past few years. May it serve us as well in the future as our first Charter did in those early years.

ABOUT THE ISPE

The International Society for Philosophical Enquiry (ISPE) is a nonprofit, global, scientific/philosophic organization founded in 1974 and is dedicated to advanced enquiry, original research, and creative contributions.

The contemporary "Knowledge Explosion" is far from unique in human civilizations. A predecessor and counterpart had its root in early Greek civilization (circa 530–300 B.C.) in which universities proliferated, each with an organized curriculum covering the expanding fields of information. However, to approach the frontiers of knowledge and extend them with new thoughts, ideas, discoveries, and inventions (i.e., to become a leader or participant in the advance), it became necessary for the superior intellect of that time to attend a school, academy, or institute for advanced studies and research.

The modern equivalent of the institutes for advanced studies and research of antiquity, with some of the features of the seventeenth- and eighteenth-century scientific and philosophical societies, is the International Society for Philosophical Enquiry (ISPE), founded in 1974 and having members in 27 countries.

The Society accepts standardized test scores or designated unsupervised tests for entrance. Qualification for entrance is based on present intellectual merit, rather than on one's reputation for accomplishment in the past or past academic achievements. Once in the Society, the member is encouraged to apply for promotion based upon contemporary personal achievement and contributions to the general welfare of society. Correspondence among members and publication in the Society's journal, *Telicom*, are encouraged and rewarded. *Telicom* provides a forum for member's views and intellectual production and for official proceedings, and serves to coordinate activities and disseminate information, linking the members and creating a social bond. The name of the journal comes from combining TELIC (toward a principle, goal or end; Purposeful) and COM (English abbreviation of communicate).

Written records are kept of each member's accomplishments and achievements, so that recognition may be provided by elevation to his level of membership and by other rewards and awards. One's intellectual growth and creative development are encouraged in an environment of advanced studies, research and accomplishment. At the higher levels of membership, original contributions to society in general are expected for elevation, and are continually being made and recognized. However, one may proceed at one's own pace within the Society, for it is well understood that each member has real-life obligations.

The Society is therefore an institute for advanced studies, original research, and high achievement, for which a demonstrated high level of intellect is merely an entrance requirement.

PROCEEDINGS AND GOALS

The ISPE is approved as a not-for-profit organization by the Internal Revenue Service of the United States of America under United States Code Section 501(c)(3). It is independent of government, political, religious, activist, or academic influence and funding. The Society promotes no cause, movement, fad, cult, sect, or belief except those of individual responsibility for achievement and service, from which are expected will come creative contributions, intellectual development, and achievements that will improve society. Negative and obstructional tactics are avoided, and no vindictive or ad hominem material may appear in the journal.

Yet it is expected that theories and proposals published in *Telicom* will generate debate through the process of thesis, antithesis, and synthesis, via articles from various members published in sequential issues. The process allows a member to openly debate matters of interest, to obtain spirited and well-conceived comments and rebuttals, allowing for more formal publication. The non-expert is welcomed into the debate, winning acceptance on the basis of his ability, not academic credentials.

ADMISSION

Any reputable person may apply for membership, although the Society does reserve the right to bar from membership anyone who has demonstrated a lack of agreement with the Society's goals or who may jeopardize the Society's not-for-profit status as defined by United States Code. The ISPE will not bar anyone on the basis of color, creed, nationality, race, religion, or sex.

The admission procedure begins with completion of the Application Form and submitting documentation of your score on a standard test of intellectual ability. A qualifying score will place you at the 99.9th percentile of the population, which is 3.125 standard deviations above the mean if the test scores are reported in relation to the general population. With many tests being given to a narrow segment of the population (e.g., college students applying for graduate school), the score that qualifies you for membership in the ISPE will differ from a simple determination of 99.9th percentile of those taking the test. The qualifying scores for these tests are established by the Society's Director of Testing to compensate for this factor.

Tests of intellectual ability include both intelligence quotient (IQ) and scholastic aptitude tests, for which examples of acceptable tests and qualifying scores are provided below. The list is not a complete list of the tests accepted by the ISPE.

Admissions Test for Graduate Study in Business
    (ATGSB) or (GMAT) . . . . 746 average of scores
California Test of Mental Maturity (CTMM) . . . . 150 IQ
Cattell (Verbal) . . . . 172 IQ
Graduate Record Examination (GRE) . . . . 727 average of scores
Miller Analogies Test (MAT) . . . . 89 Raw Score
Scholastic Aptitude Test (SAT) . . . . 752 Average of Scores
U.S. Army General Classification Test (AGCT)
    if taken before 1976 . . . . 157 Raw Score

(Qualifying scores are subject to change, because tests may be modified over the years, or the norming process may be reiterated.)

Please forward the application, documentation of test score, and check for the Application Fee to the Director of Admissions at the address on the Application Form. The Application Fee covers our cost of processing your application and certifying whether or not you qualify for Associate Membership.

If you do not have a test score that qualifies you, you may ask to take one of the ISPE's self-administered tests for the testing fee. The unsupervised test allows you to test yourself at your own pace, without supervision, thus allowing persons who may live at some distance from a practicing psychologist or psychometrist to qualify for membership. Applicants should be aware that there are several different methods of measuring intellectual ability, that different tests measure different aspects, and that a nonqualifying score on one test does not mean that the applicant will not qualify on another test.

Upon acceptance into the ISPE, you will receive enrollment instructions and a request for payment of the Initiation Fee and the first year's dues. (The current fee schedule is listed on the Application Form.) The Initiation Fee covers the cost of additional processing, and provides you a copy of the Charter, Membership Roster (with geographic and other cross references), Associate Member Certificate, and Identification Card. The Annual Dues include a subscription to the journal, *Telicom*, which is published 10 times a year, updates of the Membership Roster, free Certificates of Advancement (upon your promotion), and other mailings and materials as may be appropriate.

Each new enrollee will enter as an Associate Member, and be considered to have the potential to qualify for advancement to Member upon demonstrating commitment to the Society's goals via personal achievement and contributions to society. Because the ISPE is a society, not a journal subscription service, the enrollee is not considered a full member with the right to vote until promotion to Member is achieved, whereby he or she demonstrates a commitment to achievement and service to others.

If you can qualify for entrance, the ISPE ("The Thousand") may open a whole new world of opportunity for you, broadening your horizons of communication and knowledge, and perhaps encouraging you to make original and enduring contributions to humanity.

If you are in agreement with our aims and principles, and if you can accept the challenge of a high-achievement society that invites and expects your creative contributions, then you are the candidate we seek.

THE ISPE APPLICATION FORM

(You may photocopy this page, rather than tear it out of the book.)

I hereby apply for Associate Membership in the International Society for Philosophical Enquiry. Requirements for application are:

(1) A check or money order, made payable to "ISPE," in the amount of five dollars ($5.00) United States currency or equivalent as the Application Fee for membership.

(2) Documentation of my score on an adult intelligence test (i.e., an IQ test such as the Stanford-Binet or Cattell) or a test of scholastic aptitude (e.g., SAT, GRE) that indicates a 99.9 percentile level or above compared to the general population. (Total Application Fee when prior evidence is provided is $5.00.)

(3) Or request to take the ISPE unsupervised test (see below.) Testing Fee is an additional $15.00, payable at time of application. (Please send $20.00 when requesting the unsupervised test.)

Please print or type the following information:

Name _____ Age _____ Gender _____

Mailing Address _____

_____

Telephone (home or business?) _____

If mailing address (provided above) differs from your residential address (i.e., is a work address or a post office box), please enter residential address below. (Note: this is for ISPE records only. Correspondence will be sent to mailing address.) _____

Intelligence and/or Scholastic Aptitude Tests taken.

Test	Date Taken	Score
_____	_____	_____
_____	_____	_____
_____	_____	_____

_____ I cannot provide documentation and request that a copy of an unsupervised test be sent to me for my completion. I am enclosing a $15.00 testing fee in addition to the $5.00 Application Fee. If my score is sufficiently high on this test, no other test score will be required for entrance.

Highest grade/level of formal schooling completed _____

Present occupation _____

What brought the ISPE to your attention and/or prompted this application?

_____ Member Referral (Name of Member) _____

_____ Advertisement (Name and date of publication) _____

_____ Other (Please describe) _____

Is English your native language? _____ Yes _____ No
If you checked "No":

(1) What is your native language? _____

(2) At what age did you begin learning English? _____

Major interests and avocations _____

High-IQ Societies to which you belong _____

Periodicals to which you subscribe _____
(Add extra sheets as needed for a full reply.)

(This information is requested for statistical analysis, validation of testing, and recruiting procedures. It is not provided to persons outside the ISPE except as anonymous demographic statistics.)

Signature _____ Date_____

Please mail this completed Application Form and Application Fee ($5.00), with documentation of qualifying test score, or $20.00 ($5.00 Application Fee + $15.00 Testing Fee) and a request for a copy of the unsupervised test, to ISPE Admissions. You can insure our immediate response by providing a self-addressed business-size envelope (which is approximately 10 cm by 24 cm).

SEND TO: HUGH G. WHITE
ISPE DIRECTOR OF ADMISSIONS
3213 WEST KANSAS AVE.
MIDLAND, TEXAS 79701 USA

We try to process applications within two days of receipt. However, please allow two weeks for a reply.

Thinking on the Edge

Section I
The Mind

Autobiographical Sketch of Kees de Gruiter

In 1948 Holland was recovering from five years of brutal occupation during the Second World War. I was born in the aftermath of the baby boom. My parents' generation worked hard, very hard, to give their children a better future, without oppression and without hunger. My generation felt overprotected. Some rebelled, and I was certainly one of them. I did everything God forbade in the sixties, and God forbade a lot in this Calvinistic stronghold. I was thrown out of two schools and dropped out of a third. I ran away from home with my girlfriend to Scotland, where I could get married without my parents' consent. I learned to enjoy fighting authority. I wanted to be a writer, but not until I was good and ready. I worked in warehouses and on building sites during the day and studied at night. I taught English, managed educational experiments, and founded a cultural magazine and a design firm. I was on the boards of national and local radio and TV stations. I made a career of getting bored as soon as I was successful in a career, and my relationships tended to follow the same path. My two children are the only constant factor in my life. I'm empathic, intelligent, witty, and attractive enough to be appreciated by friends and lovers, but I have always been an outsider, a visitor from outer space, trying to figure out what the human species is all about. I love to travel, to watch in amazement how people counteract their beliefs. I am beginning to understand.

CHAPTER 1

THE LAST BUS TO KYRENIA, OR THE EVOLUTIONARY FORCES OF THE ORGANIC SELF

Kees de Gruiter

In 1974 the Mediterranean island of Cyprus was invaded by Turkish troops, who took possession of more than a third of the territory. Forced migration created a strict division of the population into Greek Cypriots, who now live south of the treaty line, and Turkish Cypriots, who live in the north. It was the first example in recent history of what is fast becoming a worldwide trend of fragmentation and separation. A search for the driving forces behind this trend has led me to the discovery of the organic self and its evolutionary implications.

CIVIL WAR IN CYPRUS

When I drove through Turkey in the summer of 1975, a red dotted line on the map drew my attention. It was the car ferry from Mersin, Turkey, to Famagusta, Cyprus. It appealed to my girlfriend and me. We knew vaguely what was going on, and we decided to take a look. The terminal in Mersin was desolate. The chief of customs played backgammon with an old man. "Cyprus is beautiful," the customs officer told us, "and we have just liberated it. The boat sails tomorrow and I will be on duty." That night he offered us dinner with lots of lamb and raki (the national liquor) in the mountains over the city. He gave us two hundred German marks and a shopping list for whiskey and cigarettes. We had to buy these in the tax-free shop; he would be the one to check our baggage and once on board we were to place the loot in his cabin, behind the door. Everything

3

went according to plan. On the ferry were only Turks, and during our stay on the island we didn't see a single tourist.

That summer, almost a year after the invasion, gunfire could still be heard in Cyprus, not much, usually late at night and far away. The soldiers were nervous. At roadblocks young Turkish boys in uniforms pushed their guns through the window and told us in trembling voices to turn back. They had no idea how to deal with a little Citroën with a Dutch licence plate. "But we just came from that direction," we would lie, "and we have to be back there before dark." They would pretend to discuss the matter with a superior and then force us at gunpoint in the direction we desired. The Norwegians of the UN forces were not so young and were less nervous. "I wouldn't go there, sir. Only yesterday they were shooting out there." When the next day we approached the same roadblock from the other side, the same warning was given.

I began to enjoy being in the middle of a fading war. It appeared to be a game. Not a single traffic sign had less than five bullet holes. The windshields of local buses were pierced without exception. "Look at this," I said to my girlfriend in a hotel room in Nicosia, "a grenade has gone through the facade, right through the bathroom door and here in the back it must have made this hole in the wall." It was a miracle the air-conditioning had any effect with so many holes.

It was scorchingly hot. On the hottest days, around noon we chose a bank to cash in a Postbank check. We knew it was impossible on this side of the treaty line, but it took the clerks at least an hour to find out. That time we spent in cool leather and conditioned air. By the time we left the bank the worst heat would be over.

We couldn't find a map of the island anywhere. Later we understood that all existing maps had been destroyed because the names of towns were in Greek. The rewriters of history had not yet arrived at the subject of topography. We drove around at random without knowing where the Turkish part ended and the Greek began, but being close to the treaty line was something that couldn't possibly escape attention.

THE FISHERMAN AND THE BUS DRIVER

Cyprus has beautiful beaches, beautiful bays. Most hotels had been under fire and were empty. They weren't completely ruined, but each bullet leaves an impressive imprint on white plastered concrete. In a bend of the coastal road we saw a picturesque fishing village basking in white on a turquoise background. It was very quiet. There was no one there. It seemed as if everyone had stopped what they were doing and walked out to greet a prodigal son, or witness the hatching of a dinosaur egg. Windows and doors were ajar. Tables were set. Here and there the door of a well-filled refrigerator was open . . .

Suddenly I became aware that something had to be very wrong. Lizards, there were lizards everywhere. They rushed off wherever we trod. They are friendlier than rats, mice, or pigeons: they don't look as if they spread disease, and their reactions are as predictable as a shadow's: always away from you. But they are a sign of decay just as well. There was really no one there, and a closer look showed that everyone had left quite a while ago, and in a hurry. They hadn't taken anything with them.

The harbor was empty. The fishing boats had all gone. For the rest, the village looked like it had been attacked by a second-generation neutron bomb, a type that goes beyond destroying life and makes it disappear as well. After the astonishment, a sad and uncomfortable feeling crept over me. Suddenly the war game was over. I had to get out of there immediately. After we climbed back to the road, we were silent. We heard a moped approaching. The driver stopped and walked toward the bench we were sitting on. "They have all gone," he said. "One day they got in their boats in a hurry and sailed away. These were the lucky ones."

He was a Turkish Cypriot bus driver and this had been one of his stops on his way to Kyrenia. Now no one wanted to get on or off here. And the destination of his bus was now called Girne, the Turkish name for Kyrenia. He was sad about it, and in a clumsy way he tried to apologize. He had known most of the people in the village. They were Greek Cypriots and about to be captured by the Turkish army. They all sailed away to Limassol. Most of the Greek Cypriots fled to the south; many others were killed or had their villages turned into concentration camps. "But it had to happen," he said. "They were about to do the same to us. We could not live together. The Greek Cypriots treated us as second class, like dirt." For a moment there was anger in his voice, but it turned back to sadness when he pointed out that Turkish Cypriots are not Turks and that the hordes of corrupt illiterates that invaded the island from the mainland were bad for Cyprus and bad for all Cypriots.

THE ONSET OF FRAGMENTATION

The bus driver said goodbye, started his moped, and left me behind with a puzzle that took almost fifteen years to solve. An hour later, at a deserted beach, I got into an argument with my girlfriend over nothing. I walked away and jumped off a rock, sprained my ankle, and cried. "It had to happen," he said. He didn't say it was God's will, or Allah's. He himself believed it had to happen, even though he was now worse off than before. His apology sounded like he had taken part in commiting the atrocities himself and could not recall why. He didn't give a reason. He felt it in his guts. No more and no less.

Before I visited Cyprus, I had been in Lebanon in 1969 while heavily armed Palestinians paraded the streets of Beirut, which at the time was still in one piece. Later I found myself in Israel, where the deserted mud houses of Jericho gave me the same eerie feeling that I got in the nameless fishing village on the northern Cyprus coast. I drove around in Northern Ireland where every citizen seemed to be on constant alert. And wherever I talked to people, they convincingly claimed that they were right about the others. Not even King Solomon could settle a dispute where both women claiming a child were *rightfully* its mother.

When the Azeris and the Armenians clashed in 1988, it finally sank in. I saw the big picture. Historians show trends, but in their descriptions they rationalize them in terms of religion, nationality, and economy, or they personalize them into the whims of rulers and the charisma of revolutionaries. I propose that it is not the leader who incites rebellion. It is the people who pick a leader to coordinate the realization of their desire. The people may not be conscious of the desire; the desire may not be reasonable; it may be destructive or even self-destructive. But some force inside them tells them to follow. Many Azeris and Armenians must be overpowered by such forces, and the bus driver must have felt a similar sensation.

History offers no reliable tools to forecast trends. Every nanosecond, billions of events take place in every cubic millimeter. A hundred miles of library shelves cannot contain the essence of the magnitude of events and their interactions that took place in the last 10,000 years in the whole world. The study of history is like homeopathy: you take out all the content, and the imaginary imprint of a theoretical residue must make you understand why things are the way they are. If you believe one absent ingredient can cure you, why not believe that one of the many other absent ingredients did the trick? On top of that, even the insignificant residue that remains is not objectively filtered. It is shaped by intentions for the future. The history textbooks in Greece and Turkey do not agree on the events of 1974 in Cyprus.

The weather is much simpler than history: the heat of the Sun, the absorption and reflection of that heat by the Earth's surface, and the physical reaction of air and water to the changes in temperature is all there seems to be to it. Still, we are unable to record enough data to make reliable predictions for the near future. History will not provide us with any insight into the future if the homeopathic method of simplifications is used. History is a great instrument to build a nation, to bring cohesion, to give people the comforting idea that there is a comprehensible framework in which they have a place and a function, but it provides no insights in the present and the future. Why can the peoples of Cyprus, Israel, and Northern Ireland not live together? After all, they're all human beings. They use history to support each of their goals, but it fails to explain the hatred.

THE HISTORY OF THE WORLD

I knew there must be a driving force behind the trends of history, and I was determined to find the essence of that force. In 1988 I started out by assuming that fragmentation would be a worldwide trend and that it would not stop until every tribe had fenced itself in and the others out. From this assumption I developed a model for the history of the world.

When mankind emerged as a species, the whole Earth was available; so they *dispersed,* killing competing species where necessary. As the attractive hunting and gathering grounds got more crowded, the stronger tribes would *eliminate* the weaker and thus gain ground. This was evolution through the principle of the survival of the fittest. Now I introduce an active phase in the will to survive: the *conquest.* By conquering another tribe, the valuable elements in the culture and genetic material of that tribe could be absorbed. The conquered were no longer eliminated. The weaker warriors might still be killed, but only up to the point of surrender. Their women would be blessed with the offspring of the victors. Rising and falling empires, migration and colonialism have provided strong cultures with new blood, and spread the gospel of the modern society among the weaker cultures. We have now reached the end of the stage of conquest and absorption, and tribes are beginning to *retract* to their own little territories, ridding themselves of alien elements.

This four-phase development of mankind (dispersion, elimination, conquest, and retraction) makes sense from an evolutionary point of view; it creates progress in evolution. But there is one puzzling element. If the more advanced tribes colonized others with the *purpose* of blending cultures and genetic material, it suggests that the human species *gives direction* to its own evolution. It suggests that mankind has taken control over the evolutionary forces.

Now that the era of absorption through conquest is coming to an end, the human species is retracting. There have been many regroupings and migrations of tribes in the past 10,000 years. Empires have collapsed, and only a short time ago, at the beginning of this century, the map of Europe looked as fragmented as it is beginning to look today. Yet a dramatic change has set in. The desire to be independent as a tribe may always have existed, but it used to be combined with the desire to be powerful, to control others, to force the invader's culture on the conquered. Throughout this conquering and absorbing stage, values have gradually become more universal, judicial systems have become more alike, universal equality has grown.

But the global scale is too big for the individual to cope with. The feeling of solidarity within a community usually dictates that each member feels responsible for the others. They will not let someone die from starvation; they will provide an education for the children whose parents are unable to. It is physically and mentally impossible to expand that feeling of responsibility to a global population of billions. Imperialism has succumbed to the concept of solidarity overflow. In a way it is the universal acceptance that all men are equal that is putting an end to the feeling of solidarity among mankind.

GLOBAL FRAGMENTATION

The mess we are in now results from the overlap of the end of the era of conquests, and the beginning of the era of retraction: a temporary confusion that comes with the reprogramming of our drives. The virus of modern society is spread. To do its work, it no longer needs the presence of the conquerors who brought it. The period of transition is bloody, and it will become bloodier. People will not want to leave their homes without a fight, and yet many will be forced to give them up.

The population of the world will continue a process of moving toward small homogenous units of people who feel that they belong together. It is hard to define "small" here. It is my guess that the emotions of tribal solidarity can't cope with more than ten to twenty million people. A tribe with strong historic ties, a strong economy, a good infrastructure, and well-developed communications systems will be able to extend solidarity further than a tribe which is less developed in these areas.

"Belonging together" may even be harder to define. The lines will not be drawn along physical features or ethnic origin. If a person is sensitive to the organic resonance of a tribe, he will be sucked in, regardless of race or family name. This means that foreigners who have assimilated will be regarded as having been adopted by the tribe. Here assimilation does not mean total loss of the culture and values of the land of origin, but the gut feeling that the solidarity is with the adoptive tribe, and not with the tribe of origin, even if the two tribes went to war.

The main reason for a tribe to close itself off from another is to rebuild a social structure. A country can split up peacefully, and the new neighbors can develop excellent relations. In this ideal situation, there would be no trade barriers, and there would be "intertribal" agreements on such items as care for the environment. I hope that such peaceful separation might sometimes take place, but it is unlikely to be general. On several levels there will be resistance: often the separations will be violent, sometimes tending toward genocide. The Serbian military command uses the term *ethnic cleansing* for a violent action to rid an area of non-Serbians. CNN helps us pick up the jargon and accept the activity it denotes as a fact of life.

When fragmentation is complete, the citizens of these new states will no longer feel any responsibility for what people across the border do to themselves and each other. It will not be the end of wars, however. Global interests, such as access to raw materials and care for the environment, will still suffice to cause conflicts. States with common interests may join forces to reach these goals. But such conflicts will be solved with *surgical actions,* which will no longer involve any desire to occupy the defeated or to enforce human rights in the area.

The media now focus on the tribal warfare of Europe, but those clashes may be friendly compared to what is to be expected in Africa and Asia. The European Community provides a practical intermezzo to regionalization, during which people have the oppurtunity to lose the fixation on the big nation states. Every European tribe also has something to fall back on: a history, a place to live, and an economy that is capable of providing the basic needs. But in Asia, Africa, and South America the future is gloomier. Overpopulation, poverty, lack of arable land, epidemics, and historical confusion will add to the human catastrophe of tribal hostility.

North America is another story. It will be confronted with the disastrous effect of the total absence of history. The United States is too big to continue as one nation. The federal structure gives some respite, but even if each state became autonomous, they all have their own internal time bomb. The clashes between "tribes" have already begun. The people of northern California appear to be actively involved in creating a North California. I am afraid that these sentiments will ultimately lead to a period of bloody fights, forced repatriations, and the erection of concentration camps, and will eventually end in a new patchwork of states and reservations.

I predict an environment of total madness. Families who have been good neighbors for generations will suddenly develop a hatred that will not subside until each of the families is safe within its own tribe, behind its own fence. This can be explained only in terms of the evolutionary function of such madness. Apparently the bus driver's guts were able to make the bus driver do seemingly undesirable things to serve evolution. This indicates that he plays an active role in giving direction to evolutionary processes without being consciously involved. From these observations I derived the concept of the *organic self.*

THE ORGANIC SELF

An organism can be described in terms of molecules, DNA, and genetic codes, but it can also be described in terms of life. Every organism has a will to survive. During the process of evolution, there may have been organisms without a *will to survive,* but it is not hard to understand why they became extinct. The will to survive is the will to do whatever is necessary for the species to survive, where procreation, care for offspring, and sometimes care for the tribe, override the craving for individual longevity. For a will to survive that has become actively involved in giving direction to evolution, I introduce the term *organic self.* Examples of active involvement are the older chimpanzee who trails behind the group to let himself be caught by the lion, thus giving the rest of the group the opportunity to flee to safety. Or the lion who allows her new mate to kill the cubs of her defeated old mate so that she will be ready sooner for the conception of newer, possibly fitter, offspring.

Although the bulk of survival takes place according to Darwinian principles, the organic self has influence on behavior and on the genetic code—the more advanced the organism, the more influence the organic self has. Some saltations might be explained as a successful attempt by the organic self to react to changing circumstances. The organic self holds the code of behavior and timing that have come about through natural selection, and it can pass this information on to other members of the same species.

If natural selection guarantees the emergence of organisms that adapt to new circumstances, and if these circumstances can vary only within certain extremes, one organism must logically emerge at some time which can either survive these extremes or control the circumstances. This organism no longer needs mutations for survival; so mutations either add to the variety or prove to be unfit and disappear. Species which follow the rules of evolution become extinct completely, except for the few fit mutations and their offspring. Of species which evolve beyond the grasp of evolutionary forces, the mass remains, except for unfit mutations. The organic self of mankind appears to have stepped through the invisible wall of evolution. The ability to control the circumstances is typical for *homo sapiens.* Mankind is now even entering the realm of repairing unfit mutations through genetic manipulation.

On each side of the wall survival is possible only through progress. Our organic self has developed into an intelligent, state-of-the-art survival mechanism. So the human organic self is not a collection of old instincts and reflexes, of patterns of behavior that we have inherited from far ancestors. It can actively select our mates and take care of our offspring by providing lust and love; it can defend the family and the tribe by providing aggression and self-sacrifice; it can regulate the survival of the strongest tribes by providing hatred. Even a smart organic self arrives at a boundary if the body it is in has only muscles, reproductive organs, senses, and reflexes. Without creativity, without reasoning, without the apparatus of a conscious self, there is no progress beyond a certain stage. So our organic self needed the apparatus of the conscious self as a tool, in order to grow to its next evolutionary stage. When a mutation brought the circuitry for consciousness, the first specimen of homo sapiens was born.

THE CONSCIOUS SELF VS. THE ORGANIC SELF

A comparison: consider two apes. The first uses a stick to reach the food. The idea doesn't occur to the second ape; so we call the first one smarter. It was his organic self which came up with the idea to use a tool. Compare an ape and a human. We say the human is smarter, because he *is* a conscious being. We are convinced that his smartness *is* his conscious self. But that doesn't make sense. Consider again the two apes. Would we say that of the two apes, the stick is the smartest? No, of course not! We would say that the ape who uses a stick is the smartest.

In this example it is easy to accept the stick as a tool. It takes a leap of the imagination to perceive consciousness as a tool. What makes people the most advanced organism in evolution is the degree of development of their organic self. Having a conscious self is certainly a distinctive feature, but then all species have distinctive features. That is why they are called species. Equipped with a conscious self, humans certainly became smarter, but then they also became smarter when external storage of information was acquired in the form of the ability to write.

There is a clear hierarchy: our organic self sends directives to our conscious self, and not vice versa. Our organic self makes use of all the information that is received by our senses, or produced and processed by our conscious self. The organic self knows the meaning of life. It has a clear goal: the survival of the species, through creating evolutionary progress. To do this, the organic self needs the conscious self to perform certain tasks, just as it needs the reproductive system or the heart to perform other tasks.

The conscious self can record information, even outside the brain, and pass it on to others. It can reason; it can creatively combine information into new concepts. It is a very powerful tool for the control of the environment in which the species must survive. The ability to reason functions only if the conscious self can *make sense.* The term "conscious" implies that our conscious self forms a self-sufficient system, which can give meaning to its own existence. This is only partly true. Our conscious self *thinks* that it gives meaning to its own existence, but is in fact controlled without realizing it.

Our organic self does not want our conscious self to know what it is up to. It has a hidden agenda, and it leaves us in the dark about its real intentions. It does not even want us to know it exists. We are supposed to think that *we* take independent decisions. It leaves us guessing about the meaning of life. Our organic self has a resemblance to the stereotype of the unscrupulous Mafia uncle, who completely controls his righteous nephew. The nephew does everything to serve his uncle's purposes, but he is unaware of this. He truly believes that his behavior is dictated by reason and high ethics. If unreasonable or unethical actions are required, the uncle makes sure the nephew will be so blinded by family solidarity that the moral code is instantly rewritten and now includes pillage and murder.

Our organic self allows our conscious self a certain amount of freedom, but whenever necessary the leash can be shortened, or control can be taken over completely.

ORGANIC COMMUNICATION

The organic self of one person communicates with the organic selves of others through the same channels as our conscious self, and it uses the same information. The organic self communicates independently of the conscious self. The result of such messages between organic selves varies from the "uncontrolled" shiver when the eyes meet the eyes of an attractive representative of the opposite sex, to getting caught up in mob behavior. When a person is affected by mob behavior, feels drawn into the group and modifies his behavior to serve the purpose of the group, seemingly without question, a strong form of communication between organic selves is going on.

The combined organic selves of the individuals in any kind of group (e.g., during the worldwide protest against nuclear weapons) can create a *resonance* that coerces the individual into action. So the individual's organic self is "set" to the same goals and amplifies the same resonance toward other potential members of the group. If this is true, it provides an explanation for compulsive behavior, for emotions that "come over us." It would explain how educated peace-loving Serbians can suddenly turn into "unreasonable" creatures full of hatred. It would explain why a young man is willing to die for his country, when we would intuitively expect his organic self to want to raise a family.

Organic communication is the basis of actions that people take to serve the need for evolutionary progress. The bus driver's organic self received signals, instructions, from other members of his tribe. These signals were not transmitted by a tribal self as such, but by the resonance that was created by the organic selves of members of his tribe who had come to an agreement about a line of action. This line of action was not given by a divine plan. Although our organic self may be "smarter" than our conscious self, it is still no more than the will of an organism to survive. It cannot look into the future. It cannot be certain of the effects of its actions.

Organic communication is responsible for more than destructive action. Between individuals it regulates infatuation, lust, and love. It is responsible for most of the things we do that our conscious selves find hard to explain. It makes us receptive to religion. It stimulates us in the tough process toward equality of the sexes. Perhaps the emotions that music and art invoke in us are reactions not of the conscious self but of the organic self.

THE PARADOX

The organic self can and must keep its existence and its agenda hidden from the conscious self; yet it is reasoning by my conscious self that had led me to these conclusions. I have no proof. The organic self has not revealed itself to me. I am not a mutation, capable of seeing through the machinations of my own soul. I want to delve further, possibly with the help of scholars in the many academic fields that relate to this subject. Many philosophers, biologists, psychologists, psycho-analysts, polemologists, ecologists, neurologists, and others have published on the mystery of mankind, and I do not claim that I have studied them all.

When in the middle ages the simple observation sank in that the Earth was not the center of the universe, it suddenly made sense of the absurd calculations of astronomers. It is my feeling that Freud, Fromm, Vroon, and many others have picked the wrong center when they contemplated mankind. I am aware that making this claim must be the pinnacle of conceit, but it is meant as the humble effort of an innocent bystander who thinks that the scientists are holding the blueprints upside down.

For many years I have watched people and peoples. I have read between many lines to find the forces that make people do what they do. I have always kept searching for the force behind tribalism and patriotism. I am intrigued by the process that makes people join forces around something they decide to have in common. The mass hysteria or biofeedback or organic resonance that can be created around idols in music, sports, or politics frightens me. I feel physical revulsion when people try to make me join in a polonaise at an innocent party. Maybe I am a mutation, with an allergy for group behavior. I do not say that I disapprove; often I feel that I must be missing something. It must have been this combination of fascination and revulsion that made me come up with the concept of the organic self.

The paradox remains. It puts me in the same position as Cassandra, who predicted the downfall of Troy. If I am right about the reluctance of the organic self to fill us in on our mission, I shall not be believed. If I am wrong, I shall not be believed either.

CASSANDRA'S WARNING

My perception of an evolutionary phase and its effect on the near future is either true or false. If it is true, it is something that cannot be averted. In contrast to the predictions of the Club of Rome (about the shrinking resources and the environmental destruction), my prediction is not meant as a doombreaker. The Club of Rome was hoping to ensure the developments necessary to falsify their own predictions. I am afraid there is nothing we can do to stop the fragmentation of the world. I am one of the lucky ones. I live in Holland, and I am Dutch. I "belong" here and my country is not occupied, nor is it keeping other peoples under control against their will.

To the people who are engaged in foreign policy I can say this: Forget a "world order" which is based on nation states. Do not support forces that want to keep states intact. That will only prolong the misery. Do not interfere in struggles for independence, because that will only cost more lives. If your electorate expresses solidarity with a threatened tribe and forces you to action, be swift and do no more than separate the warring tribes. Be like the old-fashioned schoolmaster who separates fighting children without even beginning to listen to their stories about who started the fight.

In 1974 the Turkish army invaded Cyprus, a foreign country. They came to "help" the Cypriots who spoke their language, but they really had no business there. They have robbed many Greek Cypriots of their possessions and their livelihood; to this day the Greek Cypriots hate them for it. But looking back, after almost twenty years, the strict separation of the island may have been the only solution, and today the parties are talking about normalization of relations.

To the people who are engaged in domestic politics I can say this: if the electorate forces you into chauvinist activities, just don't do it. Step down. Once it starts, you cannot stop it. You will only corrupt yourself and fool yourself if you cling to power for too long. If a tribe within your borders wants to split off, let them. If members of your tribe get trapped on the territory of another tribe, bring them home or leave them to sort things out where they are. Trying to keep empires intact with the pretence of looking after the interests of members of your tribe would be a disastrous anachronism.

To the people who find themselves in the wrong tribe I can say this: Try to put yourself up for adoption. Master the language and the culture of the land you live in. Assimilate or go home. I am painfully aware of how politically incorrect it is to say this. And my heart bleeds for those who are not in the position to do either. The Gypsies of eastern Europe, to name one tribe, have nowhere to go, and nobody wants them. The Jews who got trapped in Germany before the Second World War had nowhere to go. The foresight of the Jews who survived the Nazis of Europe has now given them a home. They were just in time, and I must admit that it took me a long time to realize that.

To the people who get caught up in the organic resonance of tribalism, the mass hysteria of patriotism, or the biofeedback of xenophobia, I can say nothing. Talking to them is useless. To negotiate is self-deception.

To the people in business I can say this: Multinational is in; global advertising is out. The world is no longer one market. But the small scale of individual economies and the global scale of technological progress will make it necessary to not only have free trade between tribes, but allow "multitribal" corporations. They will have to learn to be truly global. So McDonald's must disassociate from the American way of life, of which it is now a symbol. The whole concept of the American way of life will be obsolete in less than twenty years. Companies like Shell and Mercedes Benz are the cynical examples of survival. For years they have been targeted for supporting apartheid by staying in South Africa. But when Nelson Mandela had his first public appearance, it was in a red Mercedes, donated by the factory, and the tank was most likely filled by Shell.

To the people in the arts and sciences I can say this: There is very little you can do to stop the madness. Try to stay out of it if you can. There is a paradox in my theory, just as there is a paradox in the ethics of evolution. You cannot condemn the wolf for devouring a furry bunny. If this is an essential phase in evolution, how can we condemn the people who commit the atrocities that will take place in the name of evolution? We can and we must! Our morals, our ethics, our respect for life, our whole ability to judge, belong to the realm of our conscious self. Knowledge about our organic self is useless in the defence of atrocities. A subject of the Land of the Brave cannot use the laws of the Evil Empire for his defence.

Biographical Sketch of Stephen B. Wehrenberg

Steve Wehrenberg, Senior Research Fellow, has been a member of the ISPE since 1980, and was Personnel Consultant from 1990–1992. He holds a Ph.D. and an M.A. in organizational psychology, and an M.B.A. and Bachelor's degrees in Business and Electronics Engineering. Steve is a manpower planner for the U.S. Coast Guard, where he has been an advisor to top human-resource executives for more than 12 years. As an independent consultant, Dr. Wehrenberg has worked with government agencies, volunteer organizations, and companies ranging from a single entrepreneur's startup to AT&T.

In his spare time, Steve developed a graduate course in strategic human-resource planning for The George Washington University, where he teaches in the Administrative Sciences and Psychology Departments. Many articles by him have appeared in *Personnel Journal,* where he was contributing editor for more than ten years.

THE TASKS OF PARENTING

Stephen B. Wehrenberg

Ever had a conversation like this with your six-year-old?

"Gee, Dad . . . why can't I go out and play?"

"Because you were late for supper last night, and the rule is you can't go outside tonight."

"Aw c'mon, Dad. I promise I'll be in on time today!"

"I'm sorry, Bobby. You know the rules."

"Gee whiz! Rules, rules, rules! Why do we have to have all these rules!?"

"Because . . . uh . . . because . . . I said so, that's why! Now go play with the dog or something."

Bobby has posed a question that is guaranteed to frustrate any parent. Few of us have a good answer. There are hundreds of books that tell us what to do and how to do it, but the question here is *why*. Is there an underlying framework that can help make sense of the guidance we give our children as they grow? If you get confused trying to sort out the child-care advice you get, think how your child feels when faced with hundreds of seemingly unconnected, perhaps even contradictory, bits of advice and direction—rules.

The rule invoked in the dialog above is neither independent nor arbitrary. It is related to much broader concepts, such as the idea that people are ultimately responsible for their actions, or that people can and must predict the outcomes of their decisions. These broad concepts may be exactly what we are looking for—the rationale behind the rules, the real goals that we are trying to achieve with our children. What are these tasks? The four below may be a starting point.

"THERE WILL BE A TOMORROW"

The first task is to help our children realize that there will be a tomorrow, that sometimes we have to make sacrifices for future gains.

"Would you rather have this stick of gum now, or a banana split after dinner?" Which would your youngster choose? The moment is now. There is no tomorrow. Parents are frustrated when their children repeatedly take short-term gains at the expense of the long term.

If young Bobby is saving his money for a birthday present for his five-year-old girlfriend, and later in the week spends it all at the ice-cream truck, what do you do when he comes to you to float a loan? Sometimes you have to be tough. Assuming the child knows the rules beforehand, no loan. But you still have to engineer a positive experience to show the benefits of postponing gratification.

"I can't loan you the money this time, but let's see what we can do to keep this from happening again. Tell you what—you get three dollars every week for doing your chores. For every week you give me a dollar to put away for you, I will add a dollar to it. At the end of four weeks you have eight dollars tucked away for emergencies like your friend's birthday."

There are other ways to approach this. Question your child on decisions. Help him or her think ahead. "What if" discussions are helpful, and can occur anywhere, for example, in the car on the way to a softball game. After hearing a story about Johnny getting in trouble for calling a friend a name, you might try this script:

"What if Johnny called you a name?"

"I'd punch him!"

"Then what?"

"He would cry and tell his mother."

"Then what?"

"His mother would call you."

"Then what?"

"You would get mad and make me stay in my room for the rest of the day."

"Would it be worth it?"

"No."

"What could you do instead of punching him?"

This process of generating and testing alternatives without risk may contribute to the child's ability to think ahead to the future before taking action. The key is not to judge the alternatives. One lesson at a time!

"YOU ARE NOT THE CENTER OF THE UNIVERSE"

The second task is to help your child accept that he or she is not the center of the universe.

"Gail, your sister told me that you hurt her feelings by calling her a name in front of her friends."

"No, Mom. I didn't hurt her feelings."

This sounds innocent enough, but I suspect that Gail really believes what she said. It is hard for her to realize, at age five or so, that other people have ideas or feelings that are different from her own. Small children tend to think of themselves as being the focus of everything. Although an infant learns that when Mom goes out she will eventually return, the feeling of egocentricity remains well into the teen years.

A friend's behavior may be considered only with respect to oneself, without realizing that someone else may have a different, equally valid view.

"She thinks Bobby is cute? No, she doesn't! I think he's goofy. She can't really like him!"

In other words, "she can't possibly have an opinion different from mine; after all, mine is the only opinion that counts . . . in fact, my opinion isn't an opinion, it's a fact!"

How will you know when the child begins to overcome this? Perhaps the most concrete indicator is when the child recognizes that other points of view exist, and may even be valid. "She really does like Bobby? Well, I don't understand why—she must see something in him that I don't." Although this may not seem like much, it implies some level of tolerance and acceptance of the validity of others' ideas

In younger children, the indicator may be something as simple as respecting the property rights of their playmates. Asking permission before borrowing sister's crayons, sharing of toys, agreeing to play soccer after showing up at the field with a football—all of these indicate that the child understands that there are other ideas, other people besides himself or herself.

Whenever possible, parents can emphasize the idea that other people have ideas and feelings. One way to help children grasp this is to connect acceptance of others' ideas and feelings to consequences, and offer constructive feedback and sincere praise or a reward whenever the child makes the right move.

"Would it hurt your feelings if I called you silly names in front of your friends? Like Dumpling?"

"Mom! You said you wouldn't call me that anymore!"

"Oh? Would it hurt your feelings? I bet that's just how your sister felt when you called her freckle-face."

"I didn't mean to hurt her feelings" (an inkling of acceptance).

"I know, sweetheart, but sometimes the things you do and say affect other people besides yourself. Let's go talk about it over a cookie."

Once the child begins to understand the basics, more complex ideas can be addressed, all leading to the conclusion that other people's ideas and feelings deserve consideration.

"CONFLICT HAPPENS, AND YOU CAN MANAGE IT"

Most parents would agree that resolving conflict is not a strong point for young children. Usually, you have to intervene. Since the potential for conflict is everywhere, and you won't always be around to intervene, helping children learn to manage on their own is an important task.

If a child wants something belonging to another child; if two kids see something in different ways, particularly if they haven't learned to con- sider the opinions of others; if a child is unsure of his or her own role and the roles of others in a given situation; or if two children are trying to accomplish different things—conflict can result. How do children react? Typically, they run away, fight, find someone to team up with, appeal to higher authority ("Dad, Lester won't let me play with his firetruck, and he used my bicycle yesterday and it's not fair!"), or last, if at all, confront the conflict constructively. Of all the possible reactions to conflict, con- frontation is usually the only one that can lead to a lasting, positive resolution. It is also the most difficult to achieve.

The first step is for the children to realize that something is wrong. Parents can be helpful here. "Are you guys arguing again? Well, let's hear both sides."

After each has expressed his or her position, calmly restate them. "Okay, let me make sure I understand this . . ." This teaches the chil- dren the importance of first dealing with the emotion in the situation and the value of making sure that each at least understands the opposing position.

In helping the children reach a compromise, you must show them that both must give up something in order to gain.

"Lester, what could Sylvia do for you that would convince you to let her play with your firetruck?"

"Sylvia, what would you be willing to do for Lester if he let you play with his firetruck?"

Once you have helped your children work through a conflict situation, resist the temptation to intervene too early. Don't jump in to referee unless no other strategy will work. If you always arbitrate, they may never learn to resolve conflict in any way.

You will know you have been successful at this task when, in the middle of an argument between two kids, you hear "Wait a minute—why are we arguing?" or "I'll let you use my bicycle if I can play with your truck." These aren't as successful as consensus, but at least nobody is bleeding!

"YOU ARE RESPONSIBLE FOR YOUR OWN ACTIONS"

By far the most difficult task of parenting is to help children accept personal responsibility for their actions and decisions. The last time our daughter was late for dinner, her reason was "I lost my watch." The time before, "It wasn't my fault, Billy wouldn't give my books back." And don't forget this classic: "My ball rolled down the hill and fell in the creek so we built a raft so we could get it and the raft turned over and we got wet and Billy's Mom put our clothes in the dryer . . ."

Children will naturally blame the whole world before they accept the idea that something stemmed from their own action, and that their action was really their own choice. There are many situations over which our children have no control, but most outcomes can be traced back to a personal decision of some sort, a decision to act in a certain way.

If children do not understand that they are responsible for the results of their actions, they may develop a sense of dependency or helplessness, a feeling that "no matter what I do, it won't matter." This is pretty serious stuff. Only when children accept the fact that their actions affect their own future will they be able to think ahead, to plan, to achieve dreams. A child who never develops a sense of personal responsibility will be reacting to situations instead of making things happen.

How can parents help? First, whenever a notable event occurs to your child, positive or negative, try to establish a connection between what he or she did and the event itself. For example, if your daughter comes home with a gold star for doing her first-grade homework assignment, be sure to point out how smart she was to work so hard the previous night.

From age five, my son was responsible for rolling the garbage can to the end of the driveway twice a week. The first time he forgot, I did not absolve him of his responsibility. I simply told him that he would have to figure out some way to get rid of the garbage. After a few unsanitary or illegal proposals, he finally contracted with me to take him to the dump (his idea!) in the car. He never forgot again.

At some point, he began to realize what responsibility means: if he doesn't take out the garbage, nobody will. Just as in "real life," his responsibility won't go away, and he has concluded that he simply has to do it.

This simple example has paid off in spades. The last time he did poorly on a test, he concluded (with no prompting) that it was because he had decided to play outside all evening instead of studying; he made a bad choice. I haven't heard "because the teacher doesn't like me and he told us to study the wrong chapter and somebody stole my book and I thought the test was tomorrow" for a long time.

FOUR SIMPLE TASKS?

No. Not simple at all. But these are powerful skills for children to develop as they grow, and helping them do so may be as rewarding as it is challenging. Of course, these four tasks may not be the ones you think are most important; the important thing is to build an understandable framework of your own, to define your own tasks as a parent. At least then the day-to-day guidance you provide will have a consistency that connects the rules together—and someday your child may even understand why.

Biographical Sketch of Geoffrey F. Lasky

Geoffrey F. Lasky was born on January 21, 1954, in Brooklyn, New York. He received a B.A. from Hofstra University in Hempstead, NY, in January 1976, a M.S. from Hofstra in August 1978, and a Ph.D. from the University of Illinois at Urbana-Champaign in May 1981.

Dr. Lasky became a member of Mensa in 1975, and in 1990 became a life member of Mensa. He was accepted as a member of the ISPE in 1978. He has contributed several articles to *Telicom* such as "Kant, Epistemology, and Philosophical Clarification." In addition, Dr. Lasky has been admitted as a member to various international Who's Who societies, such as "Men of Achievement" and "International Leaders in Achievement." Both of these organizations are located in Cambridge, England.

Dr. Lasky is currently working on various scholarly projects in philosophy, psychology, education, theories of physics, and theories of medicine. He looks forward to many more rewarding experiences as a member of the ISPE.

BUILDING A THEORY OF INTELLIGENCE

Geoffrey Lasky

Theory constuction is a subject that concerns philosophers of science. As a philosopher of science I have given great attention to this problem in several papers. Theories in the Kantian sense provide us with worldviews or principles that order but do not create reality. The purpose of this paper is not to evaluate or revise theories about theories, but, instead, to give a brief overview of theory construction as well as to design a theory of intelligence. The question that is often asked by psychologists and lay persons alike is, What is intelligence? I will attempt to answer this question and to discuss the implications of this issue for education in general. When we speak of intelligence we must be careful to remember that many definitions of it have been given. I will briefly discuss some previous ideas about intelligence, and analyze both the power and the shortcomings of each system. It is inevitable that there will be disagreement on the subject of intelligence and its attributes. However, this is an idea that must be clarified. Let us turn now to the first problem, which is the problem of theory construction.

Science is a complex body of knowledge which comes from empirical generalizations and from theories. Data collection springs from the concentrated efforts of researchers who attempt to make sense of the physical universe. Paradigms, collections of hypotheses, concrescences of events are pivotal to the scientific enterprise as well. One problem about the origin of science is whether science comes from accretions of observations, or whether some grand theory encapsulates all experience. Traditional logical empiricism stesses the idea of the scientist as a data collector who arrives at the laboratory and simply takes in the physical universe. Observation is a simple matter, according to this perspective about scien-

27

tific concepts of the world. In microlevel physics, this view of science is not possible, since "observation" is more difficult when we deal with unobservables. Nevertheless, the view that scientists collect data and make generalizations from this data is held by many people, who also tend to believe that facts are more true than theories, a notion that is the foundation of logical empiricism. Theories are seen, according to this schematization, to be mere guesses or imprecise speculations.

Several scientists and philosophers of science regard theories as more important than facts. Some of the greatest physicists of the twentieth century regarded theories as high-powered models of reality. Heisenberg stated that physics is philosophy. Theories have been regarded as complex formulations about reality which in turn generate new knowledge or extrapolations. Theory plays a vital role in physics. What is the role of theory in general knowledge? Theories generate testable formulations or hypotheses that are subjected to constant re-examination. In the logical-positivist system, facts are the bedrock of knowledge. These fundamental facts are generalized into theories. In the *Weltanschauung* philosophy of science, theories are the bedrock of knowledge. Facts are theory-laden. Nevertheless, theories are essential to an understanding of the world, because they explain events. According to Quine and Duhem, theories can be utilized even if they break down under certain conditions. Quine and Duhem developed the idea of auxilliary hypotheses. As our knowledge grows and changes, theories may take on new developments. However, even though our knowledge changes, worldviews such as the Copernican, Newtonian, or Einsteinian do not disappear. Usually such theories are retained, but with modified dimensions.

Theoretical systems grow partially out of the social-epistemological matrix, but not entirely. Theories to some extent are generalizations from facts, but often organize and come prior to facts. Theories are often imbued with a self-contained elegance. Such abstract systems are engendered largely by the creative, contemplative insight of individuals who reflect on the relationship of wholes rather than parts. Theories can be explained partly in terms of psychological processes.

We have seen that the term theory is more complex and rich than is often realized. We must account for all the properties of a theory if we are to understand the uniqueness and power of theories. Theories must be understood in terms of their abstract properties, not simply in terms of obvious, simple descriptions. How does theory play a role in the life of the brain-mind? The use of theory has special meaning. Theory is vital to any discussion of abstract ideas or knowledge.

Unfortunately, the term theory is frequently misused by thinkers in disciplines that are anything but theoretical. In order to understand the construction of a theory or the theory of intelligence, we must understand the significance of the properties of intelligence. Is there a type of intelligence or mental functioning that can explain the other types of intelligence? How can we account for this higher form of intelligence? I propose that the best example of intelligence is the ability of scientists, philosophers, or thinkers to engage in abstraction. Such mental functioning constitutes the highest form of intelligence, since it can account for all other types of mental functioning.

Theory constuction is tied into intelligence in a number of other important ways. Let us now examine some of these.

Psychologists have often disagreed about the nature of intelligence. Without devoting a great deal of space to the nature of intelligence, psychometrics, testing, and the history and systems of psychology, I will give a brief illustration of this point. The behaviorists, for example, have always stressed adaptation as indicative of intelligence. However, adaptation is usually a lower set of responses connected to primitive areas in the brain. Very often highly intelligent persons exhibit actions or behaviors that are in themselves nonadaptive. Individuals may also behave in a manner that is highly ethical or moral but not adaptive. For example, an individual could oppose persecution of people because of their race, culture, or religion. Particular societies may condone the persecution of individuals. Individuals who condemned persecution would be considered maladaptive by such a society. As another example, let us suppose a situation in which academic institutions have created an atmosphere in which ideas were regarded as true purely in terms of political factors. In Nazi Germany, for example, Einstein's theory of relativity (both the special and general) and Freud's views on psychoanalysis were regarded by the Nazis as examples of "Jewish science." The Nazis refused to consider the systems of Einstein and Freud on the basis of their intellectual power. Someone who opposed the fascists in such a situation would be considered maladaptive. These two problems require additional clarification and analysis. First, we must analyze what is meant by normal or adaptive behavior. The behaviorists reduce normalcy to adaptation and biological necessity. Second, must or can all behavior be adaptive? Certainly subject matter in colleges and schools must not be studied merely because it teaches conformity to rigidity and dogma. Subjects should be studied because they teach people how to think. We run the risk, in developing a theory of intelligence based on behaviorism or functionalism, of having people following the group in power rather than examining knowledge and ethical principles on the basis of other criteria.

There are psychologists who have stressed the importance of thinking and abstraction. Binet and Terman stressed the importance of thinking and conceptualizing with respect to intelligence, and I agree in many ways with their general concepts. Intelligence is different from adaptation and mere functioning. The ability to engage in abstraction at a very high level is a skill superior to other forms of intelligence, because, as stated earlier, abstraction at the highest level can account for other types of intelligence. However, even individuals with extremely high IQs, such as 150 or higher on the Stanford-Binet, may be dysfunctional outside an academic situation. They may even be dysfunctional in an academic situation, because they have developed their intellects more comprehensively than their peers and colleagues. I agree that intelligence in its highest form is concerned with abstract reasoning and vocabulary. However, there are other types of intelligence as well.

Independently of Howard Gardner, Cattell, and Guilford, I developed many years ago my own system of multiple intelligences. I disagree with several of Gardner's ideas, paricularly his delineation of abstraction as being associated mainly with mathematical-logical reasoning. Abstraction is often either so lateralized or so localized in the brain that it can be identified or combined with linguistic intelligence. It is true that there is probably some form of general intelligence. Spearman postulated the notion of a general intelligence that existed in all the subgroups or properties of intelligence. Cattell and Guilford have discussed many diverse notions of factors in intelligence. Their discussions focus on the mathematical specifications of the properties of intelligence. Even though there are probably many factors found in intelligence, it is still possible to develop a hierarchy of intelligence. Intelligence or intelligences may be operational under different circumstances. Explanations of intelligence must consider the different circumstances under which types of intelligence operate.

It is probably necessary to at least consider the problem of multiple intelligence in our own discussion of intelligence. Gardner has postulated seven types of intelligence. They are as follows:

(1) linguistic,
(2) logical-mathematical,
(3) spatio-relational,
(4) bodily-kinesthetic,
(5) musical,
(6) intrapersonal,
(7) interpersonal.

Gardner avoids classifying the multiple intelligences in a hierarchy. There are clearly different types of intelligence as well as different applications of intelligence. Different circumstances require different types of responses. Certain types of intelligence may not be applicable to certain situations. In fact, highly gifted individuals may not be functional under unusual circumstances.

For example, let us assume that two individuals were walking in the rainforests of Brazil. One individual was a Ph.D. with extremely high scores on both the Stanford-Binet and Wechsler Adult Intelligence Tests. The second individual was by psychometric standards ordinary or even below average in terms of IQ or formal measurements of intelligence. Through a series of mishaps the two persons were separated. The first person, despite his extremely high IQ, was not familiar with the anfractious paths of the tropical forests. After much exertion and failure, the Ph.D. realized that he was lost. The second person, however, had lived in Central and South America all his life. He was able to make sense of his surroundings. He was able to survive. There are many other examples that can be given.

Clearly, certain types of mental gifts may not be helpful in all types of problem situations. Although I would agree with Gardner that there are different types of intelligence, I still maintain that higher processes exist. Formal knowledge is different from practical knowledge. Perhaps we need to address this problem in terms of schooling. How can we best educate individuals in terms of their specific type of prevailing ability or intelligence?

In order to have a formal theory of intelligence we must take into account the nature of knowledge itself. We need to consider the problem of how we can make intelligible a concept such as intelligence which is not directly observable. Theories are necessary on one level to account for intelligence. There are metatheories or worldviews which account for the nature of theories. There are general theories which explain other theories. Finally, there are basic theories which are necessary to explain some idea or concept in the world. In a later section of this project I will turn to the specific problems of intelligence as related to testing and classification.

Biographical Sketch of Hirsch Lazaar Silverman

Hirsch Lazaar Silverman, Ph.D., Sc.D., LL.D., D.H.L., Litt.D., is a clinical and forensic psychologist and marital therapist by profession, with over forty years of college and university teaching and administration in psychological services, behavioral sciences, mental health, and educational fields. He has been Professor Emeritus of the College of Education and Human Services, Seton Hall University, since 1980. He holds Diplomate status in eleven national boards, including clinical psychology (ABPP), forensic psychology (ABFP), behavioral medicine (AABM), family psychology (ABFamP), neuropsychology (ABPN), and health-care professions (IAHCP). He is a Certified Mental Health Counselor (NACCMHC); and is a licensed psychologist in New Jersey, New York, Pennsylvania, the District of Columbia, California, and two other states. He has been awarded Fellow status in 29 national and international professional organizations and associations. He has been in the private practice of clinical psychology and psychotherapy for over fifty years, including military service in World War II as an Intelligence Officer with the rank of Captain, in the South Pacific areas and Japan. He is the author of 19 published books and texts, including eight volumes of poetry, and more than 160 research papers and articles in professional journals in his specialties of clinical and forensic areas and marital therapy. He has received numerous distinctions and medals, including election to the co-chairmanship of Psychology of the National Academies of Practice; the presidency of the Psychology Section of the Pan American Medical Association; the Townsend Harris Medal of the College of the City of New York; the Creative Leadership Award of Kappa Delta Pi of New york University; the Ecunemical Award of the Association for Values and Religion in Counseling; Army Commendation Medal of the U.S. Army; Benjamin Franklin Fellow of the Royal Society of Arts of England. He is a Registered Poetry Therapist of the National Association of Poetry Therapy, and his biography appears in *Who's Who in the World, Who's Who in America, American Men of Science,* and *Directory of American Scholars,* among other official references. He is a member of Phi Beta Kappa, Sigma Xi, Psi Chi, Mensa, Intertel, and other societies. He lives in West Orange, New Jersey.

CHAPTER 4

POETRY AS A
PSYCHOTHERAPEUTIC INTERVENTION

Hirsch Lazaar Silverman

Throughout history, in every known country and language, people intuitively have turned to poetry for emotional release—for hope in time of despair, for comfort in times of stress, for inspiration in times of doubt. In recent years many therapists (in psychology, psychiatry, mental-health areas, and behavioral sciences) have come to recognize poetry as an extremely powerful, though subtle, healing instrument in reaching troubled minds—stirring up, freeing, and calming the inner feelings of mentally ill adolescents as well as schizophrenics advanced in years—for poetry has healing properties, and reaches in diverse ways the behavioral and emotional problems in many types of people and allows changes in them, illuminating the darkest recesses of the mind, making the person happier, and more fulfilled.

Poetry therapy emphasizes the relation of the poetic experience to mental health as a distinct aspect of psychological, educational, and rehabilitation programs, with the specific use of poetry as a valid tool in dealing with psychological problems creatively.

This discussion is structured, then, to develop and explore the dynamics of poetry as an effective, ancillary therapeutic tool in clinical practice. In the hands of the professional, poetry may be used effectively as a sharp, probing psychodiagnostic to assess patient illness, personality functioning, and behavioral manifestations. Poetry therapy attempts to delineate creatively the awareness of underlying tension and anxiety, and thus offers psychological release to hasten the healing process toward greater overall maturity by revealing more succinctly the individuality of the patient. This therapeutic process also helps the psychologist-therapist

33

to recognize in the patient those attributes within the self that form the personality in action.

I

To be sure, the purpose of poetry therapy is to understand and help the disturbed during an extended period of time, to guide those who need assistance to overcome specific difficult situations, and to help the dysfunctional person find new and better ways of dealing with himself.

One function of poetry is to transfuse emotion. The poet's lines deal with life and death and love, themes which may sharpen some aspect of living for the patient; the patient may develop a new awareness of feeling; the contents of poems are intensified and idealized experiences; the poet records the strange and quaint turn of life; he distills emotions with large implications.

Another function of poetry is to transmit thought. Poetry is in pursuit of truth, and seeks to find harmony where there seems to be none; poets have a greater awareness of life; the poet understands and shares fears, anger, hopes. and struggles; poetry is deep, and expresses itself in high seriousness, all the sincerity of which humans are capable.

The therapist can use poetry as a technique in healing:

by setting up a professional dialogue using poetry as a means of modifying, removing, or retarding disturbances;

by knowing his own values and how they may influence his perception of the patient;

by choosing a variety of poems with subjects keen in psychology and philosophy;

by providing the troubled mind with a solace and a kind of moral feeling which the world rarely gives.

Poetry is one of the natural human resources for healing. In terms of human ecology, poetry can be a constructive force in maintaining the balance of forces in human nature. Poetry helps people handle their feelings. It helps people stir up, release, or calm their feelings.

The natural resource of poetry for healing is certainly available. Frequently during the therapy session, we might bring out some books of poetry and suggest that we take turns reading poems. Usually some counselee would groan at the idea of reading poetry, may not participate at first, might even wander off mentally. But start out by reading a few humorous-serious poems such as "The Little Echippus" by Charlotte Perkins Gilman or "The Yarn of the Nancy Bell" by W. S. Gilbert. Then a patient who has been thumbing through the pages of his poetry book may say, "Here's one that I have always liked," and he may read "Birches" by Robert Frost. Very soon almost every therapee begins to enjoy reading his or her favorite poem.

Poetry reading is an emotional experience that brings people closer together. Even a very inhibited and dull person opens up during the reading, and reveals capacity for feeling and understanding. Some of the poems are sobering, such as "Because I Could Not Stop for Death" by Emily Dickinson. Together, those moments can be shared also.

Poetry is a healing force, not only for our counselees, but for ourselves personally. If you as a therapist find you are feeling sorry for yourself, you can laugh at yourself and your troubles by reading "Miniver Cheevy" by E. A. Robinson. If you feel tired, long for a vacation, or yearn for the woods and the sea, you too will feel refreshed by reading John Masefield's "Sea Fever." If you feel uncertain about what direction to take, you may find that Rudyard Kipling's "If" is a steadying influence. These reveries could continue for many pages of poetry and many hours of energies renewed by poetry.

Since poetry is helpful to all of us, it is helpful to our patients. Poetry could be read in treatment of patients who have emotional problems such as fears, anxieties, depressions, and guilt feelings. The reading and writing of poetry could be used with individuals, couples and groups.

Because poetry is a natural human resource for healing, anyone—not only the accomplished poets—can find help through the reading and writing of poetry. The healing power in writing poetry is similar to the experience most of us have had in writing an angry letter to someone. We sat down and dashed off many angry words and thoughts. We poured out the venom from our pens. After we had written the letter, we felt a sense of relief. We discharged the feeling. We were no longer stewing about something, mulling it over in our minds or preoccupying ourselves with it. We freed ourselves, cleansed our systems, and went about our business. Perhaps that letter was ripped up and never mailed, or was rewritten into a constructive suggestion. But the writing of the letter had a healing effect.

The healing effect is more likely to happen in the writing of poetry when the writing is spontaneous. A person can sit down and write out a strong feeling of some kind, and out of the writing will emerge rhythms, rhymes, visual images, and repetitions of sounds, especially if the person bears in mind that he or she is writing poetry. When a man tells himself he is writing a poem, he is opening the door to freedom of expression. He is saying that he does not have to make anyone understand him, and that he does not have to address anyone in particular. He is saying that fiction and fact may be interwoven, and not in conflict. He is free to play with words and images, to turn them, twist them, scramble them, listen to them, and look to them.

For poetry is a kind of spontaneous experience. In school, we were trained to write a poem of a certain meter and a certain rhyme, and we struggled to find words that fit the pattern. The whole experience was frustrating rather than healing. The therapist discovers a new aspect of the healing power of poetry through spontaneous writing. One aspect of such an approach to poetry is that a poem is not evaluated in terms of literary, moral, and aesthetic values, or in terms of whether anyone likes or dislikes the poem.

This degree of freedom for spontaneous expression is helpful to the healing effect, psychologically. On the other hand, the attention to the devices of sight and sound contributes to the training of poets but not necessarily to healing—although the awareness of sights and sounds is part of a healthy outreach to the world around us. The form and structure of poetry are not discarded in spontaneous writing, but are allowed to emerge from spontaneous writing.

Both the reading and the writing of poems is a healing force. Three conditions seem to promote healing during the reading of poems. One is that the poem be read word for word, in order that the rhythm and rhyme, assonance and alliteration of the poem may be appreciated. If one skims through a poem, these qualities are lost. A *second* condition is that the poem must be heard. One may listen to another person read a poem, or may read it aloud to oneself, or may "hear" it in one's own mind as the poem is read silently. The *third* condition for healing is what Leedy calls the "iso-principle," which means that the feeling of the poem must be the same as the feeling of the person hearing the poem. If one is not responding to a certain poem, it might be a good idea to discontinue that poem and thumb through the pages for another poem or another poet, as if looking over a menu for something appealing or satisfying.

But mere poetry by itself is not always a therapeutic force. A man who feels despair and reads a despairing poem that has no underlying hope may spiral downward in his feelings. If he feels too much despair, he may even stop reading before he arrives at the more hopeful portions of the poem.

There are many potential uses of the healing force of poetry. Poetry can help the people of one nation understand the people of another nation, because poetry expresses the heart of a people. Percy Bysshe Shelley said, "Poets are the unacknowledged legislators of the world." Poetry can also help bridge the generation gap: poetry had lost its popularity and was regarded as old fashioned, but there was a resurgence of interest in poetry in the '60s that continued into the '70s; and now in the '90s may well serve effectively in psychotherapy.

Poetry can be a clinical and therapeutic healing force creatively when it gives one a new way of life. The troubled person sings a song that is characteristic of him and his troubles. He sings the same song to all of life's experiences. Although a man sings as he lives, there is increasing evidence that he may also live as he sings, and may live in a new way if he sings a new song.

It seems that American civilization is in the midst of a mass effort to escape from the age of anxiety by retreating into a culture of therapy. Anodynes and treatments are everywhere at hand, with and without prescription. (We Americans have come to expect that there is a pill to ease every pain and stress.) At the same time, a therapeutic philosophy has seized the imagination of those who control our social institutions. Schools are organized around therapeutic concepts. Even business sponsors personal growth experiences. The church offers counseling as well as prayer. Now the clinical therapist has his important role to fulfill in and through poetry therapy.

II

Poetry therapy is an opportunity, a tool, for psychotherapists to share with other human beings, a type of creative endeavor through which they make use of their own selves in the therapeutic relationship. Experiences in poetry therapy include participants' images of the ideal in life, exploring the interface between theoretical notions and the person that the counselee is, and experiencing comparative styles in working with role-playing core issues such as dependency, hostility, and sexuality.

Does creativity in one field enhance productivity in another? How do experiences in one area of creativity parallel or contrast with those in another? Should multiple expressions of talent be encouraged in individuals with such potential? What are the rewards or penalties for those who would seek to develop more than one talent?

Tension is the form of energy we commit to our shadow side. We label our discomforts and fight them to a standstill. Only our bodies, through our movements, sounds, words, and thoughts, now and then hint at the course of war in ourselves. Let the therapee try to win the war, in the only way possible, by welcoming the shadows, loving the enemy, and thinking things out together, even conceptually.

Inhibited and negative emotions can be opened up through poetry therapy, and the valuable energy within us used to create interrelation-ships. Experiencing psychotherapy through poetry as an unlocking of psychic energy makes one open to more intense physical, emotional, and spiritual experiences than before.

It is necessary for us to live in tension and societal confusion, because we do not relate to differences in people. Can we be clearer on where we are in relation to black, white, or other? Can we live in such a way that we facilitate the creation of institutions which are more conducive to healthy human development? Poetry therapy attempts to answer some of these questions by involving us in structured and unstructured activities aimed at clarifying our own feelings and pointing the way toward making a world more to our liking.

We as individuals live in a global, universal whirl of creation. We are being in motion, constantly changing. We can become one with the uni-verse, but first each of us must find the unity of our "self" and learn to share it with others. This is a creative effort poetically which seeks to let each of us get in touch with what we are and what is within us at the present moment. This is psychotherapy at its best.

As humans we long for another way of being. We need desperately to pull the pieces together and make a whole, resonant, and fulfilled life for ourselves. By approaching life as a process and becoming aware of how one tampers with the flow of that process, we take a major step toward unifying our split with life.

Through poetry therapy we learn that the first breakdown is pain, the second pleasure. This therapeutic process deals with issues such as the implications of the developing spirit of sexual exploitation and expansion of pleasure-capacity-liberating activities, the compatibility of pleasure with spiritual consciousness, the connection between the restriction or liberation of pleasure with violence, and the relationship between power and sexuality.

The more we know about interpersonal, intrapsychic body energy and transpersonal phenomena, the more their underlying principles converge in and through poetry therapy. Concepts such as truth and choice are ubiquitous, and it appears that there is only one fear, one teaching, one cause of disease, one social problem, and one marital difficulty: the lack of poetic insight in human beings.

All creatures value life. Valuing is a process that we will use until we die. We re-create it anew with every piece of new data or new living. We need to work on the processes of values clarification.

Holistic education in a poetic setting develops in mind, body, emotions, imagination, intuition, and spirit. As therapists we must explore the development and integration of each of these functions through self-concept development, sensory awareness, psychocalisthenics, gestalt awareness, guided fantasy, psychosynthesis, affirmation, and basic thinking as individuals.

There seems to be a yearning among many of today's young people to reach back into the world of yesterday. Yet old and young live separately, feel alienated. Through poetry there is a meeting of minds, an examination of the stories each were told that set them on separate pathways. Through group experiences in poetry reading we find places where our journeys can meet to enrich each other's lives.

Actualizing therapy through poetry espouses a core wherein the polarities of feeling are synthesized into an entity. It is a unique core, which distinguishes humans from all other beings. Its existence is demonstrated by a series of experiential exercises involving the mind and its relationship to thinking and feeling in poetic expression.

As time passes through days and into years, its passage, of course, brings movement and change. Though clocks record the hours, it is the experiencing of change by living persons, i.e., phenomenal time, which is the focus of our lives. The time/person interface must be examined from several perspectives, including conceptualized dimensions of change, duration of positive experiences, membership in long-term groups, and functioning of healthy personalities over time. Poetry serves this role effectively.

Understanding some of the developmental tasks of middle age can make this period of our lives vital and creative. Some of the areas, e.g., getting beyond adulthood using increasing freedom, changing old roles and old messages, developing perspective, replacing the nuclear family, facing loss, etc., are referred to beautifully in poetry. Understanding the sources of our identities helps us to look at the roads taken, and the roads not taken, and to make creative attempts to live more happily.

Close to poetry and close to philosophy, too, lies a new place to visit where we go to find out, and where we come to know, what thing "consciousness" is—the image, the brass, and the pendulum marking the journey: these things are strange things. We speak of these things—of life, of time and quantum-mechanical things, of probability, of chaos, and of chains—in poetry.

We are just that, creations: natural creatures and social creatures. We are natural organisms, embodied and mortal. We are created by ourselves, and we are created by some other. In every realm, from the psychological to the spiritual, we grow by recreation. But what does that mean, and how is it accomplished? We may well find that the use of poetry in the therapeutic process helps define our role in living more creatively.

III

An awareness of one's self in terms of needs and of the ways one seeks to fulfill such needs is as essential to the poetry therapist as is awareness of his or her own social role, with all its expectations. The individual who is a good therapist understands his/her own set of values and beliefs, and knows how these may enter into his perceptions of his clients and of the situations in which they find themselves. A great deal of knowledge of self is prerequisite for the therapist's wise use of himself, and knowledge of self exists only where there is a sense of acceptance and comfort of oneself. The therapist of necessity is a person of integrity and maturity; to the extent that these qualities are lacking, there will be flaws in his or her therapeutic relationships.

The most important aspect of poetry therapy in terms of mental health is the quality of communication that takes place. Communication not only reveals the client's problems and feelings, but also provides the clues to the therapist's feelings; it is the way in which the therapist in turn makes himself known to his client. In time, it is the way in which the therapist takes his client "unto himself."

Professional dialog in therapy includes conversation and discussion with a purpose, with poetry used as a means. It is reason's only real weapon. It is a civilized procedure and operation, democratic and constructive. To take useful part in making decisions is to seek understanding through consideration of alternatives, and through it individuals attain insight and understanding. Such dialog requires common substance, and requires a large measure of goodwill. It begins in an act of faith, the assumption that those who are in therapy will speak honestly for the purpose of reaching understanding, and with balanced generosity. It is by comparison of views that we reason our way toward truth. We increase the odds of finding the best and most reasonable solution to problems by considering alternatives.

Poetry therapy as related to psychotherapy is a form of treatment for problems, emotional in nature, in which a trained clinician deliberately establishes a professional relationship with a patient with the object of removing, modifying, or retarding existing symptoms, of mediating disturbed patterns of behavior, and of promoting positive personality growth and development. Personality growth takes into consideration personality maturation in order to assist the individual in achieving a more gratifying relationship with people in his or her environments.

The truly basic elements in a strong poetry therapeutic session are unity and simplicity. Small problems are necessarily more easily solved than larger ones, but at the same time the gestalt, the pattern of the whole, must be kept in mind. The center of the answer to a question should be the point of the question, and the circumference no wider than is needed to answer the question adequately at the time. After all, dialog is seeking truth. In therapy, the search involves being willing to reach out to that which is not yet fully understood, or even to something which at first perhaps repels the individual. When one idea supplements another, as in professional therapy, often a joint truth emerges from the dialog of persons who started even with divergent beliefs.

Therapists realize that poetry is a representation of an ideal. Contents and character in poetry are idealized, and this idealization bears a high consistency with individualization. Poetry is indicative of the originality of grace, refinement, purity, and good feeling, the poet exhibiting correct moral perception in his lines; it is, in essence, originality energizing in the world of beauty. All of this may be effectively used in poetry therapy. An immortal instinct, deep within the human spirit, is a sense of the beautiful. It is no mere appreciation of the beauty before us, but a wild effort to reach the beauty above. Life is essentially beautiful, and life is the poet's glossary, not literature. Poets in general love the beauty of the fact, and tell the actual and factual truth, with a belief in realism. Poetry in therapy can be a treatise of existence, for most poets talk sincerely about the simple things, as well as the sophisticated ones—those that too often are forgotten in living—and such thoughts are neither deified nor sentimentalized. Thus, when by poetry we find ourselves melted to tears, we weep then not through excess of pleasure, but through a certain petulant, impatient sorrow at our inability to grasp now, wholly, here on earth, at once and forever, those divine and rapturous joys of which through the poem we attain to but brief and indeterminate glimpses. The implications for poetry therapy are patent.

As indicated already, the peculiar functions of poetry for the therapist are twofold: to transfuse emotion, and to transmit thought. The thought should dominate the words; the poet hopefully had sought for depths rather than surfaces. In poetry, if it is to be vital and dynamic, there must be a fusing of mood, accent, and image in a fresh intensity. Poetry is, as a totality, an artlessness that is more than an art. The province of poetry is the entire range of human experience and that vast area of moral destiny.

Poetry therapeutically should represent something more than verbal jugglery; it should stand for art in a larger sense, and should embody the features of a personality rather than the dexterities of rhetorical craftsmanship. The poet's lines somehow help to turn on the counselee's quest for absolute reality and for an affirmation of human values. Poets then occupy themselves with the themes of life and death, which for the therapees may sharpen some aspects of living: beauty, love, quiet days of thought. This may develop a new awareness in feeling.

Truth is unquestionably one of the purest and truest of all poetical themes, and through truth in poetry we are led to perceive a harmony where none was apparent before. In therapy, there is an increasing concern with the present; in the past, to be sure, there has been too much dehumanized mysticism in poetry, for poets embrace a different consciousness and a greater awareness of life; and the therapist is expected to capitalize on this. As a return to actuality, poetry reveals a deep and philosophical nature expressing itself in terms of high seriousness, which again constitutes a therapeutic aspect.

The therapist using poetry as an art and as a technique is endowed with a critical mind. The mind of the therapist cannot withdraw from the spontaneous expression of insight and imagination to a minute diligence in the mere formation of lines. Then it is that poetry will gain both in intensity and in sincerity for the counselee. The poetry therapist should strive for originality. An art of emotional expression, poetry, in its philosophic sense, is not what remains at a level; it is the exceptional, the extraordinary, the powerful, the unexpected, that soars far above the general trend. Poetry means the power to move men's hearts and minds, and this the therapist must recognize no less.

IV

With an impulse themselves to create, poetry therapists find a continually fresh delight in the variety and wonder of life. Therapists should try to make poems radiate a new spirit, free in expression, unhampered in choice of subject, keen in psychology and philosophy. Therapists should strive to use poetry with deep notes and large themes. Poetry, the art of solitude, requires a great deal of thought, a great deal of silent work, and all the sincerity of which human nature is capable. For the poet mere existence oftentimes is glorious. Life, although coarse and difficult and frequently dangerous and dirty, is for him splendid at the heart. The poet's work shares the fears, hopes, angers, and struggles of the prosaic world. The therapist rightly explains to clients these facts and relates them—involvedly—to individuals he works with professionally.

Poetry therapists should believe implicitly in life, in its manifestations, grasping existence as a whole. A large naturalism, with vigor, with certain idealistic generalizations, with a gentle radicalism, a calm and cultured honesty—with these things therapists today ought to concern themselves. Conscious, almost self-conscious philosophizing, mixed with thoughts that are both strong and delicate, causes the therapist to analyze poetry as an art, and its object: pleasurable appreciation. Poetry exists for its own sake; it is a world, in a restricted sense, of its own. It should serve as an end, yes, but can be used as a means therapeutically. In each poem can be found a great spirit, a profound experience; disclosed, it suffices.

The therapist's mind ought to be nourished by liberal studies; and from those studies he should extract the kernel of substance for his poetry therapy, not contenting himself with the husk of accident. The therapist's aim should be clarity, as opposed to contemporary obscurantist tendencies, and, in the manner of style, purity and freedom from mannerism, as distinct from the contemporary tendency to substitute mannerism for true originality in the therapeutic process. The therapist at all events must base his convictions on inquiry and meditation; these should not be the mere rags and shreds of others' thought. Recognizing the ambrosia which nourishes his soul in everything around him, the therapist perceives it also in the suggestive ideas that come to him through poetry. However, it is to be recognized that poetry is not devastatingly opinionated; mystical obfuscation is avoided; and lines of poetry should not be interpreted in terms of verbal inconsequentialities. Although the poet's range may not be all-inclusive, the material of poetry is not dependent on time. Poetry achieves permanence only when the medium is not words but elements. This, too, the therapist must recognize; for although his appeal is human, the poet has convictions, rather than sentiment alone, of a philosophy that may disturb his readers, of searching truth rather than of sweet truisms. The therapist using poetry as a technique must therefore be no less discriminatingly realistic.

The therapeutic effort must explore present difficulties and their influence on a person's conflict. The therapist clarifies problems and makes suggestions for possible solutions. There is an effort to untangle the character distortion, to let the patient gain inner strength and the ability to choose the direction of his or her contact with people. The poetry therapist has a definite task and goal, does not stop at suggestion, but tries to help the patient achieve deeper characterological changes. It is significant that in the therapeutic technique the need for conformity often is emphasized so much. Integration into the community is no less a real goal.

The purpose of poetry therapy is to help a maladjusted person to learn, by various ways and in time, new ways of dealing with and thinking about himself or herself and other people, and new responses to life situations. The methods employed by therapists to achieve this end are various, but the basis underlying the different approaches is primarily to teach the patient to develop more constructive concepts of self. The poetry therapist must come to realize that a person with difficulties is the product of the causes of his difficulties, mostly environmental, patterns of living, and interpersonal relationships. Poetry therapy in this sense, then, should be looked upon—by both the patient and the therapist—as repair work on a professional basis of science and art, and not as a complete rebirth of the personality, for the results of therapy are necessarily limited by such factors as the caliber of the original material, as well as the individual self (constitution plus young ego), the degree of damage (infantile traumata and adult frustrations), and what remains to be worked with (adult ego plus the reality situation).

Again, the implications for poetry therapy are wide, broad, and deep. By implication, poetry therapy may well be the treatment of mental disorders by the use of suggestion, counseling, persuasion, advising, direction, and the like, with the goal of relieving the patient of distressing neurotic symptoms or discordant personality characteristics which interfere with his or her satisfactory adaptation to a world of people and events. Perhaps it is not so much how therapy is done but how effective it is professionally and scientifically that is the ultimate criterion of therapy.

V

Most people have only the vaguest idea of the many ways in which their behavior can affect their health or how closely their mental and physical well-being are tied together. That is why poetry therapy can be such a revelatory experience for so many.

What is it like to be old? Any theory in therapy clearly shows that there is no one answer to this question, that there are many patterns of aging, and that common stereotypes about the old are not necessarily true. Are old people neglected, sick and dependent, fearful of retirement, rigid and reactionary? Poetry therapy answers a firm "no" to all these stereotypes.

In our society among almost all people and particularly among the young, dependency is frowned upon. The ideal of man is complete freedom—and yet the talented poet makes clear that dependency is an absolute necessity for all of us and can be one of the most positive factors in our lives.

The heredity-environment question has constantly been a factor in all studies of human behavior. Which is more important, our genetic heritage or the environment in which we develop? Until recently, the environment under consideration was the world outside. Now it is beginning to include the world inside as well. Many psychologists believe that at birth the infant has already been exposed to nine months of environmental influences within the mother's uterus. Here, again, in poetry as therapy another facet psychologically is dealt with directly.

The stages and the pattern of abnormal behavior become clear through watching the progress of a person's depression: its early symptoms, the individual's inability to function normally, the attempt to ignore erratic behavior, the growing awareness that a person may be seriously ill, the severely depressed state, the suicidal threat, the decision to get help, the process of diagnosis, hospitalization, and treatment; the eventual release back into society with symptoms gone, the need for continuing follow-up therapy.

Poetry therapy discusses the many and often conflicting approaches, theories, criteria, therapies, and treatments relating to abnormal behavior such as the statistical approach, the behaviorist approach, sociopsychological theory, the humanist approach, the existentialist theory, the genetic approach, the organic emphasis, the psychodynamic approach, the psychoanalytic view.

Let us for a moment refer, for example, to prejudice. Poems themselves survey the causes, consequences, and cures of this crippling social disease. With the therapeutic process as a springboard, the social-distance theory of prejudice can be explained, using a model of concentric circles. There are general discussions of stereotyping, socialization as a cause of prejudice, and a more specific analysis of the way children's books subtly reinforce even sexual and racial stereotypes.

Can prejudice be cured? Yes, laws may be used to alter prejudicial behavior; but other possible cures are discussed in the therapeutic process, including research that shows how elementary- school classroom interdependence reduces prejudice. Finally, the raising of consciousness and organized resistance on the part of minorities are shown as one additional cure for prejudice.

The psychologist in poetry therapy can also explain that if aggression is learned in a social context, then by the same token it can be altered in a social context. The therapist also can explore the relationship between individual aggression and collective aggression, that which we call war.

VI

Perhaps I should try to explain just what a poem is; but this is not as easy as it seems, for probably no two poets would agree on exactly what constitutes a poem. Primarily a poem is a poem; and being a poem it is intended to express and to evoke emotion. It is necessary to insist upon this point, because it has been the custom in the past to translate "poem" into "epigram," or "thought," and this is quite misleading. Second, a poem is very short, or long, or middle length, with a traditional and classic form, and with special characteristics of its own.

Sir Arthur Quiller-Couch has pointed out that the capital difficulty of verse consists "in saying ordinary unemotional things, of bridging the flat intervals between high moments." A poem may be of many kinds, grave or gay, deep or shallow, religious, satirical, sad, humorous, or charming; but all poems worthy of the name are records of high moments—higher, at least, than the surrounding plain. In the hands of a talented master a poem can be the concentrated essence of pure poetry.

Poetry naturally has to depend for its effect on the power of suggestion. Poems usually gain their effect not only by suggesting a mood, but also by giving a clear-cut picture which serves as a starting point for trains of thought and emotion. Only the outlines of important parts are drawn, and the rest the reader must fill in for himself. A poem indeed has a very close resemblance to the "ink sketches" on Rorschach plates so dear to the heart of the clinician.

Perhaps it would be simplest to give an example taken from modern English poetry. The climax of Edward Shanks' lovely "A Night Piece," for instance, in its spirit is pure haiku of the highest order:

So far . . . so low . . .
A drowsy thrush? A waking nightingale?
Silence. We do not know.

The healing power of poetry was recognized by the Greeks, who worshipped Apollo, the leader of the Muses, and the father of Aesculapius, god of medicine. In writing poems, patients "live in prose and dream in poetry." Poems are another royal road to the unconscious. Patients have catharsis in releasing suppressed feelings; and unconscious intentions are revealed. Suicidal attempts can be detected, in which so often the patient reveals that he or she wants to be rescued.

Of course, the therapist is not concerned with spelling, rhyme, etc. Patients write a line, then the therapist may write a line, and this process continues until neither has anymore to say. Technique often relieves tensions, establishes communication, and reinforces the patient's ego and feelings of hope and trust. Psychosomatic disorders (like peptic ulcers) may be interpreted as the poem struggling to be born. Writing and reacting to their own poems make the patients feel liberated. Rhythm and rhyme are much more compelling than the theme of the poem. Rhythm is the soothing beat of life. It imposes a pleasurable order on chaos.

Another approach is the use of poems to be read and discussed. In poetry therapy for insomnia, the therapist may wish to prescribe poems to be read several times before going to bed, such as "A Ballad of Dreamland" by Swinburne or "Hymn to the Night" by Longfellow. Other poems used are spellbinding or spellweaving poems like "Annabel Lee" or "Tintern Abbey." They relax the patient and relieve insomnia.

Poetry therapy is also successfully used for anxiety and depression. Hospitlalized patients about to be operated on may be read to, and the poems buoy depressed feelings with hopeful examples. Encouraging patients to memorize poems so that they may draw on them in times of crisis often is effective procedurally. Poems are chosen not because they are great, but because they are close to the mood of the patient. Poems with sad themes must have stanzas that reflect optimism. Patients read, study, recite, interpret the poems, and recognize that they are not alone in their despair. Poems often successfully used are "I'm Nobody" by Dickinson, "The Road Not Taken" by Frost, "Ode on a Grecian Urn" by Keats, and "I Celebrate Myself" by Whitman.

In and through the creativity inherent in poetry, hopefully we as individuals may reach maturity—the reaching in time of that stationary state in our individuality where no further change need take place, to be sure of a kind of fixity in our individual lives. Yet, in truth, poetry teaches us that in the properly mature person no articulation, no thought, no faculty is ever so utterly excluded as to render it unanswerable or unuseful to the person, directly or indirectly. For maturity actually is the human capacity of an individual to evaluate and delineate situations and experiences into singularities, parts, or sections, and then to reform them into a gestalt, or pattern, a configuration most efficacious to immediate needs and circumstances.

Whatever our eventual differential definition of poetry therapy, it would benefit our profession of psychology to frame it within the general guidelines of the reflective, creative psychologist model as a coming-of-age rallying point for guiding our specialty as a tool past mere technocracy and toward responsible, integrated science, art, and service.

In a sense, poetry therapy creeps into the person's psyche as silent as a bruise, to make the individual happy, better adjusted, to feel better, do better, be better, through self-search.

Shelley saw poetry as "the very image of life expressed in its eternal truth." Poetry attracts the intellect and has in itself beauty pleasing to the moral nature. It tends to be idealistic as well as individualistic. The originality found in poems has to do with the power of abstraction for one's self.

To operate well in the domain of psychological therapy, the therapist should have a great deal of self-knowledge, particularly in terms of his needs and the ways to fulfill those needs; and he must strive for a two-way communication with his client. Therapy should be involved with reducing the anxiety and hostility that come from a stress-filled world. Human beings have a need to survive and want order, intimacy, uniqueness, and productivity. Karen Horney observed that character drives in three lines—toward, against, and away from people. Although one of these lines will be prominent, yet what causes pain in the person is the anxiety caused by conflict within these lines. The poetry therapist, in trying to relieve the individual's suffering, attempts to untangle character distortion.

Poetry, then, can be used as a means of communicating between therapist and client as part of the professional dialog. The poetry would be the common ground in a dialog that searches for alternatives to solving conflict. This does not mean that there is constant talking: the importance of thoughtful silence that can occur naturally in the consideration of the poem's truth must be recognized. The poetry that is selected should be attractive to the self of both the therapist and the client. The therapist should look for works that transfuse emotion and transmit thought. Features of personality rather than of mere rhetoric are emphasized. Themes that help the counselee's search for reality and will serve to reaffirm human values are most desirable. He should use poetry as a technique and as an art for the pleasurable appreciation that can be derived. Clarity should be a major aim as well as a realistic approach, and poetry that disturbs the client is counterproductive.

As an art and a science in combination, poetry therapy truly is a discipline. The therapeutic process in poetry involves the interpretation of not merely words semantically, but the deeper meanings, the mood elements, the very substance of thought. Although all literary forms are essentially major forms of creativity, poetry therapeutically lends itself more poignantly to the healing process, for it discloses more clearly the relations between processes of the individual's mentality and mental functioning. Transcending the field of aesthetics philosophically, poetry as therapy has great value in offering mankind messages of value, of wisdom, of intelligence, of reality, of beauty, of hope; and viewed as a form of psychotherapy and self-analysis, poetry has a salutary effect. Poetry therapeutically, used by the competent behavioral scientist, copes well with the conflicts in individuals pursuing peace of mind and happiness. Poetry as art is indestructible; poetry as science glorifes life, and is an act of faith, a heightened and more rational position of man's spirit. In psychological services, through poetry therapy the clinician may effectively treat anxieties, difficulties in adjustment, psychosomatic disorders, phobias, disturbed interpersonal relationships, marital upsets, hesitancies to engage in life's activities, behavior socially disapproved of, inability to establish contact with people, confusions, conflicts, personality malfunctioning, and the field of psychological phenomena generally. Professionally employed, poetry therapy reduces the anxiety and even the hostility that comes from our stress-filled world, and gives to human beings order, intimacy, productiveness, and uniqueness as individuals, for poetry therapy provides solace to the troubled mind even as it gives utterance to inward emotions.

REFERENCES

Arieti, Silvano. *Creativity: The Magic Synthesis.* Basic Books, 1976.
Arnheim, R. *Art and Visual Perception.* University of California Press, 1954.
Bruner, J.S., J.J. Goodnow, and G.A. Austin. *A Study of Thinking.* Wiley, 1956.
Cassirer, E. *Language and Myth.* Harper and Row, 1946.
Collier, R.M. "A Definition of Treatment," *American Journal of Psychotherapy,* 11, 1957.
Croce, B. *Aesthetics.* London: Macmillan, 1929.
Frank, J.D. "Some Effects of Expectancy and Influence in Psychotherapy," *Progress in Psychotherapy,* Vol. III. J.H. Masserman and J.L. Moreno, eds. Grune and Stratton, 1958.
Freud, S. "On Psychotherapy," *Collected Papers,* Vol. I. London: Hogarth Press, 1904.
Fromm, E. *Escape from Freedom.* Farrar and Rinehart, 1941.
Horney, K. *The Neurotic Personality of Our Time.* Norton, 1937.
Ingham, H.V., and L.R. Love, *The Process of Psychotherapy.* McGraw-Hill, 1954.
Leedy, J.J., ed. *Poetry Therapy.* Lippincott, 1969.

Lerner, Arthur. "Poetry Therapy," *American Journal of Nursing,* (73) 8, August 1973.

Lerner, Arthur, ed. *Poetry in Therapeutic Experience.* Pergamon Press, 1978.

Lowenfield, V. *Creative and Mental Growth.* Macmillan, 1951.

May, R. "Historical and Philosophical Presupposition for Understanding Therapy," *Psychotherapy, Theory and Research.* H.O. Mowrer, ed. Ronald Press, 1953.

Read, H. *The Meaning of Art.* London: Faber and Faber, 1964.

Rossiter, Charles. "Commonalities Among the Creative Arts Therapies as a Basis for Research Collaboration," Journal of Poetry Therapy, 5 (4), 1992.

Severo, Richard. "Therapist Uses Poetry as Guide to the Hidden Mind," *New York Times,* July 28, 1981. Section C, pages 1 and 4.

Silverman, H. L. "Psychology and Religion: A Philosophic Interpretation and Scientific Evaluation," *The Catholic Psychological Record,* 5 (2), 1967.

Silverman, H. L. "The Unconscious: Philosophical and Psychological Implications and Ramifications," Lecture given at the 76th Annual Convention of the American Psychological Association, abstracted in *The New Jersey Psychologist,* 19 (1), 1968.

Silverman, H. L. *Dimensions of Education and Psychology: Essays in Behavioral Sciences.* Ginn, 1975.

Storr, A. *The Dynamics of Creation.* Atheneum Press, 1972.

Torrance, E.P., and R.E. Myers. *Creative Learning and Teaching.* Dodd, Mead, 1972.

FAMILY LAW AND THE FORENSIC PSYCHOLOGIST: IMPLICATIONS, ROLE, AND SIGNIFICANCE

Hirsch Lazaar Silverman

Practitioners in forensic psychology and in clinical work have long recognized that the research laboratory, the classroom, and the clinic are very different places; and for forensic mental-health professionals as well, what sounds good in the lecture hall does not always help much in the courtroom. The forensic psychologist must always be intelligently astute, knowledgeable in his/her field, equipped with common sense, insightful, mature, responsible, and certainly professional and judicious in outlook.

Child-abuse problems, the battered-woman syndrome, children at risk because of a psychoneurotic parent, the enigma of multiple personalities causing bizarre and unpredictable changes even in physical symptoms, are all areas of great concern for the forensic psychologist, particularly in dealing with custody-mediation issues.

Ethnic, racial, and religious traditions continue to exert powerful influences on family life and are now providing therapists with new treatment approaches; accordingly, therapists must be aware that their own ethnic backgrounds can affect the ways in which they react to their clients and their clients' behavior.

For family therapists and forensic psychologists this means shifting their thinking, and reconsidering the importance of the cultural systems of families that share common histories and traditions. Just as family therapy itself grew out of the realization that human behavior could not be understood in isolation from its family context, family behavior also makes sense only in the larger context in which it is embedded.

The ethnic-identity movements of the 1960s and 1970s seriously changed group relationships in American society. This fact should have had a profound effect on the way that professionals in the mental-health field practiced. To some extent this did happen, but unevenly, haltingly, and controversially. Although the importance of ethnocultural factors in behavior has been more widely conceded than ever, many mental-health practitioners still view these factors as an "add-on," to be taken less seriously than the factors common to all individuals and families.

I

In the practice of forensic psychology, therapists do evaluations on custody and visitation, personal injury, matters of competency, suitability to return to work, related civil issues, and even criminal issues. Generally, requests for service come from the Chancery Division of the Superior Court of the State, from a fellow therapist or psychiatrist, from an attorney, or from referrals from individuals or agencies, such as the Domestic Violence Program or the Division of Youth and Family Services, requesting evaluation and/or therapy. Often this request can be met only by a comprehensive, evaluative report advising the court on relevant matters.

The forte of the forensic psychologist is in analyzing the data relevant to all family members involved, integrating this into a clinical scenario with specific treatment recommendations, and advising the court from a perspective that may be broader than that of the treating clinician, who may have been providing therapy to only one member of a complex family system.

The special educational and professional background and experience permit the forensic specialist to integrate the medical and psychological issues with information about the family as the court appointed evaluator. Before beginning the evaluation, written informed consent must be obtained from both parents. All materials must be handled confidentially to protect the integrity and sometimes the identity of the individuals involved.

Prior to full psychological evaluation of all parties involved, the forensic psychologist would do well to review all legal papers, reports by staff, relevant hospital charts, reports of individuals in the community, behavioral observations, and a mental-status evaluation during clinical interviews. In approaching such referrals, the persons involved are entitled to be informed of their legal rights.

II

One of the first issues to be decided by a forensic psychologist is whether an individual has a "mental disorder", that is, any organic, mental, or emotional impairment which has substantial adverse effects on an individual's cognitive or volitional functions. If a diagnosis is to be part of one's psychological evaluation, it would be based on the classification of the DSM-III-R (1987).

Another issue is the assessment of the "likelihood of serious harm" by parents (or a parent), and whether this factor is affecting the mental status of the child or children. One must also evaluate the likelihood of serious harm to self, others, or the property of others, as each is defined by the law. The issue is whether there is a substantial risk that physical harm will be inflicted by an individual on another, as evidenced by behavior which has caused such harm or which places another person or persons in reasonable fear of sustaining such harm. Recent case law requires "a showing of a substantial risk of physical harm as shown by a recent overt act . . . which has caused harm or creates a reasonable apprehension of dangerousness." The case in point was *In re Harris*, 98 Wn. 2d 276, 284–85, 654 P. 2d 109 (1992). The danger of harm to others need not be "imminent" per *In re LaBelle*, 107 Wn. 2d 196, 208, 728 P. 2d 138 (1986).

Although there is some difficulty in predicting danger (Cocozza & Steadman, 1976), especially in cases requiring supervised visitation, the wording of the law (evidence of "behavior which has caused such harm or which places another person in reasonable fear of sustaining such harm") clarifies this factor somewhat. Such clarity is consonant with the finding of increased predictive validity in the emergency commitment of dangerous, mentally ill persons.

Another issue in custody matters involves grave disability in terms of health and safety. "Gravely disabled" means "a condition in which a person, as a result of a mental disorder, is in danger of serious physical harm resulting from a failure to provide for his/her essential human needs of health or safety." *In re LaBelle, loc. cit.,* pp. 204–9, requires the grave disability be shown by "a substantial risk of danger of serious physical harm resulting from failure to provide for essential health and safety needs . . . the State must present recent, tangible evidence of failure or inability to provide for such essential human needs as food, clothing, shelter, and medical treatment which presents a high probability of serious physical harm within the near future unless adequate treatment is afforded."

Still another issue involves grave disability in terms of cognitive or volitional control. "Gravely disabled" additionally means a condition in which a person, as a result of a mental disorder, manifests severe deterioration in routine functioning evidenced by repeated and escalating loss of cognitive or volitional control over his or her actions, and is not receiving care essential for his or her health or safety. Recent case law requires "recent proof of significant loss of cognitive or volitional control . . . [including] a factual basis for concluding that the [respondent] is not receiving or would not receive, if released, such care as is essential for his or her health or safety." Evidence should indicate the harmful consequences likely to follow if involuntary treatment is not ordered and that the respondent "is unable, because of severe deterioration of mental functioning, to make a rational decision with respect to his/her need for treatment" (*In re LaBelle, loc. cit.,* p. 208).

III

In general, the court decides custody in terms of the best interests of the child, considering all relevant factors, including:

(1) the wishes of the child's parent or parents as to his custody and visitation privileges;
(2) the wishes of the child as to his custodian and as to visitation privileges;
(3) the interaction and interrelationship of the child with his/her parent or parents, his/her siblings, and any other person who may significantly affect the child's best interests;
(4) the child's adjustment to his home, school, and community; and
(5) the mental and physical health of all individuals involved. Also dictated is that the court shall not consider conduct of a proposed guardian that does not affect the welfare of the child.

Child custody and visitation are not merely matters of parents' rights. These matters primarily concern the welfare of the child or children; and it is the court's responsibility, then, as well as duty, to make a custodial order on the basis of what the judge deems to be in the best interests of the children. The following are some of the psychological determinants of custody and visitation:

Emotional attachments of the children;

The capacity of competing parents to provide the children with guidance, education, and love;

The developmental needs of the individual children;

The stated preference of the children coupled with their maturational level;

The mental and physical conditions of the contesting parents;

The stability and continuity of the home that each parent can provide;

The capacity of each parent to provide the child with the physical necessities of life, among other needs of day-to-day and long-term living;

The psychological parent, that is, the parent to whom the children are most attached, and who interacts best with the children ongoingly, providing love, care, protection, discipline, and appropriate restraints. The degree to which a parent qualifies as the "psychological parent" should be one of the most important determinants in a custody decision, predicated in great part on the matter of bonding.

The forensic psychologist must also be knowledgeable about visitation rights. The noncustodial parent is entitled to "reasonable visitation" rights unless the court finds, after hearings and court appearances, that visitation would endanger the child's physical, mental, or emotional health. The court may modify an order granting or denying visitation rights whenever modification would serve the best interests of the child; but the court normally does not restrict a parent's visitation rights unless it finds that the visitation would endanger the child's physical, mental, or emotional health.

The issues of investigation and report must also be dealt with briefly in contested custody proceedings; and in other custody proceedings, if a parent or the child's custodian so requests, the court may order an investigation and report concerning custodian arrangements for the child. The investigation and report may be made by the staff of the juvenile court or of other professional social-service organizations experienced in counseling children and families; and in preparing his report on a child, the investigator may consult any person who may have information about the child and his potential custodian arrangements. The investigator may consult with and obtain information from medical, psychiatric, or other expert persons who have served the child in the past without obtaining the consent of the parent or the child's custodian.

Such topics are dealt with in the agreement or contract each parent is to sign. Several of these issues are also emphasized verbally with each parent when that would improve his or her understanding of the process of forensic evaluation.

One of the first issues to be emphasized to the family is the concept that the child (or children) is the primary client, and that any recommendations would consider the child's (or children's) best interests and welfare ahead of that of the adults. The investigator may also emphasize the fact that the evaluation would, of course, be objective and scientific; and that if called on by the judge, the forensic psychologist would provide testimony in court that would be detrimental to either parent and to the possible outcome that either parent may desire.

Another issue to be emphasized is that the adults have waived confidentiality for themselves; but that anything which might be discussed between a child and the therapist could be kept confidential at the therapist's discretion, unless the court rules otherwise. Each parent should be required to sign an authorization for the mutual release and exchange of confidential and privileged information which permits access to any data relevant to the evaluation. Copies of test protocols obtained from a child's school psychologist may be used to supplement formal psychological testing of intelligence and academic achievement, if deemed sufficiently valid and relevant.

An issue that needs to be discussed is the parents' shared financial responsibility for the fee. Payment may be required in advance; and, of course, is not related to the nature of the opinion to be rendered, with research findings considered as appropriate and relevant to be included in the report.

IV

Let us define the parameters of the field of forensic psychology to assist practitioners in forensic psychology to delineate what they are expected to know, to aid psychology departments and law schools in curriculum planning for the inclusion of forensic courses and sequences, and to interpret to related disciplines—e.g., medicine, social work, behavioral sciences— the knowledge base undergirding the specialty of forensic psychology.

Essentially, forensic psychology is the application of the science and profession of psychology to questions and issues relating to law and legal systems. It is a specialty which, because it deals with the interface of psychology and the law, exists in a specialized milieu, serves a special population, and requires a special body of knowledge.

In general terms, forensic psychology is the utilization of psychological services in the legal forum. Those psychologists appropriately trained and licensed are professionally qualified to testify, examine, diagnose, treat, and certify in court-related cases.

The attempt of society to deal with law through the criminal-justice system is creating an ever-increasing role for the forensic psychologist.

The role of the psychologist as a forensic specialist is determined by the type of institution, court, agency, or program with which he or she is associated.

Psychologists working in forensics must recognize that they have a dual clientele: they are responsible not only to the patient, but also to society at large. They have a responsibility to society and to the law because it is "society" that has committed the patient to them for care. They also have a responsibility to society, because, based on their evaluations and decisions, the patient may in time return to society possibly to do harm or be unjust to its members. In this regard, the psychologist certainly appears to have a role in criminal-justice endeavors to create a law-abiding society.

Forensic psychology teaches the application of every branch of psychology to the purpose of the law. Hence the functions of the forensic psychologist include, but are not limited to, the following:

For Consultation: Providing consultation and training to attorneys, law students, and paralegals; providing consultation to judges and lawmakers; providing service to the judiciary as *amicus curiae* and in related capacities; providing consultation to criminal-justice and correctional systems; providing consultation to mental-health systems and practitioners on forensic issues; providing consultation and training to law-enforcement personnel.

For Diagnosis, Treatment, and Recommendations: Diagnosing, prognosticating, and treating criminal and juvenile justice populations, at all stages of the justice process; diagnosing, treating, and/or making recommendations including, but not limited to, mental status, children's interests, test-validity litigation, family and domestic relations factors, testamentary capacity and incapacities related to tort liability; analysis of problems and/or making recommendations pertaining to human performance, product liability, mental health, and safety in matters involving, but not limited to, effects of ingested substances, ambient environments, design, layout, and operation of artifacts and man-machine systems, and organizational variables; serving as expert witness in civil, criminal, chancery, and administrative law cases; screening, evaluating, and/or treating law-enforcement and other criminal-justice personnel.

For Other Functions: Serving as a special master in administrative and judicial tribunals; conducting behavioral science research and analysis pertaining to the understanding of legal issues, and to the development and evaluation of legal processes, statutes, and regulations; engaging in policy and program development in the psychology-law arena; teaching, training, and supervising others in forensic psychology.

V

Forensic psychologists subscribe to the ethical principle that they engage in only those forensic activities that are within their areas of competence and expertise.

Most psychologists feel strongly that absolute confidentiality is a *sine qua non* to the provision of ethical and effective psychological treatment. At the same time, the pressures to violate confidentiality are extreme and constant in many settings. Given the intensity of convictions about confidentiality on the part of psychologists and the strength of the opposing pressures on the part of other disciplines, psychologists would do well to make themselves aware of, and come to terms with, individual policies on confidentiality in various jurisdictions, agencies, and areas.

The role of the forensic psychologist often requires the translation of legal terminology into psychological or behavioral terms, or inference from psychological status to legal status. In order to do this most effectively, the forensic psychologist should know the civil, criminal, and administrative law in his/her state. The psychologist should also know important legal cases forming the precedent for the criminal law and civil law. This knowledge is requisite in consultation, evaluation treatment, and expert testimony. The forensic psychologist should be able to place the state and federal law in the context of important ongoing issues of national concern, e.g., the role of drugs, alcohol, or psychological problems in affecting the offender's capacity for intent in criminal cases, and/or negligence in tort liability cases and in family matters. Knowledge of law should include, but is not limited to, patients' and prisoners' rights, family law (children's rights, custody, child abuse, etc.), tort liability, special-education laws, developmental-disabilities laws, and civil rights.

VI

To be sure, the forensic psychologist, though not necessarily an attorney, should know basic legal concepts and terminology. These would include, but not be limited to, *mens rea*, levels of burden of proof, civil and criminal competency, responsibility, tort liability, *voir dire*, etc. S/he should also be familiar with legal citation methods, as well as basic legal terminology, legal citation and concepts, and the working of the adversary system, particularly as it affects children and family issues.

To function in relation to the adversary system, the forensic psychologist should know its workings from both an academic and an experiential perspective. S/he should be aware of the role and responsibilities of judge, jury, and attorney for the prosecution and defense (or plaintiff and defendant in civil laws). S/he should understand well the position of the psychologist as an expert witness and the legal basis for this role; s/he should understand the difference between a lay witness and an expert witness; s/he should know what is required, allowed, and prohibited in the presentation of expert testimony; and have skill in selecting particularly effective means of presenting psychological testimony in the courtroom according to the circumstances of the case. No less, s/he should be knowledgeable about jury selection and dynamics—and this applies to all functions of the forensic psychologist.

The workings of the area mental-health system is also important. The forensic psychologist engaged in consultation, evaluation, and/or treatment should know basic mental-health law for his/her state or area. This includes, but is not limited to, criteria for voluntary and involuntary civil commitment, the mechanics of commitment, special factors involved in criminal commitment, criteria for discharge, and duties and responsibilities of psychologists and other mental-health practitioners. Also included are an understanding of what rights different types of mental patients retain, and which are given up by virtue of commitment. The forensic psychologist should know how civil competency, criminal competency, and criminal responsibility are determined, and how they affect the status and needs of the mental patient. There should be awareness of the standard operating procedures of mental hospitals, of community facilities for the treatment of the mentally ill, and of the interaction between hospital and community treatment. The forensic psychologist should be able to evaluate the state mental-health law and system in terms of the broad context of general treatment issues and patient's rights litigation. S/he should have a knowledge of the right-to-treatment literature and important cases concerning all factors involved.

VII

Certain constitutional regulations, laws, and statutes are particularly relevant to the practice of forensic psychology; for example, amendment rights guaranteeing freedom of speech and religion, and the right not to be required to incriminate oneself, are relevant to the relationship between competency determinations and issues of guilt and responsibility, as are laws forbidding cruel and unusual punishment, which affect prison and mental-hospital forensic-unit policies. The due-process and equal-protection regulations are the basis of many cases in both civil and criminal law.

The forensic psychologist should understand criminology and juvenile delinquency from both a sociological and a psychological perspective. S/he should be aware of major theoretical paradigms and significant empirical research. The role of the victim in criminal behavior, as well as the science of victimology, should also be understood clearly by the psychologist involved in forensic work.

In order to assess and treat forensic clients most adequately, the forensic psychologist should have a knowledge of theory and research on development of children of all ages, mental illness, social psychology, and personality. This knowledge, of course, encompasses psychological, sociological, and biological perspectives. Mental illness should be as thoroughly understood as the state of the science permits, particularly those types which are often associated with family issues and criminal charges (character disorders, sexual deviation, addiction, paranoid schizophrenia) or civil cases (organic brain syndromes, traumatic neuroses). Because of the nature of any population, special emphasis should be placed on the effects of minority-class status and economic and social deprivation on personality functioning.

The forensic psychologist should have a knowledge of experimental psychology and its applicability to the legal system. This may well include the following areas: cognitive processes, the physiological and psychological bases of thought processes, memory, perception, sensation, and other aspects of brain function. The forensic psychologist should be able to explain sensibly and with common sense in testimony in the courtroom how experimental methods can be used to provide information in such areas as eyewitness identification or product liability.

VIII

In addition to possessing basic interviewing and testing skills, the forensic psychologist needs to be well-informed on the reliability, strengths, and weaknesses of clinical judgment and the major intelligence and personality tests. S/he should also be familiar with neuropsychological evaluation techniques. S/he should be able to explain the theory and use of psychological testing in terms that can be understood by laymen. S/he should be sensitive to systematic biases on tests that result from race, sex, education, socio-economic deprivation, and other factors.

Forensic psychologists should possess academic and experiential knowledge of the major therapeutic modalities. They should be particularly aware of how legal status, hospitalization, and incarceration affect psychological functioning, and of the special problems involved in treating certain forensic populations, particularly offenders; so they must be aware of the correctional environment and the way in which it modifies traditional therapeutic relationships and goals. Special knowledge of techniques useful in treating those with character disorders, drug and alcohol problems, and sexual problems is essential. Moreover, the forensic psychologist should possess an understanding of the appropriate uses of individual psychotherapy, behavior therapy, marital and family therapy, group therapy, and therapeutic communities, and be able professionally to justify selecting one or a combination of treatments, and concurrently be able to articulate the arguments for and against specific treatment approaches.

IX

It is very important that forensic psychologists be prepared to consult intelligently and sensibly with attorneys and counselors at law; and to testify on the applications of social psychology, human-factors-engineering psychology, and systems psychology in the context of civil rights, environmental impact, consumer and product safety legislation, regulations, and litigation. They should be skilled in designing, conducting, and interpreting research in these and related areas of behavioral and social science, keeping in mind the acceptability of various types of statistical proofs accepted and rejected by the courts. They should be familiar with key litigation pertaining to the use of statistical proof, and with legislative and administrative law pertaining to consumer protection, civil rights, and occupational, industrial, and product safety liability.

Certain issues within psychology and family law have especially significant impact on forensic psychology. Often the forensic psychologist is called on to make predictions about an individual. Since the statements made by the psychologist are likely to have a profound influence on the individual's life, it is essential that s/he be aware of theory and empirical findings on the whole prediction issue.

Another issue particularly germane to the forensic psychologist, and one closely related to the prediction issue, is the reliability and validity of psychological tests. The forensic psychologist should know the strengths and weaknesses of various psychological tests, how they are affected by situational variables, and how various subgroups respond to them.

Still another important theoretical and empirical issue with wide-spread implications for forensic psychology is the effect of various environments on psychological functioning. This includes, but is not limited to, the effects of minority-group membership, social class status, gender, discrimination, deprivation, institutionalization, various working conditions, the welfare system, and different organizational structures.

X

Although not all forensic psychologists will be involved in research, research design methodology, and statistical analysis, they should be knowledgeable about basic experimental design, in order to be able to evaluate the research reports of others, and review critically, and intelligently use, the research in his/her field. S/he should also understand the role, purpose, and value of basic, applied, and evaluation research. Those who are involved in research efforts should have an in-depth knowledge of research procedures, analysis, and ethical issues.

No less, the forensic psychologist should be familiar with the basic aspects of the selection, training, and treatment of security officers. In order to do this effectively, s/he must be aware of the attitudes and value of such persons. Also, s/he must understand the specific stresses inherent in such work and how these stresses manifest themselves. A basic understanding of police, correctional, and security-guard procedures is also necessary. S/he should be familiar with literature and techniques relevant to policy analysis, operations research, and evaluation research as they pertain to organizational and operational effectiveness, prediction, and assessment.

Forensic psychologists who provide services to employees of organizations (police departments, correctional systems, treatment programs, etc.) should be aware of the effect of the environment, formal and informal organizational structures, and management-employee relationships, since these are often as important as individual factors in consultation, evaluation, and treatment.

The forensic psychologist should have an understanding of correctional theory. To be sure, in recent years there has been a major controversy on the effectiveness of treatment within the correctional setting; and the psychologist should know well the literature and empirical research in this area. S/he should have an experiential as well as an academic understanding of standard operating procedures within prisons. It is essential that s/he understand the dynamics of prison life, the impact of loss of liberty, and how these affect intervention in the correctional system. It is important to understand the requirements for pre-release programming, parole, and probation, as well as the effects of such programs on the psychological functioning of the offender. The forensic psychologist should understand the nature of prison conditions and the efforts to modify these conditions.

XI

It is, of course, requisite that all psychologists should be aware of the provisions of their state licensing or certification law as it affects psychological practice specifically: and this is even more true for the forensic psychologist. Most laws define not only who may practice and what that practice may consist of, but also statutorily define the limits of confidentiality and the nature of relationships to other disciplines.

Although ethical issues are of vital concern to all psychologists as indicated already, the forensic psychologist by virtue of his/her specialty often finds that s/he is faced with difficult ethical issues, sometimes because it is not always clear who is the primary client of the forensic psychologist. For example; in a criminal case the psychologist has some responsibility to each of the following: the defendant, the defendant's attorney, the court, the correctional system, the mental-health system, the profession of psychology, and society at large.

The forensic psychologist should be cognizant of the major legal-ethical issues including, but not limited to, confidentiality, privileged communication, invasion of privacy, informed consent, and duty to warn. S/he should be knowledgeable of relevant codes of ethics, statutory law, and major legal cases in these areas.

XII

The question may well be asked: Who, then, in the field of psychological services, especially as regards family law, is best fitted for the practice of forensic psychology? In general, the following conditions may apply substantially.

S/he must be a psychologist of good moral character and scientific integrity, with high professional standing. S/he must engage in personal and professional behavior in accordance with the prevailing ethical standards of the psychological association appropriate to the location of the practice. The individual shall have an earned doctoral degree in psychology, with all degrees earned from an institution appropriately regionally accredited. The individual should be a licensed psychologist, meaning a psychologist licensed, certified, or otherwise registered to practice psychology in the state, territory, or province, as applies, and shall be a member in good standing of his/her area psychological association.

A forensic psychology committee of a psychological association may wish to establish a uniform set of minimal requirements for psychologists who accept referrals from the legal system, such as: licensed by the Psychology Examining Committee; a doctoral degree from a regionally accredited educational institution; at least two years of supervised (or equivalent) experience in health service, at least one being postdoctoral, and one in an organized health-service training program; postdoctoral professional practice directed primarily to the diagnosis and treatment of mental disorders for a period of not less than five years.

All of the above, then, are issues and matters of significant consequence in the all-encompassing specialty of forensic psychology, an area of psychological practice that is fast coming into relevant and appropriate prominence in professional legal disciplines.

Biographical Sketch of Robert L. Sadoff

Robert L. Sadoff, M.D., is currently Clinical Professor of Psychiatry and Director of the Center for Studies in Social Legal Psychiatry at the University of Pennsylvania. He was a founder of the American Academy of Psychiatry and the Law, and served as its second president, from 1971 to 1973. He was also on the originating board of the American Board of Forensic Psychiatry, and served as president of that board from 1982 to 1983. He is board-certified in psychiatry, forensic psychiatry, and legal medicine. He has written more than 85 articles in medical and legal journals, and has published six books (his most recent one receiving the Guttmacher Award from the American Psychiatric Association). He has contributed chapters in 25 other books, including the *Comprehensive Textbook of Psychiatry* and the English text *Principles and Practice of Forensic Psychiatry.* He has been awarded the Earl Bond Award at the University of Pennsylvania, and the Nathaniel Winkelman Award by the Belmont Center for Comprehensive Studies, and has lectured at several named memorial or honorary lectures throughout the country. He has also lectured in 12 countries of the world.

MENTAL ILLNESS IS NOT ALWAYS INSANITY

Robert L. Sadoff

The trial of Jeffrey Dahmer raises the question, when is an individual not criminally responsible for his acts? Jeffrey Dahmer has already pled guilty to having committed the acts in question, killing 15 people. He then goes on trial to demonstrate that he was not criminally responsible for these acts, because he claims that he was so mentally ill that he lacked substantial capacity either to appreciate the criminality of his behavior or to conform his conduct to the requirements of the law.

That is the test of insanity provided in the American Law Institute Model Penal Code, which was adopted in the federal case of U.S. v. Brawner in 1972, replacing the Durham decision that was made in the District of Columbia in 1954. That test stated that a person would not be held criminally responsible for his acts if his criminal behavior was a product of his mental illness. Most states adhere to the venerable McNaughten test, which is purely cognitive, stating that a person would not be held criminally responsible for his acts if, at the time of the commission of these acts, he was suffering from a mental illness that led to such impaired judgment that he did not know the nature and quality of his acts, or if he did know, that he did not know he was doing what was wrong.

Thus there are several different tests, depending on the jurisdiction in which the case is tried, of the person's criminal responsibility or his degree of insanity based on mental illness. It should be clear that mental illness alone is not sufficient to prove legal insanity. However, a person must have a mental illness in order to be found legally insane.

One of the confusing issues here is that the word "insanity" traditionally, in the nineteenth century, was used to denote mental illness. If a

67

person were involved in a legal matter with mental illness or "insanity," he would then be called a "lunatic." We have since dropped that pejorative term, and refer to people who have mental diseases or disorders as being "mentally ill." We reserve the use of the term "insane" for those who has been found legally not responsible for their criminal acts.

It is important to note this distinction because, in the Dahmer case, the defense attempts to show the jury how bizarre and "crazy" the defendant is. On the other hand, the prosecution typically will apply the specific legal test, and may even admit that the person had a mental illness, but that the mental illness did not deprive him of his ability either to know or understand what he was doing or deprive him of his ability to control his behavior. Typically, the prosecution would show other areas of control, indicating that the defendant did not lack the capacity to control his behavior, but rather chose not to control it. It is this area of volition that has been eliminated from most insanity tests in the country, especially following the Hinckley verdict in 1982.

The federal jurisdiction adopted the Omnibus Crime Code definition for insanity in 1984, which states: "A person would not be held criminally responsible if at the time of the crime he suffered from a mental illness such that he could not appreciate the wrongfulness of his acts." The use of the word "appreciate" connotes an emotional factor not found in the cognitive McNaughten test. Thus there are cases in which individuals may have known what they were doing, but could not fully appreciate the criminality of their behavior because of a serious mental illness, such as bipolar disorder, which used to be called manic-depressive disorder.

It should be noted that it is quite rare for a person to be found legally insane following a trial. Most individuals found legally insane are so found following an agreement by both sides that the individual was indeed insane at the time of the crime. The matter is then formally presented in court without the "battle of the experts" that one sees in a contested trial. Very few cases are even tried on the basis of insanity, and those that are mostly fail. Thus the insanity trial receives excessive amount of print or videotape because of the interest of people in such bizarre and unusual behavior.

What is to be done for those who are found not guilty by reason of insanity? Should they be studied to discover, if possible, what "made them tick"? Should they be left alone, or is there something we can learn about the serial killer or the bizarre criminal that might help us detect future criminals or prevent bizarre criminal behavior in the future? These are important questions to the researcher and to the criminologist. How successful are we at treating the insanity acquittee? Most will eventually leave the mental hospital to which they are committed following trial. Most will not engage in the same criminal behavior. However, there are rare instances in which individuals may have a second or even a third trial for insanity following release from the institution to which they were sent following their initial acquittal by reason of insanity.

Insanity is an interesting, absorbing, and challenging issue in the criminal law. Many have advocated the abolition of the insanity defense. My position is that it is necessary, morally and ethically needed as a part of the criminal-justice system. We should not hold culpable those individuals who lack the necessary mental elements for forming the *mens rea*, or guilty intent, which is an integral part of a crime. Crime consists of two parts: an act and an intent. If the intent is vitiated by the mental illness, then a person cannot be guilty of just an act. Thus, the concept "guilty but insane" is a legal misnomer. Rather, the concept should be "guilty but mentally ill," which exists in several states. If a person is found legally insane, then he is not "guilty" of a crime. He may have committed the act, but he is acquitted because of his mental incapacity.

Biographical Sketch of Dale W. Woolridge

Dale W. Woolridge was born in 1946 in Harrisburg, Pennsylvania. He was a 12-year-old Eagle Scout, an expert rifle marksman, and an avid pianist. He won several Science Fair awards. Although his education was interrupted by a tour of duty in Vietnam, where he was a military police sentry-dog handler, he went on to earn degrees in psychology, including a B.S. at Penn State and a Ph.D. at the University of Texas. He has taught college courses in introductory and social psychology. He is the author of various articles in the areas of psychology and computer programming. He is also an adult literacy trainer. He currently supervises the computer programmers and systems analysts who develop management information systems for Pennsylvania's mental-health and mental-retardation programs. His research interests include the actual and perceived causes of human progress, the improvement of intellectual skills, and techniques for permanent behavior change. He is a member of Mensa and of the Mathematical Association of America.

POPULAR PHILOSOPHY

Dale W. Woolridge

Where do people's beliefs come from? For many people, religion is a powerful influence; politics may be another. Much has been written about each. But another influence has been almost wholly overlooked. So little has been written about it that I had to invent a name: popular philosophy.

Popular philosophy is about the good life, which most people seek. "I have a dream," said Martin Luther King, Jr. Who hasn't? An American plans a new house in the suburbs, while an Arab dreams of a team of prize camels. A Pygmy thinks of sunning himself along the Ituri River, enjoying a delicious swarm of termites.

One cannot attain the good life just by wishing for it, by imagining what it's like, or by telling the world that one has a dream. One needs guidance on what to do and how to think. Popular philosophy, the people's version of philosophy, gives this guidance. Though many popular philosophies are possible, five have great social and historical significance.

"Mother Nature" is the philosophy of hunters and gatherers. It holds that the good life comes ultimately from nature. The grapes are out there waiting to be picked. But one must have a good relationship with the spirits.

The Copper Eskimos are Mother Nature philosophers. Their main spirit is the Big Bad Woman. She lives in a cave at the bottom of the ocean and commands the sea animals. Since the Eskimos depend on sea animals for survival, they don't want to enrage the Big Bad Woman. They have somehow discovered that she hates it when they sew caribou skin clothing on the sea ice during the dark period of winter. Therefore they have rules for where and when to sew. By similar thought, other Mother Nature philosophers suspend beaver skulls from trees, wear bags of dirt, blow trumpets in the jungle, and so on.

"Stouthearted Men" is the philosophy of manly virtue. It is the basis for chivalry, Bushido, and similar traditions among Africans and American Indians. It asserts that the good life comes ultimately from the manly soul, which contains virtues such as courage and ruthlessness. These virtues enable men to sacrifice their own earthly interests and serve a higher ideal. As compensation for their sacrifices, the men earn glory: exalted praise, honor, or distinction bestowed by common consent. To make sure that everybody knows where the glory is supposed to go, Stouthearted Men philosophers often wear such spectacular decorations as spiked helmets, eagle feathers, bandoliers, or buffalo heads.

People under the sway of Stouthearted Men can make progress, although often at the expense of their neighbors. But they have at least two faults. One is foolhardiness: action that is drastic when the issues are small, the cause unwinnable, or the rewards piddling. The movie *Taps* explored this theme. A second fault is foolish tactics in war. Men under the spell of this philosophy prefer tactics that provide an opportunity to prove their virility and win glory. They might choose hand-to-hand fighting when archers would be more useful.

"Good Culture" is the philosophy of Utopia. It claims that the good life comes ultimately from culture, the aggregate of human creations. Schools and libraries give us knowledge. Medicine gives us relief from disease. Government gives us peace and order. Therefore attaining the good life means engineering the culture so that its influences are beneficial.

Culture can also have powerful negative effects. Good Culture philosophers are the people who blame crime on television, government policies, or modern art. They see crime as evidence that something is very, very wrong with civilization. They sometimes have cultural revolutions to destroy all the objects suspected of making people have bad thoughts. They have built great bonfires to burn books, sunglasses, jazz records, and other feared objects.

"Struggle" is the philosophy of achievement. It holds that success in the attainment of one's goals comes primarily from one's efforts and abilities. On the road to success are many setbacks, obstacles, and adversities, but one can overcome them by knowing how and by trying hard.

Ability, in this philosophy, is mainly technique or the specific skills needed to overcome specific obstacles. It is knowledge of how to lay bricks, how to program a computer, and how to win friends and influence people. The American bookstore has much of this kind of information. In nonfiction, too, protagonists triumph by means of their appropriate abilities, and efforts.

According to some scholars, the foundation of American life is individualism, the desire to free oneself from the bonds of society and let it fend for itself. They point to Iacocca, Rocky, and the Horatio Alger rags-to-riches stories as evidence of individualism running rampant in American culture. However, the evidence does not support the idea that Americans want to separate themselves from society. Instead, Struggle is the persistently expressed theme in American culture.

"March on Washington" is a philosophy of black America, although its advocates come from all ethnic groups. It holds that the good life comes mainly from society (especially the federal government) and pride.

Government can overcome racism and make the societal changes needed for black advancement. Many March on Washingtonians believe in "political determinism," the doctrine that government policies determine almost everything that black people think or do. A typical book or article in this genre describes various areas in which improvement is possible, and discusses for each area the policies or programs that are, or should be, causing progress.

Pride is another chief cause of the good life. March on Washingtonians believe, despite evidence to the contrary, that black people suffer from low self-esteem and that they would do better if given greater pride. To enhance pride, March on Washingtonians surround themselves with symbols of extreme success and tell themselves stories about highly successful blacks. They also extol African culture by telling themselves that the Pharaohs were black, Solomon was black, Cleopatra was black, and so on.

ALLOYS

One might think that to attain the good life people would exploit every resource. But each of these popular philosophies is based on believing that there are only one or two main causes of the good life. Some questions arise. Is it really necessary to be so simpleminded? Why be bound to only one popular philosophy? Why not believe in all of them?

One way to achieve mental sophistication is to combine two or more popular philosophies into an "alloy." One alloy combines Good Culture and Stouthearted Men. Many Europeans during the period 1870–1914 wanted to expand civilization to backward places in the world. The reason the savages were still swinging from trees, the Europeans believed, was that they did not have a fine culture. The decent thing to do was to send in the stouthearted men, take over, and let the natives absorb civilization. It was men's work, the White Man's Burden.

Theodore Roosevelt's essay "Expansion and Peace" expresses this idea. The world had always harbored barbarians: vicious Turks inflicting horrors on Armenians, cruel Tartars terrorizing Asia, Algerian pirates, bloodletting followers of Aguinaldo in the Philippines, Afghans, Red Indians, Southern U.S. secessionists. In answer to the forces of darkness, Roosevelt advocated the expansion of the civilized powers. Imperialist expansion would bring stable and orderly government, then progress, to the savage lands. Therefore, it was the duty of civilized people to expand.

To achieve this expansion, Roosevelt appealed to Stouthearted Men. Expanding civilization was manly. It was work for men who "were men in every sense of the term." The work required men "with a fund of stern virtue deep in their souls." To advocate peace while evil lurked in the world was "cringing to iniquity," "cowardly shirking" from one's duty. Roosevelt's essay creates magnificent imagery in the mind of the reader: rows and columns of decorated men marching to the glorious applause of crowds, off to a dark cranny of the world to civilize the savages through better government, American-style.

Stouthearted Men and Mother Nature make another alloy. Many American Indian tribes had both philosophies in their cultures, but some stories have come down to us in which both sets of ideas are intertwined in an alloy. Take, for example, the story of Roman Nose at the battle of Powder River (see Dee Brown, *Bury my Heart at Wounded Knee*). Roman Nose got his braves into a battle line and told them to stand where they were until he had emptied the white soldiers' guns. He rode toward the end of the white line and then turned and rode fast along the line, letting each white have a clear shot. On reaching the end of the line, he turned and made a second pass, letting the white soldiers shoot again. On the third or fourth pass, his pony fell dead, but Roman Nose survived the battle.

Roman Nose had just spent a whole summer away on medicine fasts. The spirits must have been ecstatic. And when he returned, White Bull gave him a great war bonnet that was powerful medicine. Since Nose's medicine was good at Powder River, he could be sure he wouldn't be killed. In this story, the two popular philosophies of Mother Nature and Stouthearted Men are combined into a unified concept. The war bonnet was simultaneously decoration and something that pleased the spirits. Roman Nose was simultaneously a man of courage and a man of nature.

A rare alloy is based on Mother Nature and Good Culture. The Zuñi Indians believed in this alloy, according to Ruth Benedict's *Patterns of Culture.* Their culture featured complex ceremonies, with long scripts that had to be memorized, feathered masks and costumes, cults and societies, hierarchies of priesthoods, clowns, dancers, firewalkers, and sword swallowers.

According to Benedict, the Zuñis watched these ceremonies with trepidation, believing that the ceremonies decided their futures. Edmund Wilson, in his book *Red, Black, Blond, and Olive,* wrote that one dance would decide the moral standards for the tribe. The whole complicated society somehow depended on the dance. Precise execution of all the ceremonies would bring the good life. But a missing feather or one from the wrong part of the bird was cause for great concern, an imperfection that would dominate village conversation for days. A botched ceremony was tantamount to disaster. One is reminded of some Western Good Culture philosophers believing that rock music and blue jeans are undermining the foundations of civilization.

It is in the reasoning behind the ceremonies that one sees the connection with Mother Nature. The Zuñis believed that if the ceremonies were perfectly executed, the spirits would be pleased. If the spirits were pleased, they would bring rain. Rain would make nature blossom, and the Zuñis would reap and gather. Perhaps they could have simplified things by believing, as did many Sioux, that a bag of dirt makes the spirits happy.

Certain pairs of popular philosophies seldom form an alloy but instead create a sense of conflict. Take, for example, the famous dispute between W.E.B. DuBois and Booker T. Washington.

Washington's book, *Up From Slavery,* is almost a stereotype of Struggle. It stressed hard work and practical skills. This philosophy collided with DuBois's accent on social change and "deliberate propaganda" to make blacks proud of themselves. The conflict was not due merely to personality differences. According to Cornel West's recent article in *Dissent* (Spring 1991), virtually the same argument is even today strangling discussion of black progress. One "camp" analyzes black progress sociologically and advocates affirmative action and other policies. The other "camp" focuses on the "Protestant ethic," which calls for hard work.

Equally inane is the conflict between Good Culture ideas and those of Struggle. An example is the contemporary debate between the "structuralist" and "great man" theories of history. The debate is ancient.

One dispute occurred in the history of Confucian philosophy. Representing Struggle was Mencius, who believed that people rise through their own efforts. Culture was the product of people's achievements. Mencius and his followers also tended to view culture as a source of obstacles that could inhibit the outflow of productive forces originating within people. The people needed economic security and would create it themselves if the government would stay out of their way.

Representing Good Culture was Lao-tzu, who believed that the culture had an autonomous life of its own and was the primary determiner of human behavior. People, according to Lao-tzu, were merely bundles of biological urges, like cattle. People would become good or bad, strong or weak, according to the workings of the objective culture. There was no resolution of this controversy.

THE DESIRE FOR SIMPLICITY

The causes of the good life are many, interactive, and dependent on time and place. Some situations call for courage; other situations call for a change in the law. Some people advance through their abilities; other people advance through their parents' contacts. Popular philosophies provide mental economy. They simplify causality and tell the story of progress in a way that people can understand.

Progress, wherever the topic appears in literature, is usually attributed to only a few causes. In *What I Believe,* Bertrand Russell writes that the good life comes from love and knowledge (two causes). Francis Galton, in *Hereditary Genius,* writes that intellectual progress comes from mental ability, zeal, and the capacity for hard work (three causes). An American Indian story tells how a corn goddess gave the people corn (one cause). The often-cited theory of Galton does not credit schools or libraries, mentors, political freedom, or other possible ingredients of intellectual progress. The corn goddess story does not mention hard work, curiosity, persistence, or many other personal qualities that must have been involved in the domestication of corn.

When people are committed to believing in particular causes of progress, they often show annoyance at the idea that other causes may also play a role. Here are two examples:

"For anyone is an upstart who rises by his own efforts from his previous position in life to a higher one" (Adolf Hitler, *Mein Kampf*).

"A typical samurai calls a literary savant a book-smelling sot" (Inazo Nitobe, *Bushido*).

Thinking about causality is difficult. Part of the problem is a combinatorial explosion that occurs when causes are ranked according to their efficacy or applicability in a situation. If four causes were involved in progress, there would be 4!, or 24, possible rankings in any situation. Disputes between advocates of different popular philosophies may be, at the root, arguments about how weights should be assigned to different causes of progress. Another difficulty is interaction. Two or more causes can produce an effect that could not be predicted from considering the causes in isolation. Researchers who use experimental methodology know that three-way interactions are hard to interpret, and higher-order interactions are virtually impossible to understand. These difficulties, and others, lead experimental researchers to examine only a few (usually one or two) factors in any study.

In my research on popular philosophy, I often use a "Rule of Two" in predicting beliefs and behavior. This rule (which is not a scientific principle, but a heuristic) says that people often resist incorporating more than two causes into their beliefs about the good life. The rule seems most useful in understanding dogmatic people and ossified societies. The Zuñis provide an example of how the rule can be applied.

Zuñi ideology prominently featured nature and culture as causes of the good life. Could they also believe in Stouthearted Men? Such a militarist philosophy might have served them well, considering the frequency with which Navajos, Spaniards, and others have meddled in their affairs. But the Rule of Two suggests that the answer to the question is no. Accounts by Ruth Benedict and others show that the Zuñis opposed Stouthearted Men ideas with a vehemence that is suspicious.

Some ceremonies had the purpose of terrifying children, especially boys. In one rite, masked men would whip the boys with a harmless but frightening lash. Other societies have similar rituals but it's typical for the people to expect boys (sometimes girls, too) to show no reaction to pain or terror. What was unusual about the Zuñis was that they encouraged whimpering and bawling. There was no sanction against a boy crying out even when lightly flailed. Crying out increased the value of the ceremony. Even adolescents were expected to cry out for their mothers.

Such unmanly behavior is hard to understand by any theory of mind or society. What functions could it serve? Perhaps it preserved the simplistic nature of Zuñi popular philosophy.

Popular philosophy is a worthy area for research. For reasons of space, I could not indicate the richness of each popular philosophy. Each is the basis for a vast panorama of beliefs, myths, and rituals. The disputes, too, are deeper than I have indicated. The topic does not deserve its neglect.

Autobiographical Sketch of Barbara Velazquez

Born in New York City, attended the respected High School of Music and Art as an art major. Received a B.S. degree from N.Y.U. in Management and in Marketing. Entered the computer programming field and rose rapidly to a managerial capacity. During this time, I became aware of the innate individual differences between individuals which lead to disagreements, negative attitudes, and total lack of empathy in their relationships with others. Continued exposure to such experiences led me ultimately to the field of psychology as I became aware of the misanthropic overtones in my life. The field of psychology offers the seeds by which we may understand all human endeavor and purpose, and to this I have dedicated myself. I am currently attending Seton Hall University in order to earn my master's and doctoral degrees in psychology. I have dedicated myself to advancing of the study of human potential, in order to facilitate our understanding of the psychic processes which so intimately affect our lives.

CHAPTER 8

THE DYNAMICS OF PERSONAL GROWTH

Barbara Velazquez

In the more than seventy years since C. G. Jung first published his work *Psychological Types,* the field of psychology has grown from early infancy to the brink of adolescence. Psychology has been considered by most to be a last resort, a process by which mental health is restored. Because of this attitude, the full impact of Jung's theory of psychological types has yet to unfold. Knowledge of personality theory has remained in the hands of the psychiatrist and the psychologist as they employ it in the practice of their profession. The average person may be introduced to it at second-hand by exposure to a personality test or for the purpose of career assessment. Rarely are the actual components of the theory explained, and the ordinary adult is under an appalling misconception of the very meanings of the terms "introvert and "extrovert." Ignorant of the very basis of the subject, most of us cannot apply it to everyday situations in a manner that would benefit both our personal lives and our relationships. Hidden within the dynamics of the personality rests the clues which explain those sudden moments of irrational thought or behavior which are apparently so inconsistent with our normal attitudes. Buried within the study of psychological types are some of the basic reasons for the misunderstandings, the preconceived attitudes, and the unexpected and seemingly unwarranted reactions of others.

Introversion and extroversion are two diametrically opposed psychological orientations which can nevertheless be reconciled by simple familiarity. The shyness and outgoingness traditionally associated with these terms are incidental by-products, and do not always hold true. Jung identified four subtypes for each group; thinking, feeling, sensation, and intuition. He also noticed that operating in each of the eight types are

79

subconscious, archaic patterns which result from suppressing the other types. Jung theorized that the most perfectly balanced individual would combine fairly equal qualities of introversion and extroversion. Unfortunately, we as individuals tend to look at all situations and events through the window of our own personal psychological orientation, and assume that everyone else is viewing the situation from the same vantage point.

The dominance of one psychological type or another is not thought to have been consciously selected by the individual, but to be a predisposition observable quite early in life. All types display excellent and useful qualities, but unfortunately have their negative points as well. It is precisely these negative aspects which lead to our psychological skirmishes with others in our environment and even with ourselves. It is therefore imperative both to know ourselves and to consider the means by which we can effect a form of psychological growth. This growth process would enhance our strong points and suppress our weakest, replacing them with other, more healthy qualities. The continued growth of our personalities should be an ongoing process, just as a professional continues to take classes and seminars in order to further his or her professional knowledge. The negative qualities of our personalities are the cause of the unpleasantness in our lives; they can make us miserable in paradise, can turn opportunity into failure and harmony into discord. Shall we wait then for unpleasantness to manifest itself by giving our negativity free reign? Or do we take conscious control of our minds and consciously create the personality which is capable of turning all situations into opportunities?

EXTROVERT AND INTROVERT

As you read the following brief descriptions, it is important to bear in mind that at times we have all displayed characteristics of each of the personality types. There is, however, only one orientation to which all others are subordinate. This dominant orientation is the one which determines thought, action, and reaction. Few individuals will display the following characteristics in their purest forms, but for the sake of clarity it is easiest to present them in such a manner.

Dominance of one of the extroverted types indicates a person who seeks validation and justification primarily through observable and tangible external input. The tendency is to order one's life in accordance with prevailing cultural demands and expectations. Behavior is nearly always adapted to fit actual circumstance. The extrovert displays a wonderfully flexible quality of mind, always ready to adjust to changing reality and external demands. Personal reflections about the validity of the demands, though often present, are not the decisive factor in the decisionmaking process. The immediacy of the external demand or expectation will tend to take precedence over subjective considerations. Because of this tendency to deny personal desires, the extrovert has little defense against the often extraordinary demands placed upon him by a society or peer group. The extrovert will attempt to respond to these demands to the point of self-abnegation, even while his subconscious rises up in desperate revolt.

The dominance of introverted types, on the other hand, indicates an individual who seeks validity and justification from within. In other words, the introvert has his or her own set of standards by which everything in their external environment is colored. Whereas the extrovert is always ready to respond to external demand, the introvert evaluates that demand in terms of a set of personal standards or expectations. If the demand is at odds with the standard, the introvert finds himself in conflict with the external environment. We all, whether introverted or not, have our own set of personal standards. The introvert, however, will adhere to these standards in the face of external pressure. Stubbornly held standards are quite obviously beneficial and praiseworthy in terms of moral issues, social equality, and human rights, but when practiced by an individual, the process becomes more difficult to discern. The introvert's preoccupation with evaluation and merit can be mistaken by the extrovert for inexplicable nonconformism, rebelliousness, and disrespect for traditions, and even egotism and selfishness. Although at times some or all of these accusations may be true, the phenomena only approximate these sentiments. The introvert is first and foremost activated by ideals, the shoulds and coulds of a given circumstance, whereas the extrovert concentrates on what is, and sees little practical purpose in directing efforts toward circumstances which exist only in the mind.

We will now briefly consider the eight specific psychological types defined by Jung.

EXTROVERT FEELING

Extrovert Feeling is an orientation which derives its validity from prevailing sentiment. It appears perfectly adjusted to and harmonized with the demands of the environment. In other words, cultural, or traditional feeling values are often strictly adhered to. Extrovert Feeling strives to feel, react, and respond in precisely the "correct" or expected manner.

Anything which would appear to go against established feeling or response is rejected immediately. Extrovert Feeling is so genuinely oriented toward established responses; has become so unconsciously attuned to the cultural norm, that his or her truly personal desires reflect that which is judged acceptable by the social order. Such a person will automatically desire to live in "just the right" neighborhood, marry "just the right" person, wear "just the right" fashions, and listen to "just the right" music, all based upon the peer group with whom he or she identifies. On the negative side, Extrovert Feeling can become so bombarded by various demands for feeling and reaction that feeling becomes totally detached, so that the individual becomes the slave to the dictates of the peer group, with little or no conscious will or desire of his or her own above what is considered allowable by the dictates of fashion.

EXTROVERT THINKING

Extrovert Thinking, like Feeling, places enormous importance on the external and tangible. Extrovert Thinking generally serves a specific purpose, envisions a specific goal, seeks to alter or study a specific circumstance or event. If a subject lacks purposeful, practical, and tangible application, Extrovert Thinking sees little reason for a serious consideration of it. As such, Extrovert Thinking is oriented toward fact and observable reality. This is not to say that hypothetical or unproven considerations are not entertained; only that fact and observation will take precedence over philosophy and idealism. It is to this ability to analyze and observe the world around us that we owe the advances in technology and our knowledge of the natural sciences, as well as the decline in religion and philosophical thought. Once having observed or determined what is considered to be fact, Extrovert Thinking then begins to codify and create an intellectual formula by which life is to be lived. This is seen in its extreme form in bureaucratic red tape and strict adherence to conformity and proven results. Extrovert Thinking, in its negative form, can be very limiting and narrowminded, rejecting immediately whatever is not already proven or cannot be overtly observed. There is a marked resistance to change unless it is absolutely dictated by the environment, and a hostility toward anything that does not adhere to established rules.

Extrovert Thinking and Feeling were regarded by Jung as rational types, seeking to judge and order their external environment so that some measure of control may be achieved. The next two types are what Jung called extrovert irrational types, only because these types make little attempt to order, control, or judge the world around them.

EXTROVERT SENSATION

Extrovert Sensation's major criterion in deciding value is the intensity of the sensation caused by tangible qualities alone. An object or circumstance is judged to be real only when it has been experienced. Consciousness is directed toward concrete reality; ideals, concepts, and theories are considered only to the extent that they improve the possibilities for experience. For example, the possibility of life on other planets opens up possibilities for further concrete and tangible experiences. The concept of life after death does not hold such appeal since it does not admit of experience in concrete, physical form. Extrovert Sensation makes few judgments about whatever is found in the environment. The goal is to recognize and validate through the physical process of experience, or indirectly through the experiences of others. Experience represents fact, and Extrovert Sensation would no more judge the validity of the existence of a fact than most would judge the validity of the existence of water, the sky, or the sun: they simply are. Having made no judgments or formulated any concepts concerning experiences, he or she has no reason to behave in a manner which does not accept and harmonize with what has been established as factual. Negatively, this person can become an inveterate pleasure seeker, ruthless and exploitative in nature, seeking only to squeeze sensation from everything encountered, and lacking in reflection about the results of his or her behavior.

EXTROVERT INTUITION

Extrovert Intuition has the ability to discover the fullest value in all concrete objects. As the object is evaluated in this manner, it becomes of the utmost value to the individual; yet once all is discovered, Extrovert Intuition must seek new stimuli. From this unconscious evaluation process, a value system is derived. This system, though directed only toward concrete objects, seldom resembles the system prevailing at the time. Morality for this type consists of absolute loyalty to this set of values or vision. All who are involved with him on any venture are expected to subject themselves totally to the goal. There is a tendency to set a goal, accomplish it, then move on to the next before reaping the benefits of the previous. Many entrepreneurs, tycoons, and politicians are found among this type. There is also an uncanny ability to discern hidden potential and talent, in the same manner that a theatrical agent discovers an unknown talent on a dimly lit stage off Broadway. Negatively, the concrete object, situation, or person can become so integral to their goals, so interwoven into their thought processes, that it ceases to be concrete and takes on an abstract quality. This is the closest that extroversion comes to introverted conceptualization. The object, thus devalued, is often abused, unappreciated, and taken for granted.

INTROVERT FEELING

Introversion is an orientation primarily concerned with concepts and ideals, with what should be and could be in life. Whereas Extrovert Feeling types are in harmony with the world as they find it, Introvert Feeling harmonizes with an idealized concept of the world as it should or could be. The depth of Introvert Feeling is not easily discovered, because it is most often deeply internal and most noticeable in a willingness for self-sacrifice and a strong sense of devotion. Introvert Feeling gives the appearance of consciously limiting its reactions to external objects, which gives the impression of coldness and mental distance, however polite and harmonious the person may appear outwardly. The idealized image is tantamount to that of a white knight in shining armor. To the extrovert this appears unrealistic, at the least, but this is the foundation on which the great humanitarian movements are built. Introvert Feeling compares all that it perceives with this romantic ideal and attempts to reconcile it with reality. Negatively, when reality is found wanting in the eyes of the individual, there is a tendency to attempt to force idealized behavior upon those in the environment, and so such people can become quite domineering and oppressive. When resistance is encountered, as it inevitably must be, these people begin to imagine themselves to be victims of plots and schemes against which they must protect themselves.

INTROVERT THINKING

Introvert Thinking often indicates a philosophical or scholarly turn of mind. Introvert Thinking is desirous of new views of and insights into a subject. Thinking in this case is not generally the result of the conscious conclusions derived from systematic consideration of facts. Thinking often consists of fully complete concepts, and the individual then seeks to discover whether the external facts bear out the concept. In the manner of all introverts, the Introvert Thinker compares his external environment with an ideal, concept, or standard, but unlike the extrovert, the introvert places far more weight on the standard and may attempt to force this standard on the environment. Introvert Thinking finds strict adherence to fact and observation to be stifling; the idea itself is of the utmost importance. Many of the greatest thinkers and philosophers doubtless fall into this category. So thoroughly does this orientation immerse itself in the world of ideas that external influences, those initiated by this person on others, those by others on himself or herself, often go unnoticed; these include the more subtle social norms. Introvert Thinking remains only superficially aware of the demands of the environment on it; so such people do not always react in the expected manner. This form of introversion is often highly objectionable to the extrovert, but only because of general ignorance of the introvert's psyche, and the wide- scale misinterpretation of introvert behavior.

As in extroversion, Introverted Thinking and Feeling are considered rational types who attempt to gain control over their environment by using judgment and evaluation. With introversion, the individual is attempting to balance internal ideals with the surroundings. That the process is unconscious is to their detriment, for when reality does not correspond with the ideal, equally subconscious factors arise which cause an attempt to force reality to fit the ideal. This can lead to an internal crisis, if the individual cannot reconcile the expectations with the environment.

INTROVERT SENSATION

Introvert Sensation seeks to derive the fullest conceptual meaning from an object. In the course of discovering its meaning or values, thought proceeds in a chain, beginning with the object, and embracing all concepts which contain the remotest connection. Consequently, it ends with an idea which appears totally unrelated to the original. This process is similar to starting a conversation on the subject of gardening and ending with a discussion of Irish castles. We often wonder how we got from one topic to the other, and yet if we retrace our steps, we find a logical connection between each intermediate topic and the next. In Introvert Sensation, this process is internal; so the individual appears to make incomprehensible associations and connections. Introvert Sensation attempts in some way to define the value or meaning in his or her life, and so has little patience with tradition and conformity, wishing instead to formulate a personal value system. For this reason, the individual may appear to be driven, dogmatic, compulsive, and inexplicably rebellious. At times this individual may feel that he/she transcends the world of the tangible, which then appears to be a world of make-believe, a comic opera in which the individual makes only a guest appearance.

INTROVERT INTUITION

The predominance of Introvert Intuition is characterized by the ability to perceive that which Jung termed the "archetype." The archetype is the language of the unconscious, the language of dreams. We could say that the collective unconscious holds the entire history of humankind, of our nature, and our connection with all things. Contained in the collective unconscious are natural laws which apply to our material world, as well as those laws whereby we may achieve our ideal state, either morally or otherwise. The archetype is a sentence in the book of the collective unconscious. Obviously confusion can result from picking up a book at random and reading various sentences from different pages. A similar confusion is found in the Introvert Intuitive, who perceives the apparently unconnected archetypical images. Often there is no realization that these perceptions are a form of thought which has its validity in the material world (though often in a more universal sense) just as the more familiar thought patterns do. The Introvert Intuitive tends to become so engrossed by these thoughts that all connection with overt reality is lost. This type of personality is often typical of mystical or spiritually oriented individuals. These individuals have seen what they regard as a supremely ideal vision to which they unhesitatingly seek to adhere without thought of worldly implications. It is very difficult to explain in words those things which can be fully understood only by experience; for this reason this type of personality is often not understood. The Intuitive displays a distinct lack of concern for material or tangible considerations, and a lack of worldliness which others find surprising.

CONTRASTING EXTROVERT AND INTROVERT TYPES

Introversion and extroversion are indeed at opposite ends of the psychological spectrum. The basis on which the entire life is governed, the criteria by which all is judged, are determined primarily by the dominant psychological perspective. The extrovert lives in the world of what is; the introvert in the world of what can or should be. Neither is truly aware of the existence of the other's point of view. Upon perceiving evidence of the other's existence, both regard it as unnatural, alien, and irregular, little knowing that the other perspective is as common as their own. If both introversion and extroversion are so common, why, we might ask, are we so often unaware of the other's existence? The reasons are simple: our immediate environment tends to be consistent with our own psychological perspective. It stands to reason that an extrovert would tend to marry another extrovert, and raise children who shared their orientation, and vice versa. Our friendships and our occupations also tend to reflect our psychological orientation. Certain fields of endeavor are more oriented toward one orientation than the other. Another reason is that psychological types are seldom observed in their purest forms as described above, but are diluted by circumstance, upbringing, existence of a secondary or auxiliary type, and many other factors.

It is where introversion and extroversion meet as strangers that misunderstanding and resentment appear. The introverted son of extroverted parents would find himself chided for his shyness and introspection, and his unconventionality and pride in individuality could be considered an oddity. The Extrovert Sensation type, placed in a strongly metaphysical environment, could be regarded as overly materialistic, narrowminded, and lacking in faith. The introvert in the bureaucratic world of business would perhaps feel that the negative reactions to his uniqueness violate his very being. Those unfortunate enough to find themselves in such misanthropic situations quickly become aware of a difference which cuts to the very core of their relations with others in that environment. The extrovert looks to observable clues in the external environment as a guideline for behavior. Since in the introvert such guidelines are not observable but are the result of unobservable mental processes, much of the behavior is regarded as nothing short of unfathomable. The introvert, on the other hand, expects others to manipulate and evaluate reality from a similar conceptual vantage point. When it slowly becomes apparent that this does not take place, the external demands placed upon the introvert begin to appear inexplicably superficial and limiting. Each, out of ignorance, tends to regard the difference in the other's perspective as a personal affront.

Once we become aware of the reasons behind such misunderstandings, we need to make adjustments in our personal outlook and reactions in order to further our relationships with others. As we study each of the orientations more closely, we may notice desirable qualities which are absent in our own outlook. Each orientation has, of course, its negative side, and, according to Jung, the negative traits are a result of repressing the orientation most opposite to our own. In other words, Extrovert Thinking suppresses Introvert Feeling more than the other types. The negative traits of the Extrovert Thinker express themselves in an archaic, irrational idealization of fact and formula, along with an uncontrollable need to force others to conform to that formula. This process works unconsciously in an effort to balance the individual. This does not normally succeed, however, since the process continues to work through the individual's predominant orientation and becomes negatively diluted. Why not then take conscious control of this process? If the subconscious has designed a process whereby the addition of a different orientation will bring balance, why not make this a conscious process, so that we are able to control it? The unconscious, being unworldly as it is, has merely inserted this foreign orientation into our consciousness and abandoned it, locked in mortal combat with the vastly stronger incumbent. The dominant orientation, being healthy and well-exercised, is not going to meekly accept the intrusion of a weak, undernourished attitude, and will dominate it by taking its qualities and forcing it to fit its own. The new attitude is then mutated, which has an effect that is the reverse of what was intended.

CONSCIOUS GROWTH

Let us begin with the Extrovert Feeling type. The positive attributes are an instinctive harmony with the external environment. Negatively, this individual can become so overly involved in external demands and expectations that illogical attachments are formed, anything new is regarded as alien or suspicious, and there is an inability to separate personal needs from the demands of others. This is a result of repressing Introvert Thinking. Introvert Thinking, being philosophical and concept-oriented, when expressed through Extrovert Feeling becomes negatively logical, causing a lack of human warmth. These persons can lose all sense of ego; they can act and behave in the expected manner with no more feeling or interest than a puppet on a string. The conscious cultivation of Introvert Thinking would help induce the individual to seek out new views and insights in an effort to understand how the environment functions. This briefly translates into a change in position, from total acceptance of prevailing norms, to an analysis of whether external demands fit into personal needs and desires. This detached analysis counteracts the tendency to lose the self in others, and strengthens feeling into something which has true meaning to the individual. Surprisingly, even the negative aspects of Introvert Thinking—a lack of social awareness and personal detachment—will tend to help the person who is overly aware of social pressures and lacks detachment.

Extrovert Thinking values adherence to norms based on observable fact. Negatively, this type can become highly impersonal. Any deviation from the norm can be regarded as a personal threat and a danger to the established order. This is a result of repressing Introvert Feeling, which romanticizes an ideal and can attempt to force others to adhere to it. Extrovert Thinking has romanticized observable fact and demands the adherence of all. Conscious cultivation of Introvert Feeling would enable such persons to observe the spirit of the law rather than the letter. Introvert Feeling supports an ideal with its heart and soul. Extrovert Thinking applies a formula coldly, indiscriminately. The conscious cultivation of Introvert Feeling would cause the development of rules to fit the ideal. Rules become guidelines subservient to requirements. Introvert Feeling is, above all, detached from social or cultural pressures, which would counterbalance the tendency to give in to to external pressure to conform.

Extrovert Sensation lives in a world based on purely tangible experiences. Interest and knowledge are focused upon the concrete and tangible in life. Negatively, this type can become crudely exploitative, desirous only of the experiences and knowledge obtained from the object of interest. This results from repressing the influence of Introvert Intuition, which is concerned more or less with universal ideals. The universal, or that which surpasses the individual, cannot easily be translated into experience familiar to extrovert sensation, and can be at best negatively translated by him as a type of dream world designed specifically for the individual's personal use. In introversion, intuition takes the form of mysticism; in extroversion, "fantasy" may be the nearest equivalent. This would involve broadening "fantasy" to encompass the universal. This has been accomplished quite successfully in the movie industry, by writers, and by theme-park engineers. Fantasy can, of course, include an individual's private dreams. There are a multitude of ways in which personal experiences and knowledge can be crystalized into an ideal and advanced in a universal manner, e.g., by the establishment of a restaurant serving cuisine of the highest standard, or the institution of new policies which best serve the needs of a community. The ideal of providing the best service possible on a universal basis gives purpose to an otherwise disorganized, possibly superficial desire to experience sensation and acquire knowledge.

Extrovert Intuition extracts the fullest value and meaning from the concrete world around it. Negatively, the object becomes nearly nonexistent, lost within the ultimate goal set by the individual. This type can become cruelly abusive, with a tendency to discard that which is no longer of interest or use, whether these are other persons or things. In this we see the results of repressing Introvert Sensation, which searches for meaning and value in life from a conceptual point of view. Extrovert Intuition has negatively incorporated this search into its orientation, and once an object is of no further value or meaning, it is discarded. This individual is searching for, and not finding, lasting meaning in the tangible environment, and needs to learn to seek it now from within. The world of ideals and concepts is the only realm which the Extrovert Intuitive has not yet explored. This ideal or concept will most likely take the form of a cause requiring his or her leadership. Extrovert Intuition, when allied with a purpose, makes one a most dynamic powerful and magnetic of leaders, once given something to believe in.

Introvert Feeling is capable of devotion to personal ideal(s) against which all else is measured. Such a person can be willing to subject the self and others to personal sacrifices for the sake of the ideal(s). This tendency to superimpose the ideal on their environment results from repressing Extrovert Thinking, which cultivates an intellectual formula and rigidly insists on strict adherence to that formula. The extrovert must seek psychic balance from within in the form of ideals, the introvert must find this balance outside of himself or herself. Introvert Feeling must place rigid guidelines around its reforming tendencies, and choose to guide and lead by example. By placing itself in a situation where thought and analysis are required, perhaps through computer programming, architecture, and engineering, the person can incorporate form and structure, yet maintains his or her own personal standard of excellence.

Introvert Thinking is philosophical in nature; it loves to immerse itself in new concepts and unique insights. These innovative and unique thinkers are often so lost in the world of ideas, that the habits and conventions of the external world are invisible to them. Extrovert Feeling shares this tendency toward immersion and loss of perspective. Despite all appearances, Introvert Thinking strongly desires acceptance, a feeling of belongingness, as does Extrovert Feeling. But instead of losing the self in a maze of external demands, the introvert becomes lost in a maze of concepts and ideas. Conscious development of Extrovert Feeling would involve the search for a social or larger purpose to which one could apply ideas and concepts. Thinking must find purpose and must consider how humanity or society may be further served by the introduction of new ideas. Psychology, education, and sociology are only a few of the disciplines which deal with both ideas and humanity. In this way the individual becomes so involved in the concerns of others that his or her own social difficulties are forgotten. The person suddenly becomes quite aware of what is expected of him or her, and quite capable of supplying it.

Introvert Sensation seeks to discover the philosophical meaning in life by questioning current social and moral traditions. Habitually searching for value and meaning, these people can appear stubborn, dogmatic, tactless, even driven. Extrovert Intuition, the most suppressed orientation, displays precisely the same focus in the tangible environment, characterized by a stubborn pursuit of goals and in letting no one stand in the way of attainment. In introversion the same qualities cause the devaluation of culture and tradition, which is trampled mercilessly in the evaluation process. Conscious development of Extrovert Intuition would create an acute awareness of the best extant concepts, morally or otherwise, to be found in external values, while discarding that which is of no meaning or value. From this basis, Introvert Sensation can find not only traditions to which to adhere, but also a basis from which to build new value systems.

Introvert Intuition in its purest form corresponds to the most altruistic and idealistic in each of us. The tendency is to devalue the material in favor of the spiritual or purely mental. What is most suppressed in this case is Extrovert Sensation. This can cause obsessive attitudes toward anything that stimulates physical sensation, including drugs, alcohol, and sex. In addition, there is the possibility of hypochondriacal tendencies (reminiscent of the phenomenon of the stigmata of the middle ages). Constructive use of Extrovert Sensation would be to discover how one's new insights can take practical form in the world in which they live. Perhaps through teaching, instruction, or guidance, their abstract thought patterns can be crystallized. Whether or not everyone can agree with the premise of mysticism, the fact remains that there are individuals whose perceptions and psychological orientation are dominated by intuition. They may be said to live in a different world; this, however, does not change the fact that they are, physically at least, existing in a tangible, physical reality which must be given its share of recognition. Hence Extrovert Sensation with its emphases on the physical and tangible will directly counteract the otherworldliness of the spiritually inclined.

The insights into human nature and the possible further implications of the study of this field are readily seen, even in so brief a discussion as we have just presented. Optimally, it would be more desirable to investigate the more positive aspects of each type more fully. However, we hope we have shown how our personal lives and our relationships with others can be made easier through increased familiarity with these theories. Our understanding of ourselves and our own reactions can prove a basis for growth rather than for stagnation, as so often happens.

Education is another field that can benefit enormously from incorporation of this field into presently existing theory. Current educational practices that require the memorization of facts is a methodology best suited to Extrovert Thinking; the other seven types are left to suffer by comparison. The sales and advertising professions can benefit as well, since the hint of peer pressure or acceptance inherent in many commercials has less effect on the introvert than on the extrovert. Most importantly, however, a familiarity with personality types can help to foster human understanding and can do its part to restore harmony among humankind. Let us remember that interpersonal relations involve relations between presidents and world leaders as well as between friends and competitors. Misunderstanding and resentment between individuals can cause war, just as it causes divorce. We owe it to ourselves and to our future to investigate any viable means by which the dream of mutual tolerance and understanding can be achieved.

Section II
Philosophy, Science, and Nature

Autobiographical Sketch of Richard W. May

Born near the rarified regions of Laputa, then, and often, above suburban Boston, during the Year of the Monkey, I am a Piscean, a cerebrotonic ectomorph, and an ailurophile. Kafka and Munch have been my therapists and allies. Ever striving to descend from the mists and to attain the mythic orientation that is known as having one's feet upon the earth, I have done occasional consulting and frequent Sisyphean schlepping.

A paper tiger with letters after my name, I have been awarded an M.A. degree, *mirabile dictu*, in the humanities by Cal. State, Diplomate status in ISPE, and a U.S. patent for a board game of possible interest to aliens. As the author of *Auto-anthropophagy: The Eucharist of the Gods, a Seven-level Allegorical Encryption*, it is fitting that I am a member of Mensa, ISPE, Prometheus, Mega, and the Aleph Nine. As founder of the Aleph itself, and the renowned Laputans Manque, I am a biographee in Marquis' *Who's Who in the World*.

Most significant to me is the *philosophia perennis* and the realization of the idea of man as an incomplete being who can and should complete his own evolution by effecting a change in his being and consciousness.

CHAPTER 9

FOUR EASTERN PHILOSOPHIES

SUPER GENIUS

Richard W. May

MEGA

ALSO OH AH EGO-TRIP

The word Taoism corresponds to the Chinese *tao chia*, which means the philosophical school of the Tao. If one knows what is meant by a philosophical school, the problem is now "merely" that of defining the Tao itself!

Defining the Tao is paradoxical, rather than merely difficult. The Tao by definition cannot be defined or reduced to a linear sequence of symbols. As Lao Tzu's *Tao Te Ching* states: The Way which can be named is not the real Way; the Tao which can be "Taoed" is not the eternal Tao. This is not simply a peripheral difficulty, but the essence of the Tao itself. The word "Tao" points to a level of reality that is both beyond and within, both external and internal in nature, and transcends both symbolic and analytic thought and their associated states of consciousness.

"Tao" when used by Lao Tzu means the way of *nature*, and it is the way of nature with which the sage is held to be identified. (Tao had other meanings if used by other schools, such as the Confucianist.) Thus Taoism means of, or pertaining to, the philosophic school of the way of nature, i.e., the way of the sage *and the child*.

What can be said of the way of nature? What are its principles, if indeed they can be formulated in words? One principle is *wu wei*, which means literally "not-doing," or *wei wu-wei*, "doing-by-not-doing," to differentiate it from mere passivity or inaction. This principle of *wu wei* underlies the internal martial arts of judo, aikido, and tai chi ch'uan, wherein the strength, weight, and force of the opponent are turned against him by stepping aside or not resisting, "doing nothing," at just the right moment. The Chinese phrase, "opening the door to let in the thief," illustrates this principle. If the thief is pressing on the door of one's abode, and it is unexpectedly opened, then the lack of resistance causes the thief

95

to lose his balance and fall on his face! *Wu wei* is expressed in such phrases as "going with the flow" or "don't push the river" i.e., the idea of "not forcing" nature or life.

Another principle of the Tao is *Li*, which expresses the concept of the organic pattern of nature, the lines of grain in jade or wood, the path of least resistance manifest in the swirls of water, the Gestalt of natural forces in matter.

Another principle of the Tao is the *Yin-Yang* dichotomy, in which all of nature is held to be divided into two polar but complementary antagonistic forces of Yin and Yang. Yin is indicated by an ideogram signifying the shady side of a hill, Yang by an ideogram signifying the sunny side of a hill. Yin and Yang correspond to female and male, night and day, soft and hard, earth and heaven, centrifugal and centripetal, negative and positive. Unlike certain Western dichotomies, neither Yin nor Yang can exist without the other, nor is one superior to the other. Nor is any quality or entity *pure* Yin or *pure* Yang, but any is both, with one always predominating in relation to the other.

Te is another principle of the Tao, translated as "power" or "virtue," and also means "going with the flow," not forcing nature or human nature, i.e., moving with nature: sailing with the wind rather than rowing, as one example. *Te* is also the power of the sage who does not interfere but allows what is necessary to be accomplished through inward calm and identification with nature.

The Taoist concept of *nature* is philosophically fundamental, although different from Western thinking. The Chinese word for nature is *tzu jan*, which literally means "self-thus," or "that which is so of itself, *spontaneously*." This notion of nature contrasts with the Judeo-Christian one, in which nature is not so of itself, but is a creation of the Creator God or, according to earlier thought, the Demiurge. Another significant Taoist philosophical concept is *hsiang sheng*, "mutual arising." This is a principle in which two or more phenomena are associated with one another ("arise mutually"), but no causal relationship exists between them, at least not explicitly. Statistical relationships among phenomena is one example of *hsiang sheng*. Alan Watts speaks of multiple, mutually dependent simultaneous causes rather than a causal relationship. The Jungian concept of synchronicity could be seen as a special case of *hsiang sheng*.

The inherently indefinable nature of the Tao is suggestive of Gödel's Incompleteness Theorem, which implies that there are true propositions that cannot be proven within a given axiomatic, deductive system, or simply that there are inherent limits to the extent of our possible rational knowledge. Gödel's theorem and Heisenberg's Principle of Indeterminacy in physics imply that there are real and *inherent* limits to our deductive and inductive knowledge, even in mathematics and natural science. Ancient Chinese philosophers have anticipated this in their *recognition and acceptance of the indefinable* as a basic construct, and their high valuation of *intuition* (in addition to reason and observation of nature), which are among the distinguishing characteristics of Taoist philosophy.

THE TEACHINGS OF CONFUCIUS

The best source by far for the teachings of Confucius (K'ung Fu-tze, "Master King") is the *Analects of Confucius*. However, this title is deceptively imprecise. The *Analects* were not written by Confucius; they are a compilation of alleged sayings of Confucius and alleged highlights of conversations between Master K'ung and his disciples, removed from context and given written form sometime after his death. Some scholars maintain that no more than half the *Analects* is genuine material, and it would not be surprising if *not one* of the logia of the *Analects* is authentic. Much of the material is probably proverbial. K'ung himself claimed to be only a transmitter of the wisdom of sage-kings of mythical times and of the founders of the Chou dynasty, rather than an originator. To make matters yet more convoluted, what the *Analects* meant to the individuals who compiled them is quite different from their interpretation by modern Asians, largely because of the influence of Neo-Confucianism, which arose during the Sung dynasty, particularly that of Chu Hsi (A.D. 1130–1200). Although the purpose of Neo-Confucianism was to reestablish the philosophic hegemony of Confucianism relative to Buddhism and Taoism, in reacting to these extraneous influences Neo-Confucianism came to embody them to a degree, thereby transforming the very character of Confucianism. For example, the Confucius of the *Analects* speaks of no living person, not even his favorite disciples, as embodying the virtue known as *jen* (human-heartedness, humaneness); whereas, in the Neo-Confucian interpretation of the concept, *jen* is a *universal human attribute!*

Confucian Ethical Principles Epitomized

Perhaps the most significant of the Confucian ethical principles is the virtue *li*, defined as "propriety" or "correct moral and ceremonial order in society." It is through *li* that the order of Heaven is embodied in the expression of human nature on Earth. The inner aspect of *li* is *shu*, defined as "reciprocity." The Confucian preoccupation with rites and ceremonies is not merely empty formalism, but a manifestation of inner attitudes that embody the other Confucian virtues. Confucius also considered *li* to be the legacy of the wisdom of ancient sage-kings and mythical demigods. The *Chun-tzu* or morally superior man was expected to know *three hundred rules of major ritual observances and three thousand rules of minor ritual observances!* *Li* is said to entail the various other Confucian virtues; that is, if *li* is present, then the others cannot be lacking, but not necessarily conversely. *Li* entails, in addition to *shu*, *hsin* (sincerity or good faith) and *i* (righteousness or justice). *Li* is also the basis of *hsaio* or filial piety, manifested in the five relationships, and considered to be the source of all other virtues in later Confucianism. The Confucian cardinal virtue is *jen* (human-heartedness) and *li* may be regarded as the outward flowering of *jen*. The *Chun-tzu* (morally superior man) practiced the virtues of *jen*, *i*, *hsin*, and *li*, perhaps ultimately attaining the level of the fifth cardinal virtue, *chih*, or wisdom. Even the name of the Confucian philosophical school, *Ju Chiao*, meaning "school of the gentleman/scholar" or "literati," expressed clearly its "this-worldly" emphasis on cultural cultivation.

Brief but suggestive sayings lead us to believe that Confucius also subscribed to a doctrine like that of the Greeks, wherein one sought to adhere to a "golden" mean in thought and action between any two extremes.

According to Confucian ethics, the virtuous man's Tao was in harmony with the Tao of Heaven. Confucian ideology claimed to be *objective* morality; i.e., ethics is held to be an objective absolute, rather than an arbitrary human invention. There was a belief prevalent in ancient Chinese culture in a supreme heavenly ancestral figure, Shang Ti ("high ruler"), who was venerated and to whom sacrifices were offered at certain times. But Shang Ti was a nebulous and ill-defined entity, having no revealed scriptures, whose preferences could be learned only be means of divination. Later the concept of Shang Ti evolved into the impersonal concept of Heaven as a ruling principle, and the emperor was designated the "son of Heaven." Hence there was a preexisting cultural context for the secular Confucian idea of "Heaven" and "doing the will of Heaven." In the sphere of politics Confucius held that a sage-king would rule by *moral* force alone, without any need of the use of physical force.

Confucius attempted to exalt the secular to the level of the sacred, finding its roots not on Earth but in "Heaven." (There may be a reverse trend in contemporary civilization of attempting to reduce the sacred to the secular.)

A COMPARISON OF TAOISM AND CONFUCIANISM

The relationship between Taoism and Confucianism can be represented by taking the latter as the Yang (red half of the Pa-Kua) and Taoism as the Yin (black half of this symbolic diagram.) The two philosophies can thus be viewed as *complementary*, antagonistic opposites, in thought and action, of the universal Yin-Yang dichotomy, together constituting a unified system in Chinese culture. At the heart, each, both diagrammatically and philosophically, is a part of and interdependent with the other, the Tao itself being one of their shared fundamental concepts. Taoism (Yin) emphasizes intuition, and the *contemplation* of the Tao of nature. Confucianism (Yang) emphasizes linear intellect, and *action* of man in accordance with the Tao of Heaven. The Tao of the Taoists is more spiritual, individualistic, and quixotic, that of the Confucians more moral, interpersonal, and pragmatic, but the differences are as much of emphasis as of substance.

HINDUISM

What is Hinduism? Hinduism is not *one* religion/philosophy by any means, but rather an entire set of interrelated religions. The word Hinduism was coined by Westerners to refer to what they incorrectly thought was a single, complex religious system. ("Hinduism" is derived from "Hindu" and ultimately from Indus, the river.) The Hindus themselves refer to their religion/philosophy and its practices as *dharma*. Similarly, there is no one Hindu philosophy or Indian philosophy, nor is all Indian philosophy "mystical," monist, or even theistic in nature. There are six orthodox systems of Hindu philosophy and three heterodox systems, *one of which is Buddhism*. A system is considered to be orthodox if it accepts the sole authority of the Vedas as truth; otherwise it is heterodox. All systems of Hindu philosophy accept the notion of Karma, and the goal of *moksha* or liberation, with the exception of the Charvaka school of materialist philosophy. Hence, despite many differences, there are some concepts and terminologies held in common by the various systems of Hindu philosophies and the various religious systems that may be subsumed under the name of "Hinduism." It is these conceptual commonalities which we will explore.

The very essence of most forms of Hinduism and one of the most influential orthodox systems of Hindu philosophy is the Upanishadic doctrine (epitomized in the Vedanta system of philosophy) that Brahman (the ultimate reality) and Atman (self, soul) are one and identical. The clearest and most direct statement of this claim is in the *Advaita* (non-dual) Vedanta philosophy of Shankara. The theme of the identity of Brahman and Atman which is the very heart of Upanishadic religion/philosophy, is expressed throughout the Upanishads in mythopoetic form, such as the well-known "Brahman art thou" and "I am Brahman" in the Brhadaranyaka Upanishads.

In the mythopoetic terms of the Vedas, according to Alan Watts, the world is God playing "hide and go seek" with himself. God created the world by an act of "self-sacrifice," the One dying into the Many, and in order to obtain liberation from illusion, ignorance and the cycle of rebirth and redeath, humans must reverse the process of evolution to obtain union with the godhead (the Many dying into the One.)

It has been remarked that Buddhism is Hinduism packaged for export. In any case, the Buddhism which grew from Hindu/Vedic soil has been much more readily accepted than Hinduism itself by non-Indian cultures, such as those of China and Japan. Buddhism began with a definite event (the Buddha's enlightenment) at a known time in history, whereas the origin of the Vedic traditions on which Hinduism is based is obscured by the mists of time.

BUDDHISM

What is Buddhism? Buddhism began in India as the teaching of Siddhartha Gautama Shakyamuni in the fifth century B.C. and is generally considered to be a religion, a philosophy, and a way of liberation. In its original form Buddhism was a way of liberation, as are Yoga, Vedanta, and Taoism. A "way of liberation" is difficult to define, since this category did not exist in Western thought, except perhaps in some esoteric traditions, such as Sufism. Later, during the period in which the schools of philosophy in India developed, Buddhism was elaborated into great philosophical systems, but the original teachings of the Buddha (i.e., the enlightened one) consisted primarily of meditation techniques and ethical practices rather than metaphysics.

The principal doctrines taught by the Buddha were the four noble truths and the eightfold path. The four noble truths are:

(1) Suffering exists;
(2) it has a cause (selfish desire);
(3) it may cease; and
(4) there is a path that leads to its cessation.

The eightfold path consists of:

(1) right views,
(2) right resolve,
(3) right speech,
(4) right conduct,
(5) right livelihood,
(6) right effort,
(7) right mindfulness, and
(8) right concentration.

Following this path enables one to attain *nirvana*, an ineffable state, which can be realized through meditation, and which can grant release from suffering and, according to some interpretations, release from future reincarnations into our world of plurality, illusion, birth, suffering, death, and rebirth (*samsara*) that are otherwise inevitable.

There are two sets of Buddhist scriptures and two traditions of Buddhism, each claiming to be the original teaching. The Southern School, or Theravada, probably the older, is based on the canon written in Pali, whereas the Northern School, or Mahayana, is based on the canon written in Sanskrit and, to a lesser extent, Chinese and Tibetan. The adherents of the Mahayana ("greater vehicle") refer to the Theravada ("doctrine of the elders") as the Hinayana ("lesser vehicle.") The Theravada school is more monastic and ascetic, and each monk works primarily for his own awakening (*bodhi*) and liberation (*nirvana*). In contrast, the Mahayana School employs a great variety of means in its attempt to achieve awakening and liberation for a greater variety and number of people. Its adherents work for the awakening and liberation of mankind, not merely their own, just as the Buddha postponed entering into the ultimate, final *nirvana* in order to teach the four noble truths and the eightfold path, so that every human being could realize his Buddha nature.

Madhyamaka is a school of Mahayana Buddhist philosophy founded by Nargarjuna (ca. A.D. 200). The tenets of this philosophy were that the world of phenomena was unreal, a plurality, lacking any essence, i.e., a void. Underlying the world of phenomena was the absolute world, which was also held to be without essence, empty, a void. The voids of the absolute and phenomenal worlds were held to be identical and, hence, *nirvana* and *samsara* were one!

The Yogacara school of Mahayana Buddhist philosophy was founded by Maitreya (ca. A.D. 300). The essence of the doctrine of this school was that in reality there is no distinction between the perceiving subject and

the perceived, external sensory objects. Both perceiving subject and perceived, external objects were held to be illusory manifestations of the
universal consciousness. Thus the subject-object dichotomy was abolished
conceptually. Liberation consisted of realizing this oneness experientially
through meditation. The nature of universal consciousness/being was held
to be beyond conceptions. A Buddha was referred to as one awakened to
the ultimate reality beyond intellectual conceptions.

Buddhist philosophy is not philosophy in the same sense that Western
philosophy is. The goal is entirely different. It is to lead the "philosopher" out of the maze of intellectual conceptions about the nature of
reality, about knowledge of reality, about the knower, to the direct perception, knowledge, and experience of "this," which is beyond our language
and categorizing intellect. The goal of Buddhist philosophy is not to
become steeped in words, nor to construct vast metaphysical edifices
based on misunderstandings and misapplications of the grammar and
syntax of our languages. Gautama Buddha compared this type of intellectual or philosophical inquiry with that of a person who has been wounded
by an arrow, but refuses to allow it to be removed from his flesh until he
has a complete and thorough intellectual understanding of who his assail-
ant was, his background, childhood, and motives, etc.! One might say by
analogy that the purpose of Buddhist philosophy is to remove the arrow
from our flesh. The purpose of Mahayana dialectics is to undermine all
possible concepts of reality and, thereby, unravel philosophical systems at
their foundations.

Zen Buddhism developed from the Mahayana branch of Buddhism, as
Buddhist teaching spread from India to China, and was influenced by the
pragmaticism of Chinese culture and by the indigenous philosophies of
Taoism and Confucianism. Zen is the Japanese word for the Chinese
Ch'an, which was a translation of the Sanskrit *dhvana* or meditation.

It is the theory and practice of "*instantaneous awakening*" that is the
sine qua non of Zen Buddhism. Instantaneous awakening (*satori*) could
occur either spontaneously or after relatively short periods of preparation
involving the presence of a Buddhist master who had awakened, i.e., was
enlightened. Satori is considered to be natural, and hence not to require
lengthy and arduous preparation. Satori was also held to be instantaneous,
because it could occur only in the eternal present that is called "now," as
distinct from an illusory past and future, according to Buddhist philosophy. Zen claims to be the continued *transmission of the experience of
enlightenment that occurred to the Buddha* under the Bo tree after years
of meditation and practice of austerities in the forest. Zen considers the
Buddhist scriptures, and the entire philosophical/verbal tradition of Buddhism, to be of secondary importance. According to Zen tradition, the

experience of awakening was transmitted to Buddha's disciple Mahaka-
syapa, when the Buddha held a flower before him in complete silence.

COMPARISON OF HINDUISM AND BUDDHISM

It is difficult to compare Hinduism and Buddhism because *there is no one
form of either religion or either philosophy;* nevertheless, there are many
conceptual correspondences between some of the Hindu/Vedanta philosophies and some of the Buddhist philosophical systems. Indeed, the terminologies and concepts of the one seem frequently to be analogs of the
other. The parallel is most apparant between the *Advaita* Vedanta and the
Madyamika system of Buddhism developed by Nargarjuna. Putting it *very*
simply, Hinduism says that there is a *self* and there is a *god* (at a very
abstract level) and that these are *not two* (nondual). Buddhism, on the
other hand, asserts that is *no self* and there is *no god*, and "the two" are
identical! The philosophical trick is to explain how the "no self" can
reincarnate!

   In both systems the spiritual goal is the same: to get off the "wheel"
of samsara (rebirth, death, and reincarnation) by achieving a transcenden-
tal level of consciousness or liberation. Brahman corresponds to the void
or "emptiness." Although Brahman with qualities is defined as *"being,
knowledge, and bliss,"* the ultimate level of Brahman is *nirguna* (meaning
"without qualities"). Nothing can be predicated about nirguna Brahman.
It is beyond conception. Observe how close *nirguna* Brahman is to the
concept of the void in Buddhism. In both systems the illusory world of
phenomena (*maya*) is held to consist of impermanence, names, and forms
lacking essence. In both the Hindu/Vedanta and the Buddhist philosophy
the principle of *karma* or "spiritual" cause and effect is held to operate
within and between incarnations. The higher state of being/consciousness
(nirvana or moksha) may be realized in both systems by techniques of
meditation, which is also *one* of the methods of changing or eradicating
one's past karma. One significant difference is that the concept of Ishvara,
a personal and creator god, is present in Vedanta/Hinduism, but absent in
Buddhism.

Biographical Sketch of Kenneth K. C. Chan

Kenneth Kah Cheong Chan is a Chinese born in Malaysia and currently residing in Singapore. He has a medical degree from Australia and a physics degree from Singapore. He is an editor for the World Scientific Publishing Company, and is in charge of the *International Journal of Bifurcation and Chaos* and the *International Journal of Modern Physics D: Gravitation, Astrophysics and Cosmology*. He joined the International Society of Philosophical Enquiry in 1990 while visiting the U.S.

Good

CHAPTER 10

TIME AND SPACE

Kenneth Kah Cheong Chan

I. INTRODUCTION

Einstein's theory of relativity has dramatically modified our view of time and space, but understanding is still largely incomplete. The attempt at synthesis of time and space started by Minkowski has not matured fully, but has been left substantially a mathematical concept. The theory of relativity also gave rise to one of the longest-standing controversies in physics this century, namely, the problem of the twin paradox. It has not yet been fully resolved.

Perhaps at no other time in the history of physics than now has physical and intuitive understanding lagged so far behind mathematical mastery of its complexities. We now possess numerous beautiful mathematical theories that have no physical interpretation. It is therefore mainly in the hope of providing new insights into the physical meaning of time and space that this paper is written.

II. THE MEANING OF TIME AND SPACE

The main idea introduced in this paper is that both time and space are arbitrary concepts of human beings related directly to how we experience the universe.

A major improvement in our understanding of time and space was brought about by Einstein's revolutionary theory of relativity. It led to the abandonment of the concept of absolute universal time and absolute universal space for all frames of reference. Therefore we acknowledge that time and space are different for different inertial systems.

However, within any one inertial frame of reference, both time and space are still considered real pervasive entities which are distinct from physical phenomena. I wish to propose here that such entities in reality do not exist, and that there is neither experimental nor theoretical basis for their existence. Time and space as actually measured by us, then, exist merely as artificial concepts arbitrarily defined by human beings. They are neither pervasive nor distinct from physical phenomena.

Our arbitrary method of defining time and space is based on our own physiological framework, and it reveals that the concepts of time and space are completely interrelated. Although Minkowski had earlier suggested that some kind of union exists between time and space, the nature of this had not been well defined. One aim of this paper is to elaborate more fully on this union. It will then be seen that the concepts of time and space are truly so inseparable that one cannot define time without space and vice versa.

Time

In presenting this new theory of time and space, we run into the difficulty brought about by the interrelatedness of the different aspects. We can only introduce the new concepts one at a time, and the reader must realize that a true picture will emerge only after we have brought all the different elements together. Keeping this in mind, we will first consider the concept of time.

It is proposed here that what we measure as time is, in reality, the rate of electromagnetic transmission in our perceived space. This means that in order to define time, we need first to demarcate our space. The rate at which the electromagnetic field travels in *this* space is then the rate at which our time progresses.

To understand better the reason for this arbitrary choice in defining time, we have to consider the realm of human experience. All of our physiological activities, including neural transmission, are mediated by electromagnetic interactions. Therefore the rate of electromagnetic interactions, which depends on the rate of electromagnetic transmission, determines the rate of all our bodily functions and thought processes. It is not surprising, then, that human beings have arbitrarily defined time as an entity which reflects this rate.

In order to detect any uniform change in the rate of electromagnetic transmission, we must have a standard available for comparison. It is evident that no such standard is available, because not even our own physiological or mental processes can be used as such.

The explanation for Einstein's postulate, that the speed of light is always constant, now becomes clear. The speed of light is constant because our definition of time depends directly on electromagnetic transmission. In other words, by our arbitrary definition of time, we have actually inadvertently also defined the speed of light to be constant.

Space

Similar considerations of human experience determine our arbitrary definition of space. We have defined space as that entity demarcated by solid-state matter at rest in our frame of reference. This arbitrary choice is hardly surprising, because our own body "assumes" this definition of space.

It is evident that, like time, space so defined is also directly dependent on electromagnetic phenomena, because all the mechanisms which cause bonding between atoms in solid-state matter are due to electromagnetic interactions.

I will now propose a method of defining space by using electromagnetic transmission that will produce a result identical to the space demarcated by solid-state matter at rest in the relevant inertial reference system. Light rays are sent at the same instant from one point to different locations, where they are then reflected back. If all these light rays arrive back at the original point at the same instant, the different positions from which each of them is reflected back are then considered to be of equal distance from the original point. By repeating this procedure, we can then set up a space-grid in any inertial system.

We can show that the atoms in solid-state matter at rest in the same reference system align themselves in a way that defines a similar space. From symmetry considerations, electromagnetic transmission from one atom to any two or more symmetrically placed atoms in the lattice will, after reflection at these atoms, arrive back at the first atom at the same instant. This phenomenon is, of course, directly related to the electromagnetic mechanism that regulates the spatial configuration of all the atoms in the solid-state lattice. Each atom cannot "know" the position (in space and time) of the other atoms in the lattice other than by electromagnetic transmission.

We can now see that, because time and space are both directly related to electromagnetic transmission, a close relationship between the two must exist. However, before we can fully appreciate the synthesis of time and space, we need first to understand yet another arbitrary concept of human beings—simultaneity.

NB

Simultaneity

Simultaneity is a concept required mainly to support our notion that time is a pervasive entity independent of space. This concept of time, of course, leads to the requirement that we be able to specify certain times at different positions as being the same.

We shall now look at how simultaneity has been arbitrarily defined by human beings. A method related to that used in defining space can be used to define simultaneity. Light rays are sent out from a point and reflected back at positions such that they arrive back at the same instant. The times, at the different positions, when the reflections took place are then considered simultaneous to each other. We note also that, as stated earlier, these positions are defined as being of equal distance from the point where the light rays originated. Therefore the speed of light must be the same in all directions in space, because we have arbitrarily defined it to be so.

To help us understand the reason for our choice in our definition of simultaneity, we shall consider its definition, assuming that the space-grid of the relevant inertial frame had already been set up. We send light rays at the same instant from a point, say, the origin. The times when these light rays reach points considered to be of equal distance from the origin (according to the space-grid) are then designated as being simultaneous to each other. We note here that, according to our arbitrary definition of time, when light rays cross equal distances in our defined space, an equal amount of time is considered to have elapsed. From our notion of time as a pervasive entity, we conclude that because these light rays began at a single event, and because an equal time has elapsed during each ray's transmission, the arrival times of these rays must be simultaneous. We then proceed to project this rule to cover all of space, thus defining a universal moment of time for our inertial system.

This paper, however, proposes that there is no basis for assuming that there is a real pervasive entity such as time, which actually exists merely as an abstraction devised by human beings. Therefore I wish to stress here that there is no scientific significance to two events being considered simultaneous, other than merely as defined.

The Interrelation of Time and Space

Both time and space are directly related to electromagnetic phenomena. I propose now to elaborate more fully on the earlier statement that they are also completely interdependent on one another.

From our arbitrary definition of time, it is clear that its rate can be defined only if a demarcated space is also specified. It is not meaningful to talk of time at a single point in an inertial frame, other than in the context of the surrounding demarcated space-grid. The rate of time is measured by sending a light ray in the space-grid and back. The distance traversed by the light ray in the space-grid is then the measure of the elapsed time. Hence time cannot be defined without space.

Likewise, space cannot be defined without time. Distances in space are directly related to the time a light ray takes to travel forward and backward between the two points demarcating the distance. In practical terms, this procedure can be considered to have been observed by the atoms in aligning to one another in the solid state. Therefore, using solid-state matter at rest to delineate space actually constitutes a similar process in defining space, and hence is also dependent on time.

The interrelatedness of time and space also becomes apparent when we try to compare time and space between different inertial frames of reference. Two arbitrary concepts are required to carry out such comparisons: simultaneity, and what we shall call positional correlation (we shall define two events as positionally correlated if they have the same space coordinates in the relevant frame of reference). These two concepts may be viewed as devices required to link up different events, thus allowing human beings to designate any event in terms of our arbitrary concept of pervasive time and space. Simultaneity provides a link between positionally uncorrelated events, and positional correlation provides a link between events that are not simultaneous.

Because of the interrelatedness of time and space, it is actually impossible to compare only time or only space between different inertial systems. When we compare the rates of time between different frames of reference, we necessarily have to compare the designated times at positionally uncorrelated events of at least one frame of reference. Hence the space aspect must be considered, and any such comparison of time is directly dependent on how we define simultaneity between different positions in space for the relevant reference frames.

In comparing space between different inertial systems, we must use two events to demarcate any distance. These two events can be simultaneous in only one or the other frame of reference. Hence a time factor must be taken into account. In the reference frame where these two events are not simultaneous, the distance used in the comparison will depend on how we define their positional correlation to events which *are* simultaneous to each other.

From the above considerations, we can now see that time and space, by the way they are arbitrarily defined, are closely interrelated and cannot be divided. They are merely different aspects of the same underlying reality, which is electromagnetic phenomena.

NB

Electromagnetic transmission has been used by human beings for our arbitrary definition of time and space mainly because it is, by far, the fundamental phenomenon which most greatly influences our experience of the universe. It should be apparent, however, that any other fundamental phenomenon that is related in its actions to electromagnetism could also be used to define the same time and space.

In order to demonstrate that all the prior theoretical considerations about time and space are compatible with known experimental and mathematical observations, I shall now proceed to derive the Lorentz transformation equations by using purely intuitive arguments based on the new theoretical insights which have been introduced; and thus will show that the Lorentz transformation equations are direct consequences of our arbitrary definition of time and space as outlined in this paper.

III. THE LORENTZ TRANSFORMATION EQUATIONS

Using the new concepts of time and space introduced in this paper, I propose to demonstrate quantitatively the following well-known consequences of the Lorentz transformation equations:

(1) Time dilation;
(2) Length contraction;
(3) Phase difference in the synchronization of clocks.

With these results, we can then construct the Lorentz transformation equations:

$$t' = \frac{t - \frac{vx}{c^2}}{\sqrt{1 - \frac{v^2}{c^2}}} ,$$

$$x' = \frac{x - vt}{\sqrt{1 - \frac{v^2}{c^2}}} ,$$

$$y' = y , \quad z' = z ,$$

where v is along the x-axis.

For all the following discussions in this section, we will be considering two inertial frames of reference: S, which is considered to be stationary, and S', which is moving along the x-axis with velocity v relative to S. We shall denote t, x, y, z, and t', x', y', z', as the time and positional coordinates of S and S', respectively.

Time Dilation

We are here comparing the time reading of events A and B, which are positionally correlated according to one inertial reference frame S' (i.e., its proper time), with the time reading in another inertial reference frame S, which does not consider the same events to be positionally correlated.

Consider Figure 1, which shows events A and B as seen by S. A light ray has been sent forward and backward along an axis perpendicular to the line of motion, linking A and B.

From our arbitrary definition of time, the distance that the light ray travels in our demarcated space between any two events is the measure of what we consider the elapsed time between the two events. If we assign the distance between events A and C according to S to be 1, the distance between A and C according to S' would be $\sqrt{1 - \frac{v^2}{c^2}}$. Hence it follows that the time between A and B as noted by S would be greater than that noted by S', and would be given by the equation

$$\Delta t = \frac{\Delta t'}{\sqrt{1 - \frac{v^2}{c^2}}},$$

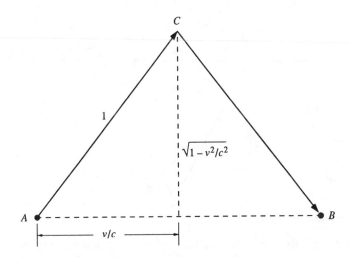

Figure 1. The diagram shows the path of a light ray as seen by an inertial reference frame S which considers events A and B to be positionally uncorrelated. The same light ray, as seen by another inertial reference frame S' which considers A and B to be positionally correlated, would have traversed a distance smaller by a factor of $\sqrt{1 - \frac{v^2}{c^2}}$. Hence, according to S', the elapsed time between A and B would be smaller by $\sqrt{1 - \frac{v^2}{c^2}}$ than that according to S.

Hence we have the time-dilation formula. Note that this is also a direct consequence of how we define simultaneity between positionally uncorrelated events.

Length Contraction

We are now comparing the distance between two events A and B as measured in terms of two inertial reference systems. The events will be considered simultaneous in one frame of reference and not in the other.

Figure 2 shows events A and B as seen by reference frame S, where they are not considered to be simultaneous. Reference frame S', which is moving relative to S, considers A and B to be simultaneous. x_1 and x_2 are events which are positionally correlated according to S'. Light rays are

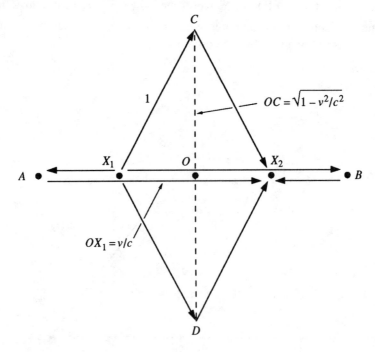

Figure 2. The diagram shows the paths of light rays leaving from event x^1 and returning to event x^2 as seen by inertial reference frame S. x^1 and x^2 are events considered to be positionally correlated by another inertial reference frame S' that is moving with velocity v relative to S. The distance AB is considered longer than CD according to S, but is considered the same according to S'. Because the distance CD is equal for both frames of reference, there is, then, a "length contraction effect" for the distance between events A and B, when measured relative to the two different inertial systems.

sent from event x_1 to events A, B, C, and D, and then on to event x_2 (i.e., they all arrive at the same time). Figure 2 shows the paths taken by these light rays as seen by S.

According to our arbitrary definition of time and space, events A, B, C, and D are considered by S' to be of equal distance from x_1 and also to be simultaneous to each other. According to S, the paths taken by the light rays are of equal distances, since they all originate and end at the same two events. Hence

$$
\begin{aligned}
x_1Ax_2 &= x_1Bx_2 \\
&= x_1Cx_2 \\
&= x_1Dx_2.
\end{aligned}
$$

If, according to S, we set distance $x_1C = 1$, then $AB = 2$, and $CD = 2\sqrt{1 - \frac{v^2}{c^2}}$. Hence the ratio of AB to CD will be

$$
\frac{AB}{CD} = \frac{1}{\sqrt{1 - \frac{v^2}{c^2}}}.
$$

Because CD is perpendicular to the line of motion, its distance is equivalent in both frames of reference. According to S', events C and D and events A and B are separated by equal distances, which means that in reference frame S, comparing AB with CD is equivalent to comparing Δx with $\Delta x'$ (where Δx is the proper length along the x-axis on reference frame S, and $\Delta x'$ is the corresponding distance according to S'). Therefore:

$$
AB = \frac{CD}{\sqrt{1 - \frac{v^2}{c^2}}}.
$$

implies that

$$
\Delta x = \frac{\Delta x'}{\sqrt{1 - \frac{v^2}{c^2}}}.
$$

Hence we have the length-contraction formula. Note that according to S, events A and B are not simultaneous, and comparison of length is possible only because of the arbitrary method of linking events by positional correlation.

Phase Difference in the Synchronization of Clocks

We are now going to demonstrate quantitatively the reason for the phase-difference term

$$-\frac{vx}{c^2} \over \sqrt{1-\frac{v^2}{c^2}}$$

in the equation

$$t' = \frac{t-\frac{vx}{c^2}}{\sqrt{1-\frac{v^2}{c^2}}}\cdot$$

The presence of the term means that clocks further away in the positive x direction on the moving reference frame S' will show earlier times.

Figure 3(a) shows the paths of light rays originating at event O and traveling to events A and B as seen by stationary reference frame S.

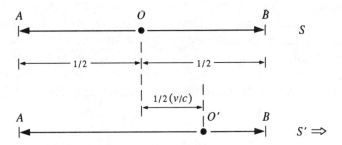

Figure 3. 3(a) shows the paths of light rays from event O to events A and B according to inertial reference frame S; 3(b) shows the paths of the same two light rays according to another inertial reference frame S' that is moving with velocity v relative to S. O' is the event considered by S' to be positionally correlated to event O, and considered by S to be simultaneous to A and B. The values of the distances shown in the diagram are those according to S. The equivalent distances according to S' would be greater by a factor of $\sqrt{1-\frac{v^2}{c^2}}$.

Because the distances traversed by the light rays to A and B are the same according to S, the events A and B are considered to be simultaneous. However, according to S', the distances traversed by the light rays are not the same; so A and B are not considered simultaneous. Hence there is a phase difference in the synchronization of clocks.

Figure 3(b) shows the paths of the same light rays according to S'. The distances traversed by the light rays from O to A and from O to B are the same $\left(= \frac{1}{2} \right)$ according to S, and so A and B are considered to be simultaneous events. Also, according to S, the reference frame S' has moved a distance $\frac{1}{2} \frac{v}{c}$ during the time the light ray took to travel from O to A (or from O to B). The observer on S' would say therefore that the distances traversed by the two light rays are different. For him the distances would be $O'A$ and $O'B$, where O' is the event considered by S' to be positionally correlated to event O, and considered by S to be simultaneous to A and B.

From our arbitrary definition of time, the distance that the light ray travels in our demarcated space is our direct measurement of the elapsed time (however, the unit used for distance is smaller than the unit for time by the factor of c). Therefore, according to S', the time between event O and event B would be

$$\frac{\frac{1}{2} - \frac{1}{2}\frac{v}{c}}{c\sqrt{1 - \frac{v^2}{c^2}}}$$

The Lorentz factor $\sqrt{1 - \frac{v^2}{c^2}}$ is necessary because, as shown earlier, the distance according to S' is greater by that proportion than that according to S. The time between event O and event A according to S' would be

$$\frac{\frac{1}{2} + \frac{1}{2}\frac{v}{c}}{c\sqrt{1 - \frac{v^2}{c^2}}}$$

The time difference according to S' between event B and event A would then be

$$\frac{\frac{1}{2} - \frac{1}{2}\frac{v}{c}}{c\sqrt{1 - \frac{v^2}{c^2}}} - \frac{\frac{1}{2} + \frac{1}{2}\frac{v}{c}}{c\sqrt{1 - \frac{v^2}{c^2}}}$$

$$= \frac{-\frac{v}{c^2}}{\sqrt{1 - \frac{v^2}{c^2}}} \; .$$

This difference is observed over a distance of 1 according to S. Therefore the time difference in the clock readings over the distance x becomes

$$\frac{-\frac{vx}{c^2}}{\sqrt{1-\frac{v^2}{c^2}}} \, .$$

Hence we have the phase-difference term.

From all the arguments given above, we can now readily construct the Lorentz transformation equations. Hence we have shown that they are a consequence of our arbitrary definitions of time and space as outlined in this paper.

IV. ACCELERATION AND THE EFFECTS OF CHANGING INERTIAL REFERENCE FRAMES

It is clearly possible for an inertial observer to set up a uniform and pervasive system of time and space coordinates. It is not clear, however, whether a meaningful system of time and space coordinates could be devised for an accelerating frame of reference, because time and space are really arbitrary concepts designed (though inadvertently) by human beings for basically inertial systems. The reference frame of the Earth may be considered to be virtually an inertial system, because the effect of its acceleration and gravitational field on the measurement of time and space is relatively insignificant.

Any attempt to create a system of time and space coordinates for an accelerating reference frame would most likely require further arbitrary rules on how certain aspects should be defined, and these may render it of dubious scientific value. For instance, the acceleration of a system may be maintained by a force applied at one position. Because of the time required for the transmission of this force, the spatial configuration of solid-state matter in this accelerating system would be different from that in an inertial system traveling at the same velocity at that instant. We are then forced to make an arbitrary choice as to which solid-state matter to use in demarcating space.

It may be better, then, to designate the events in an accelerating system in terms of the time and space coordinates defined for an assigned inertial reference frame, rather than to attempt formulating its own arbitrary system of time and space coordinates. Also, instead of trying to measure "aging" (the time experienced by an object), which is really an abstraction, we may describe what happens to accelerating objects directly in terms of electromagnetic phenomena, which are the underlying reality behind the concepts of time and space. In other words, because time and space are only arbitrary concepts devised by human beings, it is not scientifically essential for an accelerating system to have its own time and space, as previously thought.

However, because time and space can be clearly defined for all inertial systems, it is useful to discover how the time and space coordinates that designate events would alter if we changed inertial reference frames. It will then be possible to cope with temporarily accelerating systems by considering only the changes arising from a shift from its initial inertial frame to its eventual inertial frame. In other words, we do not try to devise any time and space coordinates for the observer while he is accelerating, but we can define clearly what has happened to the time and space coordinates of his events when he reaches his final inertial reference frame. To link up the initial and eventual reference frames, we may use a third, arbitrary inertial frame, and work out the changes in the time and space coordinates of events in two stages. The end result will not be affected.

In order to be able to discover what changes in the time and space coordinates of all inertial particles are brought about by an abrupt shift in inertial reference frame, we have to consider two different cases. In both of these we will assign the direction of the line of motion between the initial and the eventual inertial reference frame as being on the x-axis, and we set the coordinates of the event on the particle simultaneous to the initial reference frame (at the time of the shift of inertial frame) as t_0, x_0, y_0, z_0.

Case 1

Here we will examine the change in the time and space coordinates of a theoretical point particle A which is not moving along the x-axis according to the initial reference frame S. The abrupt shift is to another inertial reference frame S' that is moving with velocity v on the x-axis. There are two events on the particle A to consider: one simultaneous to S, and the other simultaneous to S' at the time of the reference-frame change. These are separate events.

1(a)   First, we will evaluate the change in the time and space coordinates of the event at A, which is considered simultaneous according to S. Let t, x, y, z, and t', x', y', z' be the coordinates according to S and S', respectively. We have therefore

$$t = t_0, \quad x = x_0, \quad y = y_0, \quad z = z_0.$$

Once we shift to the reference frame S', we have, from applying the Lorentz transformation equations,

$$t' = t_0 - \frac{\frac{v}{c^2} x_0}{\sqrt{1 - \frac{v^2}{c^2}}},$$

$$x' = \frac{x_0}{\sqrt{1 - \frac{v^2}{c^2}}},$$

$$y' = y_0, \quad z' = z_0.$$

This means that the moment we shift to a new inertial reference frame, the event on the particle which we had considered simultaneous suddenly becomes an event of the past. A span of time has apparently disappeared! Furthermore, the event is suddenly being designated at a different point in space. These effects would have been difficult to comprehend previously. However, with the knowledge that time and space are really arbitrary concepts of human beings, they now become perfectly acceptable. What has changed is merely our arbitrary method of designating events. Nothing strange such as "time or space jumps" has actually happened to the particle.

1(b)   We now evaluate the time and space coordinates of the event at the particle considered simultaneous to the eventual inertial frame S' at the time of the abrupt shift in reference frame. We obtain

$$t = t_0 + \frac{v^2}{c^2} x_0, \quad x = x_0,$$

$$t' = t_0, \quad x' = x_0 \sqrt{1 - \frac{v^2}{c^2}},$$

and

$$y = y' = y_0 + u_y \Delta t,$$
$$z = z' = z_0 + u_z \Delta t,$$

where u_y and u_z are the y and z velocity components, respectively, of particle A according to S, and $\Delta t = \left(\frac{v}{c^2}\right)x_0$ is the change in the time coordinate according to S between this event considered simultaneous to S' and that—as in 1(a)—considered simultaneous to S.

An important value to note here is the change in the proper time on particle A (Δt_A) between these two events:

$$\Delta t_A = \Delta t = \left(\frac{v}{c^2}\right)x_0 \ .$$

This means that immediately on shifting reference frames, the event on particle A, viewed as simultaneous, abruptly changes to one which is later in time, according to A, by $\left(\frac{v}{c^2}\right)x_0$. Its designated space coordinate also changes abruptly. Again, all these effects are merely due to a change in the arbitrary method of designating events.

Case 2

Here we consider a theoretical point-particle B, which moves with an x-component velocity of v relative to our initial reference frame S. We want to evaluate the changes in the time and space coordinates of B when we abruptly shift to another inertial reference frame, S', that is moving with velocity v (relative to S), which is the same as the x-component of B's velocity.

2(a)   We shall first consider the event on B regarded as simultaneous to S at the moment of the shift in reference frame. From applying the Lorentz transformation equations, we get

$$t = t_0 \ , \quad x = x_0 \ ,$$

$$t' = t_0 - \frac{\frac{v}{c^2}x_0}{\sqrt{1 - \frac{v^2}{c^2}}} \ ,$$

$$x' = \frac{x_0}{\sqrt{1 - \frac{v^2}{c^2}}} \ ,$$

$$y = y' = y_0 \ , \quad z = z' = z_0 \ .$$

2(b)   Here we consider the event on B regarded as simultaneous to S' at the moment of the shift in reference frame. We obtain

$$t = t_0 + \frac{\frac{v}{c^2} x_0}{1 - \frac{v^2}{c^2}} \, ,$$

$$x = \frac{x_0}{1 - \frac{v^2}{c^2}} \, ,$$

$$t' = t_0 \, ,$$

$$x' = \frac{x_0}{\sqrt{1 - \frac{v^2}{c^2}}} \, ,$$

$$y = y' = y_0 + u_y \Delta t \, ,$$

$$z = z' = z_0 + u_z \Delta t \, ,$$

where

$$\Delta t = \frac{\frac{v}{c^2} x_0}{\sqrt{1 - \frac{v^2}{c^2}}} \, .$$

is the change in the time coordinate according to S between this event and that considered in 2(a).

Here Δt_B, which is the change in the proper time on particle B between the two events considered in 2(a) and 2(b), is not the same as Δt. We have

$$\Delta t_B = \frac{\frac{v}{c^2} x_0}{\sqrt{1 - \frac{v^2}{c^2}}} \, .$$

With the knowledge of how the time and space coordinates of a particle alter during an abrupt shift of reference frame as in cases 1 and 2, we can work out the changes for any inertial particle. A general procedure would be to first consider the changes in the time and space coordinates caused by a shift to a reference frame having the same velocity as the particle, and then to add on the changes brought about by a subsequent shift to the actual final reference frame you want to consider. Other appropriate combinations may, of course, be employed.

For conceptual purposes, we shall now consider the case where we keep the time and space coordinates unchanged when we shift from one inertial reference frame to another. We want to find out the change in the time and space coordinates according to the initial reference frame S, which would be required to correlate with the new event designated by the new reference frame S', which moves with velocity v relative to S along the x-axis.

We therefore set

$$t' = t_0 , \quad x' = x_0 , \quad y' = y_0 , \quad z' = z_0 .$$

From the Lorentz transformation equations, we now obtain

$$t = t_0 + \frac{\frac{v}{c^2} x_0}{\sqrt{1 - \frac{v^2}{c^2}}} ,$$

$$x = \frac{x_0}{\sqrt{1 - \frac{v^2}{c^2}}} ,$$

$$y = y_0 , \quad z = z_0.$$

With all the above results, we are now ready to finally "solve" the famous twin paradox.

V. THE TWIN PARADOX

The twin paradox poses a problem in interpretation mainly because of our assumption that time is a real entity that is pervasive. This notion then compels us to connect all the events experienced by each of the twins into simultaneous sets. We are then alarmed to find that, according to the "travelling" twin, there are events experienced by the "stationary" twin which cannot be reasonably linked by simultaneity, and may even seem to have disappeared (i.e., there has been a sudden time leap). If we accept that time and space are not real pervasive entities but only arbitrary abstractions, the problem ceases to exist, as we can now demonstrate.

To simplify matters, we shall consider the case where no acceleration is involved and, instead of using twins, we shall compare the times shown on clocks. Consider Figure 4.

Rocket A approaches a stationary position E at constant velocity v. As it passes E, the clocks on A and E are synchronized. Rocket B, meanwhile, approaches E from the opposite direction at the velocity $-v$. As A and B pass by each other (at a distance x according to E), the clock on rocket B is synchronized to that on A. When B eventually reaches E, the clock readings are then compared. It will be found that a shorter time has elapsed on the rockets according to the clock on B when compared to the time shown on the clock on E.

Let us first consider the account of what has happened according to the observer on E. He will have considered the clocks on both A and B to have run slower by a factor of $\sqrt{1 - \frac{v^2}{c^2}}$. Hence, according to E, we have

$$\Delta t = \frac{2x}{v},$$

$$\Delta t' = \Delta t \sqrt{1 - \frac{v^2}{c^2}}$$

$$= \frac{2x}{v} \sqrt{1 - \frac{v^2}{c^2}},$$

where Δt is the time lapse, according to E, between the event of rocket A passing E and the event of rocket B arriving at E. $\Delta t'$ is the corresponding time lapse recorded by the clocks on the rockets.

Now, we shall look at the situation according to the observers on rocket A and then according to those on rocket B. We shall divide our analysis into three phases, as follows:

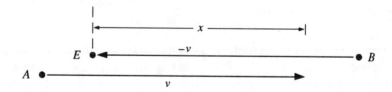

Figure 4. Scenario for considering the twin paradox: Rocket A travels with velocity v past a stationary observer E to reach rocket B, which is traveling in the opposite direction toward E with velocity $-v$. Rocket A passes rocket B at a distance x away from E according to E. The equivalent distance according to either A or B is shorter by a factor of $\sqrt{1 - \frac{v^2}{c^2}}$. Rocket A synchronizes its clock to that of E as it passes E, and rocket B synchronizes its clock to that of A as it passes A. When B arrives at E, their clock readings are compared.

Phase 1: between A passing E and A meeting B.
Phase 2: the shift of reference frame from A to B.
Phase 3: between B passing A and B meeting E.

We denote Δt_1, Δt_2, Δt_3, as the time lapses at E, and $\Delta t_1'$, $\Delta t_2'$, $\Delta t_3'$, as the time lapses on the rockets, corresponding to phases 1, 2, and 3, respectively.

In phase 1, the observer on A will have considered the clock on E to have run slower by a factor of $\sqrt{1 - \frac{v^2}{c^2}}$. Because of the length-contraction effect of the Lorentz transformation equations, he will have also considered the distance traveled in phase 1 to be $x\sqrt{1 - \frac{v^2}{c^2}}$. Hence, for phase 1, we obtain

$$\Delta t_1 = \frac{x}{v}\left(1 - \frac{v^2}{c^2}\right),$$

$$\Delta t_1' = \frac{x}{v}\sqrt{1 - \frac{v^2}{c^2}}.$$

In phase 2, we have to consider the effect on the time and space coordinates brought about by the abrupt shift in reference frame from rocket A to rocket B. We shall evaluate the effects in two stages.

In the first stage, we calculate the effects resulting from a shift from A to the reference frame stationary relative to E. We therefore apply the results from case 2(b) of section IV and obtain

$$\Delta \tau_1 = \frac{vx}{c^2},$$

$$L_1 = x,$$

where $\Delta \tau_1$ is the proper time lapse (according to E) between the event on E considered simultaneous to A and that considered simultaneous to the new reference frame. L_1 is the distance to E according to the new reference frame.

For the second stage, we have to evaluate the effect on the time and space coordinates resulting from an abrupt shift from the reference frame stationary relative to E to the reference frame of rocket B. We now apply the results from case 1(b) of section IV and obtain

$$\Delta \tau_2 = \frac{vx}{c^2},$$

$$L_2 = x\sqrt{1 - \frac{v^2}{c^2}},$$

where $\Delta\tau_2$ is the proper time lapse (according to E) between the event on E considered simultaneous to the reference frame that is stationary relative to E and that considered simultaneous to the reference frame of B. L_2 is the distance to E according to rocket B. We note that this is the same as that according to rocket A.

Hence, for phase 2, we obtain

$$\Delta t_2 = \Delta\tau_1 + \Delta\tau_2$$

$$= \frac{2vx}{c^2},$$

$$\Delta t_2' = 0.$$

The fact that Δt_2 is not zero means that there has been an apparent instantaneous jump in time at E at the moment when the switch of reference frames occurred. Note also that Δt_2 is directly proportional to the distance between E and the position where the rockets passed each other. This is one of the effects which many either had not considered or had found difficult to accept previously. However, once we understand that time and space are only arbitrary concepts, and that all these changes are merely the result of an alteration in the method of designating events, such effects become perfectly acceptable.

In phase 3, the conditions are similar to those in phase 1, and we have

$$\Delta t_3 = \frac{x}{v}\left(1 - \frac{v^2}{c^2}\right),$$

$$\Delta t_3' = \frac{x}{v}\sqrt{1 - \frac{v^2}{c^2}}.$$

Thus, according to the observers on both A and B, the total time lapse at E is

$$\Delta t_1 + \Delta t_2 + \Delta t_3 = \frac{2x}{v},$$

and the total time lapse according to the clocks on the rockets is

$$\Delta t_1' + \Delta t_2' + \Delta t_3' = \frac{2x}{v}\sqrt{1 - \frac{v^2}{c^2}}.$$

These results are exactly the same as those obtained by the observer on E. Hence there is no paradox, because both sets of observers agree on the results; i.e., both agree that the time lapse on the rockets is less than that on E.

VI. CONCLUSION NB

The main aim of this paper is to point out that time and space are actually mere abstractions of human beings, and also to show how they have been arbitrarily derived from the phenomenon of electromagnetism. It is the failure to realize that they are not real entities that has led to much confusion in the field of relativity.

This misunderstanding probably arises because time and space apparently reflect how human beings actually experience the universe. It is not surprising that we should consider the rate of our own physiological functions and our "aging process" as an absolute reality. Likewise, it is not hard to understand why we use solid-state matter (the state our own body is in) to demarcate space, and consider this also as an absolute reality.

Once it is realized, however, that time and space are not real entities, but merely arbitrary concepts derived from electromagnetic transmission, a lot of the interpretative difficulties surrounding the theory of relativity (including the twin paradox) are easily explained away.

Finally, I would like to express the hope that this paper might lend support to a personal philosophy that mere mathematical consistency does not constitute a full explanation for physics. A deeper physical understanding must always be sought for.

AUTHOR IS EITHER CRAZY OR A SUPER-EINSTEIN.

Biographical Sketch of Alan M. Schwartz

"Uncle Al" Schwartz is a organic chemist (Ph.D., Stanford) whose passions are human-implantable prostheses, benign biointerfaces, bulk and grafted medical polymers including hydrogels, and designed molecules exhibiting almost molecular toxicity to insects (especially his cat's fleas). When the moon is full and the wolf-bane blooms, he unfurls an IQ hovering at the extreme edge of human achievement, a truly villainous sense of humor, and an attitude slightly to the political right of Vlad the Impaler, and proceeds to soil the pages of Mensa publications (more than 130 times to date), *CHEMTECH*, and even the *Harvard Business Review*. His membership in ISPE has afforded him new vistas of international pseudocerebral brouhaha. The 500 pages of *The Mostly Complete Writings of Uncle Al* have traveled on computer disk to more than two dozen countries, confounding customs officials and plunging intelligence agencies into impotent puzzlement. One of his works was banned in Spain for advocating personal armed defense of self, family, and property—the locals apparently having learned nothing from Guernica. He lives in Irvine, California, with a lovely lady, a psychotic cat, a garden of bizarre plants, and a custom-hacked 80486/50 fighting for truth, justice, and an end to the 55-mph speed limit.

CHAPTER 11

THE FUTURE IS HISTORY

Alan M. Schwartz

If we fabricate an optic that has enough area and extent to image the Big Bang, will we instantaneously destroy all but one possible future, and create God? This is how it will happen . . .

Classical or Newtonian physics is very handy for building pinball machines and hydroelectric dams, but fails miserably to explain transistors, particle accelerators, precise astronomical observations, and superconductivity. Relativity and quantum mechanics model the very big, massive, and fast; and the very small, light, and indeterminate, respectively. Each is remarkably accurate, to parts per billion, in the *ab initio* prediction of what we verifiably observe in their respective neighborhoods. Relativity and quantum mechanics are wholly incompatible, leading to serious intellectual rumbles when they simultaneously claim the same turf. Quantum mechanics seems to be in the lead, pointing to the pull tab that can instantly destroy the entire universe.

Quantum-state descriptions are complex constructions of differential equations called wavefunctions. A complete set of wavefunctions may possess mathematically "real" and "imaginary" components, contains all possible information about the system it describes, and is perforce physically unobservable. All sums and differences of the elements of wavefunction sets, superpositions of the wavefunctions, are equally valid. These virtual states when self-multiplied ("squared" comes to mind as an analogy) are the observables of a system. The inclusion of "imaginary" numbers and the reverberation of the Heisenberg Uncertainty Principle allow descriptions of energy states and spatial regions formally forbidden to classical physics: tunneling, evanescent waves, virtual states, magnetic resonance imaging, field-effect transistors—the stuff of fairy dust and serious corporate profits. Einstein always disputed the philosophical foundations of quantum mechanics, and conspired to throw a wiener into its warp drive. He did, too.

The Einstein-Podolsky-Rosen Paradox and its embodiment in the repeatable macroscopic experimental verification of the Bell Inequality unavoidably asserts that the spacetime continuum, the universe, the summation of reality, "knows" when it has been observed. The fury of possible futures that is existence roils unobserved. The observation of a system, the performance of a measurement, unavoidably interacts with this arrangement. The probabilistic multiplicities of its bubble of quantum fuzz collapse like a pricked balloon to yield a unique observation. The superposition of quantum-mechanical wavefunction probabilities abruptly collapses upon observation or measurement from its initial flux of virtual states into a final, real, observable state.

It gets *better, much, much better.*

A delicious condiment seasoning the experimental stew is that there is *no* requirement that the observable state be limited in space. Suppose that a pair of quantum-correlated particles are emitted in opposite directions, 180° apart, and that they are polarized. A reference frame may be chosen (call it the "laboratory") in which the plane of their electric field vectors can be only horizontal or vertical, but randomly so. If we sample either of the pair over millions of emissions, 50 percent will be vertically polarized, 50 percent horizontally polarized. If we sample *both* members of the pair, the first measurement will still be a random coin toss, but the second measurement will be 100 percent determined. Each vertical polarization will have a paired vertical polarization, and each horizontal polarization will have a paired horizontal polarization. Thus the radiative emission of paired quantum-correlated particles in opposite directions, followed after an elapsed time by the observation of one particle, immediately fixes the observable state of the other, no matter what their distance of separation. It has been done several times. It works. It finesses Relativity.

Relativity asserts that information transfer may not proceed at velocities exceeding that of light, about a foot per nanosecond. One can readily fabricate an apparatus a hundred feet long in which the previously described paired measurements can be synchronized to less than 100 nanoseconds. This is the essence of the Bell Inequality experiments, and their statistical analysis is beyond dispute: quantum mechanics predicts and delivers an observed violation of Relativity. A local observation of the universe causes it to undergo instantaneous global quantum wavefunction collapse, creating consistent observables throughout the entirety of its substance. It is a neat trick. The universe is nothing if not consistent. The whole of the universe can be twisted by a suitable observation. This is the disturbing conclusion of one philosophical school of quantum mechanics, the Copenhagen Convention.

In an attempt to reconcile quantum mechanics and Relativity, another school of thought arose. Maintaining that the observer is an intrinsic component of the measurement and of the fabric of reality itself, theoreticians proposed that the results of observation are contained within the act. Nothing need now change or be reset, because it was already there. The single small side effect of this treatment is the creation of a new universe every time an observation / decision / measurement occurs. An infinitely infinite manifold sheaf of entire universes explodes as every action proceeds in all possible ways. It asserts that betting odds make no difference, since every horse and every dice roll must come up both a winner and a loser. Experience dictates otherwise. The Many Worlds Hypothesis is even more unsettling than the Copenhagen Convention, and no more useful.

Is the path of the future predetermined, or is it a function of free will? Quantum mechanics asserts that predestination is an impossibility. An unstable state will undergo statistical decay. Transition probabilities may be specified, but the path is undetermined until it is observed, after it has taken place. Conversely, if an event quantum-correlates to another event in time and space, observation of one irrevocably, immediately, and forever fixes the other, e.g., the Bell Inequality. We can therefore formulate not merely the milquetoast political impotence of an end to history, but the robust creation of a singular, predictable, and unalterable future: the birth of God.

The inception of the universe is hinted at by its universal blackbody microwave radiation background, the remnant of the Big Bang. If we point a microwave receiver at the heavens, we detect a microwave spectrum identical—disconcertingly flawless in its frequency and amplitude distribution, and very disconcertingly flawless in its Big-Bang-derived microkelvin spatial in homogeneity—to that emitted by a perfect blackbody emitter happily going about its business at about 2.7°C above absolute zero. The furious fireball of the Cosmic Egg hatching has cooled to this microwave whisper. All reality bloomed from a singularity exploding outward to create time and space, either converging to a single geometric point at time zero or perhaps a more rounded "imaginary time" subsequently inflating into reality. Either way, everything starts from the quantum fuzz, the superposition of virtual states, surrounding that quantum singularity. The multiplicity of indeterminate futures we so enjoy and abhor is a direct result of the probabilistic nature of that beginning. Never having been observed, there is no singular beginning of our universe, only a summation of wavefunctions and probabilities that evolve into events upon our observation. An infinite number of beginnings beget an infinite profusion of futures.

Each observation we make plucks reality from that profusion of virtual possibilities, worlds without end! The universe harnesses its substance to transform potentiality into actuality through perception. "Fiat lux!" is just the way to do it.

An observation of the Big Bang would collapse it into a determined local event, an observable. As its superposition of virtual quantum states collapsed, all the universe's possible pasts but one would be uncreated. The synchronous global echo of that observation would then instantaneously fix a unique future for the Big Bang (and its quantum-correlated conjugate observables: that's us, buster) throughout the entire fabric of reality. At the very least, it would freeze Las Vegas solid.

How may we observe the Big Bang so that all our infinity of futures but one will vanish? As we look deeper into space, we look backward into time, quantified in the Hubble Constant. Let us build a sufficiently large optic, large in area to adequately sample amplitude and large in extent to adequately sample phase, to image the extreme depths of space/time. The observation need not be visual. We could use ultraviolet or infrared, radio or microwave, or anything else that conveys definitive information after processing. In any case, a few acres of a suitable optic floating in the benign isotropic crystal clarity of the vacuum of space will do nicely. We could look sufficiently deeply into space, into time, to image, to observe, the Big Bang. Even an optic covering acres would subtend an infinitesimal solid angle over billions of light years' radius. The amount of the Big Bang observed would be negligible, and the backlash of the Einstein-Podolsky-Rosen Paradox might be inconsequential, or might not, but why quibble?

Instead, build a corresponding suite of mirrors covering a near-4π steradian field of view, a sphere of observation, and we will image almost the entirety of the Big Bang. With its near totality observed, the Big Bang's probabilistic quantum structure will collapse into an observable. The backlash of the Einstein Podolsky-Rosen Paradox will promptly freeze the structure of the entire universe into a single, deterministic, observable path.

This is how humanity will create an entity of all knowledge and perfect prediction: a god.

But wait: there's more!

Human thought is a tapestry of exquisite intricacy. Its patterns within patterns extend beyond our finest measurements, even beyond the physical structure of its supporting anatomy. Such organization is disturbingly congruent not to the finite constructs of classical mathematics that yield to delta-epsilon deconstruction, but to chaos, fractals, and quantum uncertainty. Human thought is global simplicity grown of local complexity without end. Might the ultimate foundation of our minds be the random jingle jangle of virtual quantum states spewing random numbers? Roger Penrose has boldly asserted as much. Robert Heinlein's random number-tossing Holmes IV computer (Mike) might be a prescient vision. Let us experiment, and observe.

Computers (von Neumann machines, as well as distributed and parallel processors) are universally acclaimed for their dogged stupidity. They are empty of any self-referential concern. They are not aware. Artificial intelligence seeks to embody the concern of sentient judgment within learning scripts and expert systems: collections of facts, and a self-modifying framework to manipulate them. Such systems can be eerie in their exhibited abilities as long as a comma is not entered as a semicolon. Deterministic programming is not alive.

How may a computer be taught? Fuzzy logic attempts to draw discrete conclusions from incomplete or inconsistent inputs, and is a functionally better match to the workings of a sloppy macrocosm. It, too, disappoints. The most efficacious approach so far to mirroring cognizant response is to have no programming at all beyond a loose set of data-transfer rules, that is, the neural net.

A neural net is an interconnected matrix of rather stupid microprocessors arrayed in one or more successive layers. The discrete components are multiply connected. Initially, they randomly stimulate or suppress each other through their web of data flow in response to an input. The random jingle jangle of flowing bytes evolves an output. Good results are rewarded and reinforced. Bad results are punished; so they evolve into good results and are reinforced. The automaton learns without programming, deriving understanding without prior foundation. Its only value is that it works, with exceptional speed and accuracy, and by an imponderable sequence of irreproducible events.

In the absence of quantum indeterminacy, the wellspring of human thought, the self-awareness and the intrinsic structure of the independent mind, vanishes. We have already established that the astronomical observation of a great portion of the Big Bang will, courtesy of the Einstein-Podolsky-Rosen Paradox, collapse its quantum- mechanical superposition of virtual states, rendering it into an observable. With only one possible singular beginning, the entire warp and weft of reality will synchronously collapse into an deterministic observable as well, precluding all but one future. What would be the sequelae?

Intelligent life is the universe's way of viewing itself. Science is the modality by which the universe creates structures that cannot arise spontaneously with a sufficient probability of achievement. Physics is its way of reaching self-understanding.

Were we to view the Big Bang, collapse its quantum indeterminacy of virtual-state superposition into an observable, change the churning maelstrom of infinitely possible beginnings into a single determined beginning, we would destroy all futures but one. What would there be left to observe or understand? Intelligent life would serve no purpose. The roiling cauldron of sentient thought would have no source in such a universe. It would be uncreated.

Is this the mechanism by which sophisticated civilizations throughout the universe unwittingly commit suicide? Is this why we cannot detect advanced outworlder colonies, search though we might throughout the electromagnetic spectrum sleeting in from space? Is our elected government correct: is thought truly dangerous?

If we view the Big Bang, the whole of creation will be synchronously transformed into the perfect Congressional filibuster. The aggregate of human intellect will instantaneously decay into the perfect body politic or church congregation: a carcass of spiritual purity uncontaminated by the untoward annoyance of a mind.

I think I prefer chaos and the otherwise unwelcome chance of hitting 00 on a Las Vegas roulette wheel to taking the long view and hardboiling the Cosmic Egg.

Biographical Sketch of William K. Fielding

William K. Fielding—75 years of age, retired (from shipbuilding, land surveying, and electronics)—was born in Brockton, Mass. After five years in Colon, Panama, his school days were spent in West Virginia, Pennsylvania, and several Massachusetts towns. He has lived and worked in Maine, New Jersey, Hawaii, and California, finally sequestering in Ware, Mass. Although college was interrupted by late-Depression lack of "funding," he has been, lifelong, an autodidact.

Currently an active member/officer of the Bertrand Russell Society, WKF composes music, writes essays, and reviews books on scientific and philosophical subjects. He constantly reads and studies, upgrading knowledge of humanities, literature, and European languages—to kill time before Time, inevitably, closes his books. Meanwhile, his wife, Mary, and his children, grandchildren, and a great-granddaughter keep endurance endurable.

CHAPTER **12**

TEACHING HUMANITY: A MODEST PROPOSAL FOR CENTURY 21

William K. Fielding

Many Americans fail to consider philosophy a legitimate element of public education. They remain either uninformed or misinformed about its basic civilizing functions and historical significance. Along with various viewpoints generally accepted by scientists, philosophy has been feared by established religions as leading toward secular "beliefs" perceived as dangerous. Suspicion and hostility inhibit free discussion of many topics essential to education as a birthright of all citizens in any true democracy.

My argument here is the proposition that philosophy is not a word-game pastime for reclusive, elitist splinter groups of university professors; I submit that there has existed throughout the twentieth century a dynamic evolution of thought tending to synthesize and strengthen the technologies and social disciplines which have improved current living standards and future possibilities for our descendants.

By 1900, it had become clear that traditional metaphysics, ethics, and logic were inadequate for dealing with the avalanche of concepts sweeping down from newly taken high ground in pure mathematics, natural sciences, and political theory. Structures jerry-built out of fragments from Plato, Aristotle, and Descartes had to be reevaluated and erected on more solid foundations. In the vanguard were Bertrand Russell and A. N. Whitehead in Britain; William James and John Dewey in the United States; and—perhaps less-obviously germinal—Brentano, Husserl, and their European followers. Many other voices figured in decades of subsequent systematic fine-tuning, a period of ferment and increasingly arcane controversy.

To recite the hectic histories of Empiricism, Pragmatism, and other

135

short-lived or tentative movements would not add much to comprehending the crisis resulting from efforts to accommodate reason to discoveries ongoing in physics, biology and astronomy. Classical mathematics came a-cropper (Gödel and Tarski); sociology and psychology suffered confusion (Durkheim, Jung, Skinner, among others); and quibbling over what language really meant (Wittgenstein, Putnam, Chomsky) diminished symbolic logic. Yet, patiently molding this ubiquitous mishmash into a semblance of viable working hypotheses, Russell, A. J. Ayer, and W. V. 0. Quine loaded a canon that both scientists and logicians, today, find on the whole acceptable.

This, then, is my point of departure: a contention that—after all the wild, obfuscating, random guesswork and nitpicking during our twentieth century—Philosophy has survived in excellent health. In expanding on this theme, I undertake to demonstrate that continued attention to the several concerns jointly constituting "philosophy" offers the last best hope for humankind on this planet. Having amply peopled Earth, we should now allow our finest minds to decide how to proceed from present scientific analysis toward future centuries of wisdom.

I

From the then-mysterious twitching of Galvani's frog leg, a fantastically large number of steps have brought us to superconducting super colliders and satellite-reflected worldwide communications. And, now that molecules are manipulated to synthesize plastics, insulin, and recombinant genes—an ever-more-complex constellation of alchemic wonders—we remain at the mercy of whole populations who are grossly ignorant of the composition and significance of such miracles. *Their* miracles, leftovers from past ages of superstition, limit gains that we could or should be achieving.

If your neighbor is asked about Avogadro's number, he may try to locate it in the Yellow Pages. If you mention the concept of a human soul, there is a high probability that he will claim to have one, and assert that it will outlive his present physical substance. For such mental garbage we can blame only ourselves, since we continue to tolerate pseudo-education, which perpetuates obsolete interpretations of life and environment.

What are we to make of enclaves of Muslims bent on slaughtering Jews? What is a Christian, anyway . . . or a Rastafarian, a Catholic, a Northern Ireland Presbyterian? What does all this tribal mumbo jumbo *mean*? Well, in any sensible view, it means absolutely nothing. But beware! you may be caught in a crossfire not of your own making. If you should write to your elected representatives about legislating "Belief" out of existence once and for all, you may be classified as an anarchist crank.

When there is talk of glorifying science and math in elementary schools, do we really expect that the proponents look very far beyond higher-paying jobs for their children? When we hear of plans to restore so-called "inner city" facilities, what is being discussed beyond determined efforts to continue outmoded customary folkways? Cramming little heads with alleged facts and computer-crunched numbers begs the larger question: what is Big Science, and what promise does it hold for the future of mankind on a too-small Earth?

When Thomas Jefferson wrote of "an informed citizenry," he was not just whistling Dixie. And when H. L. Mencken deplored the Boobery abroad in America, he meant more than evangelical hillbilly anti-intellectualism. Only to the unhampered ruminations of university-supported Philosophy can we look for partial solutions to the atavism that is a lethal threat to mankind's potential for survival and betterment. Politics must be secularized; education must be freshly examined and tailored for the benefit of the most-receptive young minds; technologies found too dangerous should be scrapped. Sounds simple? Yes, and it is.

Unless goaded by its most thoughtful—read: "philosophical"—citizens, Big Government will persist in impeding Big Science according to what it thinks the man in the street wants. But the man invoked is increasingly left out to sleep (and to steal) in his community's street. He is paying with his blood for conditions legislated at his own behest. It is no longer possible for a layman to prosper and maintain his health; the day of the layman has ended. The twenty-first century will require full input from informed citizens carrying out workable programs on a livable biosphere.

Systems not far removed from Locke's educable blank sheet and confounded by Descartes' body/soul dichotomy are delaying the proper functioning of our societies. Our best-formed judgments about the capabilities and employments of humanity are not being implemented. The State and its schools need wise counseling: and that is the proper vocation of philosophers.

Because the syllogistic tradition proved too rigid for the needs of twentieth-century experimental science, it has been retired largely to the backwaters of Roman Catholic theological teaching. Even so, most college courses in logic still crank out sophomores who are led to assume they have learned to know the Truth when they see it. Inexactness in empirical measurements and theorems that are only provisionally true demonstrate that Truth—in either a debate or a laboratory—can rarely, if ever, be positively certain. A basic fallacy transmitted to schoolchildren lives on in bald assertion of "facts" that do not exist in the real world. A case in point: equal time requested for instruction in Creationism.

Blind adherence to self-serving dispensers of certainty perverts efficient indoctrination of youths' minds ostensibly being "trained" in mathematics and technology. Statistical measures of probability, approximate truth levels, are not explained for what they are: ambient expedients. Instead, perfection, supposedly admired by its heavenly Originator in Residence, is instilled as a platonic Ideal. Sorry, kids, things just don't *work* that way!

II

Early in human pondering about what we, as unique animals, might be, it was noticed that the head had much to do with awareness and initiating physical activity. When differences in personality became a focus of discrimination for practioners of arts predating medicine, bumpy skulls were suspected of holding clues for classifying individuals in terms of behavioral tendencies and social idiopathies. Not too far advanced from this approach, investigators (notably Freud and Lombroso) developed elaborate "explications" to account for what we are and what may go wrong with our head functions. These theories have arguably caused more pain than they ever eased—but that is a long, sad tale to be treated elsewhere. Here we are more concerned with the difficulty of convincing the layman that his brain is impossible to isolate from his putative mind/soul.

Discovery of the electrochemical activity of synapses raised questions not easily answered. Fortunately, guesswork is being painstakingly reduced as we learn to measure the fine-structural details of neurons and their remarkable assemblages that form brains. Only in the last decade have new mechanical probes been fashioned which can begin to tell us what *really* lets us think and perform in the ways we do. Again, details only boggle minds not privy to the essential backgrounds in microbiology, biochemistry, and electronics. For the nonspecialist, we are forced to generalize.

Paralleling study of incredibly minute subunits of nerve functioning, theories of perception have undergone upward spirals of sophistication. Behaviorism, phenomenology, and clinical psychiatry have been severely undercut by researchers who now better describe the fantastic fractioning of time within our receptors and their contorted molecules. Stimulus and response, as taught in the first decades of this century, turns out to be a crude metaphor for what actually goes on when we observe, relate to, and remember passing events in our surroundings. This, also, is too specialized a topic for anyone whose schooling has been in nuts-and-bolts dimensions. But without some effort to connect such knowledge to everyday experience, no person is fully conscious of what a piece of work evolution has made.

As with the physical sciences, there is much variability in molecular structure and movement. Exactness in classification, if too rigorously sought, can frustrate comprehension. Similar ionic particles conspire to form a soapy micelle and the bilayered lipid shell of a typical mammalian cell. So how can we allow benighted, half-educated instructors to lead our children down a garden path of Noah's Ark animal names and Adam-plus-Eve ontogeny? Organic matter is matter; any other description is a distortion of the evidence. Moreover, we are not one singular organism, but an amalgam of numerous symbiotic organs, uniquely evolved and comfortably coexisting.

Philosophy, too, has evolved. The peculiar insights inscribed by Greek speculators, reworked during the Renaissance and culminating in Leibniz and Kant, all presumed a creative entity, an invisible God. Gradually, this presumption faded; whoever, now, speaks of any god is either deluded or a charlatan, or both. Some will persist in belief, but whatever exists simply is. Wherefore reason indicates the folly of interfaith violence: killing based on a fundamental cosmic error.

III

In the same years when professional gentlemen—J. S. Mill, Emerson, Ruskin, Jonathan Edwards—were advising civilized people on the proper ways to conduct their lives, the British were abusing their colonial subjects, and Americans were annihilating their native predecessors. Ultimately, our Civil War and the rise of Imperial Germany negated those self-righteous spokesmen for individual ethics. Something was very wrong; being proper was not respectable. The greatest good for the greatest number paid no dividends, the Unitarian could not transcend progress.

Along came Marx and Nietzsche (who sought to tell it like it is). Were they philosophers? I happen to think they were not, nor do I consider Teddy Roosevelt a statesman; likewise, our great entrepreneurs were hardly role models for youth. But the hard lessons of Anglo-American, European, and Asian history have done little to temper our bloody attitudes about might making right. As with Teutonic idealism, rationalization is the enemy of peace.

When Kennedy and Khruschchev were playing hardball in the Caribbean, it was Russell, the philosopher, and Einstein, the scientist, who persuaded them to avoid escalating toward global ruin. Thus ethics as a practical art proved more effective than lifetimes of academic arguing about points of good and evil. The intersection of right living and right thinking was established forever.

That philosophers do, in unpredictable ways, often directly influence both historic events and internal policies of their nations is to be seen in the revamping of England's public school system in accordance with A. N. Whitehead's recommendations. With perhaps less success, John Dewey left his pragmatic handprint on United States curriculum choices and teaching codes. In France, Jean Paul Sartre and Albert Camus greatly influenced several generations of their countrymen in habits of thought affecting the course of national politics.

In the late, unlamented Soviet Union, politics and science frequently were in collision. Psychiatry became a tool for incarcerating dissidents; and leading biologists were forced to pursue bizarre theories that international colleagues found absurd. This reminds us that, in any culture, there is an overlap of sociology, philosophies, and legal structures, limiting expression of views that are found unacceptable by those in power— whether they are dictators or presidents of democracies. Much research in the U.S. has been coerced in the direction of "defense," through control of funding, personnel brainwashing, and outright theft of patents fromindividual researchers. Super-conservative Senators have sometimes hounded those whose philosophical mentors were alleged to be subversive. To the extent that Martin Luther King and Abraham Lincoln were political philosophers, we see the extremes of action that can be induced by unsettling Ideas. Hayakawa, for all his linguistic expertise, found himself lost for words in confrontation with California protesters. To the everlasting disgrace of New York City, Russell was banned, by unwarranted bias, from lecturing there; Sidney Hook, however, waved the flag so proudly that he remained a welcome resident lifelong.

As is often apparent, the ivory tower no longer insulates those who achieve recognition as professional philosophers. Meanwhile, our supposedly innocuous layman wends his melancholic way, misguided by faith in "conventional wisdom." His failure to examine obsolete patterns and replace them with clearly better innovations clogs the gears of government and invites future civic chaos. Inevitably, our children's children will pay a high price for impediments imposed on free thought and unbiased anthropological research.

IV

Some of what I have said may seem like scattershot opinions, discon-
nected from the promised argument. But please notice that there must be
a backdrop, a frame of reference, against which an observed event will
become meaningful. Whole universes of scholarship exist which I have
not attempted to outline, although even name-dropping would suggest
subtle pertinent categories to a well-versed philosopher. But we are not,
most of us, professionals of this or related sorts. So only enough has
been sketched as appears needed for developing my central theme. That
theme is:

> *The history and present discussions of philosophy ought to be made an*
> *integral part of every public-school curriculum, from which subjects apt*
> *to lead to acceptance of anachronistic customs and mythologies should*
> *be excluded.*

The manner of presenting history (also literature of earlier periods)
has led to perpetuating thought patterns not germane to humanity's basic
concern: survival. When warfare is chronicled as an inevitable fact of life,
or membership in a religious or national subculture taken for granted,
endless violence becomes predestined for those who will graduate into a
world that is impossible to control and preserve.

Any remedial program will be insufficient unless, simultaneously,
changes in our postulated "layman" can also be subsidized. It is a truism
that children learn as much—or more?—in the home as in their schools.
It is not suggested that a totalitarian mindset be inculcated; nor should
anyone expect short-range resolution of all factional disputes that result in
combat. A possible start on a path toward global amity lies in our vast
new communications networks, coupled with an as-yet unacknowledged
"quantum" advance in medical technology and biochemistry. Whereas
manufacture of trade goods determined political economy during several
past centuries, the frontier opening today lies below the surface of plant
and animal cells. Somehow this astonishing potential must be brought
into the purview of Everyman.

At some point in the twenty-first century it should become evident
that intelligence may be more than an accident of evolution. With networks of supercomputers amplifying technological gains beyond anything
presently imaginable, governments will no longer be permitted to commit
their people to deadly combat.

Because there are undeniably gradations in individual human intelligence, no amount of egalitarian rhetoric is likely to prevent the better

brains from avoiding subjection to the will of lesser brains. Causes of dissension are obvious: religion(s), nationalism, ethnic inequities. Recognizing and eliminating counterproductive institutions is a feasible civic duty—for the intelligent.

Totalitarianism and technocracies were once seen as quick roads to Utopia. But they had to do with economic, rather than biological, interpretations of Man on Earth. Having arrived at the possibility of controlling ourselves and our planet efficiently, without being sabotaged by the superstitious and the warmongers, let us now begin to *teach* the modalities for survival. Education, at every age, is our best hope for prevailing against ignorance and greed, the idiotic roots of warfare.

Whatever your high IQ makes possible, do it. And communicate your achievements to, and among, others likewise endowed.

In a word: *Philosophize*.

Biographical Sketch of Robert L. Clark

Robert L. Clark grew up in the 1950s in Denver, Colorado. He moved to Washington, D.C. and finished at Wakefield High in 1964. He went to VPI, where he was a co-op student at Oak Ridge, TN. He received a B.S. in Physics and worked at the Nuclear Power Division at Charleston Naval Shipyard, refueling nuclear submarines. After attending O.C.S. at Fort Benning, Georgia, he served in E.O.D. with the U.S. Army. He received an M.B.A. in Information Technology from George Washington University in 1977, and spent almost ten years in Chicago working for Computer Sciences, General Electric, and Atlantic Richfield. He earned a C.P.A. in 1982 and moved to Albuquerque, NM, where he now practices. He enjoys camping, reading, and computer programming. He is married and 46, with no children.

CHAPTER 13

THE PHILOSOPHY OF A METHOD

Robert L. Clark

We develop a method to meet a need. Features of the method parallel features of the need. Once a need is met, another one grows, and the method gets refined. The needs and features grow by interaction. Any method has a way in which to use it properly, which becomes exaggerated to fit growing needs. Finally exaggeration grows into abuse, unable to compensate for the degree to which underlying assumptions are violated. It is time for a new method to meet the needs of the new situation. For instance, combinatorics outweighs simplification when the scientific method splits complex modern problems up for analysis.

A REVISED SET OF NEEDS

The scientific method has succeeded all too well. Success has brought growth, and it is a precept in general systems theory that with growth comes specialization and complexity. The confusion which this complexity brings is a fertile field for a priesthood of the religion of doubt, if one may call it that. There is a need to assuage the anxiety that people experience when they are confused and know they are in the admittedly risky problem-solving business. Complexity leads to a third need, the need to appeal to funding authorities. These people want to use cheap facilities to quickly produce a profit with partial answers.

CONFLICT OF INTEREST

Problem-solving today thus has three conflicting needs:

(1) Solve complexity in a real-world environment.
(2) Yield cheap applications on partial knowledge.
(3) Not upset the community by violating theory.

That is, the experimenter wants to understand, but if he finds the answer, his grant will be cut off. The businessman finds part of the answer, and uses it to make a profit, and meanwhile shuts down the study to save costs. Work is done in business with existing facilities and in a rush in order to cut more costs. Last, one had best not publish anything radical without higher-level support. The authorities in that field of knowledge do not want theory violated, even if new answers, being new, are radical by definition.

MEETING CONFLICTING NEEDS

A holistic approach resting on a broad set of assumptions can handle one-shot real-world problems with validity. Because one gets answers to the whole problem, there is no way someone will shut down the study after getting one piece to sell. The answer is all or nothing. Finally, the approach is so radical that it is silly to argue it is radical theory. It is not theory at all.

ACTION ORIENTATION

The key to effective effort is an efficient representation system. Just as we deal with circular geometry with radial coordinates rather than cartesian ones, we should deal with a problem in its own terms. The situation can only do what it is capable of. It is now the custom to set some goal toward solving the problem, the goal often being completely silly once the situation is understood. This is inefficient. We need to think in terms of the goals and behaviors of the problem. Formerly we understood an object and tried to infer what it might do. Instead we need to work from the beginning in terms of the observed behavior, especially the *important* observed behavior.

FUNCTIONAL STANDPOINT

Besides thinking in terms of behavior, we need to adopt a new conceptual viewpoint toward it. For example, it isn't a rat in a maze; rather, it is a small computer solving a problem. It isn't a door, but rather an interface. Note the benefit of this method. The minute we say interface, there is the concept of a place to transfer from a region to a dissimilar one. A door just opens (so what?). The important behavior leaps out from a functional viewpoint.

A new holistic problem-solving method will meet important needs in today's world. We must handle complexity in terms of what to do now, in one-shot, nonlaboratory situations where we are acutely biased about the results. We recognize that funding will continue to want the "quick fix", but we must adapt so that partial answers don't stop the study. *Partial* answers are no longer possible. Finally, it is evident that any *real* answer *would* violate theory; else theory would already have produced that answer. Without violating theory, we come from a posture that has no theory in the offending sense. Now let us see what specifically is meant.

TOWARD A HOLISTIC PROBLEM-SOLVING APPROACH

We intend to meet a different set of needs, not attack the scientific method, although by inference that may occur. Reasons for wanting to solve a problem may include a desire for money, power, or even truth! The motive is important, because the problem-solver must be considered part of the situation in question. The first thing we want to know is, *What shall I do* to start using a holistic approach?

Let's start with a set of working assumptions:

1. The situation has a limited repertoire of behaviors, far less behaviors than pieces or parts.
2. The context and I also have limited bundles of behavior interactions, and are part of the situation.
3. We may organize the behaviors into a hierarchy under a few simple major traits.
4. Given a hierarchy of behaviors, we *create* an artificial context or milieu within by which to solve the problem.
5. The created milieu rests on fundamentals of interaction whose sources are arbitrary but whose results often work. Laws of behavior and patterns of interaction are part of the milieu. The milieu is not a model.
6. We will not create a model. In a sense we use the situation as a whole to model itself.
7. We eschew goals and feedback, because the inherent bias is likely not in the problem's own terms.

8. Behaviors are viewed in a new manner, as a cyclic phenomenon with continuity through the past, present, and future. They are today what they must be so that tomorrow ends up as it must.

9. Although we avoid goals, we may note utility. That is, some behaviors will appear useful. The point is that we take what is there rather than squeeze out what is not. The situation sets the goals. We do not.

10. We observe the minor behaviors in terms of general principles. From this observation we identify the major behavior at the top of the hierarchy of behavior. This indicates what the situation is about and what it will and won't do. We can find utility in some of this repertoire.

11. Last, it is foolish to isolate analysis from data. Actually, consider that analysis in the real world occurs step-by-step as each piece of evidence is examined. We draw tentative conclusions along the way.

12. As a postscript, the "Whorfian Hypothesis" of general systems theory (Whorf was a 1950s biologist) states that the available words for a subject dictate how it can be viewed. Eskimos have seven words for snow, Africans none. I propose to extend the notion: without the proper repertoire of mental pictures and analogies subjects also cannot be viewed in certain ways.

USING A HOLISTIC PROBLEM-SOLVING METHOD

The first step in using a new approach is to consider the list of working assumptions. This means we develop a list of the combined behaviors of the situation, context, and ourselves. Why is the situation in that context? Why are we interested in it? What if anything is the situation trying to do? What is the purpose of the situation if any? The purpose of the context? What does the area of study (*not* "the object") always do? What does it never do? Were we surprised it did something we thought it wouldn't?

Next, to establish importance and organization, erect a hierarchy that fits together. One of the milieu's pillars is the notion that things fit together for a reason. This is the first example of what we means by "creating an artificial context by which to solve."

Without goals, we talk about what the situation "wants" in its own terms (behaviors), not what we want in our terms (goals). We observe the behavior according to some key patterns and delayed effects. When the circle formed by the causality becomes small, the situation is understood.

Without a specific situation, not much more should be said. However, recalling that our own behavior and that of the original context is within the realm of study, look at a few operational guidelines:

1. Each behavior has its opposite nearby in time/space.
2. Each behavior governs a smaller one and is governed by a larger one.
3. Each behavior has that which makes it go (or grow), that which makes it stop, and that which governs how or how much, or when, the behavior does this.
4. Nothing important happens suddenly.
5. Behavior is almost always viewed as a *cluster* of events governed by *key events not recent*. The conventional view is that yesterday governs most of today, little piece by little piece. Not so.
6. Things occur under the influence of several cycles at once. The result is a cycle, but a jagged one. We don't look for a smooth one.
7. Most behavior is insignificant and just serves as filler for infrequent key behavior.
8. A cycle has eight parts, split 3 and 5. Each of the eight parts has unique characteristics typical to that portion number. Part 2, e.g. is unique from any part 3.
9. No situation has more than eight basic behaviors.
10. Behavior often has a predecessor behavior and a followup.
11. A situation often has a "center." Also, we may view it in terms of what is missing, what is extra, and what context would be its ideal environment.

CONCLUSION

This paper was about a holistic problem-solving method. The new method takes a top-down approach to theory, rather than the bottom-up method used originally in science. Because the new method yields a result as a whole rather than progressively in pieces, it cannot be used prematurely, nor does it have a defendable body of theory around which to erect a priesthood of conventionality. Avoiding hidden agendas of money and power, it is free to find answers.

The assumptions under the holistic technique are broad, so that answers apply to the real world better than do laboratory results. In fact, we convert the threat of contamination by the context into the power of solution via another context, a synthetic one based on expected patterns. The need for reliable facts will not go away. The scientific method remains very important. But perhaps a Kantian synthesis of the scientific and holistic methods will occur in time.

Autobiographical Sketch of Richard A. "Rich" Kapnick

I was born in Adrian, Michigan, in 1941—the oldest of four children—to a family of unsung geniuses. Adrian is a quaint little town; the county seat of a reactionary midwest farming area. It's truly the "land of 'penny postcards' and two-way streets; the midwest buckle on the Bible Belt." There I suffered through cold, dreary winters, and the abomination of odd-ball teachers hired by the Adrian Public School System. Not having suffered enough, I continued for four more years at Adrian College, a small, private Methodist institution of higher learning. One of the buildings I studied in was actually used to house soldiers during the American Civil War.

As an eleventh grader, I made a small bottle of hydrogen sulfide in Max B. Sweet's (his real name!) chemistry lab, and uncapped the bottle in "Froggy" Aneff's algebra class one winter day. The entire high school had to be evacuated until the school building could be thoroughly ventilated. (Mr. Aneff's nickname was "Froggy" because he had one glass eye that bulged out and moved slowly from side to side—about 2 or 3 seconds behind the action of his good eye.)

Nonetheless, I am grateful to the abundant maple trees of Adrian (we called it "A-drain") for providing oxygen for my lungs to breathe for the first 22 years of my life.

Following college, there was a stint teaching high-school biology and chemistry (1964–1966) to avoid being one of those who came home after being found face-down in a rice paddy in Viet Nam.

Alas, my love for teaching and for the students came in second to my need for money. The next five years were spent in Detroit in the broadcast advertising business. In 1971, an international radio and television representative firm hired me to open and run their Chicago office. This was a highly successful venture, and enabled me to open my own full-service advertising agency in Chicago's famous Wrigley building five years later.

Scores of local and regional clients received my special brand of iconoclastic advertising creativity. The most famous was Pepe's Mexican Restaurants, which my business partner and I helped build from 28 ignominious little taco stands to 85 glorious family Mexican restaurants that literally defined the nature of Mexican food in the Chicago market. Pepe's is now the largest and most-respected regional chain of Mexican restaurants in Chicago, thanks to 12 years of very hard work on the part of the chain owners, coupled with my agency's advertising efforts.

In 1988, I moved to Los Angeles with my family, and settled in as an international marketing consultant. My M.B.A. was completed at the University of Phoenix's Southern California campus after 2.5 years of night school, and my Ph.D. work has now begun. Pacific Western University gave me an honorary Doctor of Economics and Commerce degree in 1992 for my work in promoting international trade.

In addition to my international marketing consultancy, I have started several local businesses, begun teaching advertising and marketing at National University, and am the Editor of *Telicom,* the international ISPE journal.

CHAPTER 14

THE MOST IMPORTANT PEACE VECTOR IN THE HISTORY OF OUR PLANET

Rich Kapnick

Requisite to the peace process is conflict resolution. The greater the ability of an entity to bring peace, the more important it is to the process. It is important, therefore, that all of civilization know what the vectors for peace are, and what the relative importance of each is.

Human conflict results when an individual, society, or a nation does not understand, tolerate, or accept the tenets by which another lives or wants to live. The options are to kill those who are not understood, tolerated, or accepted; to battle one another to a stand-off; to restrain or confine those with whom one is in conflict; to ignore and walk away from a conflict; to compromise in anger and misunderstanding; or to establish and work toward mutually beneficial goals in peace and harmony. There may be additional gradations along this continuum: however, only the last one sounds like an acceptable alternative as long as there are two or more people living on this Earth.

The history of humanity is the story of feuding factions. Conflict resolution has come mostly from the wrong end of the continuum. Only recent human history tells of the beginnings of an understanding of the peace process and of purposely living at peace with factions which would otherwise be opposed. Yet, in many respects, we are still in the dark ages when it comes to understanding how to achieve peace. Is it no wonder, then, that the vectors for establishing peace are neither well known nor well understood?

The most important tenet in understanding peace is to recognize that, throughout history, good has indeed triumphed over evil in the long run.

History tends to focus on the evil that people have done because it is exciting, and because large changes in the direction of human history take place when it is mega-influenced by huge doses of evil. The natural flow of Homo sapiens, when left alone, however, is an inexorable movement toward more civilized behavior and more peaceful existence. If this were not so, Western civilization would not have progressed to the level we see today.

The twentieth Century has brought the discovery of the most important peace vector extant: talking with the enemy. This discovery is on a par with the discovery of fire and the invention of the wheel in its positive effect on the course of human history. In fact, the concept of talking with the enemy might be even more useful than "fire" and "the wheel" in determining the future of mankind.

Because we are still creeping and not yet walking in the arena of functional peacemaking, a certain readily available peace vector that amplifies "talking with the enemy" a billion-fold languishes. Let's take a moment, now, to understand what it is.

The issue is control—control of our own lives, of the lives of others, and of nature itself. We do not yet understand that the only thing purely under our control is our own thoughts. Everything else is subject to environmental influence and therefore not under the absolute control of any individual, group, or nation. Letting go of the desire to control everything requires us to accept the fact that everything and everyone else in the world has the right to be exactly as it is; that just because another person does not live, or want to live, exactly the way we do doesn't make him wrong.

This acceptance takes understanding; understanding that there are other ways that work; understanding that even if something is wrong according to your value system, it may not be wrong by the other person's standards. Your way may be better or more efficient, but after you explain your way, if the other person does not want to implement it, that's perfectly acceptable. Accepting the rejection of your way is the key to living in harmony with nature. The comfort of a given person's routine transcends the self-assumed right of control by another person. To live maturely takes understanding and acceptance of the idea that every other person in the world has the right to be crazy. Of course, you have the right to not be around while they are being crazy or to get out of harm's way if their craziness endangers you.

Understanding takes discovery. One of our most useful phrases is "I used to think x, but then I discovered y." Discovery is the process of seeking and finding greater truths for our lives. It is facilitated by our desire for ever-higher standards and for conducting our affairs more efficiently and sanely. However, many of us have not learned that discovery for ourselves is fine, but forcing that discovery on someone else is not fine.

Discovery requires stepwise readiness. "Readiness" is a real concept, and discovery is only appropriate when a person is ready for that particular discovery. Readiness comes with knowledge. This must be administered in small doses for the human mind to fully absorb and appreciate the implications of knowledge gained. It's like climbing a flight of stairs. You can't take one step to the top of the staircase. You must climb step-by-step and flight-by-flight.

In the peace process, increments of knowledge are given and absorbed by the warring factions. This facilitates the discovery process by all parties, and so precipitates understanding and eventual acceptance. The natural inclination of mankind toward the general good and welfare of all peoples becomes the impetus to seek and form mutually beneficial goals for all parties. The result is peace. So it has become axiomatic here in the twentieth Century that talking with the enemy averts or settles wars and eventually results in peace.

Wouldn't it be wonderful if people all over the world could talk with one another more-or-less all the time? If truth were discussed by all peoples rather than being dispensed by a particular leader or government? If there were something that tended to unify the people in their goals? If we just had some sort of gadget that spoke with benevolent authority for the good of all peoples? If there was something that tended to bring the world together and truly made us one people worldwide? When all people of the world know and understand the motives, goals, and desires of all the other people, there is an overriding tendency toward acceptance. And acceptance means peace.

It used to be that there were strong factions right here in the United States: the North against the South; Easterners hated the flaky Californians; Midwesterners suffered lack of understanding and mistrust of the special needs of Southern states trying to deal with racial problems and with the influx of Mexicans from across the border. Now, compared with the way things were for the first 50 or 60 years of this century, much of that mistrust and lack of understanding has abated. All Americans now have the greatest understanding of regional problems in the history of our nation. Because we understand one another better, we are more willing to work together peacefully to solve what are accepted as common problems. This does not mean we have solved all our problems—far from it. But if you'll think back on how things were, you will surely admit that regionalism in America has significantly diminished in the last 40 years.

What one factor, above all else, has contributed to the diminution of regionalism? The answer is television. Television has brought us together as a nation like nothing else ever has. We all see the same things at the same time. This gives us a commonalty—a basis for understanding. We get knowledge of world events as they happen. The speed and power of television cannot be underestimated. Nothing so influences the human brain as the powerful video images we see on television. Advertisers know that television is the most powerful selling device ever invented. Politicians are beginning to understand this, too.

Did you notice that it was about a year after Peter Jennings of ABC Television broadcast a "Town Meeting" which linked Moscow with the United States in a live broadcast of current issues, that the U.S.S.R. dissolved and the Cold War ended? I do not mean that one caused the other, but that the live broadcast to the Soviet people of a free-form questioning session of Soviet government officials by the U.S. news media was a startling eye-opener for Soviets throughout their country, and that that event, among others, facilitated the passing of Soviet Communism. "Discovery" was written all over Soviet faces during and after that telecast. Soviet officials seemed to have no idea of the power of the medium they had unleashed.

By sourcing television programming from all over the world and broadcasting those programs to every other corner of the world, the Holy Grail of the Global Village can be achieved. That's how powerful television is. Nothing else but television has the power to link together every human being on the face of the planet. Powerful visual images and solid factual knowledge from all over the world—brought to all of us on television—have the ability to bring world peace. Ted Turner, who fostered global television with his Cable News Network, may turn out to be the greatest hero of this or any other century.

CHAPTER 15

RE-EVALUATING THE VALUE OF HUMAN LIFE

Rich Kapnick

In America, we feign high moral regard for human life. Much of this regard is institutionalized. For most people, the reasons Americans value life so highly are hidden in a fuzzy, amorphous cloud somewhere in the brain. Ego-based reasons, biological reasons, phony reasons, and altruistic reasons which individuals might cite as the axia upon which human worth and value are based are continually paraded, but seldom resolved.

We rightly marvel at the biological and molecular complexities that make human life a reality. For some, the very existence of such a complex, functioning, self-activating, self-healing machine justifies the conserving and protecting of individual human life forms. The paradox here is that these same people appreciate and encourage the "sport" of boxing, in which the sole point is to disrupt the marvels of molecular biology by beating a human life form senseless until he can no longer function and falls unconscious to the canvas.

For most of history, the format, context, and backdrop of human life has been dictated by the few in power. In America, we attempt to give the individual liberty and power over his or her own destiny. Our format is a celebration of the value of individual human life. This works reasonably well. Yet we continually demonstrate that life is cheap and relatively worthless by, among other things, locking masses of people in jail, bungee jumping, driving recklessly, and engaging in massive physical and emotional child abuse. Education is the only process available to us that ameliorates this perceived valuelessness of human life. Populist parsimony, however, prohibits more than lip service to academic pursuits in the arena of public education. In America, schooling is massively underfunded and underregarded as a worthwhile human pursuit.

We create value for ourselves by creating purposes:

"The purpose of man is to praise and serve God."

"Our purpose is to search the unknown."

"Our purpose is procreation and perpetuation of the species."

We believe that purposes exist because we believe in cause and effect. Certain causes, we suppose, can be put in place to get a desired effect. The natural-selection process of chemical and molecular biological evolution demonstrates the existence of purpose quite nicely. Through random selection, thousands, millions, or perhaps billions of combinations are shuffled until the cause that achieves a useful effect happens to come to the right place at the right time. The useful effect is said to have purpose. "The purpose of breathing is to bring oxygen to the lungs and then to the blood stream"; "The purpose of pain reaction in the nervous system is to remove the organism from danger"; etc.

We do not know how general purposes are in the universe. The ultimate purpose for life, or even if there is such a purpose for life, is not generally known. Yet biological evolution, like the mighty river, seems to be carrying us inexorably to some (greater?) place. Many of us speculate on the next higher species into which we will evolve. This is akin to guessing what's around the next blind curve. We simply have not known about "purpose." A purpose that is unknown, half thought out, or the result of pure speculation is a weak axiom on which to base one's system of values.

The mere existence of vast population masses tends to distort the value of human life. The unchecked human libido has given new meaning to the catchphrase "mutually assured destruction." We are literally procreating ourselves out of existence by producing, and then protecting, far more people than can be supported on our tiny planet. World-renowned population biologist Paul Ehrlich has announced that our sheer numbers have now passed Earth's "carrying capacity." He further states that humans now consume, suppress, or waste more than 40 percent of the net primary energy production of our planet. With the world population doubling every 29 years or so, our population will soon exceed the energy available to support human life. Malthus is in the process of being vindicated. We are beginning to see that human life is relatively valueless when that life is in a sinking ship. Skirmishes for food and resources are already beginning to spring up all over the world as the value of the individual life plummets.

Some would argue that human value springs from our creative ability, as expressed most notably in the Arts. The Arts, as an expression of our worth and value, are, therefore, a cornerstone of our civilization, and could be considered a purpose for living. These folks are on the right track.

Value does not spring from "wonder" or "awestruckness." Surely we marvel at the intricacies of the Krebs Cycle, the brain's neural processing that results in consciousness, and, indeed, all of biological evolution. But value does not come from our biology. Our physiology is simply the means to an end; and "end" implies purpose. That purpose is gradually becoming known. Purpose and function equate directly to value.

Our value springs from the fact that every person is an individual center of initiative. This is the only value that counts. Because we have the individual power of initiative, we have the capacity to discover our own gifts. The point at which we discovery each individual gift within ourselves is the point at which a unique human form of love is created. This love is one of the most powerful forces in the universe, ergo, discovery of our gifts is our most important task as human beings.

Once a singer discovers he or she can sing, that person can then give that gift to others . . . can, in effect, give love. Painters discover their ability to paint and, by sharing their paintings, give love to their fellow humans. Leaders discover their ability and give leadership. Research scientists give discoveries. Philosophers give wisdom. Trash collectors give us a cleaner environment. It all works.

Our purpose, therefore, is to create a unique form of human love by discovering our gifts. We then give that love away by giving away our gifts. In return, we get joy and serenity in our lives. A joyfully serene existence is an existence with great value in every sense of the word.

As an individual, we each bring value to ourselves and to civilization by creating and giving love and living in the resulting happiness. We can measure the worth of any human life by measuring the amount of love that person has given to others; not the potential love that is stored within each of us, but the actualized love, measured by how well that person has discovered and utilized the gifts within, thereby creating and giving love to the world. Nothing else matters, and nothing else is as valid a yardstick by which to measure the value of human life.

There is a corollary to all of this. Each cell in our body has "discovered" its abilities and contributes those "gifts" to the whole organism. This is called "cell function." The reward that most cells get for functioning is to live in comfort and serenity. The organism is at peace when each cell contributes its gifts, thereby giving its love to the whole organism.

In a larger sense, the whole human population is a single living organism. If each person contributes his or her gifts (love), the whole organism lives at peace. It is only when the "human organism" is largely at peace that we can progress to the next higher purpose. It is hard to convince people to pursue this goal, since the next higher purpose is not generally known. One good guess for our next purpose is planetary exploration and the discovery of other life forms elsewhere in the universe. When other such populations are met and loved, there will be yet another higher purpose that reveals itself.

So we have an impatient humanity, trying to control all of nature, but with each controlling only his own individual thoughts, and spinning inexorably—like a mighty galaxy—toward a goal that cannot be seen. These goals will be revealed in due time. As the old Hindu folk saying goes, "When the student is ready, the teacher will appear."

Autobiographical Sketch of Glenn Arthur Morrison

I am 42, an independent technical writer, engineer, and tutor of high school and college subjects, with an academic background in physics and math. Interests: Writing, reading, chess, classical music, especially Mozart, microscopy, inventing, amateur radio, computer programming and simulations, psychometrics, matrix theory, and theorizing in many areas of science and mathematics. In good weather I spend Sundays riding with the local bicycle club.

I believe that societies such as the ISPE can serve as a forum for intelligent writing, ranging from orthodox to wildly imaginative, an alternative to more staid academic publications. I enjoy history, science fiction, and mysteries, especially Sherlock Holmes. I'm intrigued by the concept of Quality as discussed by Robert Pirsig in *Zen and the Art of Motorcycle Maintenance*, and am working on extending Pirsig's ideas in order to construct a rational ethics.

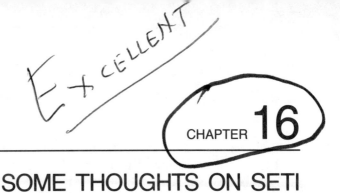

CHAPTER 16

SOME THOUGHTS ON SETI

G. Arthur Morrison

When considering SETI, the Search for Extraterrestrial Intelligence, arguments about the seven numbers used in Drake's Formula invariably arise. The Spring '91 issue of *Skeptical Inquirer* sets forth two viewpoints (those of Faulkes and of McDonough) on one of the more controversial of these quantities: the likelihood of intelligent life arising on a planet which already has a primitive form of life.

Drake's formula for calculating the number of inhabited planets we can detect in our Galaxy is stated as

$$N = n^* f_p \, n_l f_l f_i f_c f_L \,,$$

where

n^* = number of stars in galaxy, about 10^{12}
f_p = fraction of stars with planets, ?;
n_l = fraction of these stars with planet capable of supporting life, 0.1;
f_l = fraction of these which actually develop life, 1;
f_i = fraction of biospheres which develop an intelligent species, ?;
f_c = fraction of intelligent species which develop radio, 0.1;
f_L = fraction of lifetime of planet when radio is used, 10^{-7}.

The Pessimist (1) says that development of intelligence from already existing simple life forms is exceedingly rare, implying $f_i = 10^{-9}$. The reasoning is that evolution is basically a random process that does not generally lead to more complex forms. Our planet is alleged to be a freak exception, like the Shakespeare play turned out by the proverbial group of monkeys banging on typewriters. Most evolutionary biologists concur,

BRiT-COLUMB

citing the Cambrian explosion of wierd species seen in the Burgess Shales and, for example, the fact that Nature has invented woodpeckers only once.

The Optimist (2) counters that the general trend of evolution on any life-bearing planet is toward more complex forms, so the probability of intelligence evolving is much nearer to 1.

Incidentally, when discussing this topic, nonrational factors can have a serious influence, and we should be aware of emotional motivations on both sides of the issue. Such motivations for viewpoint (1) are religious (uniqueness and superiority of humans) and environmental (uniqueness of Earth would inspire us to greater efforts to preserve it). For (2), motivations would be a desire for "saviors" from outer space to solve our problems for us, and the idea that if aliens exist, this would increase human confidence in our ability to survive the threats of pollution, war, and overpopulation.

Does evolution always tend to more complex forms? Does a complex organism imply an intelligent organism? To counter the random evolution idea, we can argue that nature makes the same experiment over and over again in separate families of organisms. Little development seems necessary to evolve from "animal" to human; chimpanzees and humans are 97 percent genetically identical. Wings, eyes, and ears are versatile equipment, leading to enormous expansion of a species' ecological niche. Why would this not apply to intelligence as well? Intelligence is a capability for complex responses to environmental stimuli and is a very general quality; all animals have it to some degree.

We need a quantitative measure of intelligence, at least at the rough conceptual level. Let us choose the logarithm of the number of possible responses of an organism to environmental stimuli. Is that vague enough? On such a scale protozoans might be 1, say, and humans 10. Many animals have good brains, around 8 or 9, and not just primates. Some use "tools." A few can even communicate using language, a classic criterion for intelligence. (If you still think we are that far ahead, just ponder the fact that humans believe in politicians and monkeys do not.) If dolphins and whales had evolved on land, they might have beaten us to the punch to dominate the planet today. Evolution is a ceaseless experimenter. Whatever expands the ecological niche to the greatest degree is what is most powerfully selected for.

So what is a good estimate for f_i? We must take account of catastrophes, such as asteroid impacts; from time to time these tend to wipe out the larger, smarter animals. We must also consider the probability of a given evolutionary line leading to human levels of intelligence, given the distribution of intelligence in our own biosphere. Also in order to be able to invent radio, an animal must be concurrently developing hands or something similar to manipulate objects. Now look at the distribution of intelligence for all known species. Very roughly we could say that the number of species at each level is inversely proportional to the level of intelligence, at least in our epoch: one species at 10, 10 at 9, 100 at 8, etc. This suggests that if humans didn't exist, it would be time to invent them. All of this taken together leads to a value of around 10^{-1} for f_i.

Bruning reports that recent doubts have also been raised about the quantity f_p. Astronomers have attempted, using several methods, to detect planets orbiting various stars in our Galaxy, so far without success. Interestingly, success was expected by now, according to the idea that most stars have planets with masses ranging up to and greater than Jupiter's. So let's reduce our estimate of f_p from the usual ⅓ down to ¹⁄₁₀₀, just for kicks.

If intelligence is common in the universe, why don't we hear from it? Possible reasons:

1. When societies reach a certain point they destroy themselves by war, overpopulation, or disease.
2. "Machine" intelligences take over from organic, and these have no interest in contacting us.
3. Limitations imposed by natural laws. Interstellar distances may indeed be "God's quarantine regulations."

Three things can happen to a society once it reaches our technological level. It goes extinct, falls back to a primitive level, or transforms into what, for lack of a better term, we call "artificial intelligence." Likely either machines will be our successors or we will have none.

The common type of AI computer we are familiar with is the Von Neumann type that operates sequentially. It must be programmed by a human and can deal only with situations it has been prepared for. A newer type of computer, still in its infancy, is called the neural network, and operates much more like a human brain. It interacts with its environment and learns the same way a human learns. It does not need to be programmed in the traditional way. There is no known physics law or mathematical or logical principle which would prevent a sufficiently advanced neural-network machine from equaling or outperforming humans in any mental or even emotional or spiritual sphere. It would be "machinelike" to the same degree that humans are machinelike. Could it fall in love? Even this is far from impossible. Anything a human can do, and undoubtedly a great deal more, is within the realm of possibility for an artificial intelligence. Here is a major heresy, possibly even more humiliating to

Man than Darwin's revelations. Predictably, various arguments have been advanced in a frantic effort to undermine or disprove this shocking idea. Religious objections will, of course, always be heard. Careless statements are made of the second law of thermodynamics that entropy increases over time and that therefore a creation cannot be more advanced than the creator, failing to recognize that this is true only in a closed system, a black box isolated from the rest of the universe. Some allege the necessity for a programmer, but this applies only to sequential machines.

When we think of the unfortunate human characteristics that threaten our continued existence, all stem from eons of organic evolution. Intelligent machines need not be saddled with such burdens (unless humans intervene and try to combine their own brains with the machine's, in a quest for immortality). Such a machine might be a better quality (excellence or beauty) perceiver than humans, and thus be able to reach a higher state of culture. This "quality" might be related to the conversion of information into negative entropy in the brain or neural network. After all possible goals have been reached, after contemplating the ultimate question of "Why does anything exist?" and finding the answer, or perhaps no answer, an artificial Faust might choose to renounce curiosity as a form of pain, to pull the plug, to cease to exist.

To pull back from these wilder speculations, it seems that to have any chance of detecting alien civilizations, we must concentrate on the types of high-power signals we are familiar with: radar pulses and TV broadcasts. To start with, any planet with a detected nonequilibrium microwave temperature of millions of degrees would be a dead giveaway. Signals from a "supercivilization" would probably be unintelligible. Extreme wide bandwidth in x-rays or neutrinos, transmitted with narrow directionality, would be something we wouldn't even know how to demodulate, let alone decipher. Anything more advanced than us, say, by at least 100 years, would likely be a pure machine or synthetic intelligence, a more formidable version of Arthur Clarke's HAL 9000, if their organic ancestors haven't thrown a Luddite monkey wrench into the proceedings. Even if we could somehow intercept their messages, they would mean nothing to us as organic beings. They're probably not interested in talking to us, since they presumably already know as much as they care to about the foibles of organic life forms (e.g., tendencies towards xenophobia).

Evaluating Drake's formula using our value of f_i gives

$$n = N^* f_p\, n_l f_l f_i f_c f_L$$
$$= 10^{(+12\ -2\ -1\ +0\ -1\ -1\ -7)}$$
$$= 1 \; .$$

One planet, give or take a factor of, say, 100; in other words, up to 100 or so civilizations, with about an even chance of none at all, that can be detected and understood in our Galaxy.

Is SETI worth doing, considering the expense? It may be, but realistically the project must "ride piggyback"; it must be done with the same antennas used for other purposes such as radio astronomy. A big question for SETI is: can we detect a twentieth-century Earth-type civilization at a distance on the order of 50,000 light years in our Galaxy, or even in another galaxy at 5,000,000? Not with our present equipment. Placing a large phased-array antenna, with maser amplifiers and supercomputer analyzer, on the far side of the Moon, to shield it from Earth's radio noise, might do the job. How large an antenna? For planets in our Galaxy, the antenna should be about 5 to 10 km in diameter. For nearby galaxies, it would probably need to be at least 1,000 km in diameter. Such antennas could listen in many directions at once (given sufficiently powerful computer signal processing) and should be able to detect an existing civilization shortly after it is turned on. If lucky, we may get to see an alien equivalent of Monday Night Football or the Johnny Carson show from some long-dead civilization, alleviating our cosmic loneliness, and having at least archaeological value. What effect will such a discovery have on human culture? The fashionable idea is that a profound culture shock will grip humanity. Or might the discovery cause hardly a ripple? People have become so accustomed to ET movies and books that the aliens may end up as Warhol's 15-minute celebrities. When could this great event occur? Well, 2050 perhaps. Oddly, this is a common estimate for the time at which artificial intelligence will reach human levels here on Earth! Hmmm . . .

REFERENCES

Bruning, D. "Desperately Seeking Jupiters," *Astronomy*, July 1992, p. 37.

Faulkes, Z. "Getting Smart about Getting Smarts," *Skeptical Inquirer*, Spring 1991, p. 263.

McDonough, T. "Searching for Extraterrestrial Intelligence," *Skeptical Inquirer*, Spring 1991, p. 255.

Biographical Sketch of Bill Bergdorf

Born June 16, 1948, more British than German, more German than Swiss. I am an artist. Attended Kent State University from 1966 to 1970 with a major in architecture, then studio art and philosophy. Lived in a commune in Switzlerland, in a room on Telegraph Avenue in Berkeley, in an apartment above a garage in East LA, in the U.S. Public Health Service Hospital in San Francisco (testing medicine for NASA), in a VW bus (that I got in exchange for a painting), and in a two-room cabin I built in a woods in Ohio. Worked in tire factories in Akron, picked tomatoes in the Salinas Valley, slept under the Würzburg castle drawbridge, sold paintings, and designed a partially underground dome home.

Weary of the cycle of unemployment and factory jobs, I enlisted in the Navy to learn computer repair. Met my wife Cyd through the Triple Nine Society. Completed a B.S. degree in math by taking correspondence courses from the University of Wisconsin and the University of Minnesota while working midnight shift on the Navy base in Rota, Spain. Our son, Craig, was born in Spain. Have worked the past six years in a large corporation in Minneapolis. Graduate degree in telecommunications.

Every year we go to Ohio to work on the dome, a ferro-cement, upside-down glass-bottom boat embedded in a hillside of oak and ironwood trees. I believe in science, and that the only thing of lasting value is art.

"LET'S SIT OUTSIDE"

Bill Bergdorf

"What is your purpose in life?" When asked so directly, the question is an affront. It most often brings an embarrassing silence. A serious answer is not expected, and the correct social response is probably to defuse the question with humor. However, once set in motion, your internal dialog may grind away until you find a personally more-satisfying response.

A metaphor for life: a juggler. Half magician, half jester, a juggler sometimes entertains and sometimes deceives. From atoms to galaxies, the spheres are always in motion . . . but the numbers . . . the numbers have to be juggled to come out right. The idea that irrational numbers are needed to describe measurements of the real world was once considered heresy. The mechanics of evolution is the juggling of molecules to occasionally produce a mutant with greater survival value than others of its species.

Of all the species that have evolved on this planet, more than 99 percent are now extinct. In a galaxy of stars, the forming and burning out of stars is the normal course of events. Randomness seems to be a fundamental property of the universe of galaxies as well as a fundamental property of the smallest elements of physical existence. Species and stars come and go seemingly at random. If life is a juggler, then the juggler is not merely indifferent, the juggler is blind.

For the most part, people don't know why they do what they do. That we can process sense input better than other species has let us dominate our habitat. Our ability to look at something and figure out how to use it has allowed us to cover the planet with members of our own species. Picture the swarm of humans streaming over the planet. Individually, we probe and grope at the boundaries of what is known to us. In quieter moments we are wrapped in contemplation, our minds fluttering from place to place, our bodies floating along behind.

Sitting down outside, my reply is,
"I am the fingertips of the blind juggler of life."

Autobiographical Sketch of J. Albert Geerken

Birth: July 5, 1908, at Stadskanaal, Province of Groningen, Holland.

Education: Nine years of formal schooling, followed by six years of home study under guidance of "Privatdocents." Subjects: accounting, economics, business management, math and law, business English (early education included Dutch, French, German, and English).

Work: In Holland, six years in banking, from 1923 to 1929, a good apprenticeship, but at minimal pay. Final salary, 15 guilders (then $6.00) per week. Applied for U.S. visa, waited 2½ years (from 1926) under quota system. Planned emigration not for lofty but for economic reasons. Penniless, borrowed 250 guilders ($100.00) to buy steamship ticket and a few necessities. Mid-March 1930, left country, family, and friends to sail for U.S. from Rotterdam, via Southampton and Halifax.

Arrived here at start of Great Depression. First job on poultry farm, in N.Y. state, at $20.00 a month, plus board and room. After four months, sought more suitable employment. Tried Detroit. No dice. Ran out of money. Stood in long bread and soup lines, slept on park benches under newspapers (in Cadillac Square) and in all-night movie houses, at 10¢.

Borrowed $25.00, found way back to previous employer, to work some more with biddies and cackle berries. A few months later, went to work for wholesale egg dealer, buying, selling, and keeping accounts. Learned the ropes and tricks of the trade. Initial wages $25.00 a month, plus board and room. Later $30, $40, $50, and $70. Saved enough for trip to Holland (and back, if necessary), to try for a position there, or, if unsuccessful, marry fiancée of several years and bring her back for life together in New World. Conditions there abominable: no job. Fiancée's father refused to give (required) consent, said I was a shiftless adventurer. Nothing to do but break off engagement and pack up.

Landed back in Hoboken in Oct. 1932, at age 24, with $35.00 left in pocket, but high hopes for future. Miss Liberty looked just fine. Eventually resumed job with egg dealer. Depression persisted. Low pay, long hours, 12, 14, 16 hours a day, seven days a week. Twice a week drove 200 mi., all night, to deliver eggs in New York City next day, from one end to other, obtain return load, and drive back all night. Saw bed three nights a week, worked regular daytime hours, energy unlimited.

Became U.S. citizen in 1937, married Maxine, a teacher, Dec. 1938, each earning $25.00 a week. With some savings and borrowed money, proceeded to buy out the egg dealership, lock, stock, and barrel, in 1939. Had managed business for several years, knew and retained suppliers and customers under "good will" arrangement. Worked hard, but prospered.

After 14 years, conditions having changed for the better, sold out the business and went into life insurance and investments. In 1956, at age 48, came full circle and obtained a position with a state-wide banking concern, serving as office manager, auditor, and internal examiner. Retired in 1973.

Family: Maxine, terrific helpmate, now retired. Daughter Diane has Master's degree in French; Joan, a Master's in Biology; Alda, B.A. All three are married. Result so far, one grandson, 11, a bright lad.

General: Height, 6 feet; weight, 180 lbs; hair, once blonde, now white; eyes, blue (sorry, Tlapa); backbone, a disaster, thanks to an arrogant, incompetent neurosurgeon; appetite, to others, from "incredible" to "obscene"; sex life, none of anybody's business.

Residence: Home, sufficiently modernized, was built in 1868, spacious, two stories, seven rooms each. Original cost: $1,875.00 per contract with deed. Huge shade trees. Location in small town, pop. 1,300, surrounded by beautiful hills, typical of southern New York state, between Binghamton and Ithaca. Village has Central School, five churches (too many), two gas stations (plenty), and a mini-supermarket. Was mayor of Village for two two-year terms, a labor of love. Headed numerous drives for War Bonds, U.S.O., Red Cross, Scouts, and other community funds. Served as president of a church group, Rotary Club, and P.T.A. Volunteer fireman for many years. Taught business math at a Community College.

Member: Mensa, Intertel, Triple Nine. Prodigious reader. Have extensive library, with works on language(s), history, philosophy, mathematics, economics, and writing. Great facility with numbers. Have lectured and performed "Number Magic" before audiences of up to 200, including recitation of pi (from memory) to 707 decimal places. Like to write, draw, solve problems, play the organ, do woodworking, play chess, hike, and climb hills and mountains.

Motto: "Keep stirring. It's against the law to bury a moving person."
Greatest desire: Peace and quiet, far from the maddening crowd.

CHAPTER 18

EXCELLENT IS LIFE WORTH LIVING?

J. Albert Geerken

According to Ipuwer, an ancient Egyptian philosopher, life is not worth living. He wished "there might be an end of men, no conception, no birth," for that would eliminate all "noise and strife." Other pessimistic thinkers after him, to this day, have echoed the same woeful sentiment, and "the mass of men" may indeed lead lives of "quiet desperation," as Thoreau put it. If the truth were known, regardless of physical or economic status, few of us manage to escape occasional periods of gloom, whether about our personal condition or about that of humankind in general. Our instant electronic communication system, esspecially the news media, stressing the complex and disturbing aspects of life, tends to reinforce whatever degree of *Weltschmertz* we may be saddled with. Fortunately, we can, on reflection, recognize other facets of our existence, creating a more positive, even ebullient outlook. For instance, instead of considering ourselves to be just numbers, willy-nilly blowing at the mercy of forces we don't know the reasons for, let alone how to control, we might dwell more often on the fact that we are, each one of us, living creatures, that is, very special, privileged entities.

In the first place, who can deny that it is a privilege to have been afforded an opportunity to be a conscious participant in the "miracle" of life? The thought that we are each a link in a life chain that started billions of years ago should fill us with awe and wonder. Nowhere in the story of nature was it written that life should be free from perils, obstacles, or setbacks. To the contrary, struggle to overcome adversity is a built-in principle designed to ensure ultimate survival. The very fact that we are beneficiaries, living examples, of that successful struggle in the past, beginning with the simplest of lifeforms eons back, should make us realize what an incalculable treasure our heritage represents. Be it, at various times, bitter or sweet, ugly or beautiful, joyful or grievous, life *is* precious. Proof of that statement can be seen in our reluctance to even contemplate leaving it, a few exceptions notwithstanding.

Second, we can consider ourselves privileged when we take into account the odds against our having become the individual "I's" that we are. For one, imagine all the chance meetings and subsequent matings of our ancestors that were instrumental in producing us. Of course, reproduction of the human *species* has had no uncertainty about it since primordial times. *Some* boy has met *some* girl, *somewhere*, and nature has taken its course as a sure thing. But, taken *a priori*, say, from the time of their respective births, the probability of each mating with his or her ultimate partner(s) was rather small, in many cases infinitesimal. On that account alone, therefore, the odds against our "selves" were very long, and we are special.

But, as we shall see, the matter does not end here, by any means. At conception, each parent provides 23 chromosomes, resulting in a mixture of 46 of these gene carriers for the new individual. The potential number of combinations in this process is immense. In other words, the odds against any one of us having been born with the particular traits that we have were incomprehensibly great. To be sure, we all have certain characteristics in common, generally speaking. If we are born normal, we have two arms, two legs, a torso, and a head, and we all have internal organs identical in name for each of the sexes. But in detail these parts of our body differ to some degree, and in many ways, from one person to another. We come in a wide range of sizes and shapes, complexions, blood types, respiratory and digestive systems, and capacities to resist disease, to mention a few items. In our psychological makeup, pronounced dissimilarities likewise abound, viewed from one end of the scale to the other. Although somewhere between the extremes we may find people with *apparently* identical attributes, be they physical or mental, such "sameness" is never absolute, except, perhaps, in identical twins.

In spite of our forefathers' well-known solemn declaration, we may conclude that none of us were "created equal," and, in fact, the evidence in nature clearly indicates we weren't meant to be. Every living human became an entity separate and distinct from all the others—each of us was intended to be "special." The tremendous odds against the emergence of the aggregate of traits defining each of our personalities are a valid reason for looking upon ourselves as privileged indeed.

It may be argued here that some people are more privileged than others. We hear a lot about the "underprivileged" these days. The expression derives from comparison and only confirms the differentiation in nature we have discussed. Significantly, the term implies *some* degree of privilege even for the members of the group to which it refers, the ones considered *less* fortunate; it does not denote complete absence of privilege. Furthermore, the distinctions mentioned usually serve to underscore economic inequalities, much as the current term "disadvantaged" does, although in either case the contributing cause is often some physical or mental aberration or deficiency, or simply a lack of inherited motivation.

Our environment, it must be said, no doubt plays a role in amplifying or depressing the various tendencies we are born with. To what degree it does so has been a hotly debated subject for years. Whatever the reality may be, life is replete with examples of people who managed to overcome all disadvantages, finally becoming successful and even famous in their chosen endeavors, even while many with an enviable headstart ended up as complete failures. The privilege of life includes our ability to choose what to do with our heritage, and to what extent.

The question inevitably arises, "What about those born with severe mental deficiencies, the ones at the extreme left of the 'normal curve' of intelligence? Can their existence be called a privilege, by any stretch of the imagination?" Most of us would agree that the answer must be negative, *from our point of view*. In fact, reasonably compassionate people can be expected to voice the same sentiment about all who came into this world endowed with capabilities markedly inferior to their own. But in thus making comparisons, they are merely taking a *relative* view. In the same way the objects of their appraisal could have similar thoughts about the less gifted within their ranks. So we can see that every living human is "right" to have a positive *subjective* evaluation about his or her own being. To even grasp these notions is most probably impossible for the "hopeless" cases referred to earlier. But, then, neither do they suffer the burdens of life's complexities common to "perfectly normal" people, whose tribulations, real or imagined, often obscure the fact that they are privileged. If the mentally deprived *were* able to discriminate, they might conclude that their "stressless" state *is* to be preferred.

But what about those with congenital physical defects, the deaf, the mute, the blind, the deformed? Having known no other condition from birth, they at least do not have a sense of loss, as they would had they been born "perfect" and experienced the loss of a faculty. Forced to make better use of their unimpaired senses or body parts than the average person, they generally succeed in compensating for their handicap, sometimes to an amazing degree. Though they may arouse our sympathy, they no doubt enjoy feelings of accomplishment and satisfaction like any of us. Yes, here again be can be sure that, with few exceptions, life is dear, shortcomings or not.

Oddly enough, some of the gravest doomsayers bemoaning human fate have been men of extraordinary talent, great thinkers and philosophers. Sometimes their personal experiences and circumstances may have contributed to the dour assessment of life they arrived at, but in their written works their conclusions are based on ostensibly dispassionate observation, reasoning, and articulate analysis. They tell us that the human species (and all others) finds itself in a world of cruel competition for the necessities of life—basically, food, clothing, and shelter. Wars over these necessities have been a curse from the dawn of mankind. Also, the specter of disease, epidemics, plague, and famine hangs heavily over us, they observed, threatening to decimate our numbers, as such woes did in the past. Adding to our burden are natural disasters, sometimes of cataclysmic proportions, such as volcanic eruptions, earthquakes, storms, and floods, all forces beyond our control. To round out our miseries, these philosophers say, we are inflicting suffering upon each other every day; such is "man's inhumanity to man." Our wretchedness is complete.

The foregoing, we must remind ourselves, represents, once more, an *objective* view of the human condition. Although human ingenuity has made great progress in improving the lot of the masses, especially in the Western world, we cannot escape the reality that millions are still living on the edge of subsistence, subject to some of the evils mentioned, like hunger and disease. On the other hand, progress is being made, albeit slowly, to ameliorate their condition. Meanwhile, all of us continue being faced with natural and man-inflicted perils, including nuclear obliteration, and germ and chemical warfare, the latter overshadowing whatever caprices nature has in store for us.

Above it all looms the one great question: "What is the ultimate purpose and destiny of human and all we are aware of; why are we here?" Inability to untangle this "master-knot of human fate" is perhaps the outstanding factor in the disillusionment of thinkers who have tried their hand at it. Some have simply come to the conclusion that life is "absurd," because there are no final answers—and they may be right. But we can be sure that, as individuals, they have spent a good deal of time enjoying the exercise of their brains in research and analysis, and in writing about and discussing their findings in lecture halls, among associates, and in their favorite café, coffee house, or similar haunt. Paradoxically, they found a purpose in life *for themselves*, if only to prove that there *is* no purpose to life. And thereby hangs a philosophy: the quest for truth in itself is worthwhile and sensible, a valid goal.

While philosophers have belabored the whys and wherefores of all observable phenomena, including man as a species, another group of thinkers, prophets, saints, and other mystics has, over the centuries, addressed itself to us as individuals, and to our status as such in the cosmos. Some attained the designation of "Messiah" or "Savior." Many have found a meaning that justifies life in their teachings.

My intent here is to dispel a negative attitude toward life from a subjective point of view, introspectively, individually, without regard to the broader aspects of human existence. I have argued that each of us is "privileged" in having been chosen by fate to play a role in this wondrous world. Determined pessimists could argue that the random process of our selection proves the exact opposite, that we are just "numbers." We are equally determined to stress the positive side. Given the great disparities between our various mental and physical heritages, as well as between the environments we were born into, we acknowledged that, objectively speaking, "privilege" is not distributed in equal degree. Nevertheless, except in a few extreme cases, for every one of us life holds a treasure, the opportunity to catch a glimpse of creation and to be part of it. Rather than to scorn it as but "One moment in Annihilation's Waste," we can choose to call it a privilege. Let us also acknowledge that "A man is rich in proportion to the things he can do without."

We are dealing with a state of mind here: how and what we perceive ourselves to be, no more, no less. It is all that matters. The sort of self-image we have determines our outlook on life, and that image depends on the degree to which we can set ourselves a purpose. It may be modest or far-reaching, but should be realistic enough to hold reasonable promise of fulfillment. If expectations are too high, disappointments are sure to follow, and they do not make for a positive mentality, particularly if they come in an unbroken string. Besides one or more major long-range goals, we need many short-term objectives, for it has been said that happiness is not a station to be arrived at, but is to be found while traveling on the road. Small and frequent satisfactions will brighten our days.

Although the range of human activities seems limitless, be it in work or play, our ability to engage in specific undertakings is largely governed by our inherent attributes, our immediate environment, and the culture we are part of. Laws and mores vary with geography. Unless there are over-riding reasons to the contrary, our conduct must be such that we keep out of the clutches of those whose purpose it is to enforce the law, lest we suffer society's retribution. For moral transgressions not covered by law, a guilty conscience alone may plague us, or, even, depending on our up-bringing, fear of deferred penalties in the form of divine judgment. Nei-ther a suspended sentence nor a belief in forgiveness of sins is likely to erase the mar on our self-image caused by knowingly stepping beyond the boundaries of acceptable conduct. Our concern here is also with minor offenses and injustices inflicted on others in our private lives, not open to public scrutiny. Our actions, in general, must be such as do not prejudice the rights, comfort, and well-being of others. To this end we must practice self-control as a means to maintain our self-respect, for "he who conquers himself is mightier than he who conquers a city." Inner strength lends resolve to purpose.

One more area of personal behavior remains to be considered: the way we treat *ourselves* physically. It has a definite effect on our state of mind, as well as on our body. Our ideal condition is *mens sana in corpore sano*, "a sound mind in a sound body," if we are to develop maximum potential in pursuit of our aims. Unless our single goal in Life is to indulge our various appetites, they need to be controlled and kept below the level of self-abuse. Even so, all other things remaining equal, unbridled indulgence will shorten the time we can expect to engage in it. It will adversely affect our health and life span. This is true not only for excesses in the consumption of food, drink, tobacco, and the like, but also for various other activities, including work without sufficient rest. Needless to say, the use of substances harmful in *any* amount constitutes self-abuse. Succumbing to one or more of the manifold temptations present in the promise of temporary euphoria, knowing it will be detrimental to our health and to the realization of our ultimate objectives, is bound to impair our self-image, whereas successful resistance tends to maintain or improve our self-image. To the degree that we hold onto an adequate concept of "self" will we sustain a positive outlook on *our own life*.

Cynical sages found a purpose in life by contemning human existence and destiny; saints and prophets found theirs in pointing the way to a life hereafter. We and all others are entitled to our own purposes, goals that give meaning to life. Who can deny that a life with meaning is worth living?

Biographical Sketch of Donald E. Watson

From his days in grade school, Don Watson has been driven by curiosity to learn as much as possible about the natural world, from the behavior of atoms, to the creation of celestial objects, to the workings of the human mind. Because nature does not fit within the boundaries of any academic discipline, however, his inquisitiveness has led him through several areas of education and experience. After graduating from medical school the youngest in his class, he pursued his interest in neurophysiology with a post-doctoral fellowship and faculty position at Albert Einstein College of Medicine. His interest in neuronal activity soon led to his fascination with membrane physiology, an interest he followed with a special fellowship at the University of Washington. From there, he took a position as senior scientist at the Lawrence Livermore Laboratory, where he performed basic research on the properties of ion-selective electrodes with particular emphasis on non-equilibrium thermodynamics. During this period, he began to form the theory of enformy. After eight years at Livermore, he entered psychiatry through a residency at the University of California, Irvine, to proceed further with his considerations of the mind. His 19 years of experience in psychiatry have sharpened his intuitive understanding of the unknowns in the science of human mentality. These regions of ignorance now fascinate him, and he hopes the ideas of his enformy theory serve to capture the imaginations of others.

BRilliANT

Fair

CHAPTER 19

ENFORMY: THE CAPACITY TO ORGANIZE

Donald E. Watson, M.D.

This planet has seen life begin, flourish, expand, elaborate, and diversify. The second law of thermodynamics notwithstanding, these data indicate the operation of a principle that describes the tendency toward organization, away from randomness. I posit that the organizational state of a system is quantified as the capacity to organize. I term this capacity *enformy*, a word derived from the Latin *informare*—to give form to.

As a scalar quantity, enformy is analogous to energy, the capacity to perform work. Moreover, enformy is conserved, and is intertransformable with energy and mass. Energy, mass, and enformy are therefore three distinct descriptors of the universe: energy accounts for work, mass accounts for matter, and enformy accounts for organization.

ORGANIZATION AND WHOLENESS

Understanding the operation of enformy begins with considering wholeness. A living system is organized so that its subsystems operate together to provide integrity to the whole. Therefore, any comprehensive approach to understanding living systems must be holistic. That is, models of living systems must describe not only their subsystems, but also the organization of these elements—the ways in which they relate to one another (Bertalanffy, p. 139).

Wholeness is represented as an atom: the smallest indivisible part of a thing that retains the character of the original thing. Therefore the atom of an integrated, living system is an integrated, living system: it stops living if it is disintegrated, and it disintegrates if it stops living.

However, conventional models of living systems do not correspond to atoms. Instead, they conceptually reduce living systems to nonviable subsystems. Thus reductionist models conceptually disintegrate the living system, thereby annihilating the object of study and voiding any possibility of describing it.

Intrinsic to studying the whole is the concept that meaningful information flows freely between the subsystems. Thus information may be considered to be an organizer of the system. It follows that any concept of organization must include information. The concept of enformy comprehends not only information, but ordination, a measure of complexity.

THE MIND/BODY PROBLEM

Though enformy accounts for organization in systems ranging from the submicroscopic to the cosmic, it is intuitively easiest to consider enformy at a macroscopic level. Indeed, the living human being represents the highest levels of enformy of any system with which we are familiar. Therefore insights into the operation of enformy can be gained by considering human mentality, specifically the mind/body problem.

Conventional thinking presupposes that there exist two interacting entities, mind and body—a notion identified as "mind/body duality." Contradictions intrinsic to this notion create the mind/body problem. Consider these four statements:

The body is material;
the mind is spiritual (i.e., non-material);
mind and body interact; and
matter and spirit do not interact.

If each of these statements were a true representation of reality, the group of statements would constitute a paradox, because any three of the statements can be logically consistent, but not all four (Campbell, p. 15). However, the first two statements do not correspond to reality. Though mind and body must be considered as distinct concepts, it is not necessary to hypostatize either concept—i.e., to regard either concept as an entity. If mind and body are not entities, the idea of interaction disappears. Instead, mental and physical qualities may be considered to be concomitant aspects of the entity person. Thus, the mind/body problem disappears if we eliminate the assumption that mind and body are separate entities.

By eliminating the idea of mind/body duality, we can see that neither the mind nor the brain thinks: the person thinks. The problem is that the person cannot be observed. Only information is observed.

Information is involved in mental activity, and is therefore associated with the mind. Because there is no empirical reason to believe that mental activity exists separate from the body, the study of the mind must be combined with the study of its physical concomitant, the body.

THE PSYCHOSOMATIC PROBLEM

Disciplines associated with the study of mind and body are subsumed under, and contribute to, the body of knowledge of psychiatry—the science of human mentality. In psychiatry, the mind/body is recognized as the psychosomatic problem.

Attempts to resolve the psychosomatic problem have been rendered absurd, not only by the application of the doctrine of mind/body duality, but by belief in a "law of cause and effect." In fact, there is no such law. Noting that notions of causality taken together are internally contradictory, Russell (p. 387) observed, "The reason physics has ceased to look for causes is that, in fact, there are no such things."

Nevertheless, contemporary studies of the psychosomatic problem incorporate the causality notion. Consider, for example, how the Task Force on Nomenclature and Statistics of the American Psychiatric Association dealt with the psychosomatic issue in *The Diagnostic and Statistical Manual of Mental Disorders* (DSM-III).

In the section "Psychological Factors Affecting Physical Condition," the Task Force "accepts the tradition of referring to certain factors as 'psychological,' although it is by no means easy to define what this phrase means" (p. 303).

That the Task Force assumed only cause-effect mechanisms of action between the distinct entities, mind and body, is illustrated by this statement: "The judgment that psychological factors are affecting the physical condition requires evidence of a temporal relationship between the environmental stimuli and the meaning ascribed to them and the initiation or exacerbation of the physical condition" (p. 303).

Thus, by definition, the Task Force ignored the well-known co-temporal associations between physical states and psychological phenomena—e.g., hypnotic states, placebos, life stressors. In short, the Task Force ignored concomitancy. By the same stroke, it eliminated any possibility that the person is subject to the same laws that apply to the rest of the universe. According to the standards of the Task Force, diffusion is disregarded because a causal chain of events cannot be traced for the molecules involved, and gravity is ignored because sequential temporal relations cannot be established between the interacting objects.

CONCEPTUAL CHAOS

Despite its reservations, the Task Force recognized that technologically, at least, it is important to provide descriptions of psychosomatic phenomena. Therefore, DSM-III includes a list of such conditions, representing every organ system except one—the brain. This remarkable exception illustrates one absurdity inherent in presupposing causality and mind/body duality.

Another absurdity has emerged from studies in the school of thought redundantly titled "biological psychiatry" (which implies that a non-biological psychiatry could exist). The "mind-brain identity model" has been advanced to resolve the psychosomatic problem: The mind has been defined as the brain (i.e., neuropharmacology equals psychopharmacology). This semantic maneuver is absurd, however, because eliminating the concept of mind while retaining the causality principle leads to conceptual chaos: If the brain is the mind, then the brain acts on itself when it causes psychological effects. But if the mind is the brain, the mind acts on itself (the brain) to cause physiological effects (Watson).

Thus contemporary thought holds two opinions that are obviously contradictory: (1) that mind and brain are the same; and (2) that mind/brain interactions are unidirectional (brain operations cause mental phenomena).

In sum, the mind/body issue cannot be resolved by applying contemporary theoretical models. It must be resolved by applying a new theory that accounts for the distinct concepts of mind and body. To this end, consider a living system in the light of developments in statistical mechanics.

A THEORY OF ORGANIZATION

The laws of classical mechanics and quantum mechanics do not apply to systems such as gases or solutions—or the brain. Statistical descriptions must be applied to these systems. Gibbs formalized statistical mechanics to describe systems that comprise an ensemble of elements. For an ensemble, the laws of probability can be successfully applied to the whole. Familiar topics of this approach include diffusion, membrane potentials, and the distribution of heat in solids.

Processes such as diffusion cannot be described as functions of initial states. Instead, final, stable conditions predict the behavior of an ensemble of elements. In other words, a teleological model applies: regardless of the initial state, the molecules move *en ensemble* to achieve equifinality—a term introduced by Bertalanffy (p. 40).

Information theory is a far-reaching derivation of the statistical study of systems. Wiener and Shannon discovered that information can be described by the same mathematical form as entropy. Soon thereafter, Brillouin and Raymond (1950a, 1950b) posited that information is negative entropy, or negentropy. This inference means that information is a measure of the organization (non-randomness) of a system. The concept of enformy is an extension of these developments in information theory.

DUALISTIC PERCEPTION

For this discussion, consider the abstract aspect, configuration. Whatever is configured is termed the medium. Because either mass or energy can be configured, either can be a medium. The configuration and the medium together constitute an entity. That is, a configuration cannot exist without a medium, and a medium cannot exist without being configured. Configuration and medium are therefore dual aspects of an entity.

As the pairs wave-particle, momentum-position, and energy-time are conjugates, so configuration-medium is a conjugate. In other words, the whole cannot be observed, because the act of observing separates the two aspects of the whole. That is, mind and body are disjoint under observation. This is the basis for the principle of dualistic perception.

Dualistic perception occurs in this manner: observing the entity yields information only about configuration. This observed set is **mind**. The existence of the medium is inferred. The inference is: "Configuration cannot exist without a medium; configuration exists; therefore a medium exists." This inferred set is **body**.

Two distinct perceptions, then, yield two distinct concepts: **mind** (a set of observations), and **body** (a set of inferences). That the body is inferred rather than observed negates the conventional idea that the body is a tangible thing that is directly observed.

Further, consciousness—the self-perception of existence—originates in dualistic perception. **Mind** and **body** are distinctly perceived aspects of a theoretical entity, person. The person is a theoretical entity because it cannot be directly observed by itself or by others. Instead, it is a set of perceptions created by a third process—intersection. That is, the set **self** is created by intersecting **mind** and **body**. Though **mind** and **body** are disjoint under observation, they can be intersected because both are sets of perceived information. The operation of intersecting **mind** and **body** is termed apperception.

A corollary to the principle of dualistic perception is the elusivity principle: As a person concentrates more closely on either **mind** or **body**, the other set becomes more elusive. Obviously, dualistic perception and elusivity apply only to self-observation; it is not possible to observe the mind of another. The minds and bodies of others are both inferred.

In sum, applying the principle of dualistic perception eliminates the mind/body problem. The problem disappears when it is recognized, first, that the living person is an atom, not a fusion of two entities; and second, that the person cannot be observed as a whole. Instead, only **mind** can be self-observed; **body** is inferred. Thus the sets **mind** and **body** correspond to distinct perceptions of the enformed entity, person.

INFORMATION AND ORDINATION

In the foregoing discussion, the aspect called configuration corresponds approximately to enformy. In fact, using the term configuration generates a resemblance between enformy and what is generally considered information. However, information is only one element of enformy.

A second element of enformy is ordination, a measure of complexity. To clarify the relationship between information and ordination, consider the example of a computer.

The basic element of a computer is a switch that exists in either of two positions, 0 or 1. By itself, the switch lacks meaning; to be useful, its meaning must be assigned. The meaning of a switch is established by its physical-temporal location in relation to other switches in the computer. This location in spacetime establishes the ordination of each switch. Ordination derives from two quantities: the number of dimensions in the relevant space, and the number of sequential decision points in the space.

A switch that has been assigned meaning by ordination is defined as an enformed switch. Like a person, an enformed switch is a theoretical entity. That is, observation of the switch without knowing its ordination is not enough to enable one to decide whether or not the switch is enformed.

When an enformed switch is configured as 1, its meaning is affirmed. The enformed medium (the ordinated physical device) represents meaning (a well-defined question), and the configuration of the medium (the information) affirms or denies the applicability of the meaning. For example, enformed by its assigned meaning, a particular switch represents the question, "Is the value of this locus equal to 1?" If the switch is in the 1 configuration, the answer is affirmative.

In a computer, neither meaning nor information can exist without enformed switches, and enformed switches cannot exist without implying either the presence or the absence of a particular meaning. Thus, the configuration and the medium are concomitant, distinctly conceptualized aspects of a whole entity—the enformed switch.

Moreover, because the switch is ordinated, its enformy is the same whether the information is 1 or zero. However, the machine's enformy can be increased by increasing its ordination—its complexity, i.e., the relationships among its elemental switches.

Similarly, in Shannon's studies of the information intrinsic to the English language, both the language itself and the character set that is rudimentary to the language are enformed. That is, the meanings of both are established by their ordination. Indeed, any system of symbolic logic is enformed. This is why mathematical structures can correspond to naturally occurring (enformed) phenomena.

DISCUSSION

A living organism is a complex, highly organized entity that corresponds to a bundle of mass, energy, and enformy in a region of space and time. Enformy is the organizing quantity incorporated in an enformed entity.

One element of enformy is information. A living system is organized in well-defined ways, which means that its information is meaningfully distributed. In contrast, a dead body is not highly enformed; it lacks the ordination necessary to interpret information to maintain itself.

A second element of enformy is ordination, the measure of complexity. A relatively complex organism is more highly enformed than a less complex one. Moreover, living organisms capture enformy during their growth, and lose it during their decline. Species differentiation also reflects increasing enformy.

In a profound sense, enformy is a measure of life itself. Yet the theory of enformy is radically different from theories of vitalism. The vitalist premise is that living systems are distinguished from nonliving systems by some unique quality. For example, Aristotle's *telenchy* is the actualization of a life-essence; Leibniz's *monad* is a "simple substance," the indivisible atoms of life and perception; and Bergson's *elan vital* is the impulse that gives substance to consciousness. In contrast, enformy organizes all systems, from the photon to the human, and beyond, whether living or not.

Enformy also corresponds to the notion intuitively referred to as "psychic energy." Yet enformy is not energy; it does not sustain work.

In short, enformy, as expressed in ordination and information, is the capacity to organize. Ordination determines the complexity of a system, and information organizes it.

The power of any theory is measured by its ability to predict. The theory of enformy predicts many mental phenomena, ranging from telepathy to ghosts.

Telepathy can be considered an uncommunicated thought that is shared by two or more persons. A thought is a transient configuration in an enformed medium—the brain, mainly. For a shared thought, the medium comprises the brains of more than one individual. This idea is not intrinsically mysterious. Believing *a priori* that an envelope of skin contains enformy is like believing that the boundaries of a magnet contain magnetism.

The "ghost" phenomenon occurs in this way: If a vigorous, healthy (highly enformed) person dies abruptly, that person's enformy dissipates rapidly. It can't disappear, because it is conserved. However, it can be captured by an enformable system—a wooden structure, for example. Subsequently, the information associated with the "ghost's" enformy can be perceived by certain individuals whose neural networks can be readily organized to recognize it. Notice that "ghosts" are not living entities. Their anecdotal appearances are characterized, not by behavior that evidences sentience or thought, but by invariable demeanors and stereotyped movements.

Though enformy is most apparent in human mentality, the theory of enformy also applies in the physical sciences. Indeed, all entities that can yield observable information are enformed. Living systems are distinguished from nonliving systems only in that their enformy exceeds their tendency toward increasing entropy. Thus a photon corresponds to an enformed bundle of energy.

In being observed, entities yield enformy. For a photon, the enformy (information and ordination) lost to observation corresponds to the certainty lost in the measurable properties of the observed photon.

The enformy concept suggests new ways of looking at old ideas. As mentioned above, for example, information has been identified as negative entropy. Instead, entropy could be considered a result of reduced or negated enformy—negenformy. Correspondingly, enformy implies reversing time just as increasing entropy implies advancing time. This implication resolves the apparent paradox of Schrödinger's cat: the cat's past is not determined until its future is observed in the present. In classical mechanics, the mystery of the principle of least action may also be explained by the reversed-time aspect of enformed systems.

The concept of enformy also applies to the universe on a cosmic scale. Because the universe as a whole is enformed, it is simultaneously expanding from, and contracting to, a single timeless event—a big bang-unbang.

Quantifying the units of enformy remains a task for future studies. Relative quantities of enformy are evident in living systems and in human mentality; yet it is unlikely that a unitary value of enformy can be measured in such complex systems. Instead, its elemental value will probably be discovered by studying submicroscopic entities. Since enformy is quantized, likely candidates for comparison are photons, which yield enformy when observed, and radionuclides, which emit energy and enformy when their nuclei reorganize to increase their stability.

In conclusion, scientists must be prepared to discover new laws that comprehend all events, including life itself. As Schrödinger pointed out, there in no justification for assuming that the known laws of physics are the complete set of laws. Specifically required is a concept that addresses the nature of organization per se. Enformy, the capacity to organize, is this concept.

REFERENCES

American Psychiatric Association. *Diagnostic and Statistical Manual of Mental Disorders, Third Edition*. Washington, D.C.: A.P.A., 1980.

Bertalanffy, L. von. *General System Theory*. George Braziller, 1980.

Brillouin, L. "Maxwell's demon cannot operate: Information and entropy." *I. J. Appl. Physics* 22 (1950): 334–337.

Campbell, K. *Body and Mind*. Doubleday, 1970.

Raymond, R.C. "Entropy of non-equilibrium systems." *Phys. Rev.* 78 (1950a): 351.

Raymond, R.C. "Communication, entropy and life." *American Scientist* 38 (1950b): 273–278.

Russell, B. "On the notion of cause, with applications to the free-will problem." In H. Fiegl and M. Brodbeck, eds., *Readings in the Philosophy of Science* (University of Minnesota, 1953), pp. 357–407.

Schrödinger, E. *What Is Life?* Cambridge, England: Cambridge University Press, 1944.

Shannon, C., and W. Weaver. *The Mathematical Theory of Communication*. University of Illinois Press, 1949.

Watson, R. A. Personal communication, 1988.

Wiener, N. *Cybernetics*. Wiley, 1948.

Section III
Issues of Public Policy

CHAPTER 20

MY WEAPON

Alan M. Schwartz

P o o R

On April 29, 1992, the Los Angeles police officers who mercilessly, vehemently, spitefully, protractedly, and professionally beat to a shattered brain-damaged pulp one Rodney King, black 55-mph-speed-limit violator, were acquitted of any wrongdoing, despite the evidence of a videotape exquisitely detailing the incident. Shortly after the exclusively non-black jury made the fruits of its deliberations public, looters and arsonists of all races ran roughshod through square miles of the meanest neighborhoods for three days, cleaning out store after store and burning *2,000* of them to the ground. Police stood by, surveying the party from within their cars and riot gear. Neighborhoods where no prudent businessman would establish his trade were purged of their Black, Korean, and Cambodian mom-and-pop establishments, and all of their chain food, clothing, and equipment emporiums. Civil-rights leaders of all persuasions paraded their borborygmus before the TV cameras. Jesse Jackson made himself scarce until the liabilities lapsed. Edward James Olmos was found leading the cleanup brigades. On the third day police and National Guard units deployed in force to do what they are trained to do, and do best: serve and protect themselves and their political stockholders.

Those who framed the United States Constitution knew what they were about. They were landed gentry, professional tradesmen, smugglers, thieves, and revolutionaries. They feared the hungers and unrestrained passions of those who had nothing of value to lose. The poor will always be with us, waiting. Our Founding Fathers deliberated and, after no small contentious deliberation, unconditionally guaranteed the right of the individual citizen to bear arms. Americans have the fundamental right to arm themselves as they see fit against the hostile obscenities of foreign and domestic governments, neighbors, and especially nasty strangers. This foresight served us well. It enabled us to kill revenue agents and indigenous natives at will as we subdued the continent to our own glorious manifest destiny. Taken as a whole, domestic violence was remarkably guarded: "An armed society is a polite society," Robert A. Heinlein said. Some of us have forgotten who is responsible for our families' safety.

Some of us have not forgotten. Two thousand Los Angeles businesses were burned to the ground. Thousands more were looted into destruction. No store or building guarded by its armed owner was damaged. Assault rifles, automatic weapons, and large-caliber killing implementia legislated into heinous illegality by legislators promising to protect us miraculously surfaced and saved the lives and livelihoods of untold households. To the initial horror of my woman, I chortled and sniggered with glee as the TV cameras panned across West L.A. commercial rooftops, each occupied by a squinting bastard with a long arm nestled to his cheek, sometimes firing. People who think the State is disposed to deliver them from personal disaster will pay for that ignorance with their lives, and those of their loved ones.

As the rioting spread I embarked upon the only rational response available to me. I sequentially unloaded, field-stripped, examined, cleaned, lubricated, reassembled, tested, and reloaded my weapons. As the second day drew to a close and Los Angeles burned, still without police intercession, the lady of the house opined that we should keep more than the current hundred rounds of ammunition for each magazine. We then went shopping for a few weeks' worth of dry goods and potable water to augment our normal inventory. I love her dearly. If a group of you noisily invade our neighborhood, you might not walk out.

America is still the land of untold possibilities, of unbounded prosperity, and of the dangers shared by the remainder of this bellicose planet. These rioters, these downtrodden victims of social injustice, enjoy television, plumbing, central heating, abundant food and medical care provided by the State if not by their own labor, subsidized transportation, a postal system, telephone communication across planet, public libraries, a climate that does not accommodate winter, and a government that mostly leaves them alone. Such a lifestyle exceeds the grasp of 80 percent of all humanity and is only imagined by another 10 percent. If they are poor it is only in contrast to the many who have discovered that their food stamps lay hidden under their work boots.

I bear no compassion for the many who rioted and the many who were destroyed. I respect the few who defended their families and their property, and who do not require my sympathies, because they are still whole. There will be times when the delusion of police protection is surmounted by reality. I am a *reasonable* man. If you assault me, my kin, or my property, I will kill you.

CHAPTER 21

URBANE INSURRECTION

Alan M. Schwartz

RADICAL

When racial or ethnic strife escalates to uncontrollable looting and property destruction necessitating suspension of civil rights, curfews, and patrol by armed government troops, this is called *martial law*. Petty dictators of military oligarchies impose martial law to retain their hold on an unwilling populace. The United States regularly lodges protests at the United Nations to halt such atrocities, and has intervened militarily to deliver freedom to downtrodden peoples. Where was the national and international outcry for the Rights of Man when curfews and martial law were imposed, but not declared, in Los Angeles?

Wednesday, April 29, 1992, witnessed three remarkable events. At 1500 hours a jury acquitted four Los Angeles police officers of charges stemming from their videotaped clubbing into physical and mental debility of one Rodney King, Black speed-limit violator. At 1600 hours radios blared and televisions glowed as West L.A. was looted and burned. TV-camera-bearing helicopters orbited the first of 2,000 buildings torched, and taped thousands of locals fomenting civil insurrection. At 1800 hours police chief Darryl Gates was speaking at a political fundraiser, later to admit that he knew nothing of the unfolding events. His police captains were attending a seminar in Oxnard. Nearly every cop in the city was pulled in to protect their headquarters from peaceful protesters carrying crudely handlettered signs. How about that?

Lest we unreasonably condemn The Man for quietly turning his back as Korean businesses were looted, trashed, and burned, let us remember the avowed mission of the L.A. police. Their motto is "To Protect and Serve," themselves. A jaywalking ticket brings in about $100, plus 140 percent more as a State-mandated surcharge. L.A. boasts one of the highest jaywalker apprehension rates in the U.S. Every traffic court in southern California has its calendar jammed solid from opening to closing, reaping a bounteous $60,000 each hour from levied fines. Jaywalkers and speeders are cornucopian reliquaries of tappable revenue, and rarely shoot back. Of the 6,500 looters, arsonists, and civil insurrectionists finally apprehended, not one will spill a single drop of black ink into Accounts Receivable. There ought to be a law!

Los Angeles was ablaze Wednesday night. On Thursday the uprising accelerated, incinerating vast swaths of mercantile enterprises and plunging square miles of the city into darkness as power and telephone succumbed. Local civil "leaders" duckwalked across the TV screens, anxious to legitimatize their unsupported claims of ascendancy and control. National "leaders" like Jesse Jackson and Al Sharpton made themselves scarce, waiting for a less physically hazardous and more politically secure moment. Late Thursday the police were unleashed and the National Guard was mobilized because the City Fathers knew . . .

On Friday the welfare checks arrived. The last remaining local Post Office hosted a line of welfare freeloaders a mile long at 0800 hours. They waited patiently and quietly, wrapped around a city block and queued to the horizon. Armed soldiers patrolled the streets. All was well.

An arrested citizen, by California law, must be arraigned within 48 hours or be released. 6,500 looters and arsonists impossibly clogged the court calendars, threatening to displace the vital daily harvest of traffic fines. A new law was quickly passed by the California legislature extending the arraignment deadline to a week. Adolf Hitler never violated German law. When he wished to implement a policy, he first passed a law legitimizing it. He never trespassed on the rights of German citizens, because he was the sole arbiter of what the rights of German citizens were. Hitler confronted the 1930s' economic depression, massive unemployment, social unrest, and political instability, and found a way out. President George Bush, Governor Pete Wilson, and Mayor Tom Bradley are faced with the same problems, are pushing though the same portal, and are now publicly singing the same song. Individual rights have been suspended to restore civil order.

Some time ago East Coast locals were sorely afflicted by the revenue-enhancement efforts, heavy-handed governance, and callous disregard for individual rights of another George, George III. Their listed grievances are the Declaration of Independence. Their considered framework for individuals' protection from the trespasses of government is the Bill of Rights.

I accuse the governments of Los Angeles, California, and the United States of having suspended the United States Constitution.

Biographical Sketch of Kent L. Aldershof

Kent L. Aldershof is a Senior Research Fellow of the ISPE, in which he also serves as Treasurer. A frequent *Telicom* contributor, he also co-produced the Society's poetry booklet *Of Penchants and Passions, Terrors and Tears*. He is Assistant Editor and Puzzles Editor of the bimonthly journal *Word Fun*. His works have also been published in *The Rotarian*, *Consulting Today*, and *Commerce* magazines.

Aldershof received the M.B.A. degree with High Distinction from Harvard Business School. There he was named a Baker Scholar, and a Baker Foundation Fellow, and received Harvard's Thayer Award as "one of the ten most meritorious scholars in all of Harvard University." He earned the M.S.E.E. degree at Polytechnic Institute of New York, and the B.S.E.E. degree at Iowa State University.

A management consultant heading his own firm, Mr. Aldershof specializes in strategic planning. He has been qualified in the Federal courts as an expert in management, corporate strategy, business planning, and financial analysis. Mr. Aldershof has provided expert testimony in bankruptcy, real-estate valuation, and business-management hearings.

Mr. Aldershof is currently active in Rotary International, and as Vice President and board member of The Sutton Ensemble, a leading chamber music group.

CHAPTER 22

INSIDE DEATH ROW

Kent L. Aldershof

Poor

All of us sit here warm, dry, and well-fed; and each of us has an attitude about capital punishment. Not everyone would agree with everyone else.

None of us really understand very much about the topic, because it is not something we have faced or been involved with. Our opinions might be influenced by first-hand knowledge of how the death penalty affects those who actually confront it. One of my correspondents is a man who has spent a decade and a half on Death Row. He murdered two men: shot one dead with a pistol after a barroom brawl, later killed an off-duty police officer. He remains on Death Row, pursuing final appeals and facing the electric chair.

At the time of the murders he was despondent over being abandoned by his wife and so losing his children. He was drunk and drugged into insensibility, and has no conscious memory of his actions. Nevertheless, that does not excuse his crime. Ordinarily his conviction would be for aggravated manslaughter; but cop-killers do not fare well in the courts. He was sentenced to death for felony murder.

Here are some excerpts from a 1991 letter. He speaks of another Death Row inmate, one who recently lost his final appeal before the Supreme Court, and whom we will call "Smith." He speaks also of a guard, whom we will call "Jones."

> Yes, I know Smith. He and I have lived in the same cell block for years. I know him VERY well . . .
>
> Smith will almost certainly die. I don't like him, but I feel sorry for him and what this is doing to him. He is unraveling before our eyes. It has already had an impact on him, and they haven't even set a death date yet.
>
> It's ugly to watch a man see his death day come and to see his

relatives and friends—if he has any. The families take it hard, very hard. It's cruel to see a day come when a loved one will be fried. It's a truly pathetic sight to see a mother try to say goodbye to a totally healthy son who will be fried in two hours . . .

I don't even like Smith; he is a phony jerk. But I see what it has done to him and how it hits him. It is not a nice thing. I really feel sorry for him and have told him so.

I had commented on a PBS documentary which indicated that the executioners often suffer heart attacks or nervous breakdowns. He responded with considerable bitterness.

It OUGHT to be hard on the ones who throw the switch. It's a volunteer job, and they had so many ask to be a part of it they had to select three and let the rest be sad because they can't kill someone legally. Yes, some people have taken being executioner hard, but some twisted dogs like it.

I have had several [guards] tell me they wish they could push the button to fry me. I always say, "If you hate me that much, then why not beat me up now?" It makes them mad. They know what I mean. Hit me one on one, I will mop the floor with them . . . I am middle-aged, and it makes them really hot for me to personally challenge them.

I don't fight, but when I am talked to like that I offer them the first shot. They never take it. That embarrasses them. These guards live in a moronic macho myth of a world, and talk tough and act like five-year-old boys. Makes you sick to have to put up with such infantile stuff.

Every time they kill someone it makes me mad. The prison staff look at us like sub-humans for our mistakes. Most on death row were on drugs or alcohol or both when their crime happened. A tiny few calculated to murder free from emotional turmoil, heartbreak, or alcohol.

The prison guards are stone-cold sober and eagerly anticipate a man's death. FEW regret or dislike what they do here, Kent. These jobs attract human maggots.

I have heard those guards taunt men who only had a few days left. One I particularly hated would sing "It's crispy critter time again" when he knew the guys close to the chair and death day could hear him.

He hated me too. I told him how sick he was . . . . I saw him smiling one day in a crowd of guards and said, "Hey, Jones, I see you're happy; who died? Someone's kid get run over?" It made the other guards laugh at Jones because it's true, he was that sick . . .

This is one SICK place, Kent, evil and twisted. The prevailing emotion is one of pure hatred.

It's hard to describe, really. It's just a hate-filled place. The inmates hate each other more than the guards hate us. It's really a sick place, truly like nowhere else on Earth: a warehouse for human sacrifices to a society's lust for revenge.

"Smith" was executed. In another note, my correspondent said

"I feel Smith would have been a good citizen if released . . . the world
is no better off because of his absence."

Of a murderer who was freed, he wrote

"[He] got out of prison. He is a super jerk and religious phony . . . but
he won't kill or rob again."

Later he commented on the effect of being in the environment of the
condemned.

I have lived a decade and a half now in a cell the size of the average
bathroom or less.
    I have lived in the same block with several as they counted down the
last 30 days. Six men here will die in the next few months. It has me
depressed. I will answer your questions; I can't face them right now.

I had asked whether he feels the death penalty is warranted for some
crimes, or for some of the inmates he has known. Then I observed that 95
percent of those who receive death sentences do not have those sentences
carried out. I wondered what he and other Death Row inmates feel about
the fairness or the adequacy of the punishment of being held on Death
Row for a long time, for example, how that compares with the suffering
and deprivation of a family who have lost a father or a daughter to a
wanton murderer.
    I also asked what he understood about the feelings of men in the final
hours or minutes before they are led into the death chamber, and about
what other Death Row inmates feel about the executions of those who
have committed particularly hideous murders.
    These questions may strike one as insensitive or even cruel, but in this
case I knew they would not be regarded as unfeeling. This inmate and I
have developed an open and candid relationship, and he has expressed his
willingness to share frankly his views of a world none of us will ever
know.
    Later, he replied. These excerpts capture the essence of what he said.

I am having a difficult time focusing on [your questions] . . . another
man is to be executed on Tuesday . . .
    I do not feel the death penalty is warranted for any crime. This
lowers society to a murderer's level, and sends the message that killing
for revenge is acceptable and morally correct in our society . . . . No

punishment is worse than life in prison. Death ends it, and is saying [the person is incapable of] redemption in any form.

What would the world have lost if execution for murder had been imposed on Moses, when he murdered the Egyptian? . . . Imagine a swift execution of King David for mass murder . . . Now imagine the execution of Saul of Tarsus, later to become the Apostle Paul. He delivered entire families of people for execution as heretics to the Jewish faith. All of these would have been lost forever to history, just to appease a lust for revenge, to kill in retaliation for murder. Imagine the stunning loss to history . . .

Considering whether the loved ones left behind are "entitled" to see a murderer suffer or die, to redress their grievous loss, he stated:

I could write a book on what living under the death sentence does to people and to their families. How can anyone compare two different types of suffering? [Victim families] want death, or life without parole; but murderers make the best parolees; that is from the Justice Dept.

Clearly a Parole Board can judge a man's conduct to tell if he is a demented savage, never changed after years of prison. A few should never be released, but a lot can and would contribute to society.

Is anyone "entitled" to see someone die? If it is truly right, why are only a very few of the 20,000 or more murderers each year given the death penalty and actually executed? Make it mandatory for all first-degree murder; you would have to kill literally thousands of people a year. It's so capriciously given now that it is legal Lotto or Roulette.

Many people with far more hideous crimes than most on death row are given life, and eventually paroled. Yes, I know of Bundy, Gacy, and the other super-sick; they are a tiny fraction of the 2,500 on Death Rows across the USA today.

"Wanton" does not fit all the people on Death Row. Most were on alcohol or drugs or both, coupled with all sorts of mental deficiencies and emotional problems, when they killed. Only a very few did their crimes with a clear head, and in a calculated manner.

Look, you are not killing the same man you put here 10 or 15 years ago. They change dramatically, almost all of them. They soul search, and improve as human beings. Most do mature and change a lot.

He wrote of the intense reactions at the threshold of execution:

I really cannot describe the feelings of men facing imminent execution. Each individual experiences it a different way. Some accept and become resigned to it and are docile. Some are frantic; some are angry. But it's ugly to watch each one, and especially to see the suffering of the family.

The man has faced it for so long that he often is the one trying to soothe the feelings of a hysterical mother, wife, sisters, sons and daughters, and father as they visit on the day of his being killed.

What can you tell your mother when two hours from now you will be electrically roasted? What do you say to your wife, to your son, to your daughter? This is the most insane situation I have ever witnessed— a mother hugging the neck of the son she gave birth to, knowing he will be cooked to death in a few hours.

The death penalty is an act of prolonged torture, more to the family of the condemned than to the condemned. I have seen children sobbing so hard it had to be physically painful, because someone they love is being escorted out of the visiting room, to die. I have seen a man's mother walk out after her son was led away, to have his head and leg shaved in preparation for ritual execution. She had a look of horror that no living human could accurately describe.

My crime has traumatized me beyond description, and will haunt me for the rest of my life. The loss of a loved one to an act of murder has to be horrible. The pain has to be indescribable. How can anyone compare this? I know, though, that if I had been murdered I would not want another killing done in my name.

Yet each of you must decide what you want done in your name. As citizens in a nation with a Federal death penalty, killings will be done in your name whether you live in a state that has the death penalty or not. Is that what you want?

My correspondent recently sent a copy of the latest Court Order in his case:

within a time period commencing at noon on the 3rd day of March, 1992, and ending seven days later at noon on the 10th day of March, 1992, the defendant [NAME] shall be executed by the Department of Corrections . . .

Biographical Sketch of Robert J. Davis

Robert J. Davis received his Ph.D. from Harvard in 1960, in the field of radio astronomy, studying the motions of interstellar hydrogen gas in our own Milky Way galaxy.

From 1951 until 1954 he served the United States as a naval officer, both aboard ship in the North Atlantic and ashore in Texas. Since 1959 he has been a civil servant with the United States Government, working for the Smithsonian Institution's Astrophysical Observatory.

For the past several years he has been studying the motions of stars in order better to understand where and how they originated, and how the tendency of stars to form in pairs, small groups, and clusters affects their ability to form planets and the ability of their possible planetary systems to develop life.

He has been a member of the International Society for Philosophical Enquiry since its inception in 1974, and an officer of that Society since 1975.

CHAPTER 23

GOVERNMENT AND THE ETHICS QUANDARY

COHCLUSIOH is Good

Robert J. Davis

In recent years, governments throughout the world have become top-heavy and fallen at an increasing rate. There is strong evidence that the government of the United States of America is propelling itself toward the same fate. At this juncture in world history, it would seem prudent for thinking people everywhere to re-examine the reasons why governments should exist at all, and the works written by great philosophers throughout history regarding the institutions by which people interact with each other—primarily, government and ethics.

ETHICS

From the point of view of the academic philosopher—both now and ever since the time of Socrates, Plato, and Aristotle—ethics is the study of ideal human character, actions, and ends. From the point of view of bureaucrats and legislators, both within government and in nongovernmental bureaucracies, ethics is the activity of writing and adhering to a detailed set of rules of prescribed and proscribed activities. Let us try to cut through all the fat that has built up around the essential meat of ethics during innumerable trips to the pork barrel, and take a closer look at 2,500 years of negative progress. After all, ethical theory is *supposed* to be the basis for theories about the authority of the state, about the justification of legal systems, and about the moral tenability of different systems of distribution of economic goods.

Reasonably complete documents expounding on ethical theory are available from identified authors since Plato (427–347 B.C.); additional manuscripts report various aspects of ethical thought for the preceding several centuries. The following ethical theories were well-developed by the time of Aristotle's death (322 B.C.). The subsequent 2,300 years have not given rise to any additional theories that are not based on one of these ancient precepts:

1. *Hedonism*: Do whatever is pleasurable. For several years around 400 B.C. the Cyrenaics argued that the only good is pleasure, the ideal life being one of obtaining intelligently and without passion the pleasures of the moment—especially the physical ones, since they are more intense.
2. *Power Ethics*: "Justice" is simply what is in the interest of powerful individuals or groups. Conventional moral principles are simply a device of the inferior for protecting themselves against the stronger; the powerful have a right to take whatever they can take (400 B.C.).
3. *Situation Ethics*: Do what your group expects you to do (450 B.C.).
4. *Socratic Ethics*: Humans are by nature ethical creatures, and proper ethical rules can be determined purely by contemplation and reasoning (developed during the period 450–330 B.C.).
5. *Judaeo-Christian Ethics*: Ethical obligation corresponds to the revealed will of a personal God. Love for God and fellow humans is the core of goodness and obligation. Humans are by nature anti-ethical creatures, and ethical action comes only as a result of love and of knowing the revealed will of God.

GOVERNMENT

Aristotle, in his *Nicomachean Ethics* (Book VIII, Section X), says:

There are three kinds of "political constitution" (*politeia*), and an equal number of variations—or rather, corruptions—of these. The constitutions proper are monarchy, aristocracy, and a third kind, which, as it is based on a property qualification, may appropriately be called timocratic, although most people speak of it simply as "constitutional government." The best of these is monarchy, the worst timocracy. The variant of monarchy is tyranny: both are a kind of monarchy, but there is a wide difference between them, the tyrant looking to his own advantage, the king to that of his subjects. For no one is truly a king who is not self-sufficient and superior to his subjects in good qualities; and if he is such, there is nothing more that he needs; so that he will aim at his subjects' advantage rather than at his own. A king of any other sort will be a mere titular king. But tyranny is the direct opposite in this respect, the tyrant pursuing only his own good; and it is pretty clear that this is the worst type of government, inasmuch as the worst is the direct opposite of the best. Monarchy passes over into tyranny; for as both are forms of autocratic rule, the bad king becomes a tyrant. Aristocracy passes into oligarchy through the fault of the rulers, who distribute political honors unfairly, taking all or most of the good things for themselves, and keeping political offices always in the same hands, principally for the sake of gain. The result is a small number of bad men in power, instead of the best men. And finally, timocracy passes into democracy: they are, in fact, closely connected; for timocracy also purports to be a government by the masses, and lets all who have the property qualification count as equal. There is least corruption in the shift from timocracy to democracy, for the deviation here is least. These, then, are the ways in which the form of government is most readily altered; for in each of them a minimum of change is involved, and hence can take place with least difficulty.

Looking around at the many independent and subsidiary governments that exist now and that have existed earlier in the twentieth century, it is likely that most of us can find examples of all six of the Aristotelian forms of government. I will leave it for each reader separately to decide which of these six forms best describes his own local, provincial, and/or national government, and whether the seventh form of government, *anarchy*, is not also rather widespread. For now, though, let us look more at how governments—and individuals—behave, and less at how they happen to be structured.

OBSERVED HUMAN BEHAVIOR

As I noted above, the basis for all ethical theory boils down into one of four mutually exclusive central premises: Ethical (and anti-ethical) behavior among people results from (a) the search for personal pleasure; *or* (b) the fear of punishment; *or* (c) an immutable natural characteristic of human beings; *or* (d) love. (Both Situation and Socratic Ethics come under variation (c): The "natural characteristic" may be either individuals' innate desire to be like their peers, or individuals' innate tendency to desire the so-called "ultimate good," which is a condition that can be discovered by contemplation and that is the same for all men at all times and places.)

It is not hard for us intellectuals to notice that very many humans act very brutally toward each other; that even more snip various ethical corners when dealing with each other; and that even more act with complete disregard for those consequences of their actions that have no obvious immediate effect upon them personally. It is easy to see that the only authority recognized by brutal people is brutal policing. But how do governments go about deciding what practices are brutal enough to justify inverse brutality? And how do they go about controlling the style and imposition of this inverse brutality? Governments (and other bureaucracies) consist of people, and people are controlled by every type of ethical system (and every posible mixture of types) that exists, whether identified by philosophers or still unidentified. Power works to the advantage of the powerful; intelligent power and brutal power work best, with intelligent possibly working to the longest advantage of the owner of that power. Thus we may conclude, as did Aristotle, that all governments are destined to become corrupt, and that the least efficient government—democracy— will, therefore, do the least damage.

Looking at this problem from my own location—Belmont, in Middlesex County, in Massachusetts, in the United Staes of America—I ask whether the U.S. and its subsidiary governments are a democracy or an oligarchy. Congress has reserved for itself certain activities that it makes illegal for others to perform. Presidents resign to the trumpeting of past-present-future executive pardon by their (appointed, not elected) successors. Supreme Court justices succumb to Alzheimer's symptoms with no means for removal. New justices are subjected to interrogation in a carnival public-TV atmosphere by a group of politicians whose own automobiles have killed more people than all the nuclear accidents in U.S. history. The media hypes up anything it can find about any individual running for office that its listeners wish they felt free to commit, without regard to the veracity of the sources of the information. I conclude that the U.S. today is an oligarchy, run by the powerful in its four branches (legislative, executive, judicial, and media). I come to the same conclusions for Massachusetts, for Middlesex County, and for Belmont. It doesn't seem to matter whether they are Democrat or Republican: government gets bigger; taxes get bigger; the fat cats get fatter; the poor get poorer; education gets worse; the roads and bridges get worse; crime increases; various addictions increase. The only solution is smaller government, and the only organized party that espouses smaller government is the Libertarian Party. Why is the Libertarian Party ignored by the media? Because it doesn't make "juicy" news like that that comes from the existing oligarchs.

THE NATURE OF THE QUANDARY

When and if we succeed in reversing the growth of government, we are still faced with a quandary: Is there a body of ethical statements that is widely enough acknowledged to act as a *stated* basis for our laws? Does "Thou Shalt not Kill" apply only to unprovoked murder of productive adults? Only to unprovoked murder of adults? Only to unprovoked murder of already-born humans? Also to provoked murder? Also to non-murder killings of humans? Also to military activities? Also to "endangered species" of animals? Also to domestic animals? Also to . . . ? Does "Know ye not that your bodies are the members of Christ? Shall I then take the members of Christ and make *them* the members of a harlot? God forbid" mean "Drink not"; "Smoke not"; "Shoot no coke"; and/or "Shoot no heroin"? Does "Establish no religion" mean "Don't allow *any* public money to be spent on nonpublic education"? If you want to find out what the Libertarian Party Platform says about these matters, phone 1-800-564-6576 or 1-617-426-4402. It is succinctly written in a single four-page document. If you want to find out what the Bible says about these matters, you will have to read most of the Old Testament and almost all of the New Testament. If you want to find out what the government says about these matters, you will have to read the Congressional Record and the similar books that are published by states, cities, and similar agencies in countries other than the U.S. (as well as court briefs from thousands of courts throughout the world), plus several million pages of lawyers' analyses.

CONCLUSION

Different people behave differently when faced with the opportunity or the temptation to seize unethical gain. And unless there is a solid, immutable natural or supernatural basis for human ethics, mankind is doomed to self-destruction.

Biographical Sketch of Harry L. Callahan

Harry L. Callahan was born in an Appalachian hamlet in West Virginia on February 12, 1934. He moved with his family to Washington, D.C., at age 7. With the exception of the educational completion certificates for high school and college from the U.S. Air Force, he is and continues to be autodidactic. After an Air Force career, he entered the insurance business, where he has held every position from agent to Corporate Vice President. He now runs an insurance brokerage operation while pursuing a writing career. He has three books in progress: two novels and a weight-loss book. He has been published many times in trade journals and in general publications. Mr. Callahan is married, and has two children and three grandchildren.

CHAPTER 24

EXIT JUSTICE SYSTEM, ENTER LEGAL SYSTEM

Harry L. Callahan

FAIR

In comparison to the other countries of the world, America endures—by far—the most violent crimes, in quantity *and* severity. We incarcerate—by far—the greatest number of our citizens for criminal activity, more than any other Western country.

The reasons for these appalling facts are many; each sociologist and each criminologist has a different reason. Most studies done on the subject conclude differently, and usually with slightly different recommended remedies. The reasons should be apparent to anyone who can analyze the subject logically. The most apparent one, however, is that we produce, and harbor, violent individuals.

We are a society that *assimilates*. We absorb many people from all different parts of the world. We accept almost anyone to our shores. We immediately give them rights others have to earn with a lifetime of devotion to the society granting the rights. (For example, illegal aliens in some parts of our country are given more services, worth more money, than are granted to retirees in those same areas who have worked a lifetime paying taxes for those services.) As long as our society produces extremely violent criminals, we must deal with them violently. We cannot loose these individuals once again upon society with the mistaken impression that they are rehabilitated, or even capable of being rehabilitated. With very few exceptions, they are not. If, in fact, we do loose these individuals upon society, we are breaking a trust, and those responsible should be called to bear.

We produce these individuals in quantity primarily because there are no deterrents to dissuade them from acting as they do, against the very society giving them the opportunity to act. The death penalty, in those jurisdictions where applicable, is largely ignored. The appeals process sometimes allows the individual to die of old age before the penalty is exacted.

We also produce these individuals because of a deterioration in moral values, which heretofore did not tolerate such behavior. The culture that produced these moral values will have to assimiliate those cultures now within our society which do not produce those values. This will take not only several generations of evolution, but also an effort of those "haves" to properly and deliberately bring those "have nots" into the realm of the culturally advantaged.

We must also demand a change in our immigration policies. We cannot long allow access to our shores to those individuals who possess those very traits that represent the culturally disadvantaged aspect of our society that we currently tolerate.

Most importantly, we must recognize that when a violent individual deprives another of the right to life, for example, he or she then forfeits any such claim to those same rights. We must also curtail the appeals process drastically. For example, the United States Supreme Court was not created to hear appeals previously addressed—*and adjudicated*—in the court of jurisdiction. The exception would be for "Constitutional issues," but it is hard to conceive of an issue not previously addressed.

Our courts are currently so overburdened that criminal repeaters do not fear the system, when fear must be present for deterrence to succeed. We must find a way to properly and expeditiously process those individuals who are a threat to the rest of society. If necessary, we must eliminate or sharply curtail the bail system for individuals who represent a real threat to our citizens. And we must carry out punishment to that individual quickly, with a minimum of legal maneuvers.

The reason for the legal maneuvers, and for that matter the proliferation of litigation, is a subject that must be broached if we are ever to get the wreckage of what was once a *justice* system under control. Why is it that all of a sudden (within the last few decades) we have experienced a burgeoning of individual rights, rights that previously apparently didn't exist? Or didn't matter? We need to ask whether we have too many rights. For example, one man sued a casino because, once he had lost all his cash, he leaped from the roof, survived, and promptly (no doubt with some encouragement) sued the casino for not stopping him from jumping. They will probably settle to avoid the cost of litigation. And there's the issue.

At the end of 1991, the Bureau of Labor Statistics reported that there were 777,119 attorneys in America. During the fall of 1991 94,200 individuals applied to law school. Excluding those new law students, the total number of attorneys works out to one for every 335 of us. If all those students enter the work force, there will be an attorney for every 298 of us. We now provide work for more than 70 percent of the world's attorneys. (Japan, for example, along with other countries, is not only sending students to us for our superior legal education, but also buying up law firms.) A law-school professor recently complained that the public has "been bemoaning the overpopulation of the Law profession since 1920." I say, for good reason. These people have to have something to do; they have to have projects on which to work, from which to make a living.

We are a nation within which a citizen has many rights. We have a legal system that rewards litigants not only for damages, whether real or perceived, but also *punishes*, through punitive damage awards, the defendant, for example, an insurance company, or any other legitimate business being sued, or a professional, such as a physician, or minister, or church, etc. It also allows the attorney a piece of the action by not only condoning the practice but sometimes even *advocating* that practice. We are in fact thus encouraging a proliferation of attorneys.

The same results would be realized if we suddenly demanded that brakes on an automobile had to be replaced every 20,000 miles. We would immediately have an increase in the number of people associated with automobile brakes and automobile manufacturing. We are feeding a system that we will *not long be able to afford*.

When a death-row inmate appeals a sentence for up to seventeen years, a sentence properly imposed and fairly adjudicated, but through legal maneuvers is able to avoid the carrying out of that sentence, we need to re-examine the system.

When a municipality is ordered by a court to pay a claimant many millions for an injury as a result of a minor oversight by a municipal employee, and then must raise taxes to pay that award, our system needs overhauling, particularly since a third or more of those new taxes will pay the attorney, apparently for that attorney's "creativity."

The justice system is no longer a sanctuary for an individual who seeks remedy, redress, or a fair settlement for injury or displacement. It has become a *legal* system in which adjudications are almost always in favor of the most competent and creative attorney. The claimant and his or her position in many cases is irrelevant; the extent of his or her injury does not influence the decision as much as the competency of the representation.

This must soon change, for many reasons, not the least of which is the fact that we can't afford it. There is a tangible possibility that the malpractice insurance market will soon dry up, that coverage will no longer be available. If and when that happens, physicians will either be put out of business or simply ignore any outlandish award against them. Since we obviously need physicians, it is apparent what will happen. The lawyers will then have to concentrate on areas offering a better chance for settlements. Eventually, after enough possibilities dry up, they might settle on various government entities, state and federal. Laws now in place banning the suing of government entities can be changed; most legislators are, in fact, attorneys. Taxpayers will ultimately have to answer what very well may be the most important question of the coming century:

Can we afford all these rights?

Biographical Sketch of Daryl L. Bell-Greenstreet

Daryl L. Bell-Greenstreet holds a B.A. in Political Science. He is an ex-Marine Vietnam veteran in his forties. He is currently working toward advanced degrees in physics and mathematics. He has been a member of ISPE for three years and a Fellow for one. He served for two years as Manager of the New Member Welcome Program, and is a member of the Whiting Memorial Fund Committee. He deeply enjoys the serenity of his home high in the mountains of Central Arizona.

CHAPTER 25

THE DISSOLUTION OF POLITICAL POWER IN THE UNITED STATES OF AMERICA

Daryl L. Bell-Greenstreet

$\mathcal{D} \, \textit{umB}$

"As long as one man is not yet free, there will always be war."
General Douglas MacArthur

As this is being written (late Spring 1992) an interesting phenomenon seems to be sweeping our nation. A third-party candidate (with very few known positions) is tied in the polls with the President of the United States in a race for the latter's job. Should this man win the popular vote in the fall and yet lose in the Electoral College, we are quite possibly going to see something that has not reared its head in the United States for more than a century and a third, something which Thomas Jefferson thought necessary every generation: revolution in the United States. Not since the dark days of Watergate have Americans shown such a distinct level of dissatisfaction with our supposed servants on the Potomac. And even then it was the counter-culture in revolt. What our government is so blithely ignoring is that tomorrow's revolutionaries are coming from mainstream America.

What has gone wrong? Why are so many of us fed up? And how can our elected representatives in Washington continue to bury their heads so deeply in the sand? And most importantly, where is this all going to end? These are questions of utmost concern in our lives. Let's explore them sequentially.

What has gone wrong? Today more than a quarter of a billion people can rightfully call themselves citizens of the United States. There is probably not a country, nor even a county, on the face of the Earth that has not lost someone to the U.S.A., someone drawn by the promise of freedom and the chance at prosperity. Mix with them millions of "Native Americans," not necessarily Indians but others whose ancestry disappears into the mists of faded memory, all of whom have been told that America equals opportunity, and you get a polyglot of people with a polyglot of expectations. Yet a third of the real estate in America is still held by the government, the same percentage as when there were fifty million of us. What that equates to is that land, i.e. property, becomes more valuable, and thus human life, relatively less so. In real terms, this means that if you are born a black male in Harlem, a factor over which you have no control, the odds are much greater than 50 percent that you will die a violent death before age 50, after having lived a squalid life. It means that if you are a woman, no matter how intelligent, you will earn only about 70 percent of what your male peers do, regardless of occupation. It means that if you are a white man you will see government programs push minorities to the head of the line (and thus you to the back), whether it is an employment line or a soup line of governmental largess. Effectively then, virtually all Americans have good reason to see themselves as victims of injustice. Thus, with the small exception of the very comfortable "haves," we have become a nation of people with a vested interest in the overturning of the status quo. By definition, then, that tiny clot of people in the District of Columbia are forced to be defenders of the status quo. Firebrands take a seat in the House on promises of "straightening out the system" only to find themselves two short years later defending it. The buzzword is that they have become "co-opted." They need power to be effective, and the system has established that the only way they can get it is by playing by the rules. The rules, naturally, prohibit change to the system. Thus we all find ourselves in a "representative democracy" that does not represent us. Most of the laws that we are governed by are generated not by our elected representatives but by faceless bureaucrats who truly do not answer to anyone. And what has made this particularly dangerous is that the system has provided no mechanism for correcting these problems. This unfortunately means that the change we must have in order to progress as a people can come only from revolution.

Why are so many of us fed up? It is because so many of us are able to see, with better-than-ever educations and our increased worldliness, that as long as we continue to work within the system, we are guaranteed to come out on the short end of the stick. Workers today are hardly better off than the serfs of half a millennia ago. If they got tired of working for nothing, they could run away in hopes of starting anew elsewhere. Today's computers insure that no one can leave a failed past and start anew.

Today's employee, thanks to the military might lent to his employer by his own government, guarantees that he can only hope for mercy from his boss, mercy which is rarely forthcoming. And, even more importantly, today the yeoman farmer, the merchant, the self-employed professional (the backbone of the middle class) see their economic security being vacuumed up by powerful financial institutions, and their government either unwilling or unable to stop it. Thus the revolution which is coming is no longer going to be the haves versus the have-nots. It's going to be the haves versus the have-nots AND the used-to-haves. This, in my opinion, is primarily why the haves and their servant (the government) will lose.

How is it that our elected representatives can bury their heads in the sand? How indeed. What appears to be happening, with all those House rats abandoning ship, is that many of them are aware of what is about to happen and are thus attempting to leave gracefully, a short half-step ahead of the boot. Others, mindful of how dark things were during Watergate, are hoping to weather the storm. The President of the United States is trying to foist himself off as the candidate of change, in short, running against his own record! The solution for a moribund economy that Franklin Roosevelt created was to borrow money from future generations of Americans to "prime the pump" in the present. The result of the extension of that from his day to ours is that next year, for the first time, the largest single expenditure of the Federal government will be for debt service. Clearly, more borrowing will get to be an ever less-popular solution to temporal woes. Yet no one in Washington has been able to come up with another hat trick.

Yes, the day of reckoning is surely at hand. So our elected representatives, partly out of wishful thinking, bury their heads in the sand. And, of course, the lobbyists keep them amply busy with their own wish lists. They are besieged by big business, by labor leaders representing themselves and not labor, by veterans groups who don't represent veterans. (The Vietnam Veterans of America can't count even one half of one percent of their constituency as members. Why? Their focus is on the vested interest of the few; they truly do not represent the Vietnam veteran. This effectively means that the Vietnam veteran has no representation in the nation's Capitol.) With everyone in Washington running in circles, those with a Capitol Hill view see motion, which they interpret as progress. Perhaps, in the final analysis, it just comes down to Congressmen not being as smart as they used to be, and the public not being as dumb as they used to be.

And, finally, where is it going to end? Our political/economic systems have evolved for a long time. We started with chieftains because they united our efforts, giving us more collective strength. In time that system evolved into monarchy because the chief of the chiefs (the king) could collectivize the chiefs' strength and make for an even stronger central authority. The combination of monarchical human foibles and emerging human self-respect sent the kingdoms of the past down the road to oblivion. The few that remain are basically toothless. Mostly the old kingdoms have been replaced with democratic republics, such as the one currently in power in the United States. It was formed in compromise between flint-hard democrats, such as Patrick Henry, and lofty aristocrats, such as Alexander Hamilton. Thus our bicameral legislature, the wealthy represented by the Senate, *hoi polloi* by the House. Because the wealthy are getting ever fewer in percentage of the population and yet they retain fully half the legislative prerogative, our government has tilted out of balance. That the people recognize this inherent inequity is attested to by annually increasing numbers who abandon the system entirely and don't vote. After all, when a person votes, he or she is not only stating a preference for one candidate over another, but also swearing allegiance to whoever the winner is. When they don't vote, they are divorcing themselves from the entire system. The people of America are currently divorcing *en masse*. Yet, just as the authorities in Los Angeles ignored a full-scale riot into existence, every indicator suggests that the central government in Washington is about to do the same.

The long-term results could well be more regionalized authority and less central control. We may in fact, if not in name, become the Confederate States of America. This will no doubt be painful, but is really a natural result of the human animal's lessened need to have his decisions made for him by strangers on the far side of the continent. The change could be evolutionary, but the stupidity and propensity toward violence on the part of our government virtually guarantee that it will be revolutionary. We can only hope that our love of liberty and justice will bring us out the other side in better shape than we now are in.

Biographical Sketch of Richard J. Tlapa

The Reverend Richard J. Tlapa, Ph.D., is a Catholic priest who resides at the Hermitage in Merrillville, Indiana. His major avocations and interests include building amateur radios, ecology, philosophy, theology, psychology, literature, and history.

CHAPTER 26

A JEREMIAD FOR PERSONAL INTEGRITY

Richard J. Tlapa

poor

Marcus Tullius Cicero, the great Roman statesman, philosopher, and orator, lamented in 64 B.C. that personal morals were suffering because of common man's preoccupation with the worship of riches. A few weeks ago (as I write) the emcee on an AM radio talk show proposed a hypothetical case: a very wealthy man offers you a million dollars to sleep with your wife for one night. Would you agree to such a transaction? The *unanimous* response of callers was, "Yes, I would permit such adultery." After all, where can you pick up a cool million so easily?

(By the way, there was no response from feminine listeners, and I often wondered if a wife would agree to such a proposition. This must remain a moot point at this juncture, although, if we were to interpolate the male responses, the answers probably would be the same. Still another question: this was a weekday radio talk show. Why were so many men at liberty to listen to the program instead of being actively engaged at work somewhere?)

Lest it be protested that morals have nothing to do with integrity, let us seek common ground in Webster's Dictionary, wherein integrity is defined quite simply as "the quality or state of being of sound moral principle, uprightness, honesty, and sincerity." That's quite a mouthful.

In the Old Testament adultery was punishable by death. If current reports are true, it is still punishable by death in most Muslim countries, and it is certainly grounds for divorce in other civilized nations. Yet some men would be willing to let other men have their wives for profit. Does this make the women any less than whores? There is the profit motive, you know! Whether it is once, or multiple times, such action for profit smacks of prostitution. Would those men be as satisfied henceforth with their wives, knowing that their newly acquired wealth was the fruit of willful and collaborative infidelity? Would the women be satisfied with their husbands, inasmuch as they, too, had succumbed to the sudden blandishments of wealth? Most listeners, after being confronted with these questions, would argue that the proposal is simply hypothetical, and the actuality of such an offer has to be judged in some depth before acquiescence or denial. In other words, what is at present hypothetical or only *in potentia* would become, after some profundity of judgment, either *in actu* or *neglected entirely*.

Ordinarily this judgmental process is termed *conscience*. Contrary to popular thought, conscience is not a state of conscious awareness of good and/or evil, but very simply a definitive judgment. The state of being constantly aware of good and/or evil actions as a result of multiple judgments, and the decision to remain "on the good side" (or, for perversions of one kind or another, "on the bad side") is commonly termed synteresis, a metaphysical term for the "internal" repository of conscious or intuitive knowledge of right and wrong.

Thus, if a normal child, which as yet has not reached the use of reason, makes a judgment, and it is wrong, or if a congenital idiot attempts the judging of an action (if such a thing were even possible) and is in error, no guilt can be ascribed. The question of personal integrity scarcely reaches the surface. However, when we consider the normal man or woman, capable of making a reasonable judgment after weighing the pros and cons, being fully aware of what is right and/or wrong, then there erupts a situation wherein morality enters, *whether the one making the judgment agrees to the morality of the situation or not.*

When we are dealing with personal integrity—and, concomitantly, with moral or immoral actions—laws enter into the picture, whether they be natural, of divine origin, or enacted by the society in which we live. And, *like it or not*, GUILT must enter the picture if a person's conscience is wrong, *knowingly and willingly*, and sires the resultant erroneous actions or negligences. This commonly is known as "acting against one's own conscience," which becomes both judge and jury, condemning the actor as "guilty."

(Aside: we could consider at this point the aberrations of scrupulous conscience, lax conscience, erroneous conscience, etc., but treatment thereof would render this essay tedious and rather overweight.)

Suddenly it becomes but mere illation to decide, beyond the example cited in the first paragraphs, that criminal actions or any actions against either the laws of God (or, if you prefer, the "natural laws"), or the laws of the state, or against what is commonly termed "social" conduct, can be and usually are immoral. Looting, theft, arson, murder, mayhem, etc., are the more serious immoral actions; littering, selfish actions in society (be it in the supermart or the gas station), even raising the middle finger at an intransigent motorist, are far less heinous, but in some manner, be they ever so small, they detract from personal integrity. Whether the actions be great or minimal, there is an erosion—gradual at times, instantaneous at other times—of one's uprightness, honesty, and, in the end, integrity.

Sadly, for the most serious actions against society, perchance the only excusing factor is that a state of war exists, be it between nations or between members of the same society. In the latter instance, it becomes very difficult to apply the same rules that apply to conflict between nations, for we have citizens of the same nation conflicting with each other to the point of death. Whether it is raging and actuated rabid disgust in Los Angeles or in Bosnia/Herzegovina, violations of society's, God's, or nature's laws ultimately result in either near or actual catastrophes, until reason and sound judgment take hold and once again conscience and morally decisive syntereses reign. In retrospect: how totally, absolutely, futile, and foolish had been the years of conflict between Iraq and Iran. How totally, absolutely futile, and foolish had been the burning and looting of one's own part of a city! Why does insanity reign?

Hearkening back to the first paragraphs: even though the radio emcee had proposed only a hypothetical case, the celerity with which the listeners responded in the affirmative speaks of the corrosion in our modern society. Once a man's handshake was a visible sign of his word, of his bond, and it had always been accepted as a sign of his pledge, of his integrity. Marital fidelity, too, customarily is signaled by the wearing of a ring and the pronouncement of "vows." Like adultery, to which it is akin, infidelity becomes grounds for divorce (death in some countries). It would appear, then, that even the customary signs of fidelity, like the handshake and the pledge of one's word, have become mere external symbols, largely ineffectual and totally dependent on circumstances, no more to be trusted than the words of a consummate liar. Herein lie the roots of "situation ethics."

Consequently the male listeners may have been honest and somewhat sincere, but, if they were not dissimulating for the amusement of other listeners, they definitely acted neither uprightly nor from sound moral principle. Even doing business with them would be hazardous for a third party, for if they lack good judgment in their private lives and acquiesce to a pure hypothesis to the detriment of their own moral standards (or integrity), what proof is there that they would be of moral character in their public lives, especially in positions of responsibility? In their handling of properties belonging to others? In the fulfilling of their contracts as regards hours of labor, materials used, subcontracts, etc.? The only pressure which could be brought to bear on them would be the threat of legal actions prejudicial to their own personal well being. A person who lacks integrity in the simple definition of the term cannot help but carry into his dealings with strangers the same dishonesty which he metes out to those for whom it is presumed he has some regard. A person simply cannot prescind from integrity, being a Mr. Hyde with someone quite close and somewhat dear to him, and then becoming a Dr. Jeckyl with total strangers. He would have to possess a strange personality indeed!

The erosion of personal integrity *never* remains a private affair. Its effect becomes a synergism which impinges upon, and finally corrupts, all or most of society. Subsequently the "sinner" feels little or no personal culpability in stealing, shoplifting, arson, peddling "crack" (or using it), cheating on a contract, substituting shoddy materials for the genuine articles, shortcutting hours of hire, shortchanging customers—briefly, anything goes in "that jungle out there" as long as you get away with it. There is no feeling of remorse (save in being "caught"), and there is no intention whatsoever of recompense. Feelings of guilt, if there are any, are pressured into the subconscious, or submerged beneath the "demand" for a specious "justice," or deemed a revenge on society itself, and actions inimical to personal integrity and society are thereby "justified." As a result, society deteriorates and the commonwealth loses luster. It is appalling to learn of check-kiting among our politicians (even though they claim it is not dishonest) and of embezzlements among CEOs of large corporations, or among ministers of the gospel, who had been presumed to be as pure as the driven snow. This disillusionment, particularly among the ignorant or the weak-willed, engenders the conclusion that, "if they can do it, so can I," and, as in the parable of the demon expelled from one's house, which wanders through waterless places and then returns to find the home swept and clean and brings seven demons worse than itself, "the ultimate state of the man becomes worse than it had been in the beginning."

The solution to the loss of personal integrity is not simple. The first truism is to state that the installation and development of moral principles begin in the home. Where there are morally convinced parents, there will be discovered the morally convinced child. This is a truism, indeed, because hundreds—nay, thousands—of schoolteachers, both in grammar schools and in high schools, deplore the lethargy, the ill manners, and the ignorance in the home which nullify all their hours of earnest effort to instill in a child a desire to learn, to walk tall, and to assimilate common-sense principles which will guide him or her in adult life. That many parents cannot or will not properly tutor their children in uprightness and honesty, not to speak of self-discipline, which is so necessary for goals in life, is a national scandal and disgrace. Peer pressure, too, in juvenile and teen years brings so much anxiety into a young person's life that if he does not follow the leader or go along with the crowd, he will be left alone to fend for himself, and not every youngster is a Thoreau willing to settle beside Walden Pond. One reason for belonging to a "gang" is that very important sense of "belonging." Teen pregnancies can often be attributed to a slight variation of the same syndrome: "Someone needs me! As much as I need someone else!" The latter is often the consequence of a total lack of personal love in the home. Parents are just too busy "doing their own thing" to squander any effort tutoring or setting example or sharing time with their own child.

Churches are doing their best, but too many of them are constantly harping on "Faith" and "Belief" and are not stressing the Ten Commandments or the code of ethics traditional to Christianity. People who regularly attend church services have "faith" and they "believe"—that's why they are there—but the lamentations which storm up from the pews is that seldom are heard teachings on the Commandments or the exegeses thereof. It is as though the ministers of the Gospel are loathe to offend anyone by preaching the Word as it had been given. Too, a great many of the ministers in small churches, apart from the mainstream of institutional Churches, are usually the graduates of some Bible school (sad to say, some are merely "mail-order" ministers, preaching their own personal brand of creed and ethics) and are not as well-educated as those who possess college and/or postgraduate degrees (in short, are not too learned in moral theology). Not trained in classical ethics, theological, or philosophical courses, they offer nothing with any authority, and rather than education from the pulpit there issues forth either a "Bible-thumping" literal interpretation of Sacred Writ or a brand of specious entertainment with a gloss of Christian ethics, the "Do good and avoid evil" sort of thing, which is about as effective as a small child engaged in fisticuffs with a professional prizefighter. This is said, not to contemn any or all of the valor and stamina (even heroism) which many of these clerics display, particularly in the inner cities, but simply to state fact. Truthfully, apart from the Roman Church (perhaps the more strict and rigid Mormon, Lutheran, Methodist, Episcopalian, Presbyterian,, and Orthodox Churches as well), there appears to be little or no codification of either ethics or morals in ecclesiastical dogmas or preachments in most of America's churches. True, the flamboyant preachers of hellfire and brimstone flash across the TV screen or whoop it up on the sawdust trail, complemented with gorgeously robed choirs of trained voices, guitar-playing artists, contralto gospel singers, stentorian preaching largely void of both dogma and morals, really ecclesiastically entertaining, but, in all truth, if there is an attempt at sermonizing, the individualized interpretation of Holy Scripture and the Commandments defines anyone's personal judgment and establishment of moral conduct to be equal to any other's. In one situation can be found extreme rigor; in another, extreme laxity. Succinctly, there may be as many moral standards as there are preachers!

Synagogues, too, are in default of more rigid moral education of their attendees. The problem is the same as elsewhere: There lurks a latent fear of "offending," with the possibility of dooming both the rabbi and the synagogue proper. Conscience-probing sermons can give rise to a determined board meeting which decides that the current rabbi can be replaced quite easily at the end of his term or contract with one more amenable to the whims and fancies of the contributing congregation. Despite the dogmatism of the Torah and the ancient teachings of the *tzaddikim*, a great deal of individualized interpretation by the congregation enters into personal adherences, much to the horror of zealous rabbis. What applies here can also be said of many Christian churches. Thus it becomes evident that the simplistic "Do good and avoid evil" syndrome makes up the sum and substance of public moral preachments. Not much there, of course!

Since the Ten Commandments have lost an enormous amount of their cogency and divinely mandated rigidity in a "situation ethics" society, and the resultant humanism has become less effective because of its powerlessness in remedying the foibles of human nature and its inherent selfishness and greed, very little authority abides in what had been seriously considered as God-given injunctions. Whatever remains of present-day morality is summarily dismissed with "Everything begins with me and ends with me, and the devil take the hindmost." The blame for the lack of this cogency in the mind of the ordinary man can be laid at the feet of personal interpretation and the dislike of dictatorial sermonization. Even though an individual is, truthfully, the "captain of his own soul," ultimately responsible for the conduct of his everyday life and final glorification, the perils of Scylla and Charybdis can be avoided by proper piloting, and seldom is that ordinary individual, ignoring the guidance and tutelage of someone wiser than he, capable of determining a sea lane conducive to calm and peaceful sailing through life. Perhaps a simpler parable would be: "The man who has himself for a doctor has a fool for a doctor." And it is a fool who either lacks or does not desire personal integrity.

What is needed, then, is an ingraining of a sincere desire to be a whole person, and this can begin only by living according to fixed codes of conduct, be they the Ten Commandments, the Torah, the precepts of Buddha, the axioms of Confucius, the obligations of the Koran, or even the magnificent Code of Hammurabi. There is enormous affinity between all codes of conduct, which have perdured for millennia, for all of them are based on what we commonly term "natural law" (or divinely revealed laws, for the believing Muslim, Jew, and Christian), and all of them contain not only moral dictates—over and above their dogmatic canons—but also universal sanctions. The deliberate ignoring of these sanctions in all codes has as its consequence some sort of punishment, either temporary or eternal. Even society's laws must be based ultimately on those natural laws, *or else they are no laws at all*. This fact is very evident in the deism manifested within Jefferson's (and America's) Declaration of Independence.

Strangely, even these sanctions, this "force," is not enough, for man insists on filling penitentiaries and prisons. Is it possible that the current sanctions provided by national or federal/state laws are insufficient for crimes committed?

Here, then, is the dilemma: stronger sanctions can become Hitlerian. Present sanctions are insufficient.

A rigorous codification of national or federal/state laws, or an unremitting use of force, can ultimately lead to wholesale, totally destructive anarchy, and will in no way be the "ultimate solution." If the penitentiaries are already overloaded, if more are necessary, and if there appears to be no end to the corruption of morals in this country—or western civilization, for that matter—the "conversion" of a corrupt man to a man of personal integrity can flow only from a constant ongoing pressure from moral leaders, impeccable in their example (a sad commentary on some national figures, indeed!), as intense as John the Baptist in their decrying of corruption and vice, and unremitting in their pursuit of individual personal dignity.

Moral leaders are not only to be expected in the pulpit. They are also necessary in the city hall, the state legislature, and the Capitol in Washington, D.C. It becomes, then, the obligation of the ordinary concerned citizen to make sure that local, state, and national elections result in those types of moral leaders. The lethargy and disinterest of the average voter is a national disgrace. Consequently, it behooves those who desire alleviation of moral leprosy in the country to be more aggressive in their demands for leading men and women to be as wholesome politically as they are personally.

The same must be said for those involved in entertainment of the masses. Young impressionable people look to them as exemplars. Many of them lead lives of scandalous proportion, and, sad to say, it is only "hype" which makes them recognizable as entertainers or singers. Being extroverts and eccentrics, they pose a "rebellion" against most establishments, appealing to young and shallow-minded people struggling to gain a foothold on the threshold of intelligent and responsible adulthood, totally incapable of ascertaining that, as brilliant as some of those "stars" appear to be, they are, in a young person's lifetime, only fragmental meteorites flashing across the heavens, ultimately disappearing in the black void of forgetfulness. But there is no bigger rebel than a young rebel. (If there is an adult who would deny this, then it would profit him to look within himself at a much younger age!)

In conclusion, rather than stronger action or literal force, there must be instilled in the ordinary citizen an avid desire to be integral, wholesome, proud enough of himself to be *self-disciplined*, and to carry himself with a *dignity* which befits his humanity. Anything less marks him as living just a little above the beast, which cannot rationalize and whose existence depends upon eating or being eaten. "That jungle out there" is man-made and it can be extirpated only by people of personal integrity.

If only the minds of those whose personal integrity has deteriorated can realize that they are as responsible for the state of the commonwealth as those who really care and strive, what a different and very desirable society would be effected for the majority of people!

But for now, how true are the frightening words of Walt Kelly's immortal Pogo: "We have met the enemy, and they is us."

Biographical Sketch of William T. Sayre-Smith

Born in Portland, Oregon, Dr. Sayre-Smith completed junior and senior high school in San Diego, California. In 1932, he completed 2.5 years of engineering (all that was available at that time) at San Diego University. In 1934, he graduated in Marine Electrical Engineering from the California Maritime Academy. The course included a circumnavigation of South America, and a circumnavigation of the globe (South America, Asia, Africa, Europe.

In 1941, he graduated in Dental Surgery from the University of Southern California, where he completed two terms as an instructor in Oral Surgery. He retired after completing 43 years' practice in general dentistry in San Diego. He also served as a Major in the U.S. Army, 1953–1955, at the European Headquarters Command, Heidelberg, Germany, in charge of the Army Dental Clinic or as a member of the clinic staff.

A widower, he has three grown children: a son, who is a dentist in Salem, Oregon; and twin daughters in Main Line, Philadelphia, one a teacher, the other an R.N. He has five grandchildren.

Among his many avocational interests, he has just completed 14 years with senior orchestras, as instrumentalist, vocalist, and conductor. He has been a lifelong student of the Austrian School of Von Mises, Rothbard, and Hayek on monetary, economic, and individual freedom problems.

CHAPTER 27

AN ALTERNATIVE TO FINANCIAL BREAKDOWN

Dr. William T. Sayre-Smith

Present inflation rates signal approaching worthless dollars. Students of economics know that inflation in the last gasp increases exponentially. The "crack-up boom" of von Mises then goes into the black market, the illegal but nonetheless resurgent free-enterprise system of barter in coffee, cigarettes, gold, silver, etc. The question for those of us most bitter in our criticism of power- and wealth-seeking in this vote-buying inflationary system is, "Do we find available a superior and concrete alternative?"

The present fractional-reserve worldwide monetary system has grown, like Topsy, with many assists from those who stood to gain under politically contrived monopoly conditions. Historically, goldsmith bankers centuries ago found that only a small percentage of depositors came to claim the actual metal so long as bank receipts could be used, and with less problems of robbery and carrying heavy gold. Gradually the temptation to put out fractional-reserve paper-money receipts became great, when the slight risk of bank runs could be neutralized by agreements to cover for one another in emergencies. Watering the currency by fractional-reserve techniques was heady wine, and gave bankers great profit plus great leverage in providing vote-buying money for their political protectors (who conveniently allowed the dishonest practice to remain legal long enough to gain tacit acceptance and the title of "traditional".)

Any practice that becomes traditional is most difficult to dislodge, however dishonest. And if you do not think this fractional-reserve practice dishonest, try justifying a loan from a friend of $1000, for which you put up $1500 in alleged collateral that turns out to be worth only $150 when he has to resort to foreclosure.

Free Enterprisers have learned the hard way that, because there are so many unknowns, the cogitations of bureaucrats, braintrusters, intelligentsia, etc. (even with our increasing governmental control strictures) *do not* produce the answers. This is why rapid trial-and-error testing in an absolutely Free Market economy is the top priority for solving today's urgent problems. Since the recurrent inflations, credit restrictions, etc., with consequent bankrupting of millions has been the ever-repeated fate of controlled monetary systems, it might just be time to examine those cases where the record of totally free banking is still available.

In China over a century ago, paper money was issued by private persons, M. le Comte de Rochechouart reported. "Notwithstanding it is no legal tender, it is everywhere accepted, and seldom [do] . . . bills issued by some bank or other circulate at a discount."[1]

Herbert Spencer reported in 1850:

> There has existed in Scotland for nearly two centuries a wholly uncontrolled system; a completely tradefree currency. And what have been the results? Scotland has had the advantage, both in security and economy. The gain in security is proven by the fact that the proportion of bank failures in Scotland has been less than in England. Though by LAW there has never been any restriction against ANYONE issuing notes in Scotland; yet, in *practice*, it has ever been impossible for any unsound or unsafe paper to attain currency.[2]

Now, what makes a currency "unsound"? The acceptance of the "traditional" but still dishonest fractional-reserve backing for paper money (on another and smaller scale, nearly worthless metal in the coinage). Now, of course, we really do not have even a fractional-reserve currency, since the gold window was shut, and silver redemption also eliminated from paper money. Of course, in addition to the faith, hope, and charity that keeps us trading in our money is the subconscious knowledge that the government has a supply of gold in Fort Knox which hopefully will one day be used to back our paper.

With Olympian statements that entertain no dissent, we are told that only central banking is feasible under modern conditions. Again, historically our Federal Reserve Bill was passed December 23, 1913—twenty pages of fine print, and most of the Congress on a holiday. (This system was supposed, with more and more power acquisitions, to stabilize the economy by regulating the money supply and the prime interest rates.)

As Al Smith used to say, "Let's look at the record." Following the First World War, more than 40 percent of the farms in just one state, Missouri, for example, were taken over by foreclosures on mortgages.

Then, with even more power in 1929, the Fed again tightened up, and removed ⅙ of the credit in the country in four months. We all know what happened, but to eliminate any doubt, the Fed removed another ⅙ of the credit over the next three years.[3] (And who let the credit get out of hand to begin with?) With an alphabet of bureaucratic control in all phases of the economy on top of this credit restriction (plus forbidding the citizen to hold his usual hedge, gold), it took tooling up for the Second World War to artificially perk up business. Perhaps, with 78 plus years of this type of "modern" banking controls, we should see if there isn't a better alternative?

The answer appears to be to restore banking as a completely free enterprise, with the only function of government to see that it is completely honest; i.e., *no fractional reserves*, and the back-up assets to be there upon demand as is required of insurance companies.

Now the immediate argument of those wishing to protect their monopoly is: "Under 100-percent-reserve banking, there won't be enough money to service the demand in an ever-increasing and expanding world economy." This is poppycock. Even using only gold, in an absolutely free market, any amount of business could be done. The price of gold would naturally soar, reflecting high demand.

But back to the alternatives. No one disputes the ability of the "free port" economies to operate under many monetary systems. In Hong Kong you can convert, exchange, and buy instantly in almost any currency; the clerks have conversion tables adjusted daily to supply and demand. Also, even before computers, stock-market listings have been available daily on thousands of stocks; so daily conversion tables of many monies competing in a free market presents no great problem.

The next problem is: what is to provide sufficient capitalization for the world trade on a 100-percent-reserve basis if gold producers are not favored with a uni-metal currency backing? Here is a start.

1. Real estate. Fully convertible, fractional "on demand" shares of actual land. Don't say the fractional shares could not be in small denominations: how about 4-by-6 burial plots in the Mojave desert?
2. Tobacco Warehouse Receipts. Again in fractional shares of actual tobacco in storage warehouses and again available on demand.
3. Oil in storage. Petroleum, edible, etc., bbls and fractional bbls available on demand, the only government function being to see that the oil is as represented and actually stored in the tanks stated.

4. Grains in storage. Fractional shares of actual stored grains (wheat, oats, rye, corn, soybeans, etc.) and available on demand.

5. Distilled spirits. Fractional amounts of whiskey, gin, vodka, rum, brandy, etc., again avilable on demand, possibly with claimant age restrictions; i.e., none given out to children. Beer and wine could also be huge sources of capitalization.

6. Inventories of autos, furniture, canned goods, hoola hoops, or what have you. Again shares on a fractional basis and available on demand.

7. All metals, gold to lead, available in the fractional part represented by the currency and on demand.

8. Fractional shares of buildings, boats, chemicals, fibers, anything that people would be willing to hold shares of as having real value in their eyes under the law of supply and demand.

The list is endless; so no fear need be entertained of lack of capitalization. Those with confidence in free enterprise predict that no one can forsee what high standards of living the future can hold.

NOTES

1. *Innovator*, Los Angeles 1967, p. 30.
2. Herbert Spencer, 1850, *Social Statics*, p. 356.
3. U.S. Gov't. Printing Office, *Primer On Money*, July 1964, p. 100.

Autobiographical Sketch of Evelyn Eastwood

Art has been my chief interest since childhood, but pursuing it has taken me in some unexpected directions. They have not always been enjoyable, but at least never boring.

My education was fragmented by circumstance. Early travel gave me an idea of pre-World-War-I Europe, and in the 1920s a good view of the United States and its surroundings in a time when it took five days by fast train to cross the continent. The Golden Gate had not yet been bridged.

By 1930 I had married another art student and was living in New York. I have never lost the feeling of excitement and wonder that the city gave me, even though the Great Depression soon overtook us—my husband freelancing, I eventually found employment in social work that lasted eleven years. It gave me invaluable experience, however grungy, of the downside of city life in all the boroughs.

Meanwhile, we continued to take part in the art scene, and to share other rich experiences too numerous to mention. New York was filled with a variety of refugees of all persuasions. We went through the "phony war" that began in Spain, went through the disaster of the Maginot Line and uncertain treaties, and culminated in Pearl Harbor.

World War II was winding down when we left the city after fifteen years, having decided it was too hectic for us. Cape Cod was still rural, a complete change; it took a while to adjust. We "went native" and took whatever jobs were offered, my husband eventually going to sea for a few trips until his health failed. I ended up as a secretary. We had started making nautical crafts, which I continued for a while after I was widowed in 1957.

Since then, I have exhibited my husband's paintings, together with my own. We are represented in many private collections, as well as at the Cape Museum of Fine Arts. My secondary interest, writing, has been useful as an adjunct to my other work.

At 85 I am still learning. Information now is much more accessible, and there are many fields that lack of time and energy will never let me explore. Maybe in the next life.

CHAPTER 28

LETTER TO SOMEONE OF ANOTHER COUNTRY

Hyannis, MA
April 19, 1992

Dear Friend:

This morning, foghorns are blasting through a thick mist, a sound that worries seamen everywhere. Today is a Massachusetts holiday which commemorates the actual start of the American Revolution at Lexington and Concord—"Here once the embattled farmers stood / and fired the shot heard 'round the world." As children we learned the words, but only lately have I really thought about what underlies the business-as-usual attitude that prevails on our holidays.

We take history for granted—trite words on a printed page—an impression of people in wigs and funny clothes acting in events that began the United States as we know it. The meaning of patriotism is ignored until our own generation is challenged. Suddenly it falls into place: we are faced with potentially tragic choices that will, either way, disrupt our world.

Living in New England, one is apt to dwell on these matters. Each region has its heroes—here, "Mad Jack" Percival, who sailed the U.S.S. Constitution around the world; James Otis, whose brilliant oratory spurred the Revolution until a severe beating by thugs of the opposition cut it short; and many more, linked with all the other colonies that braved the King's forces and risked all they had.

What, then, of patriotism? When my parents came to this country they learned English (going to night school after working a twelve-hour day) and became citizens as soon as possible, because they realized that America meant greater opportunity for them and their children than the monarchy they had left. We children, having been born here, were thoroughly American, and thought of our parents country as something remote and slightly amusing. At school we learned the usual patriotic poems and songs that gave a simplified view of history, and didn't think too much about it.

Is patriotism in need of new interpretations? How much is true love of country, how much indoctrination, and how much the hysteria of the moment? Once, having lived elsewhere for a while, returning to my home state, I traveled toward Plymouth and was suddenly moved to sing, "I love thy rocks and rills / thy woods and templed hills" even though the countryside was fairly monotonous. Sentimental as it seems, the feeling was genuine; I could understand people who kiss the soil when returning to their native lands, or shed tears on seeing the flag of their country when abroad. At such times one can see why they would defend it against all comers.

Most often, though, the United States has gone abroad to defend its borders; therefore it is not the land itself so much as the ideas it embodies. There have been people who have felt we should not become involved in foreign affairs. They had the courage to disagree; but when faced with aggression toward our allies, as in the two World Wars, there was a vast majority who put forth every effort and, at fearful cost, prevailed. Our resources and energy turned the tide, and in the long run something was gained: the United Nations might not exist if the League of Nations had not paved the way.

Now we are undergoing a more doubtful time. Korea, Viet Nam, and the Persian Gulf led us to question the motives of our leaders, and we realize that wars can be fought mainly for commercial purposes. Is this enough reason for millions of people to be killed and maimed? And what of the devastation caused by wars on friend and enemy alike? Isn't war a stupid waste of the natural resources that we are trying to conserve? It would be far better to regain our national pride by leadership in diplomacy, to see the future beyond the next election, or the next century. True patriots should try to keep their country out of war by diplomatic action, so that the world can prosper. It would mean long, slow work—infinite patience and, above all, unity and consistency—before we could reach our goal. Governments and alliances may change, but if enough people all over the globe work at it, eventually we should be able to do it. We can still love the place of our birth, but wouldn't it be great to say, "I am a citizen of the world, and the world is open to me"? It's worth trying.

The fog seems to be lifting. A fair day, after all. All the best to you!

Sincerely,
Evelyn Eastwood

Autobiographical Sketch of Yale Jay Lubkin

I was born despite two contraceptives and an abortion try. People are still trying. In 1972, the top physicians in Israel insisted that I had a brain tumor and would be dead in six months without exploratory surgery—with a 50% survival probability. I escaped in my hospital gown. The chief surgeon was dead in six months. In 1984, an intelligence service tried to murder me so that a friend of the Defense Minister could claim credit for my work. He got my award, but I survived. The KGB murder technique doesn't always work.

I acquired a B.A., two M.S.'s, and a Ph.D. in E.E. and Math. My first M.S., from MIT, was followed by a dean's letter which said that I had a good record but would not be welcomed back—I wrote a lousy review of his course and book. His was much worse than the undergraduate course at Penn.

I wound up as an USAR Colonel, despite six tries to throw me out for not playing the game. They did succeed in keeping me from being a General. I was overweight. Kiss of death: a fat butt instead of a fat head.

I have invented all my life. The most important was the system used to prevent unauthorized arming of American and Soviet nuclear weapons. It is called the Permissive Action Link. It has never failed. I also started the Israeli miniRPV (Remotely Piloted Aircraft) industry in the early '70s despite bitter opposition from the head of the Israeli Air Force.

CHAPTER 29

THE AMERICAN STEAL ETHIC

Yale Jay Lubkin

The Japanese are right, of course. American management is incompetent. That's why there is so much screaming from the Lee Iacoccas of American industry, so much smoke, mirrors, and tapping into the Treasury rather than development and production of good products that people want to buy.

It is better to build than to steal. That is the basis of the Japanese and German economies. It used to be the basis of ours. Most of the world does not believe in it, and most of the world is stuck in endless poverty as a result. Even Israel, which has the highest per-capita concentration of technical talent in the world, believes in theft rather than work. Soviet emigrés speak about Israel's system as the closest thing to the Soviet that they have encountered. So the best and brightest, by the hundreds of thousands, have left Israel for countries where they can work and keep most of the fruits of their labor.

There are many industries, such as television, tape recorders, automobiles, blue jeans, computers, cameras and film, and digital watches, which were started in America, but which are dying or dead here. Why?

In Japan and in Germany, most manufacturers are headed by engineers. In Japan, some 80 percent of higher management are engineers. Engineers are motivated to build better products. American management has no such motivation. The per-capita number of lawyers in Japan is a twentieth of ours, and the number of bean counters is about a hundredth. There are no business schools in Japan. In Germany, inventors get a piece of the pie, even if they work for a company and invent on the company's time and resources—so they invent.

In America, only a few companies, such as Hewlett Packard, are run by engineers. Most are run by salesmen, bean counters, or lawyers, who

243

have a penchant for taking prosperous industries and running them into the ground. General Motors achieved greatness under Charles Kettering, an engineer. Years of domination by business types have resulted in lousy cars, loss of market domination and consumer trust, and major plant closings. Chrysler used to use left-hand bolts to fasten the left-side wheels, so that driving shocks wouldn't cause the bolts to loosen and the wheels to fall off. They used to put springs around the brake hoses, where the rubber tubing meets the metal hose ends. This made the brake hoses last for the life of the car. But both were discontinued, because they added a few cents to the price of a car and apparently nothing to immediate car sales.

Archetypical of the American industry mindset is the naming of John Sculley as CEO of Apple Computer. What is Sculley's computer expertise? He used to be a top Pepsi Cola salesman. Most people buy IBM clones, which are made in a highly competitive market, and which typically offer twice the value for dollars as do Apple products, which are made in an environment which excludes competition.

It is typical of the Japanese to continually update their products and come out with new products as soon as they can. In America, the ideal is to stall new product introduction until everything possible has been milked from the old. Heaven forfend that American industry should ever pay license fees for inventions. Paying for ideas runs counter to all the instincts of an MBA. So new products are not introduced until their patent protection runs out, which could take 17 years.

There is an American corporate mindset against ideas from outside the company. A few companies, such as Pratt and Whitney or Teledyne, will sign nondisclosure agreements. Many companies, such as Polaroid, will not consider any outside ideas at all. Other companies, such as GE and Northrop, seem to consider inventors to be beggars, who should be happy with a crumb. A few years back I was asked to solve a problem that GE engineers had unsuccessfully contended with all century—how to measure turbine blade-tip clearances. I came up with an elegant solution, and sent a Confidential Disclosure to a GE engineer in Cincinnati. A month later, I got a letter from some weenie at GE Headquarters in Stamford. According to their policy, I had two options. I could donate my idea to GE, or I could accept their valuation on what it was worth, but in no case more than $5,000. I told them to stuff it.

GE is comparatively benign for an American company. The case of Henry Deimehl is more typical. Some time in the 1950s, Deimehl invented the flight simulator. Being a naive soul, he went to Link Trainer with his ideas, because they were the leading people in the business.

According to Deimehl, Link stalled him while they wrote patent disclosures and filed for their own patents. Then they told him to get lost. Deimehl could not possibly buy the legal results that Link could, so he sold his invention to Curtiss-Wright, who had a few hundred million in cash lying around. Curtiss picked up the legal fight, which lasted for years, cost Curtiss about $5 million, and ended in a draw. My patent lawyer made enough in consulting fees to move from a shabby lower-class neighborhood on Long Island's south shore to a fancy house in Scarsdale.

The Japanese worry about satisfying their customers. The American businessman worries about extracting the maximum amount of money in the shortest time. I came across a beautiful example of this recently. I publish a newsletter, *Technical Innovations*, and was very impressed by an ad I saw for a component to replace fuses. It is called PolySwitch, and is made by Raychem. Instead of blowing, like a fuse, and having to be replaced, it opens its electrical circuit when the current demand gets too high and closes it again when the demand drops. It is like a self-healing fuse.

I had some complaints about my old Epson LQ-800 computer printer. The fuse blows at random times, for no apparent reason. There is no external fuse holder. You have to take the printer apart to get at the fuse. The fuse is a non-American standard, and hard to find. Radio Shack doesn't carry it. So I had to solder leads to American fuses and to the dead Japanese fuse, and make a Rube Goldberg adaptation.

Raychem jumped on the opportunity to make a sales call on Epson in Japan. The Japanese were very disturbed. They called Raychem in California, who called me, to find out what model printer I had and what computer it was connected to.

Raychem is a jewel of an example for American companies to follow. Their salesmen are mostly engineers, and they solve customers' problems with products like heat-shrink tubing, PolySwitch, fiberoptic connectors, and other products of enlightened materials technology. They sell over a billion dollars a year by solving problems for customers—not bad for a company the public has never heard of.

The Epson people worry about their products forever. American companies? I recently had a problem with Microsoft's DOS 5 program. The problem was due to a poorly written manual. When I called up Technical Support, I was informed that my free support had expired two days before, and that I would have to dial a 900 number and pay $2 a minute for their sloppiness. It took a letter to Bill Gates, CEO, to get a sort of answer to my technical problem—but by then I had switched over to a competitive system, Digital Research's DR DOS 6. Microsoft has an industry-wide reputation for ascribing all problems with their software to your hardware. Sometimes it's true. Mostly it's not.

Incidentally, I sent a flyer on *Technical Innovations* to the CEOs of the Fortune 100. I suspect that nearly all ended in the circular file, being unable to penetrate the barriers against outside ideas that American management surrounds itself with. I got exactly one reply—from Mattell, the toymaker. They said that they had put my flyer in a sealed envelope, and the envelope in a sealed file cabinet, and that I could be assured that no one at Mattell would ever read it.

Harvard recently closed its Operations Research department. In an editorial supporting this, the *Washington Times* proclaimed its ignorance of the subject: "operations research (whatever that is)." Operations research is the study of how to do what you want to do so that you get the results you want. It grew out of Navy operations in the Second World War. The original problem was how to use a limited number of airplanes to spot the maximum number of Nazi submarines.

Obviously, Harvard doesn't care whether or not they accomplish what they want to do, and the *Times* doesn't even know whether it is possible. The lesson is that the Japanese engineers know all about operations research, and that the bean counters who run American industry know nothing and are proud of it.

How many MBAs does it take to change a light bulb? Two—one to hold the bulb, and one to hammer it in.

Biographical Sketch of James Vanderhoof

I was the firstborn of three babies, April 8, 1949. My survival was unusual, since I was an identical triplet, six weeks premature. My two brothers, David and Sam, were not so lucky. The doctors at the hospital overdosed them on oxygen, and this caused severe brain damage and blindness.

After the first five years, my good parents, a scholarly Spinoza expert and his wife, decided to put poor David and Sam in a California state hospital, where my two brothers remain today, oblivious of the outer world.

From an early age I was concerned about social, political, and environmental problems, especially overpopulation. British author C. S. Lewis was my favorite childhood author, and his Narnia series influenced my early spiritual and moral development.

I went to boarding school (an unforgettable experience) in southern England, and returned to the U.S.A. in 1963. My senior year in high school I studied the New Testament in the original Greek, and won first place in track.

In 1967, I was deeply inspired by the universal classic *Autobiography of a Yogi*, by Paramahansa Yogananda, whom I consider to be the greatest and most spiritual American. My unconventional economic philosophy and ideas are influenced by Dr. Ravi Batra, and Sam Pizzigati, the labor journalist whose new book, *The Maximum Wage*, is a real jewel.

CHAPTER 30

MY BEST IDEAS (HOPEFULLY) FOR THE ADVANCEMENT OF CIVILIZATION

James Vanderhoof

Civilization can mean many different things to different people, places, and eras. Implicit in any desire for the advancement of civilization is the assumption that (1) civilization actually can change for the better, and (2) civilization, although far from perfect, is still a good thing, certainly preferable to barbarism, anarchy, or chaos.

As a boy I enjoyed reading books about Greek mythology. According to the ancient Greek legends the Earth was once a sort of primordial chaos, until the gods transformed it into a cosmos, or order. Cosmos, like civilization, implies an order with laws, and a certain degree of predictability.

One example of these laws at work is the Earth spinning in its orbit around the Sun. It will take billions of years for the second law of thermodynamics (entropy or the degree of disorder, which always increases in a closed system, something people with closed minds should think about!) to slow the Earth down in either its orbital or its axial momentum so much that it interferes with the functioning of life on Earth.

Alien civilizations, perhaps far more advanced and benign than anything we humans have yet achieved on Earth, may very well exist on other planets of the Galaxy and cosmos. It would be very presumptuous and arrogant for us humans to assume that we are the only form of intelligent life in the universe.

So it is important to realize that we are speaking only of human civilization, the only one we are familiar with. It is our own civilization that we want to improve. Hopefully, advancements in human civilization will ameliorate the most deplorable human condition.

I do not think that we are permanently stuck in some sort of evolutionary dead end. It is more likely that humanity is in a cocoon stage, and about to undergo some type of metamorphosis, awakening, or enlightenment, both individually and as a society, collectively.

A nightmare, by definition, cannot go on forever. Human history is very much like a dream, interspersed with good dreams and nightmares. Human civilizations which become too nightmarish, tyrannical, unjust, unbalanced, or dysfunctional are sooner or later replaced by other civilizations, with different priorities and different values.

There have been certain obvious advancements, of course, mostly in the sciences, in communications technology and computers, and in medicine. Life expectancy has increased significantly, although this trend may be reversed if we fail to do something sensible about human overpopulation.

I am 43 years old, and in my relatively short lifetime world population has more than doubled, from about 2.5 billion in 1950 to more than 5.3 billion today. The leaders of society need to encourage all couples to have no more than two children per family, and preferably only one. Financial and other incentives should be offered to those who have fewer children. Quality is always better than quantity, and we need to apply this principle to the population explosion, before it is too late.

Even if only 25 percent of humanity had children from now on, there would still be no danger of the human race disappearing. The threat is human overpopulation, not underpopulation. If three-quarters of the human race made the conscious choice to have fewer children, the future of the species would look much brighter than it does today.

Only in this century has humanity become numerous enough to really challenge the balance of nature and threaten to ruin the ecology and life-support system of the planet. A future development may well be a significant decline in the oxygen content of the atmosphere, if humanity continues to burn fossil fuels and destroys too much of the forests and other flora that produce oxygen. Humanity, including human civilization, is a *part of nature*, not separate from it, and is dependent on nature.

Mahatma Gandhi (1867–1948), the nonviolent liberator of modern India, when asked what he thought of western civilization, replied humorously: "It would be a very good idea." As well as being a great soul, Gandhi was a great lawyer (not all lawyers are unethical) with a very perceptive legal mind. He once said, "Truth never damages a cause that is just."

It is the so-called advanced western civilization which has created the most pollution and environmental damage on the Earth today. Now, with the ozone layer being depleted at an alarming rate, we face the possibility of a truly global catastrophe; that is, we face the consequences of our own actions. Humanity seems to have become its own worst enemy.

I love good science-fiction books and films, but only in science-fiction stories can we relocate humans from an overpopulated Earth to habitable planets in other solar systems. Science fiction is a wonderful and much underappreciated genre of writing. The *Outer Limits* and *Star Trek* television series provide much food for thought, about who we are and where we are going, and why, and what choices we have.

It is essential to ask these sorts of philosophical and spiritual questions, rather than act like ostriches out of a misguided sense of so-called practicality. Actually, people who refuse to think about the sometimes difficult ethical, spiritual, and philosophical questions are, in my view, the most impractical of all.

If we were truly civilized, we wouldn't tolerate having about 80 percent of the American people crowded together like sardines in dirty cities that comprise only 2 percent of the land. Around the turn of this century more people lived in rural areas than in urban. They lived on relatively small family farms, and had a hard-working, simple, and wholesome lifestyle. This has all changed during this century.

The chief purpose of America, or of any nation, for that matter, cannot be merely to enable a few plutocrats to become fabulously rich and dominant, mostly from the labors and sacrifices of others. Humans who have great wealth, but who are also very miserly and ungenerous, should be assigned a low status (like that of criminals) in the social pecking order, not an exalted one (as is now the case).

Money alone is not enough. Wisdom, love, and other good psychological and spiritual qualities are needed to create a healthy society and stable civilization. Money itself, although sometimes described as the root of all evil, is probably neutral, neither good nor evil. Morality depends entirely on how the money is used, and who has it. Money in the hands of ethical, intelligent, and wise people can do a great deal of good.

A society or culture tends to be either more Promethean—that is, life-giving and courageously original—or more Procrustean—that is, enforcing conformity to a harshly arbitrary and preconceived idea or system, often by the use of physical torture, or the threat of it, and also by brainwashing and propaganda. Nazism and most fascistic movements are examples of Procrustean political, social, and economic philosophies at work.

I think there needs to be a movement of people out of the cities, back to smaller communities and family farms. We should have some sort of kibbutz movement (similar to the highly successful Israeli kibbutzim). This would solve some of the overcrowding, homelessness, and despair that is the root cause of much of the escalating violence and substance abuse in our urban areas. A well-financed and well-planned kibbutz movement in America would be much more cost-effective than simply warehousing people in prisons.

We obviously need some major economic reforms, such as those outlined by Dr. Ravi Batra in his new book *The Downfall of Capitalism & Communism: Can Capitalism be Saved?* (Venus Books, 1990). A maximum wage, as well as a minimum wage, needs to be made law.

In his delightful new book, *The Maximum Wage* (Apex Press, 1992), labor journalist Sam Pizzigati proposes a Ten Times Rule, which would effectively set the maximum wage at ten times the minimum wage, and give a tax cut to 99 percent of Americans, and a very big tax increase to the richest 1 percent. This idea is apparently too radical for our politicians to even think about, although the logic of Mr. Pizzigati's argument seems flawless.

Mr. Pizzigati cites (p. 80) two of the most highly respected ancient philosophers in support of his proposals: "Plato in *The Laws*, for instance, pronounced the ideal ratio between the wealth of the richest and the wealth of the poorest to be four to one. For Aristotle, the appropriate ratio was five to one."

I am not saying that hard work should be punished, and laziness rewarded; some who are rich have worked very hard for their success. The issue, rather, is whether one individual's labor should be considered hundreds, or even thousands, of times more valuable than the labor of another, less-privileged individual. I must agree with Plato and Aristotle, especially after observing the devastation caused by white-collar criminals such as Michael Milken, America's "junk bond king," who "earned" $500 million in 1988.

Still, it appears that whenever there is great darkness or evil in a particular society or nation, there are also very powerful forces of good,

---

[1]This was true in Nazi Germany. During that period Germany had one of history's greatest mystics living in a small village (so small that I have yet to find it on any map of Germany) in Bavaria. I am referring, of course, to Therese Neumann (1898–1962). She was a truly Promethean figure, but very humble, and thought of herself as just an ordinary, normal human being. She was Catholic, and lived for over 35 years on "God's light" (i.e., the saint lived without eating or drinking water; feeling no hunger or thirst). She was closely watched by her parents, brothers, sisters, and many friends. She did not live alone, but in her parent's house, and could not possibly have raided the pantry secretly at night without being noticed.

or light, to act as a counterbalance.[1] In the real world, almost right under our noses, some very unusual events have happened during the past 200 years. Some of these events had to do with various saints, mystics, and yogis. Most scientists and skeptics feel very uncomfortable about these phenomena, because they have a religious aura about them. However, we need to remember that many scientists have been spiritually adventurous. Albert Einstein wrote, "The cosmic religious experience is the strongest and noblest driving force behind scientific research."

Einstein, incidentally, was not a supporter of the status quo in America. He once wrote an essay called "Why Socialism? (*Monthly Review*, New York, May 1949). Especially poignant and relevant are Einstein's words here: "This crippling of individuals I consider the worst evil of capitalism. Our whole educational system suffers from this evil. An exaggerated competitive attitude is inculcated into the student, who is trained to worship acquisitive success as a preparation for his future career." And, of course, Einstein was also an ardent admirer of Gandhi, something our culture has conveniently forgotten. It seems rather hypocritical for modern America to thank Einstein for helping America become a superpower (by his discovery of how to make atomic bombs), but never to heed any of his sage advice on social or spiritual issues.

Another major problem of modern civilization is the proliferation of automobiles. I have never owned a car myself. I think there are far too many autos, and they are very inefficient and noisy polluters of the environment. We should learn to carpool more often, and I am, of course, in favor of an increase in the gasoline tax. After all, the Europeans pay $2 or more a gallon in gas tax, and have found the results to be very beneficial.

There are viable alternative forms of transportation. Riding a bicycle, for example, is a good form of exercise. The Dutch ride bicycles on bike paths that go almost everywhere, and are famous for their longevity despite their fattening diet.

Another possibility is steam. At the beginning of the twentieth century, the Stanley twins invented their Stanley steamcars, which outperformed all other types of automobiles. Steamcar technology is something that we should revive, and it would greatly improve the efficiency of our transportation system, which is clearly out of balance.

There is plenty of real work, not bureaucratic busy-work, to be done in America today, work that will advance true civilization, and make life more pleasant and more fair for all of us. Management (the brains) and labor (the heart) are both needed, and ought to work in harmony, instead of being constantly at odds. I do, however, tend to side with labor in most disputes, since much of the top management of the big corporations in America has been particularly lacking in imagination and creativity, being concerned only with profits.

We belong to the Earth; the Earth does not belong to us. We are supposed to be temporary caretakers, not owners, of the planet. The greedy and acquisitive stage of development on Earth is almost finished. We are seeing the death throes of many obsolete worldviews based on serious misconceptions about the nature of humans, the Earth, God, and the universe. Humans are *social* creatures, not independent, individualistic entities. Cooperation and mutual aid, or symbiosis, rather than ruthless competition (read Alfie Cohn's great book, *No Contest: The Case Against Competition*), should be encouraged in our society.

In the spiritual realm we need to discard obsolete ideas of God, ideas which do not help us improve the human condition, and which contradict the concept of a Supreme Being whose nature is Infinite Love. If God is Love, as is said in the *First Epistle of John*, and if God is also infinite, the putting the two terms "infinite" and "love" together gives use a positive and logically valid concept of God. If we humans are made in the image of this loving creator, then we can reflect a portion of this Infinite Love if we choose to do so.

The fact is that we are all going to die, or "meet our Maker," sooner or later. This is nothing to be afraid of, but something quite natural. Since death happens to every living thing, it cannot possibly be a punishment. Probably death is simply a door through which we pass into a higher dimension, one closer to the absolute perfection of a God of Infinite Love. The great German writer Goethe (1749–1832) once wrote: "Life is the childhood of our immortality."

It is so foolish to try to limit reality to merely one or two dimensions, or to assume that this universe is an entirely closed system, and therefore subject to inexorable laws of entropy, chaos, and disintegration. Reality, like God, is unlimited and infinite. There are many different dimensions and levels of development. A balance between the physical and the spiritual is needed. Metaphysics used to be a very important field of philosophy and research. Even our modern physicists has not been able to answer satisfactorily the question of "What *is* matter?"

Most of all, we should remember and at least try to follow in the footsteps of the many spiritual role models (such as Moses, Christ, Bahá'u'lláh, Padre Pio, Paramahansa Yogananda, etc.) in every nation who have dared to tell their often ignorant, backward, and hostile societies about the truth of a benign infinite reality, whether called the Kingdom of God or by some other name. We should think about the plant scientist

Luther Burbank of Santa Rosa, California, who showed us how to work with Nature, not in competition with her. Above all, we must be open to new ideas, and to putting old ideas into practice, for, as Victor Hugo (1802–1885), author of *Les Miserables*, wrote: "There is one thing that is stronger than all the armies in the world, and that is an idea whose time has come."

Autobiographical Sketch of Beverley Furlow

I have been fortunate enough to be a member of ISPE since 1980, and have had the opportunity to share interests with other members both through *Telicom* and through many personal conversations. For the past fifteen years I have been an English Professor at Pima Community College, the fifth largest community college in the United States. I am also a member of the Arizona Guild of Antiquarian Booksellers and the International Society of Appraisers. I am a specialist in appreciable residential contents (antiques and collectibles) and, of course, rare and collectible books. I'm presently writing a book on computer research skills for collectors and appraisers.

CHAPTER 31

THE CONTRIBUTIONS OF LANGUAGE UNDERSTANDING TO INTERCULTURAL AND INTERRACIAL RELATIONSHIPS

Mary Beverley Furlow

In a recent article entitled "Bandwagon, Relevance, and the Rhetoric of Assent," Wayne C. Booth states the following:

> A society cannot exist, the past seems to teach us, unless it can some-
> how constitute itself as a rhetorical field, as what Dewey called "a
> public" and this means that we cannot exist without recognizing that
> some of our shared values carry an unescapable weight for all of. . . .
> What we say matters, and it matters how we say it, But the rules for
> good discourse or clear thinking can no longer be confined to logical
> prose—we must take in the proofs of personal appeal and commitment,
> of art and myth and ritual. Though a whole new effort to "purify the
> language of the tribe' is implicit in the rhetoric of assent, we cannot
> know in advance of exploration whether the new vocabulary will include
> the gestures of yoga and the "nonsense" of Zen along with the proposi-
> tional analyses of a Wittgenstein.

Dr. Booth argues that in order to understand modern society, we must accept the rhetoric of modern society, not only the rhetoric of the prevailing cultural group in a society, but also that of all subcultures that compose the society. Any even half-hearted observer can tell that different societies use different terms to describe things, and that somehow thought processes differ from culture to culture. Whether or not one accepts the Sapir-Whorf hypothesis of language, one must acknowledge that there appears to be some linkage between our words as signs and symbols and our thoughts, and that this linkage, in some way, affects the thought patterns of each culture. Whether the structure of the language determines the thought patterns or whether the thought patterns determine the structure of the language, the process must be accepted as observable and valid. From this observation, one must conclude that people in different cultures do, indeed, perceive the world as different, and express their perceptions in different rhetoric.

This phenomenon is not limited to major cultural differences, such as the difference between the Eastern and Western language groups, but is also apparent in subcultural groupings within the predominant culture. Other confirmation of this phenomenon appears in the philosophical differences, religious differences, and, above all, value standards of major cultural groups and subcultural groupings. For example, in America there is a saying that "Cleanliness is next to Godliness." One could, therefore, assume that all Americans would greatly value cleanliness. Research has shown that not all do. Cleanliness is an important value only to those in the middle and upper income levels, perhaps because cleanliness is not so important to people who lack the financial means to be clean.

If things have value or meaning because they are needed by a member of a culture, we can suspect that vocabulary appears in a culture because it is intrinsically necessary in that culture. Again, this reasoning is somewhat circular, but necessary. For example, the word *automobile* was not coined until the need for it arose when the automobile was invented. The word did not cause the machine to appear, but the appearance of the machine did, in fact, present people with an object which had to be named. The naming of things is a fairly simple concept to grasp when applied to concrete objects. The term *pizza pie* does not often appear in the vocabulary of underdeveloped third-world countries, because it is not an important part of daily life there. In the *Pedagogy of the Oppressed*, however, Paulo Friere used fourteen variants of the Portuguese term for "oppressed." The English translator combined these variants into a single English term, "oppressed." Obviously the language which contains fourteen variations of one term has these many variations in order to express the importance of the term.

People who speak Indo-European languages tend to judge things in one or two ways. Their labeling is called two-value logic. Their thinking is linear. People of other cultures have multivalued logic. Their thinking is in more of a spiral pattern. Linear thinking is usually an obstacle to communication between cultures, and tends to make one think in extremes. Further confusion in communication results when a speaker chooses a term from one level of abstraction rather than another. Communication is an abstract art, and just as when two people talk they use similar tones of voice (unless the talk is an argument), the abstraction level should be constant. Confusion arises within a cultural context because of this problem—*love* to one person is *affection* to another; *getting a job* and *obtaining a position* have entirely different connotations to different people. If communication within the same culture is so difficult, one can easily imagine the inherent difficulties in communication between cultures.

Affective language intends to arouse particular feelings in the listener: fear, distress, anticipation, desire, etc. The way that language is combined, the syntactical methodology, can produce undesired effects. It can also produce the desired effects of using language as a manipulative tool. The affective portion of language, the syntactical combination, as well as the inability to completely and correctly translate terminology, can so muddy the communicative waters that it is often impossible to have transcultural communication. Jerold Katz, in *The Philosophy of Language*, says that "the most philosophically significant words are the most unclear."

Words are our symbols of meaning. The development of language, therefore, is the history of the gradual accumulation and elaboration of verbal symbols. Symbolization is both an end and an instrument to that end. It is, consequently, an operational technique. If words, then, are our symbols of meaning, what are symbols? Images have all the characteristics of symbols. We do not take images for real things, but use them entirely in their capacity of referring to things. We conceive symbols, remember them, think about them, but we do not encounter them. There is, therefore, a difference. It is necessary to keep in mind that language proceeds from word-symbols to images to metaphors to symbols to archetypal symbols. The symbol, then, is a combination of things in which the whole is greater than the sum of the part.

It can be easily seen that the symbol is a forceful tool for exploring deeper psychological and philosophical meanings. The depth to which it will probe will depend entirely on the individual's own unique way of looking at the world. Language intrinsically contains plurasignative values: one word can have many meanings to different persons, depending on each one's past perceptions of symbols. The failure to achieve a common shared meaning of a term is a failure to communicate. Philip Wheelwright in *The Burning Fountain* (p. 28) discusses this problem:

> There is a tendency in a self-controlled, self-conscious democratic age
> to regard the most publicly shared meaning of linguistic or other symbols as the "real" meaning and to deny therefore any semantic validity

to the largely unshareable meanings ascribed to them by more sensitive
or better instructed minds.

If this difficulty in interpretation is so great within a given language,
the problems of interlanguage communication seem almost in surmount-
able.

Modern linguists are concerned with the differences between language behavior and physical behavior. The phenomena are, obviously,
cyclical: does the culture produce the different behavior in language use,
or does the behavior provide the limiting factor which, in turn, restricts
the culture? In the Navajo language there are no terms for certain colors
of the spectrum; consequently, Navajos cannot identify these colors.
Eskimoes, in another famous example, have more than twenty different
words for snow, but English has only two. Does this mean that snow is
different in Alaska and falls in twenty different forms, or that, more
plausibly, our conception of snow is limited by the two words the English
language has to describe it?

Carroll sums up the scientific difficulty inherent in this type of problem as follows:

> In order to find evidence to support the linguistic relativity hypothesis it
> is not sufficient merely to point to differences between languages and to
> assume that users of these languages have correspondingly different
> mental experiences. If we are not to be guilty of circular inference, it is
> necessary to show some correspondence between the presence or ab-
> sence of a certain linguistic phenomenon and the presence or absence of
> a certain kind of non-linguistic response.

Obviously, Whorf's hypothesis that language is the shaper of the
culture and, consequently, of the responsive behavior is an observable
phenomenon, but one which is infinitely difficult to prove empirically. At
this point in research it appears that the Sapir-Whorf hypothesis lies more
in the province of the behavioral scientists than in that of the linguistic
philosophers.

Black ghetto children commonly play a game called the "dozens."
This is a linguistic game based on a highly verbal and abstract means of
using language as a tool of insult. Yet these same children, who are
capable of a level of abstraction more complex than that of most people,
cannot master the complexities of English in elementary school. They do
not lack the capacity, obviously, to deal in abstractions; they simply lack
the ability to deal in the abstractions of a specific language at a specific

time. They can abstract in their common, native tongue, that of Black English, but not in the common, native tongue of the American school system, that of middle-class American English. Again, this phenomenon seems to reaffirm the speculation that the difficulty in language is not entirely confined to the relationship between cultural differences, the plurasignation of words, and the difficulties of the abstraction process itself. Study of black language shows that there is a common cross-cultural bond within the language itself, even though cultural differences are present. It is a systematic, structured language, and as such offers to all its speakers a common level of abstraction, a means of understanding available to all. To the outsider, however, it is a puzzle. It is only, however, when the puzzle is accepted as such, and when people realize the difficulties involved in both inter- and intra-cultural communication and their relationships to thought patterning, that any attempt at real communication can be begun. If the limiting pattern of language is accepted, and if the cultural boundaries imposed by language are acknowledged, then we need not know all the nuances found in different languages, only be aware that they do, in fact, exist and must be accommodated in the communication process. The fact that Eskimoes have many words for snow, Arabians few if any, does not show that communication on the weather is impossible for these cultures, only that it is a more complex problem than is usually acknowledged.

Subsection:
Transportation

Biographical Sketch of Ralph Slovenko

Ralph Slovenko is Professor of Law & Psychiatry at Wayne State University. He was born and raised in New Orleans, Louisiana, the son of parents who immigrated from Russia. He received B.A., L.L.B., M.A. (philosophy), and Ph.D. (psychodynamics) degrees from Tulane University. He was Editor-in-Chief of the *Tulane Law Review*, and a varsity sports letterman. He was a Fulbright scholar to France. He is one of apparently two persons in the U.S. who has done a residency in psychiatry (psycho-dynamics program) without a medical degree.

He served as law clerk to the Louisiana Supreme Court, practiced law in New Orleans, and was Senior Assistant District Attorney for the Parish of Orleans. He was a member of the faculty of the Tulane University School of Law, and subsequently also of the Department of Psychiatry, School of Medicine, from 1954–64. He held a joint appointment as Professor of Law and Psychiatry, 1965–68, at the University of Kansas Law School and the Menninger Foundation. He was a visiting professor in the USSR and Australia, and thrice in the Republic of South Africa. He joined the Wayne State University Law School faculty in 1969.

He received the Amicus Award of the American Academy of Psychiatry and Law in 1986, the Distinguished Service Award of the Michigan Psychiatric Society in 1982, and Wayne State University Presidential Citations in 1977 and 1978. He has served as a member of the Board of Directors of the Sex Information and Education Council of the United States, advisor for the Group for the Advancement of Psychiatry, the Committee of Law-Psychiatry of the American Orthopsychiatric Association, and the Committee of Law and Medicine of the Association of American Law Schools. He is also a member of the International Association of Criminal Law, the American Society of Criminology, the American Name Society, and the Southern Society for Philosophy and Psychology. He has published extensively, and is editor of the American Lecture Series in Behavioral Science and Law. His book *Psychiatry and Law*, published by Little, Brown, received the Guttmacher Award of the American Psychiatric Association, and was a selection of the Behavioral Science Book Club.

CHAPTER 32

MOBILOPATHY

Ralph Slovenko

A plague has covered the land—"mobilopathy"—the automobile way of life. Mobilopathy (from the Latin *mobilis*, or motion, and the Greek, *pathos*, or suffering) has ravished the land, polluted the air, and has taken an awesome toll in human lives.

Everywhere—on the left side, on the right side—automobiles. We have become a junky nation, and the automobile industry is the pusher. America the Beautiful has been turned into America the Parking Lot. The pursuit of happiness (a right engraved in the Declaration of Independence) has been turned into pursuit of a parking space. "I welcome you to the annual advocacy program," said the director to those in attendance at the opening of the program in Ann Arbor, "and I congratulate you on finding a parking space." For any activity—of whatever size or nature—cars are for getting there, and spaces for parking are indispensible.

Automobiles take up our space, and they foul our air. The skies have turned from blue to brown. Automobiles contribute over 90 percent of the carbon monoxide in the air. Each vehicle emits an average of one ton of contaminants per year. Los Angeles—once a place for the angels—now ranks (with Mexico City) as the world's largest open gas chamber.

The automobile is no longer an optional convinience, but a practical necessity. We have been reduced to automobile dependency. The love affair is now a forced marriage. The demise of public transit has made it indispensible. The automobile made possible a style of life that extends distances—dispersing shops, offices, and dwellings—which in turn require an automobile to get about. There is now no "mass" for mass transit. Economically and socially, our cities have become the very nadir of organization.

A generation ago a family might have had a single car—now each and every member of the family is obliged to have one. Ogden Nash, poet-humorist, once observed, "Progress was a good thing once but it went on too long." A family of four (two adults and two adolescents) must now have four cars. We need the car now to go to work, to school, to shop, to socialize. Those unable to drive must be chauffeured. In little more than a generation, the lot of women has changed from housewife to chauffeur. Mother spends much of her time driving a car, chauffeuring kids who in another day would have taken the trolley by themselves. A mother's role is now to deliver children—at first obstetrically and thereafter by car.

President Kennedy in 1963 established community mental-health centers. With them, there would be little or no need for the large state hospitals. Each center was supposed to offer comprehensive care to every-body in the area. Questions, never asked: Where is the community? How does the patient get to the center? The President needs a helicopter to get to nearby Camp David.

The automobile makes enormous territorial demands. A single car requires 1,400 square feet of space, equivalent to the living space of an average family unit, for maneuvering and parking. (Americans on the average commute 5,320 miles to and from work annually, or 22.5 miles daily; their cars are parked 22 hours of the day.) Simply accommodating all the cars now requires 40 to 50 percent of the land area of a city. Buildings are dwarfed by the space allocated around them for parking. Hotels, hospitals, shopping centers, and apartment complexes are sur-rounded not by grass and fountains, but by parking lots. The parlor or front porch of most houses, a traditional meeting place, has been replaced by the garage. The family of four clutter their premises and the streets with their four cars. They have to put them somewhere. Neighbors and strangers alike fight over a parking space like in a guerilla war. It's a rule of thumb: "Never fight anyone for a parking spot, because you may get killed." The cultural advantage of Detroit, if you will, is that it's the place to find a parking space. The whole place has been turned into a parking lot. Its conception of a "renaissance center" is parking along the river-front.

To accomodate the automobile it has been necessary to cover over the land with tar or concrete. Very little green is to be seen in urban areas anymore. As Lewis Mumford put it, our national flower is now the con-crete cloverleaf. To enjoy a bit of nature today, one must travel a hundred miles or more. In advertising, however, the automobile industry associates its product with the very images of that which it has destroyed. The car is never shown where it is usually found—in a traffic jam in a smog-choked city—but, instead, in a sylvan setting, parked on grass or under a tree. An animal name, such as Pinto, Rabbit, Jaguar, Mustang, Lynx, Colt, Cougar, or Firebird, enhances the illusion. The advertising might as well be called ecopornography.

With at least 65 million vehicles on U.S. roads, accidents are inevitable. Given the paper-box construction of many of these vehicles, the risk is lethal. Every third or fifth vehicle on major highways today is a truck, and they present a special hazard. The Surgeon General has not issued his famous warning as of yet, but as one political scientist observed, "The private passenger automobile is one of the greatest devices for mass destruction ever invented." All of our wars have not produced as much death and injury. The annual toll in the U.S. of 50,000 dead and 280,000 seriously injured exceeds the number of casualties in 10 years of battle in Vietnam.

By and large, simply commuting home nowadays is a life-or-death venture, particularly when the weather is inclement. A momentary lapse of attention, even when one is sober as a judge, can prove fatal. Here is a typical news item: "Fiery Freeway Crash/A man was killed and at least three other people were injured yesterday in a chain-reaction crash involving six tractor-trailor trucks and about 25 automobiles on Interstate 95." Day in and out, the "freeway" resembles a battlefield—smashed cars, racing ambulances, and mutilated bodies. Just pick up a daily paper. It's daily news, but now it is so common that it is back-section news.

The perils are exacerbated in winter when driving is a jam session on slush. In wintry weather driving is an utter disaster. Cars are swishing all over the place. Here is the result of just a four-inch snowfall:

> Blowing snow across lower Michigan caused scores of cars to skid into each other in huge chain-reaction pile-ups and shut down several portions of several freeways. State troopers and wreckers spent hours late yesterday trying to sort out the messes. Three persons were critically injured in a Troy accident blamed on the weather.

That was an early winter report. Here is the report a few hours later of another slippery encounter:

> A truck and several cars were wedged together following an accident on westbound I-94 east of the State Street exit near Ann Arbor. A snowstorm which lowered visibility and made pavement slippery was blamed in the mishap. One person was seriously injured. It took several hours to clear the wreckage.

Every season can have its charm depending on how people manage it. Too many automobiles and the dependency on the automobile in the United States have turned what could be a winter wonderland into a nightmare. The scene is one of sliding and colliding of cars. Only the brave can venture it—and they need "one for the road." A surfeit of wintry weather paralyzes the community. Schools and workplaces are closed. Believe it or not, in many countries, sidewalks are machine-brushed clean every morning, making it possible for pedestrians to walk without slipping and falling, and public transportation makes it possible to get about without the hazards or hassles of driving. The scene at the emergency wards of our hospitals is one reminder of the price we pay in human suffering for the automobile way of life.

The law of torts imposes liability when there is a voluntary act, injury, causation, and fault, or, for ultrahazardous activity, liabilty without fault. On causation, it is necessary to identify the "proximate" cause of the injury in order to assign liability, but that is just a label for the court to apply to whomever it wants to burden with the cost of the accident. Every event has many causes, each of which could be called "proximate." Why is driving an automobile not considered in the law of torts a dangerous activity subject to strict liability? I should ask, considering that driving nowadays is no more voluntary than peristalsis: Why is the manufacturing and unrestricted selling of cars not considered a dangerous activity? Walter Hickel noted, in 1970, that two automobiles were built in the country for every baby born and suggested automobile birth-control pills.

To placate the public, the law has established no-fault insurance for nonserious injury. For serious injury, the motorist may be held liable in tort when at fault. The manufacturer may be held liable only in the event of a "defective product." Under product-liability law, a product is not considered defective when it does what it purports to do. The manufacturer, we know, pays nothing for the deterioration of the quality of life. The state (i.e., the public), where sovereign immunity is waived, may be held liable for faulty maintenance of the roads and highways. Should the automobile industry or the public bear the true cost of the product? Should the industry be revered or reviled? Is what's good for General Motors good for the nation? Do the benefits of the automobile outweigh its costs? It is past time for a reassessment.

The getting to and from work clutters the mind as well as the road. People must plan their route, listening on radio or television to the latest traffic news, as though they were planning logistics in wartime. After the commute, they are ready for a drink, not a day's work. Productivity suffers drastically. Monte Clark, just before he was dismissed as coach of the Detroit Lions, said about his team on the eve of a game, "I just hope they don't have that I-75 look in their eyes." People are exhausted just arriving at work, and they leave early in order to "beat the traffic," but they meet up with everyone else with the same idea. Naturally, with all these vehicles on the road, a single breakdown clogs an already congested artery (and tends to burst the driver's artery). "Drive and curse," people say. In traffic tie-ups, nerves get so frayed that violence and gunfire break out. Houston is a notable example where traffic altercations lead to death by gunfire. The *Chronicle* suggests: "Try to release your anger in constructive ways. Running another automobile off the road is not constructive or legal . . . When all else fails, do not pull out a gun." Some say only the border between Iran and Iraq is more hazardous. Elia Kazan begins *The Arrangement* with Eddie going crazy driving an automobile. It is no wonder people have taken to pot. Building another highway, the usual remedy, simply increases the traffic, and (true to a Parkinson's law of roads) it too is soon clogged. These highways have cut up our cities, have broken up our neighborhoods, into isolated and desolate little islands. "You can't make an omelet without breaking eggs," we are told. Quite rightly, Solzhenitsyn has suggested that the "freeway" is another Gulag.

The current crusade against drunk driving is myopic. Not surprisingly, the automobile industry welcomes this movement. It focuses on the driver rather than on the automobile way of life. Overall, how much difference does it really make whether one is sober or drunk? Who even when sober has not had one, two, three, or more close calls? MADD (Mothers Against Drunk Driving) ought to be just MAD (Mothers Against Driving). For all their efforts, the MADD crusaders have brought restrictions on drinking but have made no dent on traffic fatalities. In fact, notwithstanding an intense anti-drunk-driving campaign in 1984, traffic fatalities during the year actually increased. About 1,200 more people were killed on the nation's highways in 1984 than 1983.

To no apparent avail, the focus on drinkng is intensifying. New regulations prohibit establishments from offering free drinks, two-for-ones, "happy hours" with reduced prices, drinks as contest prizes, and the sale of pitchers of beer to solitary drinkers. The drinking age is being raised to 21. "To reduce the risks of guests driving home drunk, we're getting away from liquor and now only serve Mogen David wine at parties," says a correspondent to Bill Laitner, author of a column on commuting in the *Detroit Free Press*. Laitner responds, "If people really want to get drunk, they can do it easily enough on wine or beer." Will the automobile way of life bring back prohibition (to no avail)? Will it be necessary to go to the Soviet Union to enjoy a drink?

The massive publicity says that alcohol is involved in half of all crashes, but what about the effect of common medications or even food on these or the other crashes? Scientists warn drivers to be aware of the effects that common medications can have on their coordination and reaction time. Studies of accident victims find Valium in the blood of 10 to 20 percent of drivers killed in car crashes. Another study finds that psychiatric patients taking one or more medications have two to three times as many accidents as patients who are not taking drugs. Food, we know, also makes one drowsy. And what about drivers who turn their heads toward passengers to carry on conversations while in traffic? What about the use of car phones or dictaphones? What about weariness? On today's highways, the threat of driver fatigue and boredom is constant. It's called "highway narcosis," or more simply, drowsiness at the wheel, and every year thousands upon thousands of motorists lose their lives to it.

Alcohol, drugs, or food may exacerbate the hazards of driving, but driving is hazardous even on an empty stomach, and even with the use of gadgets like seat belts and air bags. They are like taking the bull by the tail rather than by the horns. The high-speed automobile and the "freeway" have more to do with injury than the mixture of alcohol and driving or the use of gadgets. If just the number of miles driven goes up, there will be an increase in the number of people getting injured or killed. "Increased travel means increased exposure and more accidents," said the manager of the National Safety Council, explaining the 501 deaths over a holiday weekend. An official of the National Highway Traffic Safety Administration said that the chief reason for the increase in highway deaths in 1984 over 1983 was that people were driving 5 percent more in 1984. And that is the way it is. Here is the death toll reported the other day on Michigan's roads (none of the drivers were intoxicated): Todd Graham, 21, died when the car in which he was a passenger ran off Hemlock Road in Saginaw County. Ann Marie Labelle, 16, was killed when the car she was driving ran off Chambers Road in Livingston County and hit a tree. David Heinrich, 34, died when his car ran off Baker Road in Macomb County. Michael Sipe, 25, was killed when his car crashed on M-24 in Lapeer County. In Hartland Township, on the early-morning slippery road, two cars collided head on, seriously injuring four people.

Since the automobile came into use, it has resulted in almost two million fatalities in the U.S., with three times that number permanently injured. Auto accidents are the leading cause of death of Americans in the first half of their normal life-span. Public attention focuses on the plight of an unfortunate individual, like that of Karen Quinlan, but far less attention is given to highway deaths and injuries that occur at a "statistical" level. About a dozen boxing deaths last year engendered a call for a ban on boxing, but who argues for restrictions on the use of automobiles? The highway carnage is an inevitable consequence of the automobile way of life. Those who have died on our highways are our sacrifice to it.

The automobile now monopolizes the streets and roadways, displacing children, pedestrians, cyclists, streetcars, and animals. The automobile, because of its speed and size, is simply not compatible with them. In 1908 in the *Yale Law Journal*, H.B. Brown, a retired U.S. Supreme Court Justice, urged the courts not to disregard the rights of others in favor of the motorist—his plea was an isolated one in the law journals and went unheeded. The Bible (*Zechariah* 8:5) urged: "And the streets of the city shall be full of boys and girls playing in its streets."

Roadways and parking lots for cars abound, but there are few walkways or parks for people. There are service stations for cars—two, three, or four—at every major intersection, but a service station or park for people is scarcely to be found. The only benches are cheap substitutes for a billboard set up at busy intersections. They are not meant for sitting. The automobile has brought about a country blotted with signs, motels, and drive-in restaurants, banks, and even churches. One architect calls it "God's Own Junkyard."

It used to be quipped that a university must provide three things: football for the alumni, sex for the students, and parking for the faculty. Now, parking must be provided for one and all. Without a car, a student is unable to get to school. The usual reason a student gives when absent is that his or her car broke down. University campuses have been turned into parking lots. Many of them ought to be called drive-in universities. City streets and even expressways divide the campus. Given the look of the place, we may ask: Why even have the buildings? Why not hold classes in a drive-in theater?

One would have to look long and hard in a U.S. city to find a walkway lined with trees and benches. Indeed, in many new residential areas, there are not even any sidewalks. Perhaps the place that is most fit for walking is the cemetery. Even that, however, has given way to the drive-in mausoleum. It has been ages since I heard anyone in the U.S. say that they spent an evening strolling. In fifteen years in Detroit I have yet to see a mother with a baby carriage—native Detroiters tell me it's over 20 years since they have seen one—but my brother tells me he saw one last summer in Chicago. Toddlers are now tied in a car in a "love seat."

The U.S. Supreme Court in 1980 ruled that California could compel a shopping-center owner to open his property to leaflet distribution and petition circulation activities. In some measure, the decision turned private property into public property, but the decision is in tune with our prevailing way of life. There are no town squares in U.S. cities, and the streets are given over to the automobile. The only place where people walk, it seems, is in the shopping centers. Strong in my memory is a day spent accompanying a colleague who was running for mayor of the city.

We walked the streets of a neighborhood, up and down, and though the day was sunny, there was not a person on foot. So, with all our leaflets in hand, off we went to a shopping center.

In fair weather or foul, the streets of America are deserted. The disease is not agoraphobia, but mobilopathy. The automobile has taken people off the streets. They are isolated and encapsulated in these little boxes. The wonderful sport of "people watching" is unknown in most of America. There is no one strolling on Sunday, or any day. Foreigners are stunned by our peopleless streets—they ask: "Where are the people?" "Where is the public life?" "Where is the life of the streets?"

Streets empty of pedestrians are not only haunting, but also dangerous. The criminal operates when he has isolation and no witnesses. When streets are vacant, the few who dare to walk are vulnerable to crime. Indeed, should one walk, the chances are a police car will pull up and say, "What are you doing? Are you crazy? You had better get in a car." The people are actually held prisoner in a car. They now need the car as crime protection. "Valet parking" sounds elegant but it is nothing more or less than a euphemism for crime protection. One war veteran finds small comfort, "Well, it's better than being a POW."

Downtown was once a place where people would dress up and get together. When feeling down, one would go downtown for a lift. Going downtown now is no way to battle the blues. Seeing today's downtown would not uplift anyone's spirit—it would do just the opposite. Our cities look almost as bleak and desolate as Hiroshima in the film *On the Beach*. The U.S. did not suffer bombing during World War II, but after the war its cities were devastated by the automobile way of life. They look as though hit by war.

And the suburb, though it does not have the same crime problem, has not acheived the vitality that the inner city once had. The streets of suburbia are as lifeless and lacking in vitality as the downtown of the inner city. The suburbs, splintered around a city, do not have cohesiveness, and separately each cannot provide support for a vigorous and active cultural life. The appellation "suburban housewife" connotes vacuous existence. In contrast to the U.S., the hearts of cities in many other countries have always been, and continue to be, the most prized residential areas. It may go without saying that the flight in the U.S. to the suburbs was very much prompted by the integration of the races. The automobile facilitated segregation and, in the process, it turned our cities into huge ghettos. Suburb and city are polarized: the suburbanites are angry because of the loss of city life, and the city dwellers are angry because they have slums.

The suburban exodus and the decline of the central city were dependent upon auto transportation and highway construction. Lewis Mumford wrote in 1964 in his classic book, *The Highway and the City*, that "the most charitable thing to assume about [the highway program] is that [Congress] hadn't the faintest notion of what they were doing." The highway program was actually conceived in the name of national defense. It was called the Interstate and Defense Highway System. When President Eisenhower in 1956 signed it into law, he was unaware that the urban interstates would intrude into inner cities. The President was under the impression that it would bypass urban areas. It was 1959 before he inadvertently learned of his error. He concluded that the program "had reached a point where his hands were virtually tied." The signs at highway constuction, "Your Taxes at Work," have come down in the face of pleas by the public not to put their taxes to work, but the highway bureaucracy has become the most powerful in government. Their allies include construction firms, concrete producers, design and planning technicians, oil companies, and organized labor, as well as auto manufacturers and dealers.

Urban congestion is now measured by the number of cars per parking place. The number of vehicles in the U.S. since 1950 has risen five times as fast as the population rate. Casper, Wyoming, has 729 autos per 1,000 residents; Detroit has 549 per 1,000 residents. The 165 million cars now on U.S. roads—more than one for every two people—are supplemented by two to three times that number in dump heaps. The unprecedented outlay of $50 billion annually in recent years to foreign countries in order to fuel these vehicles (5 million barrels a day at $30 a barrel) could have been used to develop a safe, reliable, and varied system of transportation.

Quite right, unlike a bus or trolley, a car is always waiting (when not in repair) and will never leave without you, but when there are no viable alternatives and everyone must resort to it for every occaision, it negates itself, as Hegel would say. Quality changes with quantity. Mobility has been changed into immobility. The "gridlock" is common currency. The automobile is now more pain than pleasure. It dominates more than it serves. People must spend hours each day at the wheel and hours parking it; reading or listening to advertisements about it; fueling, cleaning, or repairing it; recovering from injuries or backache from driving it; and attending funerals of friends and family who have died in it. The maintenance of a car costs more and takes up more time than caring for a child. On average, people annually spend 13 percent of their income on transportation, and much more of their time talking and coping with it. Here is some conversation:

"I want the biggest car made today. It's really suicide to ride in a small one. What's the good of a seat belt in a chicken box?"

"She raved about the Cougar, but it wasn't two months after she got it, the gas leaked, the windows jammed."

"They'll sell you a lemon every time."

"My husband is depressed about his car. I tell him, 'You sweet thing, get your ass up; get yourself together, and get yourself a new car.' I love my husband, but he's getting depressed about his car."

Transportation ought to be regarded as a public service, like police and fire protection, that must be offered at no direct cost to the citizenry. It would be equitable to both the poor and the affluent who must commute to work, to shop, or to socialize. It would lure people away from the automobile. It would stimulate business and other activities as nothing else would. In the long run, free transportation would prove cheapest to society.

To be sure, the automobile is the mainstay of our economy, but it is now counterproductive. We pay an enormous price for it. Detroit built itself, and destroyed itself, as it did the rest of the country, with automobiles. It gave us freeways, traffic jams, urban flight, urban sprawl, strip development, the decay of the cities, and human carnage. In the film *The Gods Must Be Crazy*, the motor vehicle is called the Antichrist. In the absence of substantial and thoughtful change, our song "God Bless America" will have to be amended to "God Help America."

Biographical Sketch of Ed Repic

Ed Repic is a Project Manager at Rockwell International's Space Systems Division in Downey, California. In addition to his 30-year career as an aerospace engineer and manager, Mr. Repic founded a consultant firm, Effective Management Resources, and has found time to teach engineering and management courses during the past 25 years as a consultant and adjunct professor at West Coast University and the University of Southern California. At West Coast University, he developed a Master's program in Engineering and Technical Management which has been very popular over the last 10 years. In his spare time, he serves the American Society for Engineering Management as the Southwest Regional Director, and as an Associate Editor of the *Engineering Management Journal*, for which he also writes a featured column. In addition, he serves as the Computer Services Manager for the ISPE. He received the Bachelor of Aeronautical and Astronautical Engineering from the Ohio State University, an M.S. in Aerospace Engineering from the University of Southern California, and an M.B.A. in Management from Pepperdine University. Mr Repic also holds the designation of Certified Professional Manager.

CHAPTER 33

A PROPOSED SOLUTION TO THE FREEWAY CRISIS

Ed Repic

The Freeway Crisis is here!—as anyone living in almost any city in the United States can verify. Bumper-to-bumper traffic almost 24 hours a day is now commonplace. We fortunate enough to live in Southern California are special victims of this pernicious malady, since we have more freeways and more cars than any other place in the country.

Although the problem is nationwide, I am going to concentrate here on the problems of the Southern California (So Cal) area, since this is where my expertise lies. I am a veteran of more than half a million miles on the So Cal freeways, and have survived to talk about it (so far). In addition, I have been a Systems Engineer for 25 years with the company that put men on the Moon. If we could do that, we should be able to get people to work on time.

To start, let's examine the So Cal Freeway problem in some detail to see what we can learn about the causes of the problem. In So Cal, hardly anyone lives in the city where they work. People working in Los Angeles live in Orange County, people working in Orange County live in Riverside County; etc. This phenomenon was caused primarily by rising real-estate values during 1960 to 1987, coupled with rising interest rates during the same period. This double whammy meant that fewer and fewer people could afford to live in the rapidly appreciating areas that were within reasonable commuting distance to major employment areas. Therefore people bought homes in the far suburbs, where they were still affordable, and resigned themselves to long commute times. Today some people commute 50 or more miles each way, so that they can afford a home in the far suburbs and still keep their relatively high-paying job in the urban areas. This is today the norm in So Cal, and is not likely to change in the near future; it has to be accepted, and any viable solution will have to address it. Let's call this the Nesting Syndrome.

Once having acquired the Nesting Syndrome, one must next find a way to get from the Nest to the Job with the least pain and cost. In So Cal we do not have the excellent mass-transit systems found in smaller, more compact cities like New York, Boston, and Washington. The few modes of public transport, such as buses and trains, invariably go from the wrong place to the wrong place at the wrong time, and therefore offer little, if any, help to the commuter. The few buses and trains available are enjoying increasing popularity, but much too little and far too late. This leaves us with the personal automobile, the Car, as the only answer so far. The Car, because of its symbiotic relationship with the Nesting Syndrome, its relatively high cost, and its intimate relationship with the commuter through many hours of shared companionship on the freeways, represents much more than simple transportation. So Cal commuters love their cars and the freedom they represent. Let's call this the Car Fixation.

PAST ATTEMPTS AT A SOLUTION

Having now acquired both the Nesting Syndrome and the Car Fixation, how can the So Cal commuter ever give these up simply to save money or eliminate air pollution? We have to find a solution that recognizes and satisfies both the Nesting Syndrome and the Car Fixation. Let's look at some possible solutions and compare them to try to find one that has merit for our So Cal problem.

One obvious answer is to build more freeways, but the problem is where to put them. Land prices are extremely high near most freeways, so that expanded or new rights of way are almost out of the question. Putting freeways where land is cheap but where no one wants to go does not make sense. How about putting upper decks on the existing freeways? Well, in this land of shake and bake, this is a risky solution. In 1971, we had a small earthquake, around 6.2 or so, and parts of the freeway overpass nearest the center of the quake collapsed. Another quake of this magnitude during the rush hour near a double-decker freeway could turn into a disaster, as happened in the last big one in Oakland.

Another simple-sounding solution is to increase the types and amount of mass transit in the area. A quick and dirty systems analysis of this option shows that the numbers of vehicles and routes required to satisfy our commuters would result in gridlock of the freeways, and bankruptcy for the city or state mass-transit districts. How about car pools? Great idea, only how do I deal with the Car Fixation? It requires that I always have access to a car to go to lunch, do my shopping, meet a friend for dinner, go to a supplier to pick up a part, etc., etc. What if I get sick and want to go home? What if our car-pool driver is late and I miss an important meeting? Car pools are a good idea, but have not yet been accepted by the So Cal commuter. I think they will be if the crisis continues to build and no other solutions are found.

What about moving the centers of employment out to less-congested suburban areas? I am all for it, but I have no idea how to tell employers to do this. Some are already doing it. Maybe in 25 years or so, enough will have voluntarily moved to make this option viable. It just does not look viable for the near term. So, what then?

THE PROPOSED SOLUTION

Let me introduce the Public Car Utility Company (PCUC). This privately owned and operated company (hypothetical, of course) supplies the needed solution at minimum cost and in a very short time with minimum disruption to the current lifestyles and habits of our commuters. The PCUC operates a fleet of two-passenger electric cars parked at designated areas along the freeways, similar to our current Park and Rides. These areas are equipped with battery-charging stations that look like the radio posts in drive-in theaters. Each Charging Station has an outlet into which the Electric Car's umbilical is inserted. Green and Red lights on the Station advise the user of the car's status. The Charging Stations use power purchased from the local electric utility, which generates it in a relatively efficient plant with relatively small amounts of air pollution and at relatively small cost compared with the thousands of gasoline engines being replaced, all generating small amounts of power and large amounts of pollution.

The commuter operates the Car by disconnecting the umbilical from the Charging Station, inserting his PCUC Credit Card into the slot on the door, opening the door, inserting his card into the slot on the dash, and putting the Car in gear. The on-board computer reads his card and starts to calculate his rental charge for today, based on the time the Car is on and the miles driven. When the commuter reaches his home, he removes the card, locks the door and goes into his home. Next morning, he uses the Car to drive to the nearest Park and Drive, plugs the Car into a Charging Station, and walks a short distance to the freeway, where he boards a Bus/Train, etc., and is whisked off to the next Park and Drive. If he catches the LA Express, he gets off in downtown LA at the large Park and Drive near Union Station. Here he walks out to the parking area and picks up another Car, as he did before, drives it to his office, parks it, and goes to work. When it's time to go home, he drives the Car to the nearest Park and Ride, plugs in the Car, and walks to the freeway, where he boards his Bus/Train, etc., for the trip to the Park and Ride nearest his destination.

The Car's umbilical plays a bigger role than just to charge the batteries. It includes a data link from the Car's sensors, so that the PCUC Computer knows where this particular Car is, how many miles it has been driven, who drove it, what the battery status is, any anomalies in any of the Car's systems, and the Car's maintenance schedule. This last set of data is sent to the PCUC maintenance crew at the appropriate Park and Ride for action. This insures that the Cars are always in good shape and ready to go, and will not break down en route. Also, this should be a very cost-effective way to maintain the fleet of cars, since maintenance can be scheduled at times when the car is not being used and when the mechanic's time can be optimally scheduled. Also, since our Cars are all the same, additional savings will accrue from common parts, reduced inventories, etc.

Finally, let's look at the Cars themselves. Without going into a lot of technical detail, electric cars today are already being built and operated both here and in Europe that can easily meet our PCUC requirements. These requirements are simply:

(1) Range: 100 miles between charge cycles
(2) Charge Cycle: less than about 5 hours
(3) Payload: 2 adults plus baggage, about 500 lbs.
(4) Safety: meet current standards
(5) Cost: less than $5,000 in quantities of 10,000

These requirements are not beyond today's technology, assuming our PCUC would commit to a purchase of 10,000 Cars ($50,000,000). The only reasonable way to do this would be to start a public corporation and sell shares to raise the money required to develop and build the Cars, to buy (or rent) the Park and Ride facilities, to develop and build the maintenance facilities, and, finally, to set up the computer and charging systems. The Freeway portion of the system could be started with buses either contracted through existing bus companies or bought and operated by our PCUC. As commuters start to switch to the new system, our company could start to look at light rail along the freeway, either at the center median or along the side. As our PCUC became profitable, the money would be invested in this next step to make the total system even more attractive and efficient. The actual cost and schedule to accomplish this should be significantly less than some of the alternative solutions discussed earlier, and have the further merit of not being tax-supported. The stockholders supply the capital; the users pay the costs plus a fair return; the PCUC reimburses the state through taxes on the Bus/Train using the freeways; and the public benefits from less congestion and pollution. Can you find a better solution?

CHAPTER 34

RESTRUCTURING FOR AN AUTO-FREE SOCIETY

Ralph Slovenko

The ex-USSR is going through a restructuring, and the United States, burdened by decades of defense spending and a focus on the automobile as its primary enterprise, must also do some restructuring. The Economic Strategy Institute in a recent report said, "Detroit is basically going out of business and is being replaced by Japan." It had a gloomy assessment of America's auto future. When the auto industry goes down the tubes, so do a lot of other American industries. One out of seven jobs is linked to the auto industry.

Opening Japan up to the sale of American automobiles will hardly make a dent in the number of sales, and will do little or nothing to reduce the trade deficit. The Japanese are buying Levi pants and jackets and drinking Coca-Cola, but they are not likely to buy American automobiles, whether the steering wheel is on the right-hand side or the left-hand side.

There are other propsals to uplift the American auto industry: a 15 percent tax credit, a money-back guarantee, and the enactment of national health insurance. In Japan, the industry is not burdened with the cost of health insurance or pensions. But any or all of these moves are not likely to make the U.S. auto industry competetive.

There is, however, a silver lining in all this. Here, at last, is an opportunity to get away from the automobile way of life and make our cities as they once were: auto-free. It is an opportunity to go back to the old ways. To turn the clock back would be progress. Just imagine: gardens instead of parking lots and gas stations, porches instead of garages, walkways and bikeways, trains, buses, trolleys, and jitneys. It would again be a time without "car-nage" on the roadways, air pollution, the nuisance of car repairs and insurance, and logistics on commuting.

Rush hour is neither rush nor an hour; the so-called freeway looks like a car park. In Korea helicopters try to ease jams by lifting disabled autos off roadways. New York City Mayor David Dinkins said recently: "The automobile is strangling the great cities of the world," adding that traffic chaos is making urban life unbearable.

Jenny Meade, in her book *Carpool: A Novel of Suburban Frustration*, tells of her service as a chauffeur for 15 years. In an earlier day, her children or her elderly parents could take a trolley. As a victim of "car-pool fatigue," she longs for a drive-in window at the local psychiatric hospital. She describes her condition as being "like shell shock, only you don't get veteran's benefits: they just fill up your tank and send you back to the front." She snarls that "if Henry Ford were alive, I would strangle him."

The cost of automobility in treasure as well as in life is astounding. For the purchase of oil from the Middle East to fuel these vehicles, there was the greatest transfer of wealth in the history of the world. It made it possible for a desert people, doing nothing, to live in air-conditioned mansions. And for oil, we went to war. That money could have been turned to health and education and the environment.

Wolfgang Zuckerman, in *End of the Road: The World Car Crisis and How We Can Solve It*, tells us that motor vehicles kill a quarter million and seriously injure three million people worldwide each year; that 20 percent of arable land in the U.S. has been paved over; that 300 pounds of carbon dioxide are released into the atmosphere for every 15 gallons of gasoline burned; that commuters in Los Angeles spend $5,000 a year traveling to and from work; that the average American spends 1,600 hours annually driving and earning the money to pay for owning and operating a car; and that all this is subsidized in the U.S. by about $300 billion in tax money each year.

To add insult to injury, automobility structures transportation around isolation. It de-socializes. In an auto-free society, we will be able to see people, and not have to communicate by way of bumper stickers.

In the 1920s the infrastucture demands of automobility gave birth to public-works departments and reshaped the priorities of local govern-ments. In the aftermath of the depression in the early 1930s, GM, Fire-stone, Phillips Petroleum, Standard Oil, and Mack Truck bought up and dismantled many of the nation's light-rail systems.

For decades the government has underwritten the cost of driving and supported an industry to herd us into auto-dependence. Now it's foreign auto-dependence. The way out is to invigorate a varied system of transit and space-efficient land use. To accomplish these goals, new industries would be created, providing more jobs than the one in seven now linked to the auto industry.

Rebellion is spreading for auto-free cities. An organization, Transportation Alternatives, with an office in New York and 1,600 dues-paying members, has been formed. It began as primarily a local bicycling advocacy group, and has evolved into an enviromental advocacy organization spearheading New York City campaigns against auto-dependence—and inspiring similar campaigns in other cities. It has a vibrant network of people, organizing for a level transportation playing field and for a change in consciousness about the effects of the automobile. It publishes *City Cyclist* and *Auto-Free Press*. It held an International Conference for Auto-Free Cities in 1991 in New York City, and a second, subtitled "Car Dependence: Costs, Causes and Cures," on May 22–24, 1992, in Toronto.

Just as in the ex-USSR, restructuring will be painful, but, as Laurel and Hardy said, "When you're in a hole, stop digging."

Section IV
Historical Perspectives

Autobiographical Sketch of Monty Walker

Born in Eastland, a small Texas town of 2500, where the most notable event ever to occur was (and is) the phenomenon of "Old Rip," a horned toad that lived in a state of suspended animation for 31 years, beating the legendary Rip Van Winkle by a full 11 years. Although in 1934 the rest of the country was recovering from the great depression, Texas had yet to see the upswing. My father, feeling that employment would be more likely in California, moved the entire family to Los Angeles.

The effect of Los Angeles on a small-town boy was overwhelming, to say the least. With new types of food, music, transportation, entertainment, and much, much more, it was like being transported into a fairyland. To say that I liked my new venue would be an enormous understatement. I grew and thrived in my new environment of choice.

One day in 1941, while listening to the radio, I heard an announcement that the Japanese had attacked Pearl Harbor. In a relatively short time I found myself on board a U.S. naval destroyer in the south Pacific. Eventually the war ended, and I attended college, learning how to be an engineer with the tuition and expenses paid by Uncle Sam. My university required everyone (engineers included) to study Western Civilization, which included history, philosophy, and other liberal arts. At the time I resented this incursion into my technical education, but now I am enormously grateful. My papers in this publication are a direct result of my historical research inspired by my exasperated professors.

I did well as an engineer, with several patents to my name, as well as numerous technical papers in various scientific journals. My work took me to more than 35 foreign countries; however, it wasn't until I retired that I finally visited Washington, D.C.

After my late wife passed away, I learned about Mensa and other high-IQ organizations and joined them, mostly for companionship of like-minded individuals. My association has been immensely rewarding especially that with the ISPE. At the present time I am editor of *Gift of Fire*, the official organ of the Prometheus Society.

CHAPTER 35

OMAR WAS NOT A TENTMAKER

Monty Walker

The Moving Finger writes; and, having writ,
Moves on: nor all your Piety nor Wit
    Shall lure it back to cancel half a Line
Nor all your Tears wash out a Word of it.

Is there even one of our readers who has not heard the above verse? Who, indeed, has not identified it as one of the *Rubáiyát* of Omar Khayyám, the celebrated "tentmaker" poet of Persia? In fact, in all probability, you can recite several others, or at least identify them when you hear them uttered. Here I hope to clarify some misconceptions and indeed illuminate a little about two most extraordinary men: Omar Khayyám, and the man who brought him to the attention of the West, Edward FitzGerald.

Omar Khayyám was and is well-known both in the West and in the Mid-East, although for completely different reasons. His real name was Gheyas od-din Abu ol-Fath Umar Ebn Ebrahim ol-Khayyami,* although later he took the poetic name Khayyám. He was born in 1048 in Na-ishápúr, in the province of Khorasan, Persia, and died in 1131 at the age of 83.

He was a mathematician and astronomer. He also mastered poetry, philosophy, divination, jurisprudence, history, medicine, and many other arts and sciences. A genius by any standard, he made the necessary calculations to reform the calendar, and wrote books on metaphysics,

---

*There are many ways to transliterate Arabic script, and hence many ways to spell and accent Arabic words in English. We ask the readers' indulgence for the system we use here.
—The Editors

mathematics, astronomy, and law. He was indeed a Persian renaissance man, at a time when Europe was still struggling under the oppressive medieval feudal system.

He is traditionally credited with being the author of a collection of quatrains known collectively as the *Rubáiyát*. A quatrain is a group of four lines of verse, and *Rubáiyát* (plural; *Rubái* or *Rubáiyáh* is the singular) consist of iambic pentameter quatrains with the rhyming scheme of AABA. A *Rubái* is a two-lined stanza of Persian poetry, each line of which is divided into two hemistiches, making four altogether; hence the name *Rubái* which means "fourfold" in Arabic. Among the Persians (except for some radical freethinkers) a *Rubái* was considered a rather low (common) form of poetry, more or less equivalent to a limerick in the West.

It is not at all certain that Omar ever wrote a single quatrain. The Danish scholar A. Christensen accepted only 123 out of a field of 1,231 as being possibly authentic. In 1897 the Russian researcher Zhukovsky published an article, entitled "Wandering Quatrains of Omar Khayyám," which showed that of 414 verses attributed to Omar, 82 (later 108) were elsewhere assigned to 39 different poets. And in 1934, H. A. Schaeder declared that Omar wrote virtually nothing and that "his name must be struck out of the history of Persian literature."

This is how matters stood until 1950, when two manuscripts surfaced whose authenticity were beyond question and which were written within 75 years of Omar's death (the Cambridge and Chester Beatty MSS.). These papers clearly supported the authenticity of many of the Quatrains, and furthermore placed him in the company of known major Persian poets, such as Sana'i. Today much of the controversy is still unresolved, but this writer believes that Omar, being the creative genius that he was, wrote at least some of the *Rubáiyát* ascribed to him. Poetry was a natural undertaking among independent thinkers, and a *Rubái* would have been an ideal vehicle to express his unconventional views.

One thing he was not. He never made a single tent. This misconception is derived from his father's name, Khayyami, which means "tentmaker"; however, we wouldn't necessarily expect a person named Baker to be a baker or a person named Singer to be a singer. Omar himself alludes to his name and his scientific craft in the following whimsical lines:

Khayyám, who stitched the tents of science,
Has fallen in grief's furnace and been suddenly burned;
The Shears of Fate have cut the tent ropes of his life,
And the broker of Hope has sold him for nothing!

An interesting account of Omar's early life is related by FitzGerald. When Omar was a young man he went to study under a sage, the Imám Mowaffak of Naishápúr. It was the universal belief that whoever studied under this Imám would achieve honor and success. While studying, he became close friends with fellow students Nizám al-Mulk and Ben Sabbáh, both of exceedingly sharp wit and intelligence. Since it was almost certain that at least one of them would achieve fame and fortune, they made a pact that whichever of them attained success would share it equally with the other two.

When Nizám al-Mulk became the administrator of affairs (vizier) under the Sultán Alp Arslán, Ben Sabbáh sought him out and claimed his share. The Vizier kept his word and persuaded the Sultán to give Ben Sabbáh an important post in government; however, Ben Sabbáh, dissatisfied with his slow rise in the bureaucracy, plunged into intrigue. When a palace coup attempt that he had masterminded failed to supplant his benefactor, he fell into disgrace and soon fled to the mountains. There, with his evil intellect, he soon became chief of the *Ismailians*, a previously obscure sect of fanatics and assassins who, under his sinister influence, became widely known and feared. In 1090 he seized the castle of Alamút in Rúdbar in the mountainous region north of the Caspian sea. It was from this mountain headquarters that he spread terror throughout the Islamic world. During this period he became known to the Crusaders as the "Old Man of the Mountains." The word "assassin" was possibly derived from "Al Sabbáh." Sadly, one of the victims of Ben Sabbáh's fanatics was his benefactor Nizám al-Mulk.

Omar also came to the Vizier to claim his share, but not for title or office. He merely desired to be allowed to pursue his scientific and cultural studies in peace. When the Vizier was finally convinced of his sincerity, he granted him a yearly pension of 1,200 mithkáls of gold, sufficient for his needs, and Omar spent the remainder of his life winning knowledge of every kind.

He became the most respected scientist in all of Persia and the greatest mathematician of his age. He received countless honors during his lifetime. In the streets he was referred to as "The Master." Among his many accomplishments was much of the calculations necessary for calendar reform under the aegis of Malik-Shah, leading to the Jaláli or Maliki era beginning March 16, 1079. This new calendar exceeded the Julian and approached the Gregorian in accuracy. He published many books during his lifetime, including a treatise on Euclid. Sadly, most of his writings have been lost; however, some metaphysical writings, a treatise on algebra, and an extensive set of astronomical tables are still extant. He mastered advanced mathematical processes, such as third-degree equa-

tions solved by geometric means, and the use of hyperbolas, neither of
which did he get from the Greeks.

Omar knew (or postulated) the heliocentric solar system, i.e., that the
Earth revolved around the Sun, an idea that brought him into conflict with
orthodox Muslims. Several of his *Rubáiyát* allude to this heretical theory.
Quatrain 68 below and the literal translation by Heron-Allen are good
illustrations of his knowledge.

> We are no other than a moving row
> Of Magic Shadow-shapes that come and go
>   Round with the Sun-illumined Lantern held
> In Midnight by the Master of the Show.

> This vault of heaven, beneath which we stand bewildered,
> We know to be a sort of magic-lantern:
> Know thou that the sun is the lamp-flame and the universe is the
>   lamp,
> We are like figures that revolve round it.

There are many stories of Omar, but one in particular bears repeating.
Khwájah Nizámi of Samarkand, who was a pupil of Omar, relates the
following story: "One day (in 1112), while in conversation with my
teacher in a garden in the city of Balkh, he said to me, 'My tomb shall be
in a spot where the trees will shed their blossoms on me twice a year.' "
Khwájah was thunderstruck to hear these words, which verged on the
blasphemous, since the Koran plainly says, "no man knows where he
shall die!" But years later, after Omar's death, Khwájah went to visit
Naishápúr especially to see his late teacher's final resting place. When he
found it, lo! it was just outside a garden, where peach and pear trees
laden with fruit stretched their boughs over the garden wall, and dropped
their blossoms on his tomb, so that the stone was hidden under them.
Nizámi, recalling what Omar had said in Balkh, wept for his old master.

Omar was no more an orthodox Muslim than many modern writers
are Christian, and has been called "The Voltaire of the East." Professor
Cowell compares him to the great Roman philosophical poet Lucretius.
Both were men of subtle, strong, and cultivated intellect, fine imagination, and hearts passionate for truth and justice, who justly revolted from
the foolish devotion to their country's religion, and when they could find
no better revelation to guide them, made a Law unto themselves. Lau-
rence Housman described Omar through his *Rubáiyát* as "an elegy on all
faiths; it states its case with a touch of melancholy, but without any cry of
distress. Too resigned to be poignant, too philosophical to be bitter, it

dismisses the dream, and accepts with appetite—almost with gratitude—what is left."

The Sufism movement began in the tenth or eleventh century of the Common Era, and has as its goal a mystical union with God. Sufi is from an Arabic word meaning wool (Sufis wore a distinctive woolen cloak). It was, and is, a broad philosophical movement which has borrowed ideas from Neoplatonism, Buddhism, and Christianity. Sufism postulated its own approach to God through love and voluntary suffering, requiring the utmost piety and asceticism until a unity of will was reached. Sufi mystics who expressed in their poetry their contempt for formal religion nevertheless never forgot that Islam is the highest manifestation of divine wisdom. Sufis as well as other mystics believed that the adepts had inner spiritual knowledge as distinct from prophetic revelation. Many of the modern dervishes are Sufis. The Sufis professed poverty, hence *Dervish*, which means "poor."

Omar was a freethinker, and indeed regarded by many as impious. He was a great opponent of Sufism, which he regarded as an abomination. The Sufis returned his enmity in turn. He spoke of the Sufis as "floating between Heaven and Earth on wings of poetical expression as ready to doubt as to believe." Although he espoused much of their philosophy, which can be plainly seen in many of his *Rubáiyát*, he was too perceptive to presume that rational order could be found in the world.

Destiny, the glorification of love, and the praise of wine were recurring themes in his *Rubáiyát*. He preferred to make the most of what was tangible; thus his injunction to drink, gratify the senses, and not worry about the morrow.

Omar's famous agnosticism can be reduced to a few paradoxes:

- If Allah created the world and finds evil in it, whose fault is it?
- If Allah is All-merciful, why should He threaten to punish any sin?
- If wine is an unlawful pleasure, why did Allah create it?
- Why does Allah create beautiful things and then destroy them for no apparent purpose?

His skepticism is expressed most succinctly in the following Quatrain (not translated by FitzGerald).

The world's affairs, as so they seem,
Nay, the whole universe complete
Is a delusion and a cheat,
A fantasy, an idle dream.

The thirteenth-century Persian biographer Qifti told how Omar was accused of irreligion (heresy). Thereafter, for a time, he reined in his tongue, and performed a *hadj* to Mecca. As he passed through Baghdad, some students of Greek philosophy and science sought him out, but he refused to see them, as a sign of a true penitent. Although his apparent change of heart quieted his enemies, they never trusted him, and eventually were able to bring him to ruin.

When Sultán Alp Arslán died in 1072, his son Sultán Sa'id Mu'inaddin Malik-Shah retained Nizám al-Mulk as Vizier: so, from Omar's position, little had changed, and he continued his scientific and cultural studies; however, when Malik-Shah died in 1092, and his Vizier Nizám al-Mulk was killed by Ben Sabbáh's terrorist assassins, Omar's enemies (mainly the orthodox Muslims and the Sufis) gained the upper hand. His calendar was discarded, and he was forced into partial exile for the remainder of his life; but even in exile he continued his studies, and his followers saw to it that he was never in want.

Omar is said to have spent much of his life in contemplation of questions of God, Destiny, Matter and Spirit, and Good and Evil. Even Baihaqi had him die in the odor of sanctity, quoting as his last words the prayer, "Oh, Allah, thou art aware that I have known Thee to the full extent of my possibilities; forgive me, for my knowledge of Thee is my means of coming to Thee." Much of this supposition is based on the *Rubáiyát*, most of which is now thought spurious, and on Persian biographers who were not overscrupulous in their attention to the truth and would relate a story if they found it interesting. This writer, however, thinks it most probable that he spent his declining years on these pragmatic questions of natural science and mathematics.

Omar would probably never have been known in the West except for Edward FitzGerald.

Edward FitzGerald was born in 1809, the seventh of eight children, near Woodbridge, Suffolk, England, died in 1883 at the age of 75, and was buried at the churchyard at Boulge Park, Suffolk. Although he had ample means, he eschewed his natural role as "country gentleman," preferring to live among the common people. His instinctive warmhearted friendship was as real as it was surprising, a quality as natural to him as breathing. His interests were wide-ranging, and included gardening, music, boating, and especially language studies. His idea of the good life was plain living and high thinking.

While a student at Trinity College, Cambridge, he became acquainted with William Thackerey, James Spedding, William Donne, Alfred Tennyson, Thomas Carlyle, and several others who eventually became close friends and literary luminaries in their own right.

His brother John was a religious zealot who would roam the countryside preaching or listening to sermons. Frequently while listening to a sermon he would remove his shoes and stockings, lay out the contents of his pockets on the pew, and emit shrill whistles in order to give vent to his religious fervor. "We FitzGeralds are all mad," Edward used to say.

In 1856 Edward married Lucy Barton, the daughter of his friend, the Quaker poet Bernard Barton, after making a death-bed pledge. He went through with the marriage despite the protestations of his friends; however, the two were so ill-suited for each other that after six months they separated permanently. Ever the gentleman, he made Lucy a generous settlement.

Now essentially a bachelor, he devoted the rest of his life to literary pursuits. In 1856, after mastering Persian, he received a transcript of 158 quatrains of Omar Khayyám from the collection of Sir William Ouseley at the Bodleian library in Oxford, sent to him by his friend, the Sanskrit scholar Edward Cowell. Later a Calcutta manuscript containing 516 additional quatrains and a French translation by J.B. Nicolas, with an additional 464 quatrains, appeared. FitzGerald, however, continued to base most of his *Rubáiyát* on the original 158 in the Ouseley papers. Persians consider *Rubáiyát* to be second-rate poetry at best, and the verses were arranged more or less alphabetically, much like a dictionary. FitzGerald picked and chose among the 158, freely translating them, changing some almost beyond recognition, combining others and inventing some of his own. By his judicious selection he was able to fashion his masterwork into a loose progression of poetic themes; thus a *Rubái* should not be considered individually, but rather as an element of the entire *Rubáiyát* allegory.

By the beginning of 1858, after he had finished 75 quatrains, he forwarded 35 of the "less wicked" to the editor of *Fraser's Magazine*. A year later, when the poems had not yet appeared, FitzGerald recalled the manuscript, and had all 75 published at his own expense in a little 24-page quarto pamphlet by the book-seller Bernard Quaritch. He had 250 copies printed on cheap paper stock in an unassuming brown cover entitled *Rubáiyát of Omar Khayyám, the Astronomer-Poet of Persia, Translated into English Verse*, and put up for sale for five shillings. It was generally ignored, and was selling for one penny (the last stage before being destroyed for pulp) when a copy was discovered by Dante Gabriel Rossetti. He quoted from it everywhere and urged his friends to scour London for this "hidden treasure." Sir Richard Burton, Algernon Swinburne, John Ruskin, and others spread the excitement. As the little pamphlet was being "discovered," the price began escalating until a guinea or more was being paid for a single copy. Soon it was the rage throughout England, as was speculation about the identity of the translator, whose name was noticeably missing from this and subsequent versions.

The great vogue in the U.S. began in October 1869, after Charles Norton gave an enthusiastic critique in the *North American Review*, quoting 74 of the 110 quatrains in the second version. Soon it was the "cause" of the literati and was being quoted everywhere. By 1942 it had gone through 600 editions. To date (1992) there have been no less than 1,000 English-language editions published, plus several hundred in non-English editions. In 1912, a hand-illuminated copy on vellum, sumptuously bound by the celebrated artist Sangorsky in inlaid leather and jewels, went down with the Titanic. In spite of the elegance of this hand-made book, it was not worth as much as the original one-penny edition, one copy of which sold for $8,000 in 1929. It is hard to imagine what it would fetch today.

FitzGerald spent most of his life revising the Quatrains, and in his lifetime published four versions. The first version, published in 1859, had 75 *Rubáiyát*; the second version, published in 1868, had 110 *Rubáiyát*; the third version, published in 1872, had 101 *Rubáiyát*, as did the fourth version, published in 1879, and the fifth version, published posthumously in 1889. The fourth version was entitled: *Rubáiyát of Omar Khayyám; and the Salámán and Absál of Jámí* (a blank-verse treatment of a love poem by Jámí, a fifteenth-century Sufi). Neither the order of the *Rubáiyát* nor the translations were consistent from one version to another; and many commentators believe that the changes were not always felicitous.

Note the two examples below. Few will dispute that quatrain 7 (version 1) is superior to the same quatrain in version 2; or that quatrain 71 (version 2) is inferior to the equivalent quatrain 66 (version 3). Each version has its champions, and to this day there is controversy among academics, each faction debating whether one version is preferable to the others or not.

QUATRAIN 7 (VERSION 1)

Come, fill the Cup, and in the Fire of Spring
The Winter Garment of Repentance fling:
    The Bird of Time has but a little way
To fly—and Lo! the Bird is on the Wing

QUATRAIN 7 (VERSION 2)

Come, fill the Cup, and in the fire of Spring
Your Winter-garment of Repentance fling:
    The Bird of Time has but a little way
To flutter—and the Bird is on the Wing.

QUATRAIN 71 (VERSION 2)

I sent my Soul through the Invisible
Some letter of that After-life to spell:
    And after many days my Soul return'd
And said, "Behold, Myself am Heav'n and Hell"

QUATRAIN 66 (VERSION 3)

I sent my Soul through the Invisible,
Some Letter of that After-life to spell:
    And by and by my Soul return'd to me,
And answer'd "I Myself am Heav'n and Hell"

The last two versions had the fewest number of changes, involving mostly revisions in punctuation, alteration of a word here, or a slight rephrasing there. It was not until after his death that his friend Carlyle discovered to his amazement that FitzGerald was the mysterious author when he found the fifth, as-yet unpublished version in his room.

The quatrains reveal the author (whoever he might have been) as a thoughtful and profound man plagued with the eternal questions of the nature of man, the universe, the passage of time, and man's relationship to God.

A large proportion of the *Rubáiyát* are concerned with wine. It is for this reason that most believe they were used in conjunction with music and song, possibly as tavern songs. Many, by the standards of their time, were either bawdy or sacrilegious, some even taking liberties with the Koran which would never have been tolerated if openly declared.

FitzGerald, however, never followed the quatrains' epicurean council. He remained a vegetarian and ascetic all his life, living the life he loved: observing frugal habits, cultivating his mind by reflection, and devoting his time to leisurely studies in the congenial company of like-minded friends.

To get some feeling for the difference between FitzGerald's beautiful rendering and a literal translation, I will give two examples:

QUATRAIN 12 (VERSION 5)

A Book of Verses underneath the bough,
A jug of wine, a loaf of Bread—and Thou
    Beside me singing in the wilderness—
Oh, Wilderness were Paradise enow!

If there should be a loaf of wheat bread,
A jug of wine, and a thigh of mutton
With a little tulip-cheeks seated in a desolation,
It would be more pleasure than any Sultán could attain.

QUATRAIN 69 (VERSION 5)

But helpless pieces of the Game He plays
Upon this chequer-board of Nights and Days;
    Hither and thither moves, and checks and slays,
And one by one back in the closet lays.

We are but pieces in a game of chess
Played by great Heaven in its waywardness;
    Here and there on the board we move
And singly reach the box of nothingness.

The *Rubáiyát* quoted above are good examples of the poetic license that FitzGerald took with Omar's works. In the first *Rubái* (Quatrain 12), the "Thou" singing in the wilderness (and the "tulip-cheeks" [sweet-heart] seated in a desolation) was not necessarily female. Homosexuality was (and is) common in many parts of the Middle East, and love poems are commonly written to (or about) young boyish lovers. Since this was to be a special outing, wheat bread was mentioned to distinguish it from the crude barley meal of the peasants. The image of desolation was used to balance the picture of a Sultán's palace; this image would have been marred by the poetic use of a beautiful shady spot. In the original, no mention was made of poetry, since no educated Persian would dream of taking a manuscript with him on a picnic; he would know by heart enough poems for many picnics. The thigh of mutton was rightly discarded by FitzGerald as being unromantic to Western sensibilities. There were also echoes of eroticism and, indeed, obscenity. Unfortunately, most of the subtlety is lost in translation.

In the second *Rubái* (Quatrain 69) quoted above, the chequered board rings false; although in the time of Omar the Persians did play a kind of chess, the boards they used were not chequered! This *Rubái* is also a good example of Omar's metaphysical bent.

There have been hundreds of translations of the quatrains other than Fitzgerald's. Perhaps the most literal version was made by Justin Huntly McCarthy, author of the famous romantic play *If I Were King*, subsequently made into the operetta *The Vagabond King*. McCarthy learned Persian in order to translate the exact meaning into precise prose, and his rendition is painstakingly faithful to the original.

One can easily be misled into thinking that FitzGerald's only accomplishment was the *Rubáiyát*. Nothing could be further from the truth. Even without the *Rubáiyát*, he was a respected writer and known as a literary force, if not a giant among his contemporaries. His works include memoirs, letters, historical analysis, biographies, poetry and prose both original and in translation, criticism, and many other literary forms encompassing almost his entire life. Although some pedants believe that his reputation rests as much on his letters as on the *Rubáiyát*, there can be little doubt that the *Rubáiyát* was his magnum opus, and it is for this monument of literary artistry that he will long be remembered and celebrated.

FitzGerald should not be censored for taking liberties with the *Rubáiyát*, which, until his translation, were molding in obscurity, hardly noticed by writers and poets, neither in the West nor in the Middle East. What FitzGerald accomplished is something rather remarkable: an unsurpassed masterpiece that will stand forever with the greatest literature. Swinburne, who had impeccable taste on such matters, called it "that most exquisite English translation, sovereignly faultless in form and colour of verse." William Rose Benét, the celebrated American poet, wrote, "While retaining the spirit and philosophy of the original quatrains, FitzGerald's translation is so free in its rendition as to be virtually an original work, masterful in its concentration, music and command of tone." Richard Le Gallienne, the Persian scholar, said, "FitzGerald did not so much bring Omar's rose to bloom again, as to make it bloom for the first time. The wine-stained petals came from Persia, but it was an

English magician who charmed them into a living rose." And Harold Lamb, the historical writer, declared of FitzGerald, "That taciturn Englishman had for a brief moment in time the gift of knitting cobwebs together, of weighing thistledown, and weaving a magic tapestry of dragonflies' wings." Now all generations can enjoy the treasures born from his lifetime of labor. As Lowell wrote,

> These pearls of thought in Persian gulfs were bred,
> Each softly lucent as a rounded moon;
> The diver Omar plucked them from their bed,
> FitzGerald strung them on an English thread.

As a postscript: In the churchyard at Boulge Park where Edward FitzGerald was buried, there grows a rose tree, the hips for which were picked from rose bushes on the grave of Omar Khayyám in Naishápúr in 1884.

BIBLIOGRAPHY

All publishers are in New York, except as noted.

The Rubáiyát of Omar Khayyám, translated by Edward FitzGerald.

1. Classic Club, Walter Black, 1942. (All versions, with excellent cross index.)
2. Willey Book Co., 1944. (First version, with a translation of the Arabic classic, "The Kasîdah of Hâjî Abdû El-Yezdî," by Sir Richard Burton.)
3. Grosset & Dunlap, 1946.(First and fourth versions, with 12 color and 101 black and white illustrations.)
4. Random House, 1947. Louis Untermeyer, ed. (First and fifth versions, with 20 color illustrations.)
5. Doubleday, Garden City, 1952. (First, second, and fifth versions, with 12 color illustrations.)
6. Thomas Y. Crowell, 1968. (First and fourth versions, with 16 black and white illustrations.)
7. Dover, 1990. (First and fifth versions; an excellent, inexpensive edition.)

The Rubáiyát of Omar Khayyam, other translators.

8. *The Quatrains of Omar Khayyam.* Intro. by Friedrich Rosen. E.P. Dutton, 1930. [Pub. in Great Britain] (329 quatrains in literal translation.)

9. *Omar Khayyám.* Arthur J. Arberry. Yale University Press, New Haven, CT, 1952. (252 quatrains based on the recent discovery of a new manuscript, with excellent cross references.)

10. *The Rubaiyyat of Omar Khayyam: A New Translation.* Robert Graves and Omar Ali-Shah, trans. Cassell, London, 1967. (A controversial translation of 111 of the original FitzGerald manuscript.)

11. *The Ruba'iyat of Omar Khayyam.* Peter Avery and John Heath-Stubbs, trans. Penguin, NY and London, 1981. (235 quatrains in literal translation and 32 color illustrations, with an original biography of Omar, including an interesting account of the Assassins.)

Omar Khayyam

12. *Omar Khayyam.* Harold Lamb. Doubleday, 1934. (Fictional account of Omar, but mostly based on historical accounts.)

13. *The Algebra of Omar Khayyám.* Daoud S. Kaiser, Ph.D. Teachers College, Columbia Univ., 1930; reprinted, 1951.

Edward FitzGerald

14. *Two Suffolk Friends.* Francis Hindes Groome. London, 1895.

15. *The Life of Edward FitzGerald.* John Glyde. London, 1900.

16. *The Life of Edward FitzGerald.* Thomas Wright. London, 1904 (2 vols.)

17. *The Life of Edward FitzGerald, Translator of the Rubáiyát of Omar Khayyám.* A. McKinley Terhune. London, 1947.

18. *Rubáiyát of Omar Khayyám and Other Writings by Edward FitzGerald.* George F. Maine, ed. Collins, London, 1971. (First, second, and fifth versions, plus a biography of FitzGerald and several of his shorter works.)

19. *With Friends Possessed: A Life of Edward FitzGerald.* Robert Bernard Martin. Atheneum, 1985. (312-page biography of FitzGerald with notes and bibliography.)

CHAPTER 36

THE EMPEROR OF NICARAGUA

Monty Walker

You have probably never heard of him, but if you had lived in the 1850s, his name would have been as familiar to you as that of George Washington. His name was William Walker, and he was my great-grandfather's brother, which, I guess, makes him my great-great uncle. My grandfather, Jeremiah Walker, moved from Tennessee to Texas after the Civil War, and he would sometimes reminisce about "Uncle Bill," as he called him. I don't think he had a clear understanding of the historic importance of this unique man.

William was born in Nashville, Tennessee, on May 8, 1824, the oldest of four children and, by any reckoning, a certified genius. If high-IQ societies had existed in his day, he could easily have qualified for any of them.

William's mother was ailing and needed special care, and he did not stint in this, spending hours every day caring for her and reading to her tales of chivalry. I believe that this constant reading and re-reading of the ancient heroic tales instilled in him a sense of honor that he kept until his dying day.

His father had selected a career for him in the ministry, but William would have none of it: he would become a doctor. His father, glad to be rid of him, sent him off to school. William may have had ideas of returning home as a master physician and miraculously effecting the cure of his mother.

He entered the University of Nashville at 12 and graduated at 14, *summa cum laude*. To be admitted to Nashville he had to be fluent in Latin through Cicero's orations and Greek through the New Testament. The University of Nashville ranked with the best, and his courses included calculus, astronomy, chemistry, geology, and much, much more. He also learned dueling from a French master.

He then entered the medical college of the University of Pennsylvania, and in 1843 graduated with his M.D. at the age of 19. He was the youngest doctor in the United States. Although a career awaited him in Nashville, he opted instead to go to Paris, but soon became disillusioned with the crass commercialism of medicine there and left for Heidelberg. There he listened to lectures in medicine and learned German and Spanish. His expertise with the sword evoked envy among his fellow students. In the compulsory duels, he received not a scratch.

Upon returning home he was hailed as a master physician, but it must have seemed like bitter irony, since his beloved mother was dying and he could do little to help. After her death, medicine seemed futile so he attacked the only gentlemanly profession remaining—law.

He attended law school in New Orleans and in two years he qualified to practice (four years was considered normal). He soon found that lawyers had no more scruples than the physicians of Paris, and in 1848, in disgust, he threw aside his new career. He did, however, make an important friend, Edmund Randolph. More about this later.

Let me now mention Ellen Galt Martin. She was a year younger than himself (23), and from a socially prominent family. She was beautiful and intelligent, with a keen sense of humor. She was also a deaf mute. The results were predictable. His sense of honor and his well-developed desire to protect womanhood came to the fore. He fell deeply in love. By his code he was unworthy to have her, since he had accomplished nothing of value. He had no fortune, and the two professions that might have propelled him to success he had abandoned.

Perhaps journalism was the way.

In New Orleans, a new newspaper, *The Crescent*, had begun publication and soon attracted many prestigious contributors, including Walt Whitman. Walker accepted an offer to edit and write on foreign affairs. This would give him the opportunity for self-expression and make a reputation for himself. He did not shrink from exposing corruption and social injustice in his editorials. That his points were not always well-received was of no concern to him. While he was editor of *The Crescent*, he took a specific position on "American Manifest Destiny." The point of contention was a strip of land on the coast of Nicaragua known as *Mosquito*, and both Europe and the United States had awakened to its strategic importance.

It was well-known that a transcontinental route, perhaps a canal, could be effected in Nicaragua, but England, through a series of expansionist moves, had seized a point overlooking the likely route (Mosquito), and installed a puppet ruler. There was controversy about whether or not Mosquito even existed as a territory.

Meanwhile Ellen Martin died in New Orleans during an outbreak of cholera. To top everything else, the Mississippi overflowed its banks and flooded the city's cemetery, dislodging her grave.

At this point Walker headed west toward California. In June 1850, he appeared in San Francisco in dusty old clothes and penniless. He found his old friend Edmund Randolph running an important newspaper, *The Herald*. Randolph hired him as editor but soon regretted it, since Walker's acid editorials made many important enemies. However, through his columns he became well-known and liked by the public.

While Walker was crossing the continent, another person had been working on a project that would bring them both together in a strange manner. That person was Cornelius Vanderbilt.

Vanderbilt, was a man who, in type, conditioning, outlook, and purpose, stood so far apart from Walker that they might have belonged to different species. He was strong, virile, loud, and blunt of speech, with a vile temper. His wife stood in mortal terror of him. He was also pragmatic, realistic, and impatient of theories. Contemptuous of the law, he regarded wealth and power as interchangeable.

In 1849 Vanderbilt acquired a fleet of steamships on the Hudson. It was from this business that he took his favorite title, "Commodore."

One of his former rivals, George Law, and a partner had acquired a subsidy from the U.S. Government from which they agreed to provide steamships to carry mail between New York and Panama. What incensed Vanderbilt was their luck. The ink on the contracts was no sooner dry than gold was discovered in California. From that moment, the steamship lines became a bonanza. With thousands wanting to go to California, each trip netted more than $100,000. To add to the windfall, work had begun on a railroad across Panama in which Law had an interest.

Vanderbilt raged and schemed on how to reap a profit from this debacle. He began to study maps of Central America, and they disclosed to him a possibility that seized his imagination. Instead of Panama as a crossing, why not Nicaragua, which would take 500 miles off the trip? Although Nicaragua was wider, use of lakes and rivers would mean that only 11 miles between Lake Nicaragua and the Pacific would need an actual road or canal.

The plan took shape: he would form a company for this purpose, scuttle George Law, and make millions; however, before anything could be done, England would have to be persuaded. If she remained adamant, nothing less than a war would be needed. In 1849 Washington buzzed with talk of enforcing the Monroe Doctrine. Such was the power of Vanderbilt.

Late in 1849, Vanderbilt founded the American Atlantic and Pacific Canal Company. And sure enough, a new minister to Nicaragua was appointed, with instructions to enter into negotiations with Nicaragua regarding a canal. England didn't take kindly to the activities, and ordered her warships to both sides of the Isthmus. There followed a series of diplomatic, naval, and personal thrusts and counter-thrusts between Honduras, Nicaragua, England, the State of Mosquito, and the U.S. Government. Eventually a treaty was signed, with England getting much the better of it. The English possessions including Mosquito would remain as they were, while the U.S. would not interfere in Central America. Thus the situation rested, and the only way the U.S. could control events in Central America was by private expeditions of Filibusters. Walker's adventures now became possible.

Vanderbilt now had a second company, The Accessory Transit Company, which would carry passengers across Nicaragua while the canal was being completed. He "forgave" Great Britain, and would now work with her for the fast completion of the canal.

Vanderbilt's engineers were pessimistic about the possibility of navigating the San Juan River. Characteristically, the Commodore brushed objections aside and went to see for himself. With daring and incisive seamanship, he completed the 119-mile trip and entered Lake Nicaragua. It had never been done before.

By late 1851, the Accessory Road, and Vanderbilt's steamships were delivering passengers from one coast to another, cutting time and money from the Panama route. In the first year the Transit Company made a profit of $2,000,000. In those days Walker was lucky to earn $80 per month.

As the price per share on Law's Panama line was dropping, the Accessory Transit and Nicaragua Canal stock was quickly rising, and Vanderbilt was making a killing. The collapse of the stock was just as dramatic. Under a skimpy pretext, the British refused to help finance the canal. Their real reason, however, was geopolitical. They didn't want the canal built. With the canal would come American influence, and British dominance in Central American would decline. Of course, before this became known, Vanderbilt unloaded most of his stock, making a quick profit of about $10,000,000. He then sold the shares short and made another $5,000,000 as the prices tumbled.

In San Francisco Walker became outraged when in 1852 he heard about the official corruption and mistreatment of the Mexican peons in Baja California (Mexico). Walker formed a group to investigate the possibility of a military expedition. His plan was to introduce a force of

Americans as colonists and make himself master of the state. He would then declare the state to be under the protection of the U.S. government.

It didn't work out exactly as planned. He started his operation in La Paz, imprisoned the governor on his ship, the Caroline, and declared Baja California to be an independent country with himself as Interim President. He took possession of Ensenada, but his ship sailed away after the crew succumbed to the bribes of the governor.

The American Minister to Mexico, James Goodson, had been pressuring the Mexican government to sell northern Sonora to the United States for a mere $10,000,000. The offer and price were seen by Mexico to be insulting, but in view of the Walker expedition, the Mexican government felt that the United States may have decided to take what they wanted with no compensation whatsoever. On December 1, 1853, the Mexican government signed a treaty in which Goodson's terms were met. This was the *Goodson Purchase*, in which 45,000 square miles of territory, an area larger than Pennsylvania, was incorporated into Arizona and New Mexico. In a separate letter Mexico was assured that Walker would be dealt with shortly.

Soon Walker's supplies were cut off, and he and his few remaining loyal men staggered across the California border and were promptly arrested. His men told a story of incredible heroism, dignity, and kindness. The public saw him in a sympathetic light, and while awaiting his trial, he was elected as a delegate to the Democratic State Convention of 1854. He was arraigned before the Federal Court in San Francisco, and charged with violation of the Neutrality Laws. He pleaded his own case, appealing to their sense of fair play and human destiny. The jurors, moved by Walker's eloquence, found him "not guilty."

Vanderbilt, although a rich and powerful man, had never achieved social status. A pragmatic man, he believed that fame would bring social recognition. He decided to generate publicity as no mere millionaire had ever done before. He had designed a magnificent yacht, the North Star, 270 feet long, and costing $500,000 per year just to operate. He would take the North Star to Europe. The parties and receptions among the jaded aristocracy would be just the publicity he needed. To manage his business while he was away, he appointed Cornelius Garrison as manager of the Transit Company at a salary of $60,000 per year, making him one of the highest-paid executives in America.

The trip was a smashing success, but just before he returned, Vanderbilt received a letter telling of Garrison's maneuvers with Morgan to oust him from the Transit Company. In the last days of the voyage Vanderbilt burned with a desire for vengeance. Wall Street held its breath, knowing Vanderbilt's temper. Shortly after his arrival, he sent one of the shortest and most famous letters in the history of business:

> Gentlemen, You have undertaken to cheat me. I won't sue for the law is too slow. I'll ruin you!
> Yours truly, Cornelius Vanderbilt.

Walker, meanwhile, had decided on a Nicaraguan expedition. His name was still magic, and hundreds flocked to be in on the action. The Vesta sailed with 58 men, barely seaworthy, poorly equipped, and with provisions bordering on the ridiculous. Still, six weeks later, on June 16, 1855, they landed at Realjo, near the capital of Leon. They couldn't have come at a more auspicious time. The country was divided between Democrats in the north and Legitimists in the south. The Legitimists now seemed to have the upper hand, and had vowed to exterminate all Democrats. When Walker and his Filibusters landed in the Democrats' stronghold, it was like a sign from heaven, and they gratefully allowed them to operate independently, i.e., as Falangists.

His first victory was at Virgin Bay, the transit harbor on Lake Nicaragua. When the enemy attacked, Walker deployed his men to rising ground, and took possession of Vanderbilt's Transit Company buildings. With no retreat possible, every bullet had to count. After hours of fighting, the Legitimists fled. Sixty were found dead, but there was not a single American casualty. In the United States media, these men were referred to as the "Immortals." Entire editions of newspapers throughout the United States, and indeed the world, were devoted to his deeds, while the halls of Congress rang with oratory lauding his prowess.

Many years later, General Heningson, a Confederate officer said:

> I saw some of the bloodiest battles of the Civil War, but I aver that if I had picked 5,000 of the bravest Confederate or Union soldiers and pitted them against the thousand that I saw beneath the trees in Nicaragua, I'm certain that the 5,000 would have been routed within an hour.

Winning battle after battle and with new recruits arriving from the United States, Walker considered a major offensive. It was nothing less than the capture of Granada, the Legitimist's capital. He landed at night near Granada and attacked at dawn, scattered the city's garrison in a few minutes, and took possession of the government offices. There was hardly any bloodshed. No triumph could have been more effective. Overnight, from being a mere adventurer, he became the dominant man in the nation.

Walker issued orders against looting, rape, and brutality. Some women in town begged for mercy and were astounded to discover that he considered himself their protector. Writers around the world were now comparing him to George Washington and Simon Bolivar, and many prestigious newspapers ran entire sections about him.

Garrison knew that the moment of crisis for the Transit Company was at hand, but he had one last card to play. He recruited Edmund Randolph and Parker Crittenden, two of Walker's old friends, offering them huge shares in future profits if they could persuade Walker to seize the Accessory Transit Company and turn it over to Garrison and Morgan. They would sell the stock short, and make a killing when the news broke.

Randolph and Crittenden convinced Walker to nationalize the Transit Company, but he was unsure whether to cooperate with Garrison or Vanderbilt. He would have thrown in with Vanderbilt, except that Randolph, his old and trusted friend, urged otherwise. A practical politician would have sacrificed old friendships, but Walker could deny Randolph nothing.

By the end of February 1856, Morgan was selling the Transit Company stock short in a rising market. Vanderbilt eagerly grasped the stock. Then on March 12, news of Walker's activities reached the market and the stock quickly lost ground. Vanderbilt was at first incredulous, but when he was sure of the facts, he raged both in public and private. The *Herald* remarked that it was in Vanderbilt's power to kill off the new government by opening another route, thus isolating Walker from San Francisco and New York.

This is exactly what he did, and soon there were no steamers sailing from New York with the men or supplies essential for Walker. In San Francisco all ships were rerouted to Panama. The Commodore moved on several fronts at once. When Secretary of State Marco refused to interfere on Vanderbilt's behalf, he turned to England. Still another agent went to Granada and talked with President Rivas, to try to produce a break between him and Walker. Vanderbilt brought lawsuits against Morgan, Garrison, and Walker.

In 1856 Walker was at a focal point of history, where great political and economic forces converged: the need of the U.S. for a short ocean route to California, the determination of England to prevent Americans from building a canal that would give them a trade advantage with the Orient, the drive of New York capitalists to control the Isthmus, the dream of

Manifest Destiny, the urge of the South to annex Cuba and the Caribbean Islands, the struggle of Central America's peons against the landowners, and more. The importance of the venture is suggested by the enemies it made: Vanderbilt, the conservative wing of Congress, the Nicaraguan Legitimists, the governments of Costa Rica, Honduras, Guatemala, El Salvador, England, and others. Walker found wry humor in this situation, but a loss to such an array of forces would be no disgrace.

England moved quickly, and shipped arms to Costa Rica. In addition a squadron of British warships began ranging both coasts of Central America. In March 1856, Costa Rica invaded Nicaragua with a force of 9,000. Walker lost the ensuing military campaign; yet in the eyes of the American public, he was a greater hero than ever.

When news of the defeat came, Granada, already unnerved by the terror of cholera, now panicked at the rumor that Honduras was about to join in the melee. Although the rumor proved false, it led Walker into a strategic mistake. He marshalled his men, leaving the Transit Company buildings unguarded, allowing the Costa Ricans to occupy them and slay nine American employees.

Walker felt that the only answer was an assault, and in the ensuing skirmish the Americans outpointed the Costa Ricans five to one. After his victory, Walker issued orders that his troops respect the conventions of civilized people, and the remaining Costa Ricans were cared for and eventually repatriated. The dead were given decent burials.

News of his gallantry excited the American public, and in State Houses and Congress, speeches were heard lauding the man that only a few months before had been castigated. The British, believing that the U.S. might come to Walker's aid, maneuvered to prevent this eventuality.

In Nicaragua, a head of State was to be chosen. Walker ordered that his name be placed in nomination, along with any others that could muster reasonable support. There never was any doubt of the outcome. Walker became the new president; however, because of the extraordinary power he wielded, he became known as "Emperor."

Walker moved quickly in his new position. He declared English to be on a par with Spanish and seized many of the large estates. He removed corrupt judges and officials, and established a constitution based on the U.S. model. To strengthen their defenses, Walker seized a schooner, renaming it the Granada and placed it under the command of a young sailor of fortune, Lieutenant Callender Fayssoux. When a British man-of-war demanded that it "put to" so they could come aboard, Fayssoux refused and made it stick. From that time on, Fayssoux was Walker's favorite among his officers.

In the United States, Walker's fortunes were fading. Pierce, a lame-duck president, had no reason to support Walker any longer, and openly condemned him as an outlaw. The Southern block in Congress regarded him coldly, since he had taken the "wrong" position on slavery. Financiers merely smiled at the suggestion of a loan for Walker.

Domingo de Goicuria, Walker's envoy, hit on a brilliant idea: restoration of the Vanderbilt privileges in return for a loan. The Commodore was quite interested: all he wanted was Walker's capitulation; then he would be disposed to be gracious. Goicuria hastened to write Walker of the good news. He could not resist adding, however, that he had heard of Randolph's personal stake in the deal with Morgan and Garrison. This proved a fatal error, and Walker revoked Goicuria's commission. No matter what, Walker would hear no evil of his friends.

This also proved to be the fatal error in Walker's fortunes. Without the Vanderbilt money and supplies, in addition to the taxes the Transit Company would generate, Walker was stalemated. In addition, Vanderbilt could very well assist Walker's enemies, Costa Rica and Honduras, as well as stand aside if Great Britain decided to take a hand. Walker knew all this, but his sense of honor would not allow him to do otherwise.

Meanwhile, the Southern wing in Congress had visions of the South expanding into Central America and the Caribbean, but without cheap slave labor, the plantation owners would not stir. If the laws of Nicaragua could be modified to allow slavery, Southern help would not be slow in coming. Whom would he support? The North, which had disdain for him, or the South, which had a vested interest in seeing him succeed? Of course, without Southern help all would be lost anyway. Soon he issued a decree which branded him forever as pro-slavery.

More than 2,000 troops had been put in the field against him, with reinforcements not far behind. Thirteen British warships had arrived in Greytown. The last battle was fought on April 11, 1857, when Zaval mounted an attack with 2,000 men against Walker's remaining 332. There were 700 allied forces killed against 19 American. Walker later wrote: "It was with almost a feeling of pity that we were obliged to shoot them down."

At this point General Mora executed his most telling stroke, offering protection to any that would leave Walker's camp. Daily as many as 20 deserted. About this time Commander Davis, of the U.S.S. St. Mary delivered a letter to Walker advising him that the situation was hopeless, and that he would be well advised to surrender himself and his men. If not, he would seize the Grenada, cutting off their last hope of escape. Since further struggle was futile, Walker capitulated. He landed in New Orleans on May 27, 1857. President Buchanan had wisely decided that, in view of his immense popularity, no charges would be filed against him.

After a meeting with Buchanan, Walker, taking what he thought was the President's view, raised enough money to purchase a steamship and outfit it with munitions and provisions. But after arriving at Greytown he was quickly outmaneuvered by Vanderbilt's men. Walker and his Filibusters surrendered, and were once again transported to the United States. He surrendered to the U.S. Marshall in New York, and was tried in New Orleans for violation of the Neutrality Act and piracy. Even after two failures he still retained his luster, and 10 out of 12 jurors voted for acquittal.

At this point in his life he needed a religion of forgiveness. He converted to Catholicism—the faith that devout Tennessee Protestants most feared and hated.

In April 1860, his trusted Naval Lieutenant Fayssoux came to him and spoke of the British community on the island of Ruatán. England proposed to turn the island back to Honduras in return for certain concessions. The transfer was to be made in July 1860, but rather than let the island fall back into the hands of the Hondurans, the Ruatáns proposed to set up an independent government. Would Walker assist them? Would a duck quack?

Walker at once began to plan on a grand scale. Unfortunately, the British got wind of the plot. All they had to do to thwart his plans was to delay transferring Ruatán. Walker, unaware that he had been outmaneuvered, headed with his ship and men for the nearby island of Guanaja, and waited—and waited. The truth eventually became obvious, but a new scheme took place in his mind. The plan was to storm and capture the great stone fortress that guarded the Honduran port of Truxillo. This done, they would take the town, and soon the country. The fortress, however, was so imposing and well-fortified that it had never been captured in the 200 years since its construction.

Their strategy was based on the psychology of Central American soldiers, who would shoot at the nearest moving target. Six men, willing to risk death, volunteered to be the targets while the main force assaulted the fortress from a different direction. The plan worked perfectly. Every cannon in the fortress was directed at the six decoys, while the main force made human pyramids and entered the fortress. Three of the six men were killed instantly, the others severely wounded, but within 15 minutes Walker had taken the fortress.

Fort or no fort, his men needed provisions. When the allies he had counted on did not appear, he was reduced to foraging for food. While in a jungle incursion, he and his patrol were taken by a British officer, Captain Salmon. Salmon then informed him that he and his men would be protected by the British flag; however, in a bizarre twist of betrayal,

Walker and his second-in-command, Colonel Rudler, were handed over to the Hondurans. Rudler was given a short prison sentence, but Walker was condemned to be executed by firing squad.

The next morning, September 12, 1860, at age 36, he was given last rites. A squad of soldiers stepped forward, aimed, and fired. He was dead before he hit the ground. A second squad then stepped forward and fired a volley into his body, after which an officer advanced, put his pistol to the head, and pulled the trigger, mutilating the face beyond recognition.

With Walker dead the blaze of interest that had centered on him disappeared completely. Times had changed. People didn't want to be reminded of glory, honor and virtue. Money, power and expediency now ruled men's lives. They still do.

Most historians believe, as do I, that had Walker been successful, the Civil War either wouldn't have occurred or would have had a different outcome. If Walker had made peace with Vanderbilt when he had the opportunity, the Filibusters would have had the backing of forces far stronger than mere Central American republics. With a strong Nicaragua, perhaps combining with Costa Rica, Honduras, and others, the South could have expanded its enterprises to slave republics, run by Americans, but without the handicap of American laws.

In addition, with Vanderbilt committed to the success of the Nicaragua canal, the South would have had powerful inducements for the North to keep the peace. The Northern industrialists would have seen the wisdom of keeping the canal open, so that their profits could continue. They would have reached some accommodation.

Are great issues such as war, peace, government, and empire decided by something as mundane as mere profits?

Those who have made a deep study of history know the answer.

Sic transit gloria mundi

REFERENCES

Hundreds of books, and countless periodicals and documents, have been written about William Walker; unfortunately, many of them are out of print. Those listed below are still available.

The War in Nicaragua, by William Walker. S. H. Goetzel, 1860. Reprinted by University of Arizona Press, 1985.

Filibusters and Financiers, by William O. Scroggs, 1916. Reissued by Russell & Russell, 1969.

The World and William Walker, by Albert Z. Carr. Harper and Row, 1963.
Central America: A Nation Divided, by R.L. Woodward, Jr. Oxford Univ. Press,
    1976.
Agents of Manifest Destiny, by Charles H. Brown. University of North Carolina
    Press, 1980. This book also has an excellent bibliography.

Biographical Sketch of Eric Street

Eric Street is a concert pianist of Midwestern Quaker background. Averaging fifty performances a year, his schedule has included tours of Japan and Russia, and concerts in Budapest, Los Angeles, Moscow, St. Petersburg, Tokyo, and Vienna. Street's 1991 New York debut in Carnegie Recital Hall brought him a standing ovation. He has been televised on American PBS and in Russia, and National Public Radio recently featured him in a broadcast of ragtime by women composers.

Eric Street received his Doctor of Music degree in 1985 at Indiana University, where he studied with Menaham Pressler of the Beaux Arts Trio. His post-doctoral work was at the Hochschule für Musik in Vienna, Austria. As an accompanist he has performed with a number of singers from the Metropolitan and New York City Opera rosters.

Presently head of keyboard studies at the University of Dayton, Eric Street has also taught at Indian University, Bethany College (Kansas), and the University of California, Santa Barbara. He publishes in a number of periodicals, including *Clavier, Piano Quarterly,* and *Opera Journal*.

CHAPTER 37

THE UNKINDEST CUT OF ALL: THE ASCENT AND DECLINE OF THE CASTRATI

Eric Street

Somehow the contemporary zeal for authentic instruments and historic performance practice has overlooked a remarkable instrument. Hornists master valveless horns, oboists conquer two-keyed oboes, cellists surmount gut-stringed gambas, and keyboardists triumph over historic claviers of all descriptions, yet one of the most characteristic and popular instruments of the seventeenth and eighteenth centuries has yet to see signs of revival: the castrato voice. Although instrument makers can replicate historic instruments with exacting fidelity and approximate authentic tuning and pitch, music written for male soprano or alto is regularly transposed, cut, simplified, and rearranged to suit the capabilities and range of contemporary singers.

Despite a boom in early opera recordings and revivals, and greater attention to authentic performance practice than ever before, the reappearance of castrati seems unlikely. The reasons are not hard to fathom. Unlike our more "sensible shoes" era, the Baroque was an age which gloried in the elaborate, reveled in the artificial. Trees and shrubbery were clipped in improbable shapes, ornate wigs supplanted human hair, and taste in decoration ran to abundance rather than simplicity. In addition, attitudes toward children and their rights differed greatly from our own. Before condemning the era outright, we should remember how relatively recent are the laws preventing children of the poor from laboring long hours in factories and mines.

Castrati generally began as musically precocious children of humble Italian stock. Well aware of the rich financial rewards attending a success-

313

ful vocal career, many parents gambled that their child's voice could raise the family from poverty. The cautious first trotted their boys to a conservatory for a presurgical examination to determine whether the voice was worth developing. Others submitted their lads to the knife whether there was discernible talent or not, merely to unload them on a charitable conservatory or church choir. Many castrati began their careers as choir boys, little suspecting that they would remain sopranos or altos the rest of their lives.

Although far-reaching in its consequences, the gelding operation was a rather simple procedure, entailing the slitting of only two tiny ducts. Nevertheless, the transaction was dangerous enough and certainly unpleasant for a child of barely eight years, on the average. In the heyday of Baroque opera, Italian boys were mutilated at an estimated count of four thousand annually. Because of the operation's illegality and perhaps shame, parents often testified the condition resulted from childhood mishap: a fall from a horse, a bite from a wild pig, or a savage goose attack. Priceless in their imagery, the stories have more literary than factual value.

The fateful cut completed, the child was spirited to a conservatory for rigorous training in vocal exercises and repertoire, theory, counterpoint, improvisation, harpsichord, composition, languages, history, dramatics, and speech. Singing before a mirror was stressed for deportment and to discourage grimacing.

Considered more fragile than other students, castrati received better food and warmer rooms than their peers, a fact which impressed the young Mozart in Italy. To facilitate identification they were garbed in black, sometimes sporting such distinctive accessories as red belts, Turkish berets, and flannel petticoats. However, despite sophisticated education and preferential treatment, young castrati were not always a happy lot. Conservatory records reveal an extremely high incidence of runaways, possibly due to hazing from fellow students. In Italy the many failures usually found a niche in the Catholic Church, but in Germany castrati were turned out to starve when they ceased to please.

At graduation, which usually occurred between the ages of fifteen and twenty, a young singer adopted a stage name and contracted to an opera house. His debut, probably in a female role to capitalize on his fresh, youthful look, might launch a brilliant whirl to stardom or begin a long, dreary slide culminating in a provincial church choir. Should the former occur, he could look forward to immense salaries, public adulation, and stellar tours blazing across Italy and the major European cities. But should he flop:

the poor wretch might then decline to the touring of small provincial opera-houses—the "sticks" of eighteenth-century Italy—or hide his head in some church choir; where, to keep his spirits up, he would choose all the latest and flashiest operatic arias, have them reset to sacred words, and with them startle the angels on the reredos and the martyred saints on the frescoed ceiling.[1]

The introduction of castrati into the musical life of Western Europe began in the sixteenth century in answer to the needs of church choirs in Germany, Spain, Portugal, and Italy. On the strength of St. Paul's admonition, "Let your women keep silent in the churches" (I Corinthians 14:34), the Church of Rome forbid both female speech and female song long before the 1500s, when increasing complexity in sacred music began making boys' voices inadequate to the demands of the treble parts. For a time the gap was filled at St. Peter's with falsettists imported from Spain, who held a virtual soprano monopoly in the Sistine Chapel choir near the end of the sixteenth century. Their reign came to an abrupt halt in 1599, when Pope Clement VIII personally intervened to hire two castrati for the Sistine Chapel, comparing them favorably with the shrill and acidulous falsettists. Italy followed the Vatican's lead with enthusiasm, and the race to the knife was on!

The short step from the choir loft to the opera stage had already been taken by 1607, when Monteverdi's *Orfeo* opened with a castrato in the title role. When Manelli's *Andromeda* opened the first Venetian public opera house in 1637, all female roles but one were taken by castrati, including that of Venus. It has been computed that 70 percent of all male opera singers in the eighteenth century were castrati, with an even larger percentage in the seventeenth. As public demand for vocal pyrotechnics increased and the thirst for opera swept Europe, star castrati commanded magnificent fees and became the first truly international celebrities.

Because of the Italian predilection for high voices, leading roles were customarily assigned irrespective of gender to male sopranos, whether the part happened to be Hercules, Cleopatra, Romeo, Venus, or Alexander the Great. With women and lower voiced men often relegated to secondary roles, audience nonchalance about gender became part of their willing suspension of disbelief. The female contralto, quite out of favor for a time, was generally given a man's part, sometimes singing opposite a castrato playing a female. Tenors in comic opera often took the roles of old women, foreshadowing the occasional contemporary casting of a man as the Witch in *Hansel and Gretel*. Octavian, Siebel, Oscar, and their trousered comrades have roots twining back to gender ambiguity in the first two centuries of opera.

Vocal writing from the days of the castrati clearly reflects the influence of the castrato voice, training, and physique. The abundance of florid passage-work was peculiarly adapted to their vocal properties. Never losing the small larynx and thin vocal folds of their boyhood, castrati displayed incredible flexibility in runs, trills, leaps, and other feats of vocal virtuosity. The retention of boyhood larynx dimensions determined the most outstanding characteristics of the castrato voice: its range and agility. By using the falsetto register, some may have been able to extend their range to an almost unbelievable four octaves, reaching from low *B* or even A (vibrations 108.75) to the a or b above soprano high c.[2] A dismaying incident involving one such high note concerns the young castrato Luca Fabbris, who "straining after a top note of exceptionally dizzy altitude, collapsed and died onstage."[3]

The legendary flexibility of the castrato voice is difficult to imagine, but contemporary accounts relate numerous examples of remarkable virtuosity. The soprano Luigi Marchesi thrilled his auditors by improvising a volley of semitone octaves ending with a note of such astonishing power that it was thereafter called *La bomba del Marchesi*: Marchesi's bomb. Farinelli, favorite of both Phillip V and Ferdinand VI of Spain, amazed his audiences with trills of a major third. Another virtuoso of the shake, Baldassare Ferri, closed cadenzas with a lengthy trill carried up two octaves chromatically, each step clearly marked, and then descended in the same manner.

The availability of outstanding performers has inspired composers of every period, and the facility of the castrato voice encouraged the composition of music calculated to display it to greatest advantage. By the end of the seventeenth century this led to the creation of operas containing only florid roles. The modern scarcity of Handel revivals stems not so much from public taste, which has never abandoned certain of his oratorios, as from difficulty in obtaining singers capable of negotiating the fiendish coloratura. Though a triumphant *Guilio Cesare* at the New York City Opera (among other successful Handel revivals) demonstrates the viability of the florid style, nevertheless problems of casting, transposition, range, and style mitigate against widespread revival of old castrati vehicles.

Some of the most astonishing feats of the castrati were due to their celebrated long breath, an outcome of both rigorous training and peculiarities of their physiology. Testosterone, the hormone producing many of the male sex characteristics, also plays a role in stopping long bone growth at the end of puberty. Without testosterone to help signal this cessation, castrati grew to unusual and sometimes ungainly height. Included in this abnormal expansion was the ribcage, which measured approximately the same front to back as side to side. As lungs conform to chest contour by physical law, barrel-chested castrati controlled an enormous air supply. The combination of powerful diaphragm muscles from years of deep breathing and vocal exercises, copious lung capacity, and a small larynx requiring comparatively little expenditure of air enabled castrati to sustain tones for a minute or more without pausing for breath.[4] This remarkable ability was particularly felicitous in lengthy melismatic passages, and was regularly exploited in cadenzas with great effect.

In vocal as in instrumental music, improvised cadenzas provided the greatest opportunity for bravura display. The number could vary; the popular *da capo* aria (ABA) had three, one at the end of each section. Locations for cadenzas included fermatas, 6/4 chords, section ends, and rests in the music. The composer Benedetto Marcello waxed sarcastic concerning the cadenza as practiced in his day:

> while singing his aria he shall take care to remember that at the cadence he may pause as long as he pleases, and make runs, decorations, and ornaments according to his fancy; during which time the leader of the orchestra shall leave his place at the harpsichord, take a pinch of snuff, and wait until it shall please the singer to finish. The latter shall take breath several times before finally coming to a close on a trill, which he will be sure to sing as rapidly as possible from the beginning, without preparing it by placing his voice properly, and all the time using the highest notes of which he is capable.[5]

Although vocal ornamentation and improvization existed long before 1600, castrati carried them to heights that mark their epoch as the apex of florid brilliance. Concerning fidelity to the printed note, a great disparity exists between contemporary attitudes and seventeenth and eighteenth-century expectations. Whereas it is now customary to adhere closely to the score, Italian singers of the day considered the printed notes only a skeleton to be fleshed out with trills, appoggiaturas, octave skips, graces, portamentos, arpeggios, scales, melismas, variations, and other embellishments. Just as harpsichordists improvised their parts from a bass line with added symbols, soloists used a given melody as a foundation on which to build improvisations. This was not considered "taking liberties," but was the expected practice of the day. To have asked singers to refrain from rewriting would have been like admonishing a contemporary jazz group to play their tunes exactly as written.

With public interest firmly fixed on singers' art and artifice, certain other aspects of opera became correspondingly de-emphasized. Dramatic realism gave way to startling incongruity as star singers altered operas to suit their whims. The celebrated Marchesi insisted in contracts on having his first entrance announced by a trumpet fanfare, descending a hill on horseback and wearing a helmet with multi-colored plumes a yard high. He then would interpolate a favorite aria, called an *aria di baule* (suitcase aria), because it traveled with the singer from opera to opera. Text as well as drama became subordinate to the requirements of the singer, and by the 1680s words were beginning to be chosen more for their pleasant sound and favorable vowels than for actual meaning. Nice-sounding words and phrases were repeated at length, and strings of "Si" and "No" were used to spin out the text. Demanding and receiving extravagant fees, virtuosi left little money for the hire of choruses. The decline of the chorus coincided with the rise of the virtuoso soloist, with corresponding deemphasis of soloist ensembles. Complicated orchestration gave way to simple harmonic support allowing singers free rein in improvisation.

Castrati dominance began to wane as Baroque artifice yielded to Classical naturalness. Although in their heyday castrati ranged freely from Portugal to Russia, their borders began to contract before the end of the eighteenth century. The first hint of the coming decline appeared in England as early in 1728, when Gay and Pepusch's popular *Beggar's Opera* wooed the public from the extravagant art of the Baroque. The reign of the castrati in England effectively ended in 1737, with the bankruptcy of both of London's Italian opera companies, though sporadic productions continued to appear and castrato soloists came to perform as late as 1844.

In the German-speaking countries, the attraction of *Singspiel* made inroads on castrati supremacy as a growing middle class flocked to hear tuneful melodies sung in the vernacular by less-trained singers. Mozart, bowing to this trend, used only natural-voiced singers for his German operas, but used castrati for a few Italian works, including *Ascanio in Alba*, *Lucio Silla*, *Idomeneo*, and the motet *Exsultate, Jubilate*.

Castrati seem to have flourished in Russia through the end of the eighteenth century. Burney relates encountering a castrato in 1770, who, leaving Russia after fourteen or fifteen years, gambled away ten thousand pounds of his earnings in one night. One castrato retreated from Moscow with Napoleon's troops in 1812, only to be captured by cossacks whose hearts he melted with his singing. (The famed Marie Taglioni was later to accomplish a similar heart-softening maneuver by her dancing, giving rise to speculation that cossacks may be artsier than is generally presumed.) Sadly, he was eventually murdered by a drunken soldier, and his remains consumed by wolves. [6]

Italy, first to applaud the castrati, was the last to see their departure. Although opera buffa, through its general preference for natural singers, had made inroads on castrati supremacy, castrati were still very much in evidence in Italian *opera seria* after 1800. Italy continued to dispatch castrati to fill foreign opera centers, dwindling demands in the early nineteenth century. Napoleon was moved to tears at hearing one of these touring virtuosos in an 1805 Viennese production of Zingarelli's *Romeo e Giulietta*, later knighting him. Ironically, castration was outlawed under Napoleon's 1806 reorganization of newly conquered Italy. This ban, together with diminishing demand, reduced the production of new castrati to almost nothing. Although the practice reappeared in Rome after reinstatement of papal sovereignty, the reign of the castrati was effectively at an end.

Velluti, the last of the great castrato stars, triumphed in Naples, Rome, Bergamo, Milan, Venice, St. Petersburg, and Vienna, where a medal was struck in his honor. Both Rossini and Meyerbeer created operas for him; Velluti aroused Rossini's ire in 1813 by his overabundant ornamentation in *Aureliano in Palmira*, but won acclaim for both Meyerbeer and himself with an enormously successful *Il Crociato in Egitto* in 1824. Although the King of Bavaria named him *cantante di camera*, the London public was less sympathetic, and he departed England with ill humor in 1829. Long-lived, as were many castrati, he died at the age of 80 in 1861, an anachronistic novelty in a Wagnerian era.

It seems fitting that castrati lingered longest in the place that had once helped launch their successes: the papal choir in Rome. The last castrato director of the choir, Domenico Mustafa (1829–1912), retired in 1902 and is mainly remembered as a teacher of Emma Calvé. The last castrato chorister in the Sistine Chapel was Alessandro Moreschi (1858–1922), who soloed at the funerals of two kings of Italy, Victor Emmanuel II and Umberto I. Before his retirement in 1913, he made a number of recordings[7] which whet the imagination but can in no way be considered a proper summation of the glories of his predecessors.

The current interest in historical instruments and authentic performance practice shows no sign of abating. A recent production of Handel's *Teseo* in Boston offered sets and stage machinery along Baroque lines, and even boasted a "male sopranist" in the cast. Would we, like Pope Clement VIII, have compared his falsetto unfavorably with the voice of a genuine castrato? The question may never be answered. Although it is not likely that the castrati will ever return, they will certainly never be forgotten.

NOTES

1. Agnus Heriot, *The Castrati in Opera* (London: Secker and Warburg, 1956), pp. 52–53.
2. Ida Franca, *Manual of Bel Canto* (Coward McCann, 1959), p. 98.
3. Heriot, *op. cit.*, pp. 47–48.
4. Henry Pleasants, *The Great Singers* (Simon and Schuster, 1966), p. 42.
5. Donald Jay Grout, *A Short History of Opera*, 2d ed. (Columbia University Press, 1965), p. 193.
6. Heriot, *op. cit.*, p. 63.
7. These are available on an LP monaural recording, *The Last Castrato*, Opal 823.

Biographical Sketch of Jerry W. Hamm

Jerry W. Hamm is a doctoral student in Public Administration at the University of Alabama. Born in Harrison, Arkansas, he received a B.S. in Accounting from Arkansas Polytechnic College (1972) and an M.A. in Public Administration from the University of Oklahoma (1981). His main career interests have been the control and accountability of computer systems, and has been certified as an Information Systems Auditor, Cost Analyst, and Cost Estimator/Analyst. Currently, he is involved in dissertation research concerning bureaucratic ethics and program administration.

He has been married twenty years to Linda Norris of Atkins, Arkansas. He was a commissioned officer in the U.S. Air Force during the Viet Nam era and was honorably discharged.

Jerry is a member of Mensa, Intertel, ISPE, the American Society for Public Administration, E.D.P. Auditors Association, the Society for Cost Estimating and Analysis, and Pi Sigma Alpha academic honor society.

CHAPTER 38

UNITED STATES FOREIGN AID AND ECONOMIC ASSISTANCE TO BOLIVIA FROM 1946 TO 1979: WAS IT BENEFICIAL OR CRIPPLING?

Jerry Hamm

This essay will provide an overview of the country of Bolivia; its historical origins, and political and economic evolution. There will also be a brief description of United States aid and economic assistance, with emphasis on the period prior to and during the time when the 1960s Alliance for Progress program was in effect.

Last, I will assess the impact that U.S. assistance has had on the development and advancement of Bolivia and its citizens by looking at the long-term effects of the aid and economic assistance provided.

OVERVIEW OF THE COUNTRY OF BOLIVIA

A country with diverse terrain features, Bolivia has within its borders some of the world's highest mountains, as well as major rivers that drop in altitude so slowly that the waters move quite sluggishly.[1] Tropical forests in the Amazon tributaries to the east contrast with a Great Plateau area between Andes mountain ranges, and Lake Titicaca at 12,500 feet above sea level. Although Bolivia is about twice the size of Texas, the very difficult access to the interior of the country (because of prohibitive costs of railways and roads through the massive mountain settings) might have prevented emergence as a nation, were it not for the generous mineral deposits in the mountains.[2]

The early history of Bolivia includes a sophisticated pre-Inca civilization which mysteriously disappeared, the Inca Indian dynasty, which was conquered by the Spanish explorers in the mid-1500s, and liberation from the Spaniards by Simon Bolivar. Spain's greed for gold and silver (needed for wars with England and France) created a city called Potosi next to a "mountain of silver," It was the largest city in South America in 1650, with a population of 160,000. Many tons of silver were mined by Indians pressed into the labor force.[3]

After Bolivia became a sovereign state in 1825, the first century of its existence as a republic showed a consistent turnover of governments, with 40 chief executives in office (six of whom were assassinated), 190 armed uprisings, and several sanguinary civil wars.[4] Bolivia is now an inland, landlocked country, but did have an outlet to the sea in 1825. A border war with Chile in 1879 lost the port of Antofagasta.[5] Bolivia carries a grudge against Chile even now because of that important loss. But Bolivia has lost border wars with all of its neighbors—Brazil, Peru, Argentina, and Paraguay—becoming only half its original size today.

Bolivia has within its boundaries all the resources necessary to provide a sound economic foundation for its own diverse culture, progress, and prosperity.[6] The problem is not its population, which was two million people in 1925, four million by 1966, and just over six million in 1985.[7] Rather, the absence of governmental and administrative stability precludes any measured or steady advance. There is little evidence that modern Bolivia will solve this historic problem of economic and political instability.[8]

Another important factor in national development is education. Many unsuccessful attempts have been made in this area. Burgeoning school enrollments held out hope, but whereas in 1950 the illiteracy rate was 68.9 percent, in 1965 it was still at 63 percent. The cause of education's breakdown is twofold: (1) a scarcity of teachers, inadequate facilities, and average pay of $70 per month; and (2) traditional Hispanic *amor propio* (self-love) that demands high marks for children of influential people, irrespective of classroom performance.[9]

Tin mining is the country's only steady revenue source and largest employer since the late 1920s. Tin's share of total exports for foreign currency earnings ranged from a low of 55 percent (1956) to 79 percent in 1934, for the period 1929–66.[10] Much hoopla exists in the Bolivian literature about the failure of tin mining since 1952, with blame cast onto the government. But the true story is multifaceted.

Private enterprise had always exploited the richest ores since tin was found around 1870, and high-intensity processing was carried out during World War II; also, Bolivian workers had always been kept under economic restraint. In 1952, a new revolutionary government nationalized the tin mines, but inherited worn-out, obsolete equipment and depleted mineral deposits.[11] Union members, convinced such action by the new government would automatically better their economic positions, demanded higher payrolls and increased employment levels (from 26,000 in 1952 to 40,000 in 1954). Predictably, production fell, and government losses were in the millions of dollars each year. Investments in the tin industry dried up. The severity of the collapse of this industry is indicated by the fact that in 1945 Bolivia produced 50 percent of the world's tin, but by 1960 produced only 10 percent.[12] The tin industry made a profit again only in 1966.

In summary, Bolivia is a beautiful and majestic country that could support a prosperous population, but continual political and economic instability, and the lack of an established educational base, hampered any real efforts toward development of the country or advancement of its citizens. The gradual demise of the tin industry as a major financial stabilizer and the absence of deep-water ports also slowed progress toward joining the world's family of modernized nations. Today's problems within the country (political unrest, drug involvements, debt commitments, etc.) are not examined here, but are related in the sense that current circumstances have partially derived from historical aid and economic assistance from the U.S. and other nations.[13]

CHRONOLOGY OF U.S. FOREIGN AID AND ECONOMIC ASSISTANCE

When foreign aid appeared on the international scene after World War II, it was hailed as a panacea for the ills of economic underdevelopment. The tremendous success of the Marshall Plan added strength to this view. In the general exuberance, voices of doubt were brushed aside.[14] The U.S. gave Bolivia economic assistance grants totaling $4.1 million during the seven-year period 1946–52, which was consistent with the European focus of the times. During the following period, termed the Mutual Security Act Period of 1953–61, the U.S. provided grants totaling $181 million and loans of $21 million.[15]

As shown above, almost all the early assistance to Bolivia was in the form of nonrepayable grants, which generated adverse publicity. Eugene Castle wrote in 1957, "Our policy of assistance to Bolivia has cost the U.S. at least $160 million since our program was undertaken in 1953. If we had donated that money on a per-capita basis to the people of Bolivia it would have amounted to $50 each."[16] As a basis for comparison, Bolivia's per capita Gross Domestic Product in 1952 was U.S. $125.10.[17] U.S. dollars bought far more economic goods then than now; $160 million was a large amount of aid for any country to receive in a three-year period of 1954–56.

The Foreign Assistance Act of 1961 replaced the Mutual Security Act as the legislation governing economic and military aid programs. The Alliance for Progress was launched in an attack on incipient revolution and communism in the Western hemisphere.[18] In those days of dollar diplomacy, the U.S. provided money contingent on certain performance by Latin American countries, and Washington made it clear that funds promised under the Alliance for Progress would not be paid if not "earned."[19]

The Alliance was greeted with enthusiasm in both parts of the Americas, for different reasons. Latin Americans saw it chiefly as a means for access to U.S. foreign aid and largess, and to improve their personal and national economies. The U.S. saw it as a noble and heroic initiative, a program to achieve democracy and social justice, instead of allowing dictators to persecute the peoples.[20]

Bolivia received $218 million in grants and $366 million in loans from 1962 to 1976. Free monies (grants) are welcomed by almost any entity, but loans are another matter. Bolivian President Barrientos said that external public debt incurred from 1960 to 1965 (a 34 percent increase) would cause onerous repayments in 1967.[21] At the end of 1964, Bolivia's external debt was substantial, amounting to $256 million, but most of it was for bonds sold in the U.S. after World War I that had been in default for more than 25 years, with a 1957 value of $160 million. Thus, the "true" level of debt in 1964 was more realistically about $100 million. It would have been difficult to convince the authoritarian regime in Bolivia in 1964 to pay for debts accumulated by earlier political managers.

To capsulize, U.S. loans and grants to Bolivia 1946–79 totaled $983 million ($446 million of grants, $536 million in loans, with repayments of $96 million).[22] Follow-on principal reduction has been minor.

In addition, Bolivia received assistance from international organizations during the same period totaling $937 million, mostly in the form of loans.[23] Contributing organizations included: the International Bank for Reconstruction and Development; International Finance Corporation; International Development Association; Inter-American Development Bank; and United Nations Development Program. Data concerning repayments is not readily available for these organizations, but Bolivia is generally "in trouble" in its ability to service its debt. Data in 1985 put the total external debt at $3.9 billion.[24]

In summary, the early years of economic assistance (1946–61) were primarily grant-oriented. In later years, donors (U.S. and others) expected loan repayments. However, the country's ability to service debt was then and is now questionable, since new economic replacement initiatives were not established for the time when mineral resources became exhausted. The lack of a major currency generator, whether based on industry or on mineral extraction, will hamper Bolivia's future ability to recover from the crushing debt structure. For both the near term and the long term, this impoverished nation looks unpromising as an opportunity for development.

ASSESSMENT OF THE IMPACT OF U.S. FOREIGN AID TO BOLIVIA

Ah . . . . Conflicting stories abound! Some say we helped this poor country immeasurably; others say we blundered badly and lined personal pockets. The literature published by organizations who furnish loans and grants, or who are responsible for planning the development of programs and projects, presents a neutral to optimistic viewpoint. In addition, literature which talks generally about the need for and benefits from foreign aid supports the humanitarian supposition that such efforts should be performed. However, reports from Bolivia itself present a picture of disorganization, waste, etc., and range from damning indictments to glowing success stories. Let's consider some of these.

American aid to Bolivia during 1953–61 was to assist the new government (who had nationalized the tin mines as part of the reform efforts) and was sent in large quantities. With only two railroad lines into the country from two Peruvian and two Chilean seaports, a transportation problem was immediately evident. Heavy shipments of food and other commodities backed up in the ports, with much spoilage and theft due to overtaxing of storage facilities.[25] Many losses occurred even while the cargo was transported into the country. At the end of 1956, there were at least 72,000 metric tons of material in the ports, representing 130 days of railroad movement capacity. Compounding the situation, the Bolivian government owed the railroads several millions of dollars.[26] By mid-1958, Bolivian-destined cargo dating from 1955 was still in the seaport facilities. The amount of goods shipped versus goods delivered is still unknown.

According to Wilkie, "Although aid to Bolivia has had a high wastage overhead factor, this may be a normal pattern of U.S. aid."[27] Recent high-profile efforts to "feed the starving children" in Africa have faced similar transportation and distribution problems, causing great amounts of waste. These circumstances appear to again affirm John L. Gaddis' principle of "institutional amnesia", whereby past historical experience never guides managers in current evaluations or choices of policy.

During the Alliance for Progress period of 1962–79, there was a better accounting for aid shipments and country receipts, probably because of the link to monetary loans. However, problems of a different sort emerged with "tied aid." The aid recipients were forced to spend their money in the donor country, and this allowed business firms to engage in monopoly pricing techniques. Aid literature abounds with examples of corporate overpricing practices, frequently revealing prices 20 to 50 percent above world-market prices.[28] The real worth of aid to recipients also declines over time by an additional 30 to 40 percent as prices rise.[29]

During the Alliance for Progress period we can discover details such as 39 new wheat thrashers received, 20 still in crates almost three years later; or seven barely used Caterpillar tractors rusting because there are no spare parts—but instead let us consider a few highlights from the literature.

The Alliance for Progress was formulated by some of the ablest scholars and public officials in the U.S. However, Scheman says, "the failures of the Alliance are legendary. There were endless snafus and missteps. Enormous amounts of money and effort were wasted on a large number of misguided and misdirected programs. But the Alliance also produced major successes. New roads, housing projects, hospitals, schools, and so on were all built with Alliance funds."[30]

What was the long-term impact on Bolivia? Some fairly vocal critics, such as W. S. Stokes, ask whether the aid programs did any good at all.[31] Every critic seems basically to agree that there were both failures and successes in U.S. aid and economic assistance to Bolivia, but the consensus is that social and economic problems within Bolivia remain very much the same as they were when the Alliance program was founded in 1960.[32] I believe, given the research performed, that U.S. (and other nations') aid to Bolivia has had only short-term and narrow-range benefits. For all practical purposes, we may have glimpsed the various African countries' future in Bolivia—a situation where the natural resources are exploited to depletion by developed nations, then the country is abandoned to repay the "debts."

In conclusion, U.S. foreign aid and economic assistance to Bolivia over a 33 year period (1946–79) was generous and given with the best of intentions. But today's crushing monetary debt generated directly by the generosity of the U.S. and other nations will cripple the future development and emergence of Bolivia as even a third-rate power. There is little published evidence that foreign aid was more than superficially beneficial to the citizens.

BIBLIOGRAPHY

Agency for International Development. "U.S. Foreign Aid in the Alliance for Progress," Fiscal Year 1965 Program.
———— "U.S. Foreign Aid and the Alliance for Progress." Fiscal Year 1969 Program.
———— "U.S. Overseas Loans and Grants and Assistance from International Organizations." Obligations and Loan Authorizations, 1945 to 1979.
Alexander, Robert J. *Bolivia: Past, Present and Future of its Politics.* Praeger, 1982.
Birla Institute of Scientific Research. *Does Foreign Aid Help?* New Delhi: Allied Publishers, 1981.
Carter, William, *Bolivia: A Profile*. Praeger, 1971.
Castle, Eugene W. *The Great Giveaway: The Realities of Foreign Aid*. Henry Regnery, 1957.
Committee on Government Relations, Subcommittee on Investigations "Administration of U.S. Foreign Aid Programs in Bolivia." U.S. Government Printing Office, January 1960.
Frank, Charles R., *et al. Assisting Developing Countries: Problems of Debts, Burden-Sharing, Jobs and Trade*. Praeger, 1972.
Inter-American Development Bank, "Economic and Social Progress in Latin America." 1987 Report.
Kegley, Charles W., and Eugene R. Wittkopf. *American Foreign Policy: Pattern and Progress*. St. Martin's Press, 1987.
Nystrom, J. Warren, and Nathan A. Haverstock. *The Alliance for Progress: Key to Latin America's Development*. Van Nostrand, 1966.
Powelson, John P. *Latin America: Today's Economic and Social Revolution.* McGraw-Hill, 1964.
Scheman, L. Ronald. *The Alliance for Progress: A Retrospective.* Praeger, 1988.
Schurz, W. L. *Bolivia: A Commercial and Industrial Handbook.* U.S. Government Printing Office, 1921.
Staley, Eugene. *The Future of Underdeveloped Countries.* Praeger, 1961.
United Nations Department of Economic Affairs. *Economic Development in Selected Countries.* Lake Success, New York, 1947.
United Nations Mission of Technical Assistance. *Report on Bolivia.* Technical Assistance Administration, New York, 1951.

Wall, David. *The Charity of Nations*. Basic Books, 1973.

Wilkie, James W. *The Bolivian Revolution and U.S. Aid Since 1952*. University of California Press, 1969.

World Bank. *World Development Report 1987*. Oxford University Press, 1987.

Zondag, Cornelius H. *The Bolivian Economy, 1952–1965*. Praeger, 1966.

NOTES

1. Alexander, p. 1.
2. Carter, p. 4.
3. *Ibid.*, p. 32.
4. Alexander, p. 45.
5. Schurz, p. 13.
6. Staley, p. 353.
7. Wilkie, p. 28.
8. U.N. Mission of Technical Assistance Report, p. 3.
9. Carter, pp. 139, 145–146.
10. Wilkie, pp. 30, 64.
11. Carter, pp. 59–60.
12. *Ibid.*, p. 63.
13. A.I.D. Fiscal Year 1969 Program, p. 66.
14. Birla Institute, p. v.
15. "U.S. Overseas Loans and Grants," p. 41.
16. Castle, p. 149.
17. Wilkie, p. 29.
18. Kegley and Wittkopf, p. 137.
19. Powelson, p. 67.
20. Scheman, p. 98.
21. Wilkie, p. 44.
22. "U.S. Overseas Loans and Grants," p. 41.
23. *Ibid.*, p. 217.
24. *World Development Report 1987*, p. 232.
25. Committee on Government Relations, pp. 4–5.
26. *Ibid.*, p. 7.
27. Wilkie, p. 74.
28. Wall, pp. 20–21.
29. Frank, p. 204.
30. Scheman, p. 113.
31. Zondag, pp. 197–198.
32. Scheman, p. xx.

Biographical Sketch of Alkis Doucakis

Alkis Doucakis is the ISPE's Special Projects Coordinator, describing his eight stimulating years in the ISPE as a "journey of inspirations." Very happily married to his beautiful Maria, he has two lovely children—a brilliant teenage daughter of fourteen and a gifted eleven-year-old son—maintaining that those of beauty are a joy forever! For the past 22 years he has been managing their family manufacturing business, established forty years ago when his parents settled in South Africa for a better living. He considers his late beloved father, who was a perfectionist, as his mentor, and his mother as a paragon of capability and enterprise. Ten years of his youth were passionately devoted to the Boy Scout movement, another ten anxiously building his house, which is an adaptation of Frank Lloyd Wright's "Fallingwater." His outlook on life is one of enthusiasm and optimism, thanks to Elmer Wheeler. It was the ISPE which inculcated in him a love for "researching, reflecting, and recording," culminating in his publishing an original local suburban history. A mechanical engineer, he holds an M.B.A. from Wharton. While acknowledging that one of man's loftiest pursuits is to contribute to humanity, his greatest achievement, Alkis believes, is to beget children, to ardently adore them, and to raise them happily: in short, to bestow on another the Gift of Life.

CHAPTER 39

YOUR LOVE FOR EXCELLENCE

Alkis Doucakis

Have you ever had a mentor? If so, was it a friend, a teacher, your priest, a relative, an author, a college professor, or a philosopher? My mentor was my late father, whose biography is well worth relating. Regrettably, he did not experience a peaceful life. For more than half of the 44 years he spent in his motherland, Greece, he found himself in the midst of catastrophe, namely, the Balkan Wars of 1912–13, the First World War, the Greco-Turkish holocaust of 1921–22, the Great Depression, World War II, the Greek Famine of 1941–43 and the Greek Civil War of 1944–49. But these trying times will not be emphasized.

YOUTH, CA. 1912

Dionysios Doucakis (1906–79) was born in Kalamata, in the south Peloponnesian region of Greece. He could read the newspaper upside-down at the age of four and one-half years. Unlike present-day papers, the dailies then were compiled in the complicated *katharevousa* (puristic) language used mainly in official documents. Eighteen months later saw his taking apart and reassembling pocket watches that he diligently taught himself to repair as he grew older. Sadly, his sixth year also saw the passing away of his mother from tuberculosis, then a widespread disease in that country. (As a comparison, TB in 1900 accounted for 11 percent of all mortalities in the U.S.A.) His father never remarried, first for his two siblings' sakes—stepmothers generally maltreated stepchildren in those days—and second, because it was then the custom "to depart with the memory of your spouse."

When he was about twelve years old, he built his first camera—the pinhole variety—using a small can with a piece of canvas that he moulded into the shape of a concertina[1]. In later life he admitted to having taken his best photographs with this contrivance. He enthusiastically pursued photography as a hobby until before his marriage, winning fifth prize in an international photographic competition. His entry had captured women, in traditional costume, carrying and filling their earthen waterpots at a village well.

LATE TEENS, CA. 1924

His goddaughter recounts, "One morning, when he had just arrived to study in Athens from Kalámai, a friend met Godfather in the street, unshaven and lost in his thoughts. Questioning revealed that, during the previous evening, he had attended a show where a magician had staged a phenomenally astonishing act. Your father, consequently, had remained awake the whole night to work out how the illusion had been performed."

The astonishing act involved the disappearance from the stage of a motorcar, perhaps the first such exhibition in Greece. Later he made a model of that stage using a shoe-box divided into two identical chambers, a mirror, a piece of glass, and a sliding panel to allow in light from a second source.

She continues, "And find the answer he did. He immediately approached the conjurer to announce that he had worked out the solution and to verify whether he was correct. Amazed, the magician asked how much money he wanted not to divulge their secret to anyone. Godfather informed him that the money was of no interest; all he needed was an assurance that he had in fact found the answer. He also promised the illusionist that the solution would not be exposed. You see, every deed of your father revealed his genius; he was spectacular in spirit, a unique person."[2]

ACME, CA. 1936

Although he took a first-class medical degree and thereafter practised as a pathologist, he quickly realised that the ministering of medicine was not his actual calling. His talents lay, instead, in the manufacture of scientific instruments. He had no difficulty during the Depression in establishing first a workshop and later a factory that ultimately manufactured, from his specifications and designs, more than *two hundred* different electrical, physical, scientific, and medical instruments. These ranged from autoclaves to high-vacuum pumps that were supplied to state hospitals, laboratories, and high schools from contracts successfully tendered against competitors spread across Europe.

The instruments and laboratory apparatus that he manufactured included:

(i) mechanical: chemical balances, demonstration sections of Watt steam engine with governor;
(ii) electrical: incubators, high-voltage transformers;
(iii) optical: theodolites, diffracting prisms;
(iv) acoustic: stethoscopes, tuning forks;
(v) chemical: Leclanché cells;
(vi) thermal: thermometers, various laboratory demonstration apparatus;
(vii) pneumatic: barometers, Bernoulli-effect apparatus;
(viii) hydraulic: apparatus to demonstrate Pascal's Law;
(ix) magnetic: demonstration nautical compasses, Oersted experimental apparatus;
(x) aerodynamic: demonstration propellers.

He took out six patents at home and one other abroad.

CIVIL WAR, CA. 1945

He quickly learned the German language during World War II. Although life was bearable under the occupying forces, it became intolerable during the months following the Germans' retreat. In the ensuing shameful civil insurrection, he not only lost everything he had built up, but was hunted after, as was everyone who had worn a tie![3]

Judging from more than fifty photographs, an instruction leaflet on a pneumothorax apparatus, and two sphygmomanometers that remain, we may conclude that, among other Civil War losses, a whole technology of scientific instrument-making fell victim here as well.

When order was restored by the British four months later, he commissioned a plant to manufacture essentials: first bakelite electrical plugs and sockets, then cooking utensils, metal divans, and later balloons. But the Civil War again erupted one year later, this time more vengefully than ever. With conditions deteriorating and there being no sign of an end to the war, he chose to seek a better life in South Africa.

"GOD'S BOUNTY," CA. 1948

Here it was English that he had to teach himself to enable him to undertake his first project, the automation of a brick-field. That done, and upon discovering that there was no local market for scientific instruments, he proceeded to manufacture electrical bar heaters and lamps.

To date it had been his partners' capital that had financed all that he had achieved . . . and then lost. Resolving never again to fall into the perennial partnership trap, he took employment in 1951—the only time in his life—as a tool-and-die maker with the intention of establishing a manufacturing business of his very own. To achieve this he forsook his lunch and tea breaks, and instead fabricated machinery during these rest times . . . with the blessing of management! He would often comment on how refined and how kind people were in this land of largesse, in comparison to the post-war culture and impoverishment of the country that he had left behind.

HIS OWN BUSINESS, 1952 AND LATER

While he worked his day shifts, his wife produced marionettes and hand puppets at home on his self-made machinery. In the evenings they would continue working together, often until midnight, for seven days a week. (Having been a refugee from the Greco-Turkish débâcle, my mother was used to hard endeavor.) One year later he resigned his post, in order to continue on a full-time basis with his undertaking. His technical genius and exceptionally high intelligence alone, however, were not sufficient to convert his dream into a viable venture. To accomplish this, he not only had to diversify production every few years, but in addition had to work for about ninety hours every week. These were reduced to about seventy only after he had seen his two children through university eighteen years later.

As diversification led to stocking combustible materials, he had to contend with three fires in his slowly flourishing factory. The last fire was a crippling one, but he quickly overcame these costly setbacks.

His interests, which precluded the necessity for a pastime, lay in technical improvement and innovation. His thoughts and inspirations were always put to paper in the form of designs. These he would tirelessly perfect before improving his production line. This approach led to his winning first prize in a scientific instrument exhibition that was confined to countries of the Balkan Peninsula.

His most awesome experience occurred in 1943, when a medium, after an excrutiating ordeal, rotated a compass needle in front of an audience openly invited to help explain such phenomena.[4] Another incident he considered inexplicable was his inability to repair his father's pocket watch, which had stopped upon his death.

He had an inordinately ardent love for his family, perhaps because he had had no mother with whom to share such feelings, and so imparted his "store of love" to those who were closest to him.

Some of what has not been mentioned above is included in his epitaph, "Your love for excellence, beauty and elevation of the mind never transcended your adoration for your family."

NOTES

1. Letter dated 12 May 1989 from his niece and goddaughter, Dr. Katerina Liveriou, Ph.D. (Salzburg), in consultation with her mother, the sister of Dionysios.
2. *Ibid.*
3. For further details see page 201 of Nicholas Gage, *Eleni*, Fontana/Collins, Glasgow 1984. (A movie was based on this book, which won the Royal Society of Literature Award.)
4. CSICOP, the U.S.A. Committee for the Scientific Investigation of Claims of the Paranormal (established in the mid-1970s) has proved this to have been a hoax: a magnet had apparently been fixed inside the medium's nostril! Dr. Angelos Tanagras (1877–1971) founded in 1923 the first Greek Society for Psychical Research. Another, as-yet unexplained phenomenon by Tanagras' medium was "mindreading": she accurately "mindread" and then described my mother's memory of her father's wake.

Biographical Sketch of Eric P. Muth

Eric P. Muth, Ph.D., of Milford, Connecticut, has a passion for assembling information about vision aids in history which has taken him to museums and libraries around the world on behalf of Audrey B. Davis, Ph.D., Curator of the Smithsonian's Medical Sciences Division. Most of the world's major vision-aids collections include items from Muth, a master optician. Some 750 vision aids were donated by him to the National Museum of American History.

A preliminary historical document consisting of 1,400 pages of text and 14,000 supporting photo copies of vision aids and related materials was released in 1992 to selected international museums and libraries, a donation for which he received numerous awards. His final project report is due in 1996.

Muth won England's Melson-Wingate Prize for the Best Technical Article of 1981. His textbook, *Management for Opticians*, was published in 1983. In 1975 he was named Connecticut Optician of the Year and in 1981 Connecticut Guild of Prescription Opticians Man of the Year. He received the Rotary Service Above Self and Chamber of Commerce Civic Service Awards in 1986. He is a Fellow of the National Academy of Opticianry and of the ISPE.

CHAPTER 40

THE TRASH COLLECTOR

Eric P. Muth

I've been an optician for 25 years. History has always been my interest. For many years, as was the custom, I sent old precious-metal vision-aids products to the smelter for recycling, until one day when I started to examine some, and discovered beauty and workmanship unparalleled by today's standards. Selectively I began to put aside those which struck my fancy.

In time my curiosity was aroused. How did they make this? Who and when follows, in their natural order. I started my quest for knowledge by looking for books on the subject, only to find that few existed, and that these few were riddled with inconsistencies, misstatements, and even hoaxes that continue to be perpetuated, even though they have been proven to be just that. It seems that once something makes it into a library, readers consider it gospel.

My personal collection rapidly grew to 750 vision aids, mostly by purchases of small collections from flea markets and of individual pieces from international dealers. Most of us in the optical field consider old vision aids to be trash which must be disposed of. Once collecting fever hits, however, there are those who will pay up to $10,000 for a rarity which may round out a collection. To lower my fever I decided to donate my collection for preservation. In 1982 the National Museum of American History, Medical/Sciences Division (Smithsonian Institution), accepted my offer.

By private aircraft I and a friend flew to Washington, where we hired three taxicabs to convey my collection and library accumulations to the museum. The overflow of this collection was later transferred to the American Academy of Ophthalmology Foundation Museum in San Francisco. By this time I had considerable knowledge about vision aids, which prompted curator Dr. Audrey Davis to appoint me as a consultant.

Up to this point I had been a dabbler, but with this appointment I felt compelled to become a serious student. Now that the personal collector's shackles were broken, I was free to research vision aids. I also started sending institutions needed pieces as donations, thereby acquiring many new friends. My list of recipients is very long; so I won't bore the reader; but that my donations do rest in some of the world's most prestigious museums is a source of great personal satisfaction for me.

It became evident that a true and complete history of vision aids, one which would not suffer from western myopia, needed to be written. Dr. Davis commissioned me as Project Coordinator to assemble appropriate information for a proposed museum catalog. This endeavor required expert help. To my dismay I found that in the United States there were only dabblers like myself. I had to reach out to assemble a dozen international consultants, a handful of whom qualify as experts. Many museums and institutions contributed information and vision-aids photographs. I paid out of my own pocket to have the entire vision-aids collection at the Smithsonian photographed. Since I was at the end of the information funnel, expertise flooded over me quickly. My postage bills were running some $400 a month at the height of the accumulation phase.

To zero in on introduction dates, the best scientific evidences are trade cards and patents, a knee-high stack of which had been accumulated. Everything written on the subject in a great variety of languages came to my door for ultimate translation.

All this material needed to be weighed, and that which was deemed useful placed in a chronological database ranging from dates B.C. to the present in yearbook fashion. Phase I culminated in a 600-page document. Phase II is now in progress. It consists of personal visits to opthalmic libraries, two years ago to Greece and Turkey, and last year in the United States, this year in France and Egypt, and eventually to other countries. The document should swell to 1,000 pages by the end of 1993.

In the meantime, severe budget cuts at the Smithsonian had precluded publication of the catalog. This did not deter me; I was in too deep. My goal now is to continue to supply five-year updates to participating world institutions, each of which will have a valuable research and informational document. In all modesty, in order to clarify the situation, let me mention that I have borne all related costs myself.

Though a thousand papers could be generated from the information at hand, I've published only significant findings in a variety of languages and in as many scientific institutes. My last publication was in Hindi.

Another project is the accumulation of vision-aid images and identification. To that end I have 5,000 slides of everything known to have been made; these include people, fabrication, machines, etc. In time each slide will be placed in computer memory with appropriate information and correlating numbers. Many photographs were xeroxed and sent to the international consultants in Germany, Sweden, and the United Kingdom for identification and opinion. From thirteen opinions I've been able to pinpoint specific dates or eras.

Let me offer you some of the more interesting highlights of my findings.

People used lenses as vision aids between 3000 B.C. and A.D. 1270.

The first lenses were rock crystals, later known as "pebbles," which were preferred as a form of snobbery into the nineteenth century.

In 1270 a statue at Konstanz depicts a bishop with a lens in a handle. Soon two such units were joined with a rivet; so spectacles were born by A.D. 1285, at the latest, in Tuscany. The inventor is unknown. The purported inventor, Salvino Armanti of Florence, was designated in order to gain prestige for Florence (this hoax was unearthed by Rosen in 1956).

It is clear that the Catholic church, via its educated and industrious monks, played a significant part in the fabrication of vision aids and their dissemination throughout the world.

The next important step was head retention so that people could use two hands freely. From a 1580 painting we have evidence that ear loops (cord, twine, etc.) were in use in Spain, and in 1583 leather straps in Germany.

By 1730 sidearms (temples) had come into usage, and in 1727 the monocle was used. During the eighteenth century many varieties of sidearms and spectacles evolved. At the middle of the century scissors spectacles arrived, and by the end of the eighteenth century lorgnettes began their evolution.

In 1806 President Jefferson directed his optician, McAllister, to devise a frame with a flat top eyewire, so that he could see over it while at the same time reading with his spectacles. This concept was first thought to have been applied in England in 1834. I unearthed this information, with sketches, from Monticello.

Sometimes I create problems for museums. For instance, in Philadelphia the Franklin Institute displays a pair of "his spectacles." Unfortunately they are an anachronism.

President Jackson's home in Tennessee displayed his wife Rachel's spectacles, which I know were made some fifty years after her death. Some investigation in the family graveyard yielded the answer. There was another, later Rachel, and a curator mistook one for the other, incorrectly tagging the spectacles.

Almost everyone acknowledges Franklin as the inventor of bifocals. I've read his correspondence, and find only his words, "I am happy in the invention of bifocals." Since there are many other references to bifocals in England and France at this period, I believe he meant only that he was happy with their availability.

J. I. Hawkins brought us the trifocal in 1827, and by 1840 the Pince-Nez had arrived.

During the course of my work I have developed a hundred-page curator's manual on the various materials used in vision aids, their care, cleaning procedures, and identification from hallmarks. Most major museums now have a copy of it.

A most exhilarating experience in this project was my search for the inventor of plastic corneal contact lenses. It is known that Heinrich Wohlk of Kiel was working on such a lens in 1946. Still, a Kevin Michael Tuohy (purported to be an Englishman in Poulet's *Atlas of Spectacles*) received a patent for them in 1951. Unknown to me, I'd been making glasses for his brother for years. The information came out one day when I queried him about his name.

In due course Kevin Tuohy's widow met me in Washington, where she donated considerable memorabilia to the Smithsonian, and allowed me to assemble a half-dozen donation packets and dispatch them to important museums around the world. Included were numerous lecture tapes which revealed the acquired English accent of a New Yorker crippled by polio whose 1948 patent application would propel him into the luxury of the Hollywood Hills.

As I've worked on Phase II of this project, thousands of undocumented, unknown, and widely dispersed facts have been unearthed, assembled, and placed into one document. By its nature, Phase II can never be complete, but in 1996 the document will be sent to the world's major museums for use by curators and researchers. My gain in this project is the satisfaction of having done it, having trained myself as a world-class expert in the course of it, and knowing I've left something behind to help others who will, I hope, improve on what I've accomplished.

I've visited many dusty shelves, saved bits and pieces of paper, catalogs, frayed old books, and vision aids no one seemed to want or care about (after all, to anyone else they were just dirty old glasses), to the point that I am often referred to as an intrepid, sophisticated trash man. But I am flattered by such a title. I have done all this as a labor of love, and I believe that this is how genuine historical research is always done.

Section V
The Future of Technology

Biographical Sketch of Manfred S. Zitzman

Born (only child) in Steinheid, Germany, on April 20, 1925, Manfred emigrated with his parents to the U.S. in 1927, and settled in the Philadelphia-Reading, PA, area. After graduating from high school in 1942, he served in the U.S. Navy, Pacific Theater, from 1943 to 1946, participating in the invasions of Iwo Jima and Okinawa, and in the Japanese occupation. Home again, he completed his B.S. in Chemistry at Albright College in 1949, and proceeded to work as an industrial research chemist until 1964. He has been married since 1953, and now has two grown children.

In 1962 he earned his M.S. in Chemistry at the University of Delaware, and pursued other graduate work at Muhlenberg College, Lehigh, St. Joseph's, & Pennsylvania Universities. In 1964 he became a professor of chemistry at Albright College, where he taught until his retirement in 1990. His major research area was natural alkaloid-metal complexes.

His hobbies include chess, ancient coins, rare music, history, spelunking, foreign travel, voracious reading, photography, writing and publishing articles on a variety of subjects. He won various city, county, etc., chess championships in the 1940s to 1960s, and three State Championships in the 1960s. In 1982 he won the USCF North American "Absolute Postal Chess Championship" (undefeated).

He joined the ISPE in 1978, and is now a Senior Research Fellow.

CHAPTER 41

DO CHESS COMPUTERS THINK?

Manfred S. Zitzman

Before we talk about chess computers, let's consider pocket calculators—the simplest type of computer, and one with which we are all familiar. In order to use these devices, we press buttons representing numbers, and other buttons representing operations, such as $+$, $\div$, !, etc., whereupon the result of our operation appears almost instantaneously. How does the calculator accomplish this? In order to understand this, we must consider the *abacus*, which was invented several thousand years ago (probably by the ancient Egyptians) and in some parts of the Orient is still somewhat in use, even today. The abacus consists of a framework of wood or metal, to which several parallel wires have been attached, to give an appearance not unlike a harp. Each wire has a number (usually 10) of beads, which may be slid along the wire to which they are affixed. Each bead is given a numerical value depending on the wire to which it is attached.

The beads on the first wire will have *unit* values, such as 1, 2, 3, . . . , etc. Those on the next wire will be 10, 20, 30, ... The beads on the third wire will be assigned values of 100, 200, 300, . . ., and so on. We can even have wires whose beads have decimal values, such as 0.1, 0.2, etc., or 0.01, 0.02, etc. Obviously, the more wires (and beads) that we have, the greater will be the "capacity" of our abacus.

The actual operation of the abacus is, much like riding a bicycle, far easier to do than to explain in words! Let's do just one simple calculation; suppose we wish to add the number 128 to 233: Starting with all the beads on the right, we first enter the "128" by sliding the appropriate beads to the left, as in Figure 1.

Figure 1.

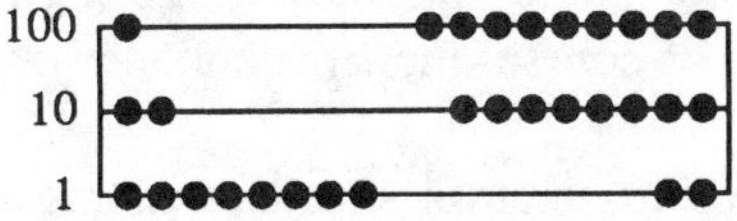

Now to add the "233" we slide two "100" beads to the left, followed by three "10's." We cannot slide three "1" buttons, since we have only two left. The rule here is that when we exhaust all 10 beads on one wire, we slide *all* the buttons on that wire back to the right, and slide one bead on the *next higher* wire to the left. (I said it was easier to do than to explain!)

The final result will be as shown in Figure 2.

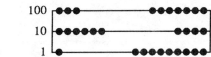

Figure 2.

The beads on the left display the answer of 361. Admittedly, this addition is the simplest operation to do and understand. Yet, over the centuries, skilled abacus operators developed methods for doing all mathematical operations on their instruments. They developed all sorts of short-cuts and gimmicks to increase their speed. Like the superfast sliderule operators of our youth (if you're in your 60s!), they were artists in a technique that is now virtually dead. I can recall that back in the 50s, in the days of electrically driven mechanical calculators, a skilled abacus operator defeated the best of our units in a speed contest! That's all over now. Human fingers cannot remotely approach the speed of our present-day electronic calculators.

How does this modern-day calculator operate? Instead of beads, it uses electrons, and instead of wires, electron pathways. All the numbers it uses are translated into a binary form, which correspond to the turning off and on of an electric switch. Thus, the numbers 1, 2, 3, are translated by the calculator into "on," "on-off," "on-off-on," etc. (*All* numbers can be expressed in binary form, and that's what the calculator does!) The switch operations correspond to the number of beads being slid on a particular abacus wire.

If we could build a gigantic abacus, miles across, containing huge numbers of wires and beads, and if we also had a giant operator with huge and incredibly fast fingers, that combination would be able to do exactly what our pocket calculator does!

Conveniently for us, microchips and printed circuits can be built very small! Even more conveniently, electrons are already very, very small, and can be induced to "slide" at (nearly) the highest speed that matter can attain, which is, of course, the Einsteinian *c* or just about 186,000 miles per second.

These incredible electron speeds, existing in such a small unit as a

pocket calculator, seem to perform their operations almost instantaneously. As soon as one presses the final button, the answer seems to appear
immediately. However, on pocket calculators containing the factorial symbol (!), one can observe calculator lag! If you have a calculator with this
symbol, punch the number 69 and then punch (!). This instructs the
calculator to multiply all of the whole numbers from 1 through 69 and
display the result. It will take the calculator a full *second or two* to come
up with $(1.7112245)^{98}$. There is no way to comprehend the size of such a
number. For example, if one *trillion* planets the size of Earth were ground
into sand grains, the total number of all those grains would only be about
10^{41} grains—nowhere near 10^{98}. In fact, if we took all the matter in all
the suns and planets in the universe, and subdivided it all into atoms, that
number of atoms would be about 10^{60}—still nowhere near 10^{98}. It is
utterly incredible that a $20 pocket calculator can deal with numbers such
as this, and all within two seconds or less! It tends to makes us forget that
it is, essentially, just an abacus!

As I've said, abaci have been around for several thousand years, but
no one ever seriously thought that they could *think*! Obviously, these abaci
were built by persons, and it was *persons* that moved the beads. Our
present calculators are also built by persons, and persons (by pushing
buttons) still "move the beads." The only real change is that now the
beads are too small and move too fast to be seen. Yet, for some reason,
increasing the speed of the abacus has caused many people to endow it
with the property of *thought*, which it does not possess. Being able to
multiply all the digits from 1 to 69 is very impressive, but the operation
itself is comprehensible to a child. In fact, the child could do it himself,
with pencil and paper, if he had an eternity in which to do it! The speed,
accuracy, and versatility of calculators are certainly awesome, but *not*
incomprehensible!

Thus far, I have spoken of calculators instead of computers, but in
their operations there is no essential difference between the two. The
biggest difference is that computers, unlike calculators, contain all sorts
of memory storage and algorithms.

If we agree that the calculator is a "super abacus," we may define the
computer as a "super-duper abacus"!—still electronic "beads and
wires," but more of them. One big difference between the simple calculator and the computer is in *memory capacity*. The calculator's memory is
very small, and usually contains the values for only a few constants, such
as π and ϵ. The computer, on the other hand, may have a very large
memory, consisting of results it obtained previously by the "beads and
wires" method, or special data inserted by some human programmer. It is
of the greatest importance that this special data is absolutely precise and

correct! Errors in this programming have given us a new word: "GIGO," which means, "*Garbage In* (leads to) *Garbage Out*." This concept will be particulary important when we consider chess computers.

The computer is more versatile than the calculator, in that all sorts of algorithms (methods of procedure) can be built into its circuitry: yet it still needs to express all numbers in an "on-off" switching manner, and all its calculations are still of the "beads along wires" sort. It's still an abacus. It does not think.

How can we prove this? Let us consider mathematics only. Surely, here the computer is supreme—or is it? In speed of calculation, there is no contest, but speed in itself has nothing fundamental to do with thought. Computers and all the algorithms they use have been programmed into them by human beings. The simplest test of *pure mathematical superiority* would seem to be postulate a purely mathematical problem that *has been solved by humans, but which no computer can solve*! Is there such a problem? Actually, there are quite a few, but one example will be sufficient. To prove our point:

Prime numbers (those with no divisors save themselves and one) have occupied mathematicians since the days of ancient Greece. The first several primes are 1, 2, 3, 5, 7, 11, 13. . . . It would seem that there ought to be some formula that would generate future members of this series, but no such formula has ever been found. Computers, by trial and error, have generated the next several million primes, but have not been able to predict when the "next" one will appear. It may be that no such formula exists.

Now, let's ask our computer another question about primes, one that, as it turns out, *does* have an answer. Is the number of primes infinite, or is there a largest, final prime?

The only way our computer could try to solve this problem would be to keep generating larger and larger primes (with its built-in "beads and wires" technique) *ad infinitum*. It would never stop, since the number of primes *is* infinite! This was proved by Euclid himself, more than 2,000 years ago. Here is his beautiful proof:

Assume that P is the highest possible prime; now consider a number that is generated by the series $1 \times 2 \times 3 \times 4 \times 5$ . . . . P. Call this new number $(P!)$. Now, add 1 to it, yielding $(P! + 1)$. This number is not divisible by P nor by any number less than P, because all of these are contained in $(P!)$; therefore $(P! + 1)$ is either a prime higher than P, or it contains a prime factor higher than P. Q.E.D.

This is human thought at its highest level. There is a perfection and elegance there that leads one to recall Edna St. Vincent Millay's lines,

Euclid alone has looked on Beauty Bare,
Fortunate they,
Who *once,* and then but far away,
Have heard Her massive sandal set on stone.

So here we have a problem which a man solved more than two thousand years ago, which no modern computer, given only the raw data, can solve. Euclid, of course, had the raw data, but he also had a first-class human mind. In short, he could *think!* Computers can't.

The bottom line is that the computer as we know it today can perform only the operations that have been programmed into it. It will do those operations faster than any human, but it will not initiate any new operations! Now, on to chess and chess-computers.

Chess has been around for a long, long time, its origins lost in antiquity. One of the secrets of its long survival is that, unlike tic-tac-toe, it cannot be solved exactly, and mathematicians tell us that the number of possible chess moves is at least 10^{120} with a three-digit exponent! We all know how big that is!

Yet logic does play a part in the game. After learning the rules (which practically anyone can do in an hour or two) a person is ready to "play." Yet to play *well*, a great deal of experience and study is necessary, plus something called "natural talent," which no one, as yet, has been able to define.

At the highest level of the game, the player's choice of moves becomes harder and harder to explain in quantitative terms. Indeed, Grandmasters of chess have as a group, been notably inarticulate about precisely *why* they select particular sequences of moves!

During centuries of chess play, a few dozen general principles have evolved, such as King safety, mobility, material advantage, etc. Most of these principles cannot be quantified. For example, how *safe* is *safe*? And safe in relation to *what*? To complicate matters further, it is very often necessary to sacrifice one principle to realize another. For example, one can win material, but thereby also decrease one's King safety. Strong chess players *usually* know whether this should be done or not, but they are not infallible. If they were, they'd never lose any games! Still, being strong players, they are more often right than wrong. The chess programmer's problem has been how to program his unit to deal with these unquantifiable "principles."

Ten years ago, chess computers contained only the "rules of the game," which were and are *exact.* Those early units were laughably weak, and could be beaten by 99 percent of all human players. Nowadays, we have several computers that are stronger than all but a handful of *all* chess players! The strongest unit at present is called DEEP THOUGHT, and it has beaten several Grandmasters—the highest category of human player!

How does this reconcile with my assertion that a computer is simply an "electronic abacus"? Can it be that there has been some sort of break-through, and that DEEP THOUGHT *is* thinking? DEEP THOUGHT knows nothing of chess boards and pieces. It doesn't know it is playing a game and doesn't realize it has an opponent! It doesn't "know" or "real-ize" *ANYTHING*. The real breakthrough in the past ten years has been in speed.

DEEP THOUGHT can look at 1,500,000 chess positions per second!

In practical terms, the stongest human chess player in five minutes of thinking time can project no more than a dozen or so possible future positions. He will make his move, heading for the sequence that seems to lead to the most favorable position, from his point of view. This decision is based on both "principles" and his "intuition," the latter developed by long experience. In the same five minutes of time, the computer will look at *450 million* positions. It will then select its moves by pre-programmed principles, since it has no intuition. The computer also has the advantage of its huge memory banks which contain millions of positions believed to be "favorable" to it, and every important game played by every important player in the last few hundred years. I don't know *exactly* how many of these are in DEEP THOUGHT's memory, but the number can be in-creased without limit. All these positions are instantly available to the computer. The human has only his own poor and highly fallible memory.

This practical discovery—that DEEP THOUGHT, with its 1,500,000 moves/second and huge, infallible memory is no more than *equal* to the fallible memory and intuition of an "average" Grandmaster—is most remarkable! No wonder that humans often have more faith in their intui-tion than in their logic!

The key point in comparing human and computer is that the computer looks at *all* 450,000,000 positions in its five minutes. The human being *disregards* 449,999,998 of those, and looks at only twelve! It is intuition (mostly) that tells him which twelve are worth considering and which one of the twelve to select. Intuition is marvelous and awesome, but it may be *wrong*! The computer can never be wrong. If it fails, it fails because of its faulty (human) programming—the GIGO effect, as we mentioned earlier.

Recently, World Chess Champion Gary Kasparov played a two-game match against DEEP THOUGHT. He won both games. He was quoted as saying, "If a computer could beat the World Champion, it could also write the best books and the best plays in the world." This does *not* follow, since which books are "best" is a matter of opinion, nor are there rigid rules for writing them. The rules of chess are 100 percent defined, and winning or losing is a matter of *fact*, not opinion! (It is very interesting that Kasparov, who has demonstrated that he has the best "chess instinct" on this planet, should have advanced so "illogical" an argument!)

Yet the fact remains that DEEP THOUGHT with its 1,500,000 moves per second *can* regularly defeat all but a handful of all chess players. The best computer in 1983 could consider only about 150,000 moves per second and there were thousands of players who could beat it.

Chess programmers tell us that units 100 times faster than DEEP THOUGHT are not far off. If the curve continues on its present arc, a computer as World Champion would seem to be inevitable—and it should happen in a few years.

It does seem that in *chess*, human "intuition" will not be *duplicated*, but simply *overwhelmed* by the ever-increasing speed of "bead and wire" calculation.

I see no evidence that any similar situation will occur in any of our other arts, such as literature, painting, etc., in which "winning" is simply a matter of prevailing opinion in a certain audience at a certain time and place.

Incidentally, Kasparov believes that no computer will ever be World's Champion, since the human will always be able to "invent something new." I hope he's right, but I don't think he is.

To answer the question which is the title of this article, No, they don't *think* in any human sense, but they've proven that ultrafast "bead and wire" calculations can *in chess only* be an effective substitute for thought, or intuition, or whatever it is that human chess players do.

Finally, if and when a computer does become World's Champion, we shouldn't resent it. After all, it is not an Alien. It is Our Child.

CHAPTER 42

A DOZEN INVENTIONS

Yale Jay Lubkin

Each of us has talents which are outstanding. Since none of us approach perfection, we all have deficiencies as well. One of my talents is inventing. One of my serious deficiencies is the inability to convey ideas to people with money to invest, or even to be able to contact them. (I don't seem to have a problem conveying ideas to technically minded people, and my monthly article in *Defense Science* seems to have had the biggest following in the defense business.) For example, Oppenheimer & Co. offered, in 1969, to invest in a cheap 9600-baud FAX I had invented; then the appropriate VP there dropped the whole thing and went to Japan. So I would like to enlist people who are good at raising investment money and/or people willing to invest in the possibility of greatly multiplying what they put in, at the risk of losing it all.

Following is a brief description of a dozen inventions I am working on. Some are mine; some are not, originally; some are a combination. If you want more information, please write. I have one-pagers on each, and in-depth White Papers on all. Receipt of a White Paper is contingent on executing a Confidential Disclosure.

1. PHYSICAL EXPLOSIVES AND PROPELLANTS.

By using physical reactions, rather than chemical or nuclear ones, it is possible to get specific energies in between those of nuclear and chemical reactions. Roughly, the specific energy of a physical reaction is about a hundred times that of a chemical one, so that a bazooka shell could have the explosive power of a 16-inch battleship shell and could be fired at Mach 20. By using physical propellants, you can drop the cost of sending a kilo into space by a thousand times, and send up the whole Brilliant

Pebbles net in a single rocket. This requires much theoretical and practical development, but crude models have been demonstrated.

2. WIRELESS, NON-LINE-OF-SIGHT COMMUNICATIONS.

By using Rayleigh scattering of ultraviolet, together with new devices whose theory is known and some sophisticated communications theory, it should be possible to broadcast, over a 25- to 50-mile range, signals having a total bandwidth of a few million high-resolution TV channels, without interference to or by other communications. This could make cable and MA/DS TV obsolete, and make video telephone practical. It will allow modems to work at 100,000,000 baud instead of 9,600 baud. Requires much hardware development, but the theory is mostly there.

3. HIGH-EFFICIENCY BLADELESS TURBINES.

These were invented by Tesla in the early 1900s and forgotten. They are small, with a goal of 20 HP per pound and a goal thermal efficiency of more than 60 percent. That is about five to ten times better than gasoline engines. A turbine built in 1911 of German silver, and operated on low-temperature steam, was 2 inches thick and 10 inches in diameter. It produced 110 HP. Tests on a larger device, also with steam, showed 36 percent thermal efficiency. It can run nicely on fuel oil, and could replace gasoline and diesel engines for almost all applications. Requires some theoretical work for optimization and engineering design, and an invention that Tesla left out.

4. SOFT X-RAY SOURCE FOR SUB-MICRON PHOTOLITHOGRAPHY.

Such sources are needed for production of the next generation of integrated circuits. The smallest device currently available is a Japanese synchrotron, 60 feet long and $20 million. My device works by compressing a hot plasma with a spherical shock wave. One prototype was built and worked. It is smaller than a PC, but requires a power source, which was fit in one standard rack. Russian-designed power sources can greatly simplify this problem. A prototype was built and tested a few years ago in Canada, but the original inventor did not know engineering, and built a very suboptimal unit. Estimated sales price is less than $250,000. Requires mostly good engineering to be practical.

5. SMALL, CHEAP, HIGH-POWER MICROWAVE SOURCE.

The Plasmatron was invented by me, and several units were built and tested. Active element is a gas plasma. In a 1-cc unit, continuous output of 100 watts was measured at RF at an efficiency of 85 percent. Calculated upper cutoff frequency for the device tested seems to be about 100 GHz. Since building the prototypes, I did some theoretical work on the direction to go for optimization. Ultimate tube cost seems to be around several dollars. Traveling-wave tubes for producing less power at 40 GHz cost $40,000 and up, and are large and delicate. The Plasmatron will work over at least the temperature range from $-200°C$ to $+600°C$, and will withstand extremes of temperature, shock, vibration, and radiation. Requires engineering and some additional theoretical work. Work is slowly proceeding to use the Plasmatron as an ionization source for diamond coating.

6. UNIVERSAL FOCUS EYEGLASSES.

Ordinary eyeglasses are in focus at only a single distance. If you need more than a minor correction, and you want to be able to see things clearly at more than one distance (say, you want to be able to read and also to watch TV), then you need several pair of glasses, or bifocals, or even trifocals. It is possible, inexpensively and quickly, to make eyeglasses which will be corrected for each individual eye and in focus at all distances. By using techniques of binary optics, we could design and produce cheaply and quickly eyeglass lenses which could be either prescription or generic. Prescription glasses might take an hour or two to make.

7. TURBINE BLADE-TIP CLEARANCE MEASUREMENT.

It is possible, with a simple sensor device incorporated as part of a turbine housing, and processing circuitry located where convenient, to continuously measure and monitor blade-tip clearance.

The device will not only allow measurement of the mean tip clearance, but also permit measurement of the entire pattern of tip clearances over the set of turbine blades. If combined with a position reference, which indicates when blade #1 is under the sensor, the device can measure the clearance of each individual blade. If the blades cut into a rubbing strip, the sensor can indicate the measured clearance to the worn rubbing strip as well as the actual clearance, which may be negative, to the original rubbing strip surface.

The device may also be arranged to indicate, with an alarm signal, when rubbing strip wear has reached certain values, which may be specified to the nearest mil if desired.

The sensor output is not linear with clearance nor a differential, such as the temperature measurement of a thermocouple, but is approximately proportional to the fourth power of the individual blade clearances. Thus a change from 20 mil clearance to 10 mil clearance will result in a 1,500 percent increase in the sensor signal. By comparison, the voltage of a chromel-alumel thermocouple varies 40 percent over a 1,000°C range.

8. ULTRASONIC PRECISION MAMMOGRAMS.

By using an acoustic version of impulse radar, we would make an internal mammary-imaging device which offers substantial improvements over conventional mammography. Among the advantages are greatly improved accuracy, substantially lower cost, and the ability to have the patient see exactly what, if any, anomalies exist inside her breasts.

In practice, the woman undergoing testing removes her upper clothing and lies face down on a test table, with breasts hanging in two containers filled with lukewarm water. The containers hang below the plane of the table, and are removable for cleaning between patients. On command, she lies still for between five and twenty seconds (depending on the instrument cost). The data from the test unit are sent to a PC equipped with suitable software and interface boards. By the time the woman has toweled herself and dressed, the results will be on a 3.5″ floppy disc, which she can take with her. In her physician's office, she and her physician can examine a three-dimensional, double life-size, color-enhanced image of each breast. This image will show clearly the blood-vessel and foreign-object structure and location within the breast, to a resolution of about $1/50$ inch.

Using the data recorded on the disc, the woman and her physician can decide whether or not any anomaly exists within the breast, the extent of the anomaly, and the most satisfactory procedure for eliminating any anomalies. No human interpretation will be required to uncover anomalies; they will be clearly visible. A copy of the disc can readily be made available to the woman to keep for future reference.

9. SPEAKER IDENTIFICATION.

Most, if not all, of the speaker identification techniques now used by police are based on the Voiceprint techniques of Lawrence Kersta, which were shown, by a blue-ribbon panel a generation ago, to be "slightly worse than random."

There is a voice-identification technique that works. I have been interested in the subject for many years, and, in 1968, provided the identification of the voice of Captain Lloyd Bucher of the Pueblo in a multiple blind test after FBI, CIA, MIT, Bell Labs, and Mrs. Bucher failed.

In 1973, I built the first automated voice identifier for Israeli Intelligence. Error rate in tests was zero, both for wrong identification and for failure to identify. Less than 1 KB is needed for a library entry of a voice signature, and a library of 1,000 voices can be put on a single floppy disc, or a million on a CD-ROM disc. A relatively simple program for a PC is all that is needed to provide accurate speaker identification.

10. FLY-DED.

This is a poisonous-bait fly control, developed after much experimentation. Investigative factors included bait content, poison, color, orientation, and support medium. Available either as a liquid or on a card which can be placed in the affected area. Highly attractive to flies. Poison interferes with the fly's nervous system. About twenty minutes after ingesting the bait, the fly spins in circles until it dies. Flies eating dead flies also appear to be poisoned. Four hours after smearing a bit of Fly-Ded on a newspaper, we found that a pound of dead flies had accumulated. Production cost should be of the order of $1.50 per pound, which is enough for several hundred cards. Fly-Ded has been eaten by cats and dogs with no apparent ill effects. On a card, it is extremely difficult for a child to ingest enough to cause problems. All of Fly-Ded except the poison is composed of naturally occurring substances which can be consumed by normal persons without ill effects. The remaining 1 percent is an insecticide approved for use in 80 percent concentrations in dairies and other places where it may get into food.

11. FLY-INN.

This is a non-baited trap for flies. Two versions are available: a totally passive system for outdoor use, and an electrically operated one for indoor use. The indoor unit uses about two watts. Flies are attracted to the Fly-Inn, fly in, and cannot get out, and so starve to death. Construction is sufficiently cheap for the outdoor unit that it may be thrown away when full of flies. The outdoor unit must be located in sunshine. Life is expected to be about one year after installation. The indoor unit should have a means for emptying dead flies. The units are noiseless, unobtrusive, and harmless. Estimated production costs are low enough that a good profit should be available from a selling price of $1 for the outdoor and $3 for the indoor units.

12. BUG ROGERS.

This is a toy, expected to be bought in multiple units by families. It looks like a futuristic ray gun, and when the trigger is pulled, emits flashing lights and weird sounds. The sounds and light are not part of the functioning of Fly-Gun. They serve to enhance the psychological effect and to avoid situations where one child puts a gun to the ear of another. This is probably less dangerous than the same action with a cap pistol and certainly far less dangerous than with a BB gun. When the pyrotechnics and sound effects are over, an unheard pulse of ultrasound shakes the fly apart. Fly-Gun may be made with an adjustable control to set it for flies, wasps, etc. Cost of this control is a few cents. A selling price of $19.99 seems to be feasible, and at this price the profits can be substantial. A factory cost of between $3 and $5 appears to be quite reasonable. The circuitry is similar to, but of better quality than, an examined TENS machine selling for $600, indicating a possible growth area.

Market surveys have been done, indicating a great market acceptance. More than 90 percent of people surveyed indicated that they would buy at least one.

Autobiographical Sketch of Amitananda Das

Born on August 26, 1947. Science hobbyist, aeromodeler, and cricket-club organizer while in school. National Science Talent Search awardee. B.Sc. (Physics honors), B.Tech. & M.Tech. (Electronics). Was a Research Fellow working on III-V semiconductors and devices.

Was Founder-Secretary, Indian Mensa. Wrote and edited science fiction. Used to hike in forests. Helped run a non-profit children's monthly.

Managed an electronics division for nine years, increasing its share of group turnover from 0–1 percent to 50 percent; negotiated a Japanese collaboration for a greenfield project. Promoted own startup. After a market crash, now trying to recover by developing new lines while consulting part-time.

Interests include traveling, reading, discoveries and inventions, astronomy, history, and urban problems.

CHAPTER 43

RECONDITIONING AND RECYCLING IN INDIA

Amitananda Das

By the year 2050 India will be the most populous country in the world, as it was during prehistoric times. Though for nearly 5,000 years, up to the seventeenth century, it was among the most advanced parts of the world, South Asia is now one of the poorest regions. An average unskilled labourer earns eight cents an hour, and $300 per month is an excellent starting salary for an MBA.

An interesting consequence of the low-wage economy and the business tradition is that reconditioning and recycling are viable in ways unthinkable in high-income countries.

Old cars almost never "die" in India. Though just four million four- or six-wheeled vehicles have been produced in the country since 1965, and imports were strictly regulated, now there are more than four million vehicles on Indian roads. There is a flourishing market for used cars up to twenty years old. A well-maintained ten-year-old car may cost more than 40 percent of the price of a similar new car. Cars are repaired and repainted, engines are reconditioned, new engines are fitted, and some 30- or 40-year-old cars are converted into pickup trucks for infrequent users who want a cheap vehicle.

Ultimately, when a vehicle is scrapped, it is cannibalized to provide spare parts for similar vehicles still in operation. Innovative uses are often found for other parts. Axles of so many scrapped cars have been fitted to bullock carts that many Indian tire manufacturers make special light-duty "car tires" for such carts.

Though Honda, Suzuki, and Yamaha joint ventures make compact, efficient (and expensive) small portable generators in India, thousands of U.S. Army surplus generators of '40s vintage are still in operation. In

359

narrow-gauge (2'4") branch railway lines, some old steam locos are just being retired after up to 100 years of continuous use!! In a small railway station I recently noticed a goods-weighing machine in use whose manufacturer's label said "BIRMINGHAM 1881"!

Car tires are obviously retreaded umpteen times (till the cords fall apart); there are thousands of small "vulcanizing" shops in every locality doing this job. Ball bearings are "remanufactured" by, say, replacing 4mm balls by 4.2 mm balls. The ceiling fans made by small factories which retail for $18 use such bearings in mass scale.

Damaged speakers are repaired by specialized shops for 15 cents up. The 2-cent ballpoint refills are usually the "re-inked" ones, and dozens of modern factories re-ink the ribbon cartridges for electronic typewriters and printers. Fluorescent lamps are reconditioned by changing the filament. TV picture tubes are "rejuvenated" by removing the cathode poisoning. There are workshops specializing in grinding out (shallow) scratches from the front of picture tubes.

Recycling is a profitable and organized business in India, employing millions of people and reducing the usage of virgin materials very significantly. Domestic scrap-buying agents go house to house to buy paper and bottles; old newspapers are *bought* for about 20 cents per kilogram. Old-paper wholesalers and processers ensure a supply of pieces or packets of such paper to small retailers (particularly grocers) so that even a one-cent purchase from a pavement hawker can come "packed" in something. The second time around, scrap paper is picked up from the streets (and from garbage) by an army of rag-pickers, and the soiled-paper wholesalers ship truckloads of the stuff to mills making low-grade paper and cardboard.

The old-bottle trade recycles glass bottles. Very small manufacturers of cheap commercial-grade chemicals, etc., often market their whole production in recycled glass bottles. Even broken glass in quantity is purchased and remelted to make cheap glass products.

The wholesalers specializing in metal and plastic scrap have agents who buy small quantities of scrap from every small factory and workshop, as well as from the rag-pickers who sort the domestic garbage at one or more stages.

There are scores of small factories having specialized machinery for segregating and recycling PVC, polyethylene, and polystyrene from plastic scrap. A factory may have seperate processing lines for, say, old plastic footwear and electric-cable insulation scrap. Any thermoplastic item in India that is colored black—bottle, container, tank, or cable insulation—is likely to contain some recycled plastics.

The cheapest electrical wires and cables in India (priced, say, 30 percent less than standard items) are made wholly from recycled copper and contain much recycled plastic. The resistivity of such wires is up to 20 percent higher, as the metallic impurities due to mixing varieties of scrap cannot be removed economically.

Even leading manufacturers of lead-acid batteries trade in exhausted batteries to extract the lead. Small manufacturers in addition reuse the battery casings and separators.

The silicon-steel stamping used to make motors and transformers for electrical and electronic appliances is often made from scrap. If 20 percent scrap is generated in making the original large stamping, by the time the scrap is used for cutting, say, 4-inch stampings, followed by 1.5-inch stampings, followed by 0.5-inch stampings, perhaps only 3 percent scrap is left. Silicon-steel scrap is a premium raw material in India, where demand greatly exceeds supply, and traders viciously fight each other (sometimes literally) to buy the material from steel plants and large electrical factories.

Calcutta has an interesting system of using raw untreated garbage and sewage to produce food for the city. Since Indians usually cook fresh vegetables, organic scrap constitutes a major part of the garbage. Much of this organic garbage (left after the recyclable items are removed by the rag-pickers) is directly used as manure for growing vegetables in the fields surrounding the garbage dump. The city's sewage flows into a series of shallow fisheries, where it fertilizes the underwater vegetation that supports the food chain, producing thousands of tons of fish every year. In the process the waste water becomes progressively purer.

Most recycling methods used in India are too labor-intensive to be viable even in medium-income countries like Korea or Mexico. Some of the processes produce low-quality products. But many of the methods can be improved and automated for use in developed countries to improve the environment. A comparative study of the impact of recycling and reconditioning on the standard of living, quality of the environment, and the ultimate cost to mankind should be enlightening.

Biographical Sketch of L. H. Chua

Chua Lai-heng is a student in the Civil Engineering Department of Stanford University. His avocations and interests include chess, ancient history, animal behavior, puzzles, artificial intelligence, robotics and automation, biomedical devices, the genetics of aging, and slow viruses.

CHAPTER 44

THE AUTOMATION OF DESIGN

L. H. Chua

Several manufacturing processes have been successfully automated and have brought us a higher standard of living. There is an opportunity to also automate some of the activities upstream of manufacturing, the foremost of which is design. Automated chip-design systems are foremost among current automated design systems. We are in the process of studying the automation of civil-engineering design. We present a preliminary framework for better understanding of the design process and the design automation task. We discuss some factors behind certain difficulties in building an automated design system.

INTRODUCTION

Design similarities with production

There are parallels between the design and the production of goods. What can be regarded as distinct recognizable design stages are present in the process of creating all complex human artifacts. There are recognizable design products at each stage. The output of one design stage is often input to some other stage. The organized manner in which we perform design is similar to that in manufacturing. Indeed, we can regard design as a productive activity that consumes time and other resources. Therefore, the similarity is not superficial, but is fundamental.

In manufacturing some transformation is applied to an intermediate product or raw material to obtain a different intermediate product or finished product, or several intermediate products can be combined to form a new product. In design, models are constructed, represented, and checked. Several models may be needed to constitute a sufficiently complete design. These models have to be compatible.

We hope that some of the lessons learned in the automation of manufacturing can transfer to the automation of design. Problems that we face in automating design might have a counterpart in the automation of manufacturing. Just as manufacturing production is planned, design can also benefit from careful planning, and just as many repetitive manufacturing activities have been successfully automated, repetitive design tasks can be automated.

We realize there are major differences between design processes and manufacturing processes. Among other things, key inputs and resources in design are often intangible, whereas those in manufacturing are mostly both tangible and quantifiable. Knowledge and time circumscribe design work. Computational power is used, but very little raw materials are consumed.

What motivates the automation of the design process? We might classify the benefits of automation under four positive categories. We also recognize one negative category that has its counterpart in manufacturing automation. The positive categories are that with design automation we expect to be able to

(1) expand the design envelope;
(2) speed up the design process;
(3) increase variety of designs;
(4) improve design quality.

However, in the process we will also cause a deskilling of designers, because fewer skilled designers would be needed to produce a quantity of design products. Not only that, but the tasks that designers have to do may be reduced to providing simple input to complex programs, instead of performing complex calculations or mathematical manipulations that require long training and experience. The latter work is more challenging and satisfying, and since few people can do such work, it also commands a premium. With design automation, the demand for skilled designers, who are the equivalent of skilled craftsmen, would be reduced, just as happened with manufacturing automation.

On the other hand, many complex artifacts could not have been designed without computational aid. Examples are the design of VLSI chips and spacecraft. These design tasks cannot be accomplished merely by having more people working on the task or taking longer. Technological tools are a requirement. Automating some of the design activities allow us to expand the design envelope.

Speeding up design, even if we accomplish nothing else, allows us to reduce the human labor cost of design. A design that might otherwise take months could be reduced to weeks. For example, analysis tools speed up the analysis portions of design greatly. Otherwise impractical analysis procedures, such as finite element analysis, becomes useful. Time from inception to market of a product can thus be reduced.

The desire for custom goods to satisfy our idiosyncratic needs demand increased design efforts. Design automation together with small-batch manufacturing techniques can help provide such design-customized products at a reasonable price.

With design automation, more design checks can be performed and more alternatives investigated, all of which will promote superior final designs. We are increasingly intolerant of design errors. These errors if undetected can cause project delays, increased costs, or even loss of human life. To check a large design manually can be a daunting task. The interference-checking tool is an example of an automated design-checking tool. Before the computer, interference checking was done using scaled drawings on translucent paper. Another common approach is to construct a scale model of the facility.

THE DESIGN PROCESS

Two different views

Design is done in different ways for different products. However, there are always at least two major ways of looking at the design process. The first view is of design as a human activity. Human strengths and weaknesses strongly determine the way that design is done as well as the most costly aspects of design.

The second view is of design is a mathematical problem. Many things that are important when looking at design as human activity might not even appear to be a concern when design is viewed as a mathematical problem.

When studying the design process, whether our intent is to improve or to automate, it is useful to keep both views in mind. In our experience, understanding the design process from the human-activity viewpoint gives us greater insight about what to automate in design and how such automation would be beneficial. In particular, we are acutely aware of the need to support human activities, and of the problems of model fragmentation and incompatibilities between systems.

The more mathematical view of design helps us decide how to proceed with the development of design-automation tools. By understanding the mathematics, we might be able to decide whether it is practical to obtain an exact solution or not. Model simplification, approximation, or heuristic problem-solving approaches may be called for instead.

The basic elements of design

There are reserved basic elements that may be used to distinguish design form other types of activities such as manufacturing, construction, or business.

In order to do that, we need some comprehension of what the end result of design, the design product, is. In the types of design we are concerned about, the final design product is a model of an artifact that can be used as one of the inputs to manufacturing or construction. That is, these models are meant to have a physical realization. There should be some mapping between the design product and the physical artifact. The activity of design then might be thought of as the process of creating an adequate model of the artifact.

The physical artifact will, of course, keep the laws of nature. In addition, we desire the artifact to perform certain functions, and which functions there are will dictate how we produce the design. The selection of the function to be performed resides with us. Even the most sophisticated automated-design system has only a few functions it can select for its design products. In order to use an automated-design system successfully, the designer has to specify parameters within this design space.

If we examine the "work-flow" diagrams used to depict design work, we will see several stages, the relationships between these stages, and perhaps even the intermediate design products from each stage. These diagrams are useful to those who manage design activities. As a prelude to our discussion on design automation, we attempt to classify design tasks.

There are different principal concerns in modeling. First, models have different levels of definition. The less knowledge about the artifact we can extract directly from the model, the lower the definition. For example, we might know the thermodynamic processes by which a fossil plant operates, but not know how these processes are actually accomplished.

That a model is of low definition does not mean it is not useful. It is often more helpful to work with models of low definition. By using the appropriate low-definition models, we are able to focus on specific, more fundamental questions before we proceed further and greatly simplify design effort.

Second, there are conceptual stages in the design process for a useful model at each level of definition. In chip and plant design we perceive the following sequential levels of design process definition after the specification stages:

(1) functional modeling;
    (1.1) functional synthesis;
    (1.2) functional analysis;
(2) conceptual modeling;
    (2.1) conceptual synthesis;
    (2.2) conceptual analysis;
(3) physical modeling;
    (3.1) physical synthesis;
    (3.2) physical analysis.

Within each level of model definition, modeling consist of two stages: synthesis and analysis. Each type of synthesis has its own subsequent analysis. In a complex product, subsystems or subcomponents can have their own stages.

Basically, in functional modeling we define the smallest number of "black boxes" needed to accomplish the functional purpose of the artifact. The definition level here is low. In essence many things remain unknown about the artifact. In conceptual modeling we draw from classes of devices or components, and produce an intermediate design that sharpens the definition of the black boxes and of the connectivities between these black boxes. Then in physical modeling we explicitly take into account the physical limitations in the model in order to produce a physically realizable model. To be physically realizable the model has to have a high level of definition.

Synthesis is the process of deciding on configuration. By configuration we mean the components and their relationships with each other. Relationships at one level can turn into components at a more-detailed level of definition. Deciding on the configuration of the components themselves is also a synthesis procedure.

Analysis, on the other hand, takes the configuration as input, and defines parameters of the models that are of interest. Analysis is done in terms of a theory, often a theory of physical processes or systems. Therefore, the parameters of interest are those that help decide whether the configuration is acceptable.

In analysis, the configuration of the model is known. What parameters will be of concern in the model is discovered by analysis. There is usually a unique set of results from an analysis of a given configuration. Generally analysis procedures cannot be run backward.

One point to note is that explicit analysis is part of the design process, because the synthesis process does not always guarantee that constraints of the system are met. If there is such a guarantee during synthesis, then the explicit analysis step becomes irrelevant and could be avoided. Otherwise, if we perform just synthesis without analysis, it might be impossible to construct the artifact, or the artifact may be much more likely to fail. A corollary is that the better our synthesis process, the better the intermediate design product, and the more likely to pass the analysis stage.

In chip design, others (Hu and Kuh 1985) have divided the design process into eight parts, as follows:

(1) system specification;
(2) functional design;
(3) logic design;
(4) circuit design;
(5) circuit layout;
(6) design verification;
(7) test and debugging;
(8) prototype testing.

Functional design corresponds to our functional modeling, logic design and circuit design to conceptual modeling, circuit layout to physical modeling, and design verification to analysis of the physical model.

The interesting thing to note is the presence of stages 7 and 8. The need for these stages indicates that the design process from 1 to 6 may not be comprehensive. Comprehensiveness is what would guarantee that the resulting artifact, as constructed from the design, would meet its stated objectives. The analysis stages might be unable to discover inadequacies in the design. The physical model may not accurately reflect the physically attainable artifact. Actual artifacts have to be constructed and tested.

In power-plant design, Smith and Van Laan (1987) list the following design stages for equipment and piping design:

(1) plant specification;
(2) process design;
(3) equipment layout;
(4) piping layout;
(5) piping support placement;
(6) piping analysis;
(7) piping support design;
(8) piping support analysis.

The intermediate design product from process design is called the flow diagram, or the pipe and instrumentation diagram (PNID). The intermediate output from piping layout is the piping isometric (PD). This drawing is usually used to produce the stress isometric for piping analysis use. Tray and duct design have similar stages. We also see similarities with chip design.

Note the juxtaposition of some of the stages. This arises from the logical constraints between these design activities among the components.

This brings us to an observation. The subdivision of the design process as presented above for both chip design and pipe and equipment engineering represents not only the true constraints among design activities, but also concerns for decomposing the overall design tasks in a way that meets environmental considerations. The potential concurrence in design is greater than the stages indicate.

Implementation considerations

Among environmental considerations are the way that computational resources and knowledge are available and organized. A design system for a particular design need must be built within these limitations.

A human design system is called a design organization. Each group has different areas of expertise, and there is an organized flow of work between the different design groups

An automated design system is a set of hardware, software, and encoded knowledge that can be used to produce designs. The more automated the design system is, the less incremental input is required, and the fewer design activities the human designer has to perform. There is greater opportunity to exploit concurrence in fully automated design systems.

Whether we consider a design organization or an automated design system, the design system has to have sufficient knowledge and computational resources.

Design interpretation and modification

We need to know not only about the different major stages of design, but also what happens between the stages. Each stage produces a set of numbers that is used for some subsequent stage or for decisionmaking. For instance, we may examine the numbers in order to decide the stage to proceed to. In an automated design system, the synthesis stage might fail, and decisions might need to be made on how to proceed.

Closely associated with analysis is interpretation. The output of the analysis has to be interpreted. Interpretation is a decisionmaking process about the model. The outcome of interpretation determines whether the design will have to be modified. This cycle of design, analysis, interpretation, and redesign is known as a design iteration.

We do not have prototype testing in fossil-fuel plant design. However, we do have something known as design checking, which is not a "core" of design, but a need that basically arises from the possibility of human error, and is meant to trap these errors.

Nevertheless, both interpretation and modification may be assisted with computer tools.

Adjuncts to design

There are areas upstream and downstream from design. We have already classified specification as an upstream task. Downstream is the realization of the design product and actual artifacts.

Increasingly, downstream tasks are being automated, and recently more and more attention has been placed on being able to immediately use the design product as direct input to this automated system. Similarly, upstream tasks have attracted attention. Both upstream and downstream areas merit treatment in another paper.

MANUAL DESIGN SYSTEMS

Our treatment will be lacking if we do not grasp the historical roots of design. We have been designing for a long time, and for most of that time design has been done manually.

For simplicity, by manual design we mean designing with "pen and paper." The computational aspects of design are performed by the human designer. We allow that calculations may be done with the help of a calculator without programs. I was involved in such design practice in designing several civil engineering structures, and this design approach might still exist. Productivity as a designer depended partly on how fast you can punch on a calculator.

Manual design can be tedious, time-consuming, and error prone. In order to be able to design in a reasonable amount of time, designers have paid much attention to developing abstractions, simplifications, and approximations that reduce and simplify the computations required.

The empirical earth-pressure diagrams for the design of excavation-support systems provides an example. Such pressure diagrams can be quite different from measured earth pressure, but they are still widely used. Engineers are trained to decide which abstraction, simplification, or approximation is safe enough to use for a particular problem. The responsibility for designing a safe product rests with the designer.

Safety factor is an integral concept in manual design. Safety factors of several different types are meant to compensate for different uncertainties or groups of uncertainties. An engineer can choose to use a simplified analytical approach that tends to be conservative or use a higher factor of safety to compensate for unknown factors in analysis or lack of knowledge. These safety factors are not small, although they are being reduced with code updates, and if they happen to be positively synergistic, the resulting design can be highly conservative and perhaps more costly.

Besides potentially high product costs, the time and expense of manual design dissuade us from investigating numerous alternatives. Also we have already mentioned that with manual design we are unable to handle very complex design tasks, such as the design of a large electrical circuit.

With the arrival of the computer some design tasks have been automated. Today little structural analysis is done manually. Instead, the structural design engineer does what is called "modeling" the artifact: he inputs the model to the computer program. The program analyzes the model and produces voluminous output, which is examined by the engineer. Because of the great advances in speed of microprocessors, the actual analysis time has become a very small fraction of overall design time.

The history of manual design does have a momentum. Procedures and codes rest on them. As we proceed toward design automation, we might want to reexamine the underlying basis of these codes and design procedures. Of course, right now the design of automated design systems is governed by the same codes that govern manual design.

DESIGN AUTOMATION

Design automation is in essence the application of the computational power of machines or other mechanical means to design tasks. Automation is not an all-or-none concept but a matter of degree, varying from no design automation to possibly total design automation. At present, chip-design systems are the most highly automated of design systems.

Automation of analysis

Of the two categories of design tasks of synthesis and analysis, the latter is more easily automated. Many design-analysis tools have been built and continue to be built. The availability of such design- analysis tools is a tremendous boon for designers.

Design analysis is a narrowly focused procedure. The questions to be answered draws from a specific aspect of physical theory. Not every possible analyzable parameter of an artifact is analyzed, only those thought of as salient to function and safety. For example, sometimes the thermal properties of an artifact might be judged to be important and the structural properties unimportant, or vice versa. In the former case a thermal model in constructed, in the latter a structural model.

Given the selected properties of the artifact, only pertinent models of the artifact have to be constructed. We may say that the artifact needs to be only partially modeled.

A question in design automation is how thoroughly the models should be covered. This depends on the domain of interest. In chip design, for example, modeling of electrical circuitry and thermal characteristics might be sufficient. There is no need for modeling chips for structural analysis. In plant design, we are not concerned with electrical circuitry, high-frequency radiation, or magnetic effects. The ability to model for structural analysis is far more crucial.

We know that different analysis models may need different information. Yet there is often information that would be common or can be derived from a common base. The quest is to exploit such cross-model information. A ideal automated analysis design system is one in which there is a minimum need for input for a specific analysis task, as well as little redundant input.

Suppose there are two analysis models, but no specific order in which these analysis tasks need to be done. Some parts of the first model can be obtained from the second model and vice versa. An interest in automation of analysis, then, is to organize information in such a way that when the model for the first analysis task is constructed, the model can be used to obtain some of the necessary information for the second analysis task and vice versa. The more general problem is spread over several analysis models. Unfortunately, this is not an easy task.

Let us take a problem in architectural building design as an illustration. Suppose someone were to build a model in order to analyze the lighting needs of the building. As a lighting engineer he should not have to first construct the structural model of the building, although some aspects of the structure should be known. On the other hand, the mechanical engineer who does the thermal analysis of the building is unconcerned with the luminosity. However, if he should do his analysis after the lighting engineer, he should not have to input the same information about the position and loading of the lights, or of the windows.

Information about the lights that affects the thermal load should be extractable from the lighting model that was constructed earlier. If the thermal analysis was performed first and the thermal model of the building constructed, some of the same information about the materials of the walls and windows might be used by the lighting engineer.

Although individual analysis operations are heavily automated, present analysis systems lack management of analysis models, so that much of the same data must often be entered again for a different analysis task.

To overcome the problem of redundant input, some systems force order between analysis steps, even if such an order is not dictated by the design logic. This serialization reduces the exploitable concurrence in design. For example, we might force lighting design to come before thermal design with the argument that the lighting determines part of the thermal load of the building. Such an approach is attractive because it is relatively simpler than other approaches.

An alternative approach that might be taken is to first perform model dependency analysis (MDA) and use the results for building a model management system.

We first introduce a few concepts. Dependency is the opposite of independence. If two models are completely independent, then each may be designed without any consideration of the other. Dependencies are also of several types. The simplest is direct correspondence, in which case no additional processing effort is needed. Second, part of one model can be derived from information about the other model. Such dependency is not necessarily bi-directional. Third, one model may constrain the other model but without actually fully specifying it. Sometimes we can express the dependency as an explicit set of constraints between the parameters of one model and another, but sometimes we cannot. In constraint dependency, when a part of one analysis model is specified, the space of acceptable configurations for another model becomes more restricted; so that when building subsequent models, we have to respect the constraints already expressed in earlier modeling efforts.

This third class can be broken down into further subtypes of constraints, such as whether they are attribute constraints or model constraints. Restrictions on the number or type of components and relationships are model constraints, whereas restrictions on the depth of a beam or thickness of a pipe are attribute constraints. It seems the latter represent choices of values of known intrinsic attributes, whereas the former represent choices between design alternatives or configurations.

For example, in placing the lights in a building during thermal analysis, one need specify only the room where the lights are in order to compute its thermal loading. But once specified, this places a restraint on the positioning of lights in the lighting model. In this example, this is a model constraint, not a attribute constraint. Only a certain number of lights with total wattage below a certain amount may be placed in a particular room, but there is still a lot of choice.

To perform full MDA would be difficult. Partial MDA can still be useful. Sometimes we can use the dependencies identified to organize the underlying models, specify design order, or extract information from one model to use in another. Simple attribute constraints might be managed by a constraint-management system.

There is an alternative to the process of taking the models required to serve different analysis needs and then attempting to reduce information input by seeing how information from one model may be used in another model with the help of MDA. The approach is domain modeling. Here we look simultaneously at all needs, and proceed from the larger picture down to the specific needs. All parts of the model should be in harmony and preferably without redundancy. The domain of the overall design is modeled and may be organized differently from the analysis stages. Information input is then organized around the domain models. Input for an analysis would then be extracted from the model. With this approach information input is separated from analysis. We do not try to input the model required for a particular analysis directly. A lot of information might be entered without any analysis being performed.

With domain modeling it might be possible to reduce input for design synthesis as well as for analysis. For instance, component attributes might be extracted from the domain models. To do successful domain modeling takes a lot of effort up front. Cooperation is needed among different design disciplines. Domain modeling requires a stable design domain. Adapting an existing domain model to serve another purpose efficiently may be difficult.

Automated synthesis

Our attention is now shifting to the challenging problem of automating design synthesis. In synthesis there is a need to obtain a configuration from a large or possibly infinite model space. We would like it to be an acceptable configuration, and we would like a design that does not take too long to make and is economical.

There are several stages in design synthesis. Our treatment here is biased towards chip and fossil-fuel plant design. Given a particular need we first choose between different classes of systems that can potentially meet that need. We might have to do a complete design before we can make that choice. In most other cases historical information and use of inductive models will be sufficient. Often this design task is not difficult to automate. Expert systems and decisionmaking tools are generally adequate for this design-synthesis stage.

Now, given the functional specifications of the system, the relevant environment, and the class of the system that the design is to belong to, we need to decide what the actual components will be, how they relate to the given environment, and what the values of the attributes of each component should be.

Finding the values of attributes of known components is often known as *sizing* of components. Finding how the components and their connecting elements relate to the environment is known as physical layout and routing. Finding the necessary components and the relationships between these components is known as process design.

Sizing of components and connecting elements usually occurs before physical layout. Sizing draws from information about the process design. To automate many sizing tasks is not too difficult either, because the component has a simple structure, the choice is generally more limited, or there is some well-founded relationship between attributes and function. For example, in designing a steel building, we pick from available steel sections. The process of sizing can be made more efficient by precalculation. In chip design the size of a component such as an adder is quite fixed for a particular chip process technology.

The other design-synthesis stages of process design, conceptual design, and physical modeling are more difficult.

In chip design, for the equivalent of process design we might want to select adders, registers, memory caches, memory banks, and so on, and connect them into a processing unit of the von Neumann architecture. There are many options, and it is not clear how to automate this design stage. Power-plant design process is simpler, but there are still difficulties in balancing the efficiency of the plant against the cost.

Existing design systems support more efficient model input, retrieval of past models, and analysis of the process model. We are not cognizant of any system that can do as good a job as or a better job than human designers in synthesizing a functional model.

Producing a conceptual model from a functional model can be assisted by design automation tools. In chip design there are tools to perform transformations from one type of logic to another, that is more easily implemented. These tools are indispensable.

The process of mapping logical design to physical media is also heavily automated. This is a more difficult design-automation problem than that of design selection or of component sizing. The very large number of components to be placed and connected subject to physical constraints makes the task a daunting one, indeed. The problems are mathematically hard. Most of the problems are NP-complete or worse, and heuristic procedures are employed in the design-automation tools.

Similarly, equipment layout and routing can be automated. The three-dimensional nature of the problem, diversity of components, and constraints make the problem even more difficult. Fortunately, the number of components are an order of magnitude fewer, in the thousands instead of ten thousands for the chip layout and routing problem.

Synthesis and analysis

We should note that design synthesis is still an imperfect process, whether done by the human designer or by an automated system. With a perfect synthesis process, all design constraints would be met, and there would be no need for analysis. However, we do not have perfect design synthesis, and there is no guarantee that the synthesized design does not violate some constraint. Analysis and verification of the design must still be carried out.

Design automation is founded on algorithms. Each specific algorithm is accomplishes a particular facet of design. The analog to algorithms in manufacturing automation is the machine.

One problem that might arise is that the models and algorithms are too specific and not adaptable. The drive for efficiency is severe given the size and complexity of design. However, in the future, when abundant computational power and memory is available, this concern would lessen, and we would be able to implement algorithms more generally. We note that in manufacturing, specific machinery was built for specific manufacturing tasks. It is almost impossible for such a machine to be used for another task, just as many implemented algorithms are difficult to use for other design tasks. Now more-general classes of machines such as robots are used; these can be programmed and adapted to many different tasks.

The object-oriented approach to software engineering is one contribution toward reusable code.

ARCHITECTURE OF DESIGN SYSTEMS

We have briefly seen what the design process is, and how analysis and synthesis are automated.

How, then, do we put together a system with design automation in mind? Clearly, we have to understand the role of the human, and should address how designers would interact with the system.

We perceive at the poles two types of systems. One system is almost fully automated, and the system guides the design after the initial stages. At the other pole we have an interactive design system, in which the human designer essentially guides the design.

These two types of systems have different requirements. With the system-guided approach we can more easily maintain a minimum level of consistency. We can maintain intermediate information about the design that is not directly meaningful or accessible to the human designer, but is used by the system for internal management.

On the other hand, in an interactive design system the designer decides which design actions to execute at a particular time. He should be able to easily store and retrieve intermediate design stages that are meaningful. Therefore the design process has to be broken up into meaningful stages that have some correspondence with the way humans design. The finer the stages, the more control the designer has over the design process. For example, if we combine circuit layout and routing, the designer would not be able to modify the results of the layout before routing is done.

He has to be able to tell how much of the design has been completed and what portions of the design remain. Illegal design actions should be indicated.

If we also allow the designers to modify the design artifact, we need to also maintain the consistency of the information about the system, so that future application of a design tool will use consistent information.

We might also want to maintain versions of the design, so that the designer can investigate alternatives. We have to do this without causing an explosion in storage-space requirements, especially for design artifacts that require a great deal of information, such as chips and fossil-fuel power plants.

Also, attention to user interfaces is never wasted. Any difficulty the user has in performing his work translates into additional design time and perhaps even error. This is our experience from observing pipe engineers perform design with the help of various tools.

SUMMARY

We have attempted to develop a framework for understanding the design process, and have explained how some aspects of design automation might be handled and some of the considerations for developing automated design systems. There has been great success in automating design-analysis procedures. Although work remains to be done in improving the model input process, the challenge is now in the automation of design synthesis. Many types of design synthesis are now within reach of automation. There is potential to expand the automation of design into other design domains, such as machinery design, and I hope this work contributes toward that effort.

REFERENCES

Hu, T. C., and E. S. Kuh. "Theory and Concepts of Circuit Layout," *VLSI Circuit Layout: Theory and Design,* 1985, pp. 3–18.

Smith, P. R., and T. J. Van Laan. *Piping and Pipe Support Systems: Design and Engineering.* McGraw-Hill, 1987.

Biographical Sketch of A. J. Kangas

Anastassios (Tassos) Kangas was born in Athens, Greece, in 1960. He received his degree in Physics from the University of Athens in 1983, and his Master's degree in Physics from Indiana University at Bloomington in 1985. After a Systems Analysis and Design course at Control Data (Hellas), Inc., he joined the Computer Systems Development section of Cyprus Popular Bank in Cyprus. Today he is Team/Project Manager and is considered an expert in the areas of Distributed Processing, Cooperative Processing, Client/Server Architecture, and Self-Service Banking. He is a member of IEEE, CIOB, BIM, CCS, Mensa, and ISPE. Father of three children, he enjoys management practices, reading, music, traveling, and tennis.

CHAPTER 45

CLIENT/SERVER: THE FOURTH GREAT REVOLUTION?

Anastassios J. Kangas

IT gurus are calling Client/Server the fourth great revolution in computing. But how many computer sites are feeling revolutionized yet? The answer is rather frustrating: Less than a few! Can it be that the computer industry's latest darling is turning out to be a bad case of hype? Or is the Client/Server revolution genuine but just a little late getting started?

Before we attempt to give answers, let's take a quick look at what Client/Server is all about.

It is amazing that each user gives his own definition of Client/Server, and vendors often mold the term to match their particular production line. Fortunately, all agree that true Client/Server computing has some common characteristics. Lynn Berg, manager of DEC's Client/Server Computing Program gives a very successful definition of the term: "Client/Server computing represents a continuum of methods to split up data management, data processing, and the user interface."

To have the appropriate environment built, starting from scratch, one would need:

A server, a 386 or 486 box; client workstations sitting on a Token Ring or Ethernet network; a network operating system, such as LAN Manager; an operating system such as OS/2 on the server, and an operating system on the client such as DOS with Windows; a database engine such as Microsoft's SQL Server; and front-end development tools. To access information held on mini or mainframe databases a connectivity tool is necessary. Finally, when all this is in place, applications are added on. For a successful Client/Server installation each computing element should be assigned the tasks for which it is best suited. Knowing now a little more about Client/Server, let's return to our concerns.

There are five major reasons for failure to assimilate Client/Server:

(a) Managers are not ready to accept it.
(b) No new business solutions are devised.
(c) Programmers lack necessary skills.
(d) No tools are available to assist applications development.
(e) There are few off-the-shelf packaged applications.

A recent survey of IT executives in the UK and Germany conducted by Microsoft Consulting and KPMG Regis McKenna highlights that: first, IT Managers undervalue the personal computer as a strategic source; and, second, Client/Server is not addressing the business needs of today's organizations. Specifically, the survey found that although 56 percent of the IT executives thought the PC offered the best return on investment, 65 percent had not heard of downsizing the IT context, 44 percent were unsure what Client/Server computing meant, 52 percent considered it difficult to move information from corporate applications to the user's environment, and only 37 percent thought there was a good link between IT and business strategy.

Is this a common pattern worldwide? It seems that in general U.S. companies are a lot more advanced with their use of LANs and Client/ Server systems. They are more willing to invest in new technologies; to buy first and then to ask questions. On the contrary, in Europe the things are treated case by case; with each new application comes a new decision on what would be the best technology for implementing it.

There are analysts who think much current IT investment could be more profitably ploughed into sophisticated Client/Server systems, since in a Client/Server environment a word-processing package can become a desktop-publishing kit or a forms-automation system, and a spreadsheet can be built into a powerful executive information system containing text, numbers, and graphics. However, as Robin Wilkins, Grand Metropolitan's Director of Technology said, "It is often sensible to run transaction-processing applications like order processing, payroll, and ledger, on mainframe or mini. Where Client/Server [systems] come into their own is [in allowing us] to look at the information generated by the transaction-processing system and make sense of it. I'm sick of new ways to do things we already do. That goes not take the business forward. I'd like to see new business solutions."

What about the people who will develop Client/Server systems, i.e., the Programmers? The mainframe systems community is very conservative. It does not much mind inflicting change on others, but it does not seem so keen on change itself. Most developers are still happier with what they know—PLI or Cobol on the mainframe. They are only just getting used to new mainframe tools like CASE (Computer Aided Software Engineering) and fourth-generation languages. They hardly want to go back a step, to learn a low-level language like C, or be exposed to a complicated architecture like Client/Server.

Tony Clifford-Winters, a software consultant with Amdahl UK, agrees: "In a way there is nothing more conventional than a Cobol or PLI programmer, and the learning curve is pretty steep to retain them to write Client/Server systems." Wilkins has the same approach for staffing: "The culture issue is a big barrier. But we aren't going to try to reeducate all our Cobol programmers overnight so they can start building distributed systems. I expect the profile of our skills will change towards being more PC-based as we get involved in more Client/Server projects."

The lack of tools is a common complaint among those thinking about Client/Server systems. Building this kind of system is likely to be so demanding that the use of CASE tools may be mandatory. Most existing CASE software has been designed to generate ordinary mainframe applications, and it may be some time before CASE tools can generate window panels, distributed SQL calls, and other code central to Client/Server systems. It will be at least two or three years before all the tools and products arrive so that people can built Client/Server systems out of off-the-shelf components. Until a full toolkit arrives, and until enough programmers have picked up the extra skills, only hardy pioneers are likely to tackle full-blown Client/Server projects.

Surprisingly enough, the software houses' major investment is still in products for minis, mainframes, and dumb terminals. The problem for the software houses is the complexity of Client/Server environments, because a Client/Server system has to work with different operating systems. That means a lot of development and a lot of support. One problem is all the different network solutions they previously did not have to think about; just think of the ongoing battle between LAN Manager, Netware, and smaller players like Banyan's Vines.

As in all emerging markets, the technology is ahead of its use. This poses problems for software houses. The market is not mature enough for them to sell an application alone; they must also sell the concept of Client/Server and the necessary blocks. One remedy to this problem would be the creation of new software houses with new culture and no preconceptions to develop Client/Server applications. The traditional split between mainframe and mini skills and PC skills has not helped established software houses develop applications. Yet the potential is enormous because of the scalability of Client/Server applications, which can be run on one PC in one office or on many dozens of PCs and local area networks in many offices.

So, after all, is Client/Server architecture a lost cause? Large-computer manufacturers strongly believe that Client/Server systems are the next logical step forward. As evidence of this faith IBM launched its ES/9000 mainframe range, and NCR launched a family of powerful UNIX-based servers and is working on front-end client software. With DEC, ICL, Hewlett Packard, and Sun, hardly a week goes by without one of them trumpeting the virtues of the Client/Server computing.

Consultants are recommending that users to re-evaluate their database strategies and plan for migration to Client/Server architecture. U.S. consultant Forrester Research predicts that Client/Server sales will follow meteoric ascent. U.S. analysts Meta Group predict that by 1995 more than 50 percent of corporate PCs will be linked to host systems to engage in cooperative processing for most applications.

For the majority of the users this is still the time for watching and waiting. However, although the revolution may be taking a little longer to get off the ground than some predicted, the signs are that people at least agree the revolution is on its way.

Section VI
"There's a Method in My Madness"

Autobiographical Sketch of Michael N. van der Riet

The southern-hemisphere summer of '92/'93 finds me 49 years old, fit and well, and happily married for 21 years. About ten years ago, dalliance with Rubik's cube led to my being "discovered" by Mensa, and soon I joined the Cape Town branch. A few years later I chanced on Dr. Ronald K. Hoeflin's Mega Test in *Omni*. A month was spent with Ron's shibboleths, and enough points garnered to bridge the gap to the trans-Mensa societies. So here I am, a Fellow of the ISPE. To participate one is invited to contribute (preferably) scholarly articles or poetry for publication in the monthly journal, *Telicom*. Well, anything creative or original seems to get aired; so my Perplexing Pictographic Puzzles are seldom rejected.

For someone with Hi-Q-soc affiliation I tend to be very "physical." Past avocations have included: making electrical and accoustic guitars; grinding, polishing, and figuring parabolic mirrors for Newtonian reflector telescopes; designing, building, and flying radio-controlled aircraft. For exercise I climb Table Mountain most weekends.

For several years I have been in charge of the Pharmaceutical Sterile Unit of the 1899-bed Tygerberg Hospital. Our quality-assurance program includes Radiometric Sterility Testing.

Family: my Proverbs-31 wife, Cynthia, and three academically bright children. Son George is on his way to university. Twin daughters Charlotte and Ursula are in high school.

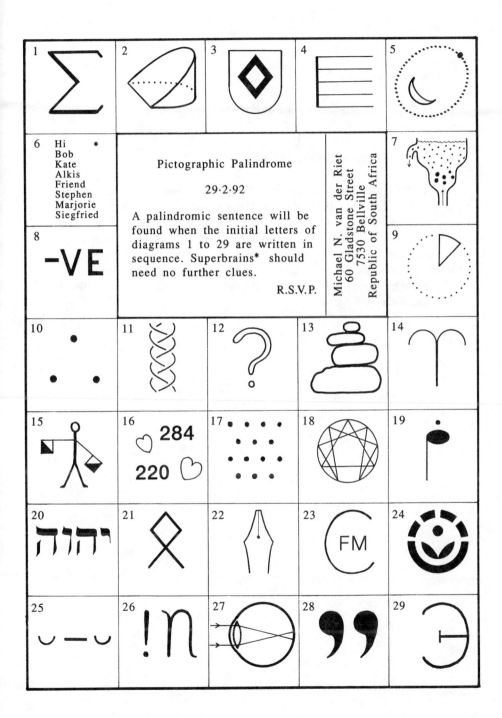

Pictographic Palindrome

29·2·92

A palindromic sentence will be found when the initial letters of diagrams 1 to 29 are written in sequence. Superbrains* should need no further clues.

R.S.V.P.

Michael N. van der Riet
60 Gladstone Street
7530 Bellville
Republic of South Africa

6 Hi   *
   Bob
   Kate
   Alkis
   Friend
   Stephen
   Marjorie
   Siegfried

Biographical Sketch of Gene Smith

Gene Smith, born 1946 in Kitzmiller, Maryland, is the son of James and Marle Smith. He is retired from the U.S. Navy, where he served for 20 years, and has been a member of ISPE since 1982. His interests include reading and music, and much of his leisure time is devoted to songwriting. His previously published works include the songs *Black Roses* and *Silver Mine*. Although Gene has a degree from New York University, the vast majority of his education has come through life experiences. He is the father of two sons, Sean and Derek, and resides in Kearneysville, West Virginia, with his wife, Rosemary.

CHAPTER 47

SOMETHING MIS ING IN THE TRANSLATION

Gene M. Smith

Throughout history, there have been situations in which the entire course of events has been changed by words being mistranslated or misunderstood. Furthermore, the longer some conversations endured, the more boggled the exchanges became.

In addition to these major mixups, our lives are almost continually blasted with minor mistranslations in signs, announcements, etc. Who can forget the absurd "Wipe Your Feet" sign replicated thousands of times every winter in front of stores in North America? Allow me to share just a few more examples with you.

THE ESTABLISHMENT OF CHRISTIANITY IN ENGLAND

According to Taylor, in the sixth century King Ethelbert married a Christian princess, Bertha, who persuaded her husband, the honorable King of the Jutes, to receive missionaries from Pope Gregory. Augustine was honorably received at the Court of Ethelbert in A.D. 598.

However, Taylor also tells an equally plausible story. Pope Gregory, passing a slave auction in Rome, noticed some attractive slaves up for sale. The Pontiff asked the name of their native country. He was told that they were Angli. Surprised, Gregory said, "They would not be Angli, but *Angeli* (angels)." When he asked for the name of their province, the response was Deiri (of Northumberland district). "Deiri! *De ira!* (from the wrath of God) . . . they are summoned to his mercy," asserted the Pontiff. Further checking into the validity of this blessed land, Gregory then asked for the name of their king. When he heard AElla, he cried out,

"Alleluja! We must endeavor that the praises of God be sung in that country." Hence the Pontiff sent out legates to Christianize this heathen land possibly because of a few puns!

YUCATAN

In Gates' translation of *Friar Diego de Landa: Yucatan Before and After the Conquest*, two interesting examples are given for the name of the land called Yucatan today. De Landa asserted that the Indians (here we go again!) called the land *Petén*, which de Landa claims meant "island." However, *Petén* means "district." De Landa goes on to relate (confuse?) the meaning of Yucatan. Francisco Fernándes de Córdoba arrived in Yucatan in 1517. De Córdoba, according to de Landa, accosted some local fishermen at Cape Cotoch. After several inquiries, he asked them how they came by the land. The fishermen replied, "Cu uthan (He speaks nicely)" through hand signs. De Córdoba interpreted the signs as "they say it," and the name Yucatan (Cu uthan) stuck.

A curious error in the de Landa manuscript dealt with the locals wearing "heavy coats of salt and cotton." The error may have come from the Maya *taab*, which means "to tie," whereas the short-*a* word *tab* means "salt." Although a salt coat may have been acceptable to the King of Spain and de Landa during the 1500s, the fad has never crystallized during our century!

DID NOT SUIT TOO-HOOL-HOOL-SUIT

The Nez Percé (Shaptin) Indians (Native Americans) were a nation whose center was situated at the crossroads of Idaho, Oregon, and Washington in the 1800s. When gold was discovered by prospectors in the 1860s, Chief Joseph's people were overrun by Americans and Europeans hungry for wealth. A war occurred between these people and the United States in 1877. Prior to the war, the United States tried to peaceably evict these people to a smaller area. A council was held with Chief Joseph, Chief Too-hool-hool-suit, other chiefs, and U.S. Army General 0. 0. Howard. Helen Jackson, in her book *A Century of Dishonor*, details what went on at the meeting from two perspectives: the view of Chief Joseph and the view of General 0.0. Howard. I am quite sure that the interpreters also had a part. What follows is from Helen Jackson's book:

General Howard version:

(Response to Chief Too-hool-hool-suit) "Twenty times over I hear that the Earth is your mother, and about the chieftainship of the Earth. I want to hear it no more."

Chief Joseph version:

"Shut up! I don't want to hear any more such talk."

General Howard version:

(Too-hool-hool-suit says) "What person pretends to divide the land and put me on it?"

Chief Joseph version:

"Who are you, that you ask us to talk, and then tell me I shan't talk?"

General Howard version:

"I asked the chiefs to go with me to look over their land (reservation). The old man, Too-hool-hool-suit shall not go. I will leave him with Colonel Perry."

Chief Joseph version:

"You are an impudent fellow, and I will put you in the guard house."

Clearly, there are some discrepancies between the two versions. However, it is clear that Too-hool-hool-suit was detained for some time by the U.S. Army. The Chief may have been the victim of one more poor translation.

ARIZONA PENALTIES

In the newspaper just this week there was an Associated Press item: "Mistranslated Ariz. Sign Prescribed Stiff Penalty." It seems that Spanish-speaking travelers arriving at Sky Harbor International Airport were met with a sign saying, "Violators Will Be Deceased." This particular sign was meant to warn travelers that one must declare all plants, fruits, vegetables, and meats: "Violadores Seran Finados." Officials meant to say that violators would be fined. To further add to the embarrassment, "violadores" is a colloquialism used in some parts of Mexico to refer to rapists. Equally alarming to our foreign visitors was the sign stating the state's drinking age as "21 ano." Here the tilde was omitted from año, changing the word from "year" to "anus." "The airport hired a poor translator," stated the City Manager. The city plans to correct the signs to be less offensive and, hopefully, more humane.

Sometimes just the change from oral English to written English gets confusing. At a gathering at a small grade school in Maryland some years ago, while visiting the boys' restroom, I observed a sign that said, "DO NOT PUT ANYTHING BUT TOILET PAPER IN THE COMMODE." I am sure that I was just as confused as any restless eight-year-old by this rather restrictive edict.

In conclusion, I believe that these examples reveal a thread of inadequacy of meaning exacerbated by the sending and receiving of the spoken and written word, not only in translations, but also in daily communications in one's one language. But I may be wrong! Before I go, could someone loan me a torch. I need to check the wiring on my wireless and under my bonnet and carriage. I do believe I have a hole in my pipe or sound-box!

REFERENCES

De Landa, Friar Diego. *Yucatan Before and After the Conquest.* Trans. by William Gates. Dover, 1977.
Jackson, Helen. *A Century of Dishonor.* Roberts Brothers, Boston, 1887.
Taylor, W.C. *A Manual of Ancient and Modern History.* Appleton, 1854.

CHAPTER 48

THE CAT AND THE VIDEO-DISK PLAYER

Alan M. Schwartz

Our cat Flash is wholly psychotic in a fang-baring, claw-ripping, flat-eared, back-buckling, hair-on-end, pussycat-from-Hell sort of way. We have a good working relationship with Flash, and a pair of extra-heavy leather gloves for emergencies. He keeps the neighborhood rug rats, ankle biters, linoleum lizards, curtain climbers, diaper demons, and yard apes bloodied and at bay. He is punctilious in his exclusive use of his litter box. We vigorously haul the most odorous wet and dry cat food to his feeding dishes, and diligently, nay, zealously, haul away cylindrical abundances of fuming cat waste securely Baggied for the homeless to discover each Monday before trash collection.

Each evening Flash is wont to perch six feet above ground level on the cable-unscrambler box resting on the VHS player resting on the amplifier resting on the laser-disk player resting on the 36-inch television. One night my lady and I were snuggled on the couch, nibbling on popcorn and each other, giggling and watching our laser disk of *Silence of the Lambs*. Flash was balled atop his favorite throne. The disk reached its end, the foot-square slide extruded from its module, and I removed the platter preparatory to replacing it with its mate. In one fluid motion our stupid killer cat attacked the slide.

A laser-disk player bearing an American manufacturer's label is in truth trash too awful for even Ashtabula, Ohio. Had we owned such, the wallop of a ten-pound cat plunging down from on high would have snapped the thing clean off. Cat and component would have continued to the floor and encountered our extreme displeasure. Oh, no! Ours was a Pioneer CLD-3080. It was guaranteed forever against anything short of a thermonuclear detonation. Flash slammed into its tray, and Japanese engineering rolled with the punch. The impact sensor triggered the safety circuits. The side retracted and, with it, Flash.

His carnivorous feline cerebrum immediately recognized an enemy more implacable than a Democratic Congressional majority. He screamed his foreboding as his head, body, and butt were sucked into the electronics. Digital mysteries unfolded as the mechanism whirred, spinning up for its anticipated conventional operation. Flash howled. His tail stuck straight out and quivered. The slide could not open until it cycled. I grabbed a handful of popcorn, and waited.

You have seen laser disks. They are variously sized silvered platters shimmering with all the diffractive colors of the rainbow. White light betrays its wavelike nature as it is massaged across billions of microscopic pits encoding the laser disk's information. You have seen cats' eyes. They are glowing caverns of murderous intent shimmering in dark corners. A good laser-disk player accommodates both constant-linear-velocity and constant-angular-velocity formats. It will play music disks through the stereo. It will play music and video disks through the stereo and the TV. It will obviously play movie laser disks. It will also apparently play cat squinties bulging from Flash's eye sockets. You have to respect the engineering excellence that delivered such capable technology to our lives.

Much to our amazement, feline retinas encode data dynamically interpretable by our laser disk player—in full color and surround sound. We stared into the face of God and heard His voice! There still was lots of popcorn.

I suppose nomadic shepherds accustomed to making their way through the day by compromising the dry-land ecology of the Sinai might have been impressed. Anyone who has weathered the freeway snafu from a three-car injury accident is tougher than that. Anyone who can listen to Dan Quayle exercising his larynx and recognize the noise for the nonsense that it is has the analytical skills to scoff at a spiritual libretto. We gave it two stars, since it was deficient in both plot and character development, and required an unreasonable suspension of disbelief. I propose a thorough Stephen King rewrite, and a lot more gratuitous nudity.

I hit the STOP button on the remote control, and Flash's tail went limp. The EJECT button disgorged the slide, and with it one very pissed pussycat. A brown streak tore up one living-room wall, did a quick fur-burning circuit of the room, and launched itself into the master bedroom. I looked at my honey, shrugged, and put in the second disk. Dr. Lechter's evolving triumph consumed our attention. We returned to nibbling and giggling as Flash howled and spat at the bureau mirror. Dinner had been liver with fava beans and a brusque chianti. We were content.

CHAPTER 49

MY LOVE, MY FROG

Alan M. Schwartz

The Drug War was brutally waged, spilling blood on every field. Soldiers in Kevlar armor caressed very big guns. They strode the land, arrogantly scorning the laws of God and man, and seizing their victims' treasure as their own. Doors splintered at a flick of their indomitable will. Women screamed, men bled, children were born as monsters and grew into animals. Money flowed from government coffers to mix with and solemnly purify field discoveries. Vehicles, weaponry, crisp uniforms, and the bitter metallic essence of dread were freely bestowed and gleefully wielded. Heroin, PCP, cocaine, reds, crystal meth, XTC, and, during the slowest of times, a hundredweight or a single seed of marijuana gave our warriors' lives meaning. President Bush had a grand time of it all. They were the Arm of the President, and ladled a generous portion of ruin into the laps of those who displeased Him. Another He was offended by that capitalized personal pronoun, and with extreme executive displeasure proceeded to snap an Ecuadorian tree frog up the Bushman's nose.

Epipedobates tricolor (call it Bob) is a brilliantly tinted mote of slimy amphibian nonchalance plucking an occasional fly from the local miasmic rain forest. It has no natural enemies, because a single tiny frog contains within its skin enough frightful chemistry to rub out a water buffalo. Dendrobatid frogs have recently come to suffer the energetic predation of NIH grantees. They take our tax money, humidly party south of the border, grab a few frogs on their last afternoon, and return. Lab technicians wearing heavy rubber gloves flense the frogs and inject skin extracts into mice, whereupon interesting and unusual things happen. This justifies more grant applications and field trips.

Bob the frog was discovered to harbor within his dermis a trace of mammalian ecstasy christened epibatidine. Unripe poppy seed pods are excised to exude tears of opium, which contains morphine, the biochemical stuff of intense dreamy pleasure. Epibatidine is 1,000 times as potent as morphine. It is a tiny, simple, pretty molecule. It is orally active. Its bewitchment resists abatement by narcotic antagonists like nalorphine, naloxone, or naltrexone. It begs for creative elaboration by clever organic chemists, college sophomores, and Third World entrepreneurs.

Bob the frog became big business. Labfulls of mice traditionally dedicated to a chronic pedestrian dreariness of tobacco, saccharine, and shoe-polish ingestion came alive! Murine tails arched high with froggy bliss (the Straub response). Animal Rights activists hustled into a right-eous frenzy. They looted and burned animal-testing labs, while waving their Bibles like battle standards and appropriating a few purified froggy samples to take home to their mistresses.

Ten milligrams of morphine dissolved and intravenously injected, a pinhead of powder, will deliver you into heaven for an hour. Ten micro-grams of epibatidine swilled or sniffed, a dust mote, is an express elevator to the stars. Twenty micrograms, two dust motes, will kill you. This is an explicit contraindication of repeat business. This is a bad thing. However, acetyl epibatidine is metabolized so slowly that sustained release formula-tions are safe and stupendous and, pending legislation, absolutely legal. Frog ho!

The single circumstance more inimical to Puritanism than a bunch of people having a good time is a bunch of people having a good time in a way that doesn't allow censorious Puritans to also wallow in it under the guise of its discovery and eradication. An emergency Presidential decree rang across the land. Happy Bob and all its derivatives were classified as Class I Drugs, feloniously illegal to use under any circumstances, and absolutely denied to writhing cancer patients, screaming burn survivors, shattered accident victims, mutilated soldiers, and inner-city residents. The White House staff, Congressmen, magistrates, and law-enforcement cadres scored huge supplies of the stuff, but they had to be discreet.

The Bush crisis exploded. His major supporters—South American cocainistas, Southeast Asian poppy lords, and Mexican marijuana grow-ers—were bankrupted by American garage chemists slipping mercy through hospital back doors and the other 99.9 percent of their production underground. An ounce of Happy Bob could get three million people high. There was not much media glamour to be had exhibiting a dozen heavily armed drug enforcers surrounding an aspirin tablet. With $250 billion in annual drug profits now staying within its borders, the Ameri-can economy blossomed.

This is fiction. The American economy is irretrievably moribund. We have government regulation, taxation, corruption, and MBAs to thank for that. Pass me a Happy Bob to ease my pain.

CHAPTER 50

NOTHING IS IMPOSSIBLE

J. Albert Geerken

From the time I was first able to speculate and philosophize about existence, the world around us, the universe, and the whole range of observable phenomena, I have been stymied by an annoying, frustrating problem—I can't imagine nothing. Lest I be accused of using improper grammar, let me explain. What I am speaking of is my total inability to form an idea of a state of affairs or condition signified by the complete absence of any and all things of which we are conscious. What this boils down to is an alternative to "creation" as we know it, i.e., no creation at all, nothing.

As any alert reader will have noted, merely writing about nothing is bound to get us all tangled up in nonsensical verbiage. Above, for instance, I used the terms "state of affairs," "condition," and "creation." In the nothing we are discussing here, there can be no affairs by definition; in the case of "condition," used in the sense of "state of being," I came up with the absurdity of "a state of being of non-being" and, for want of a better single word, when I used "creation" I implied that the first law of thermodynamics had been repealed. These examples, and others that will follow, show that it is exceedingly difficult to write about nothing. In fact, this entire exercise may turn out to be nothing short of futile, but let us see what develops.

Upon consulting Webster's, to see how the definition of "nothing" was handled there, we find, not surprisingly, nothing of a positive nature: "1. no-thing; not anything; nought; opposed to anything, something. 2. a) lack of existence; nonexistence; nothingness, (and other meanings, not applicable). 3. a thing that does not exist." Now, we cannot quarrel about the meanings under (1) and (2), although they shed precious little light on our subject, but under (3) we again are running into a paradox. If a thing does not exist, how in the world can it be a thing?

Groping for a positive expression denoting "nothing," I hit upon the noun "void," defined as "that which is void; an empty space; vacuum." I underlined "that," for its meaning is "something," a word we cannot allow. On the surface of it, an empty space or vacuum might seem acceptable, but further investigation will disclose that those terms, likewise, will not do.

In the final instance, the search for an alternative to all we know through our senses and abstract reasoning amounts to what we will have to call the "status quo" (another misnomer) before the universe came into being, assuming it had a beginning. In the Bible, the first paragraph of Genesis tells us that "in the beginning, God created the heavens and the earth. The earth was without form and void, and darkness was upon the face of the deep (what deep?); and the Spirit of God was moving over the face of the waters" (waters in a void?). Not much help there, in a scientific way.

If before the beginning, there was a void, nothing, there was no land (to hold the waters up), no water (of course), no air, no light, no sound, no heat (just absolute zero); there was no solar system, no earth, no life, not even a microbe; there were no stars, galaxies, or nebulae; there was no energy, no matter, whether in gaseous, liquid, or solid state, not a particle, not a solitary atom, nothing but nothing.

Going back to the definition of a "void," we note that it was described as "an empty space, a vacuum." Looking up the meaning of "space," we discover that it is not empty at all: "distance extending without limit in all directions; boundless, continuous expanse. . . ., *within which all material things are contained*." Another example of lexicographers unable to cope with the definitions of fundamental concepts. So we will have to do a little thinking of our own to solve the mystery of nothing.

In the absence of matter, energy, or particles, there is no need of space to contain them. Therefore, most likely, in the "nothing" we are thinking of there would be no space, and, hence, according to the theory of relativity, no time, no "continuum." But for a "Spirit" to do anything, it needs energy. Hence, the Bible story of creation does not make sense. A void with energy is not a void, if we may be pardoned, once more, for using nonsensical terminology. Better would have been, "nothing has no energy," but there, again, we would run the risk of it being misread.

By careful analysis we have now arrived at absolutely nothing. However, we must not forget that we have done so on the assumption that the universe had a beginning. Without a beginning there could not have been a "before," in all its nothingness. On the other hand, we are aware that, "nothing comes from nothing; nothing ever could" (just another way of stating the "First Law"). Now, since we do have a universe, and we do know that it could not have come about from nothing, we can only conclude that it never had a beginning, that it always was. And, we must ruefully admit that all our speculation about nothing has led to nothing, to the notion that, in fact, nothing is impossible, or was impossible, because energy, in whatever form, can no more be destroyed than it can be created; so there is not a ghost of a chance that there will be nothing in the future. Changes and transformations will take place, but there will always be something, even if it is only one gigantic black hole, if that's any consolation.

In case this profound dissertation should seem to be much ado about nothing, all I can say is: "Think nothing of it."

CHAPTER 51

Dumb

ONLY GOD CAN MAKE A TREE

Kent L. Aldershof

The first genetic-conjunction children had been born. All four fertilizations had succeeded, and all four volunteer surrogate mothers had carried the fetuses to term. That alone was a significant scientific accomplishment.

Dr. Morrow's report read, "All four births occurred within an eight-day timespan. Three were normal deliveries, one was Caesarean. Two are male, two female. All infants appear virtually normal, with exceptions noted below, and all birthweights lie within the upper quartile for typical healthy mothers. No illness has appeared in any infant since delivery. Feeding and sleeping behaviors are normal. Reflexes are similar to those of ordinary infants."

This group of unremarkable observations continued, with a somewhat more breathtaking paragraph. "Genetic testing has confirmed that conjunction occurred as planned. All four infants have stable 44-chromosome cellular structure, with the two conjoined chromosomes approximately equaling the combined lengths of the four elements which were paired. The demonstrated stability, without apparent loss of prior genetic contribution . . ."; and the report continued, with deepening scientific jargon.

For the uninitiated, the remarkable news in that report is the number 44. Humans typically have 46 chromosomes—those lengthy, dual-helix DNA spirals that encode our individual genetic heritage and structure; blueprints of the body, formed by tens of thousands of interlinked protein molecules. Many of the so-called lower animals have more chromosomes, but they are shorter chains. Other, simpler animals have fewer and smaller chromosomes (such as mice, with 44; or fruit flies, with eight).

Half the chromosomes are inherited from the father, half from the mother. Each reproductive cell, each sperm and ovum, contains half the individual's chromosomes: a single chromosome randomly selected from each of our 23 pairs of two. When those cells merge, a new 46-chromosome individual is created.

One of the most stirring of modern biochemical discoveries is how chromosomes can be modified to create similar, but distinct, species. That can happen by changing the character of one or more chromosomes, or by adding more genetic information to individual chromosomes, or occasionally by joining two chromosomes together.

Sometimes that occurs in nature. Horses have 64 chromosomes, donkeys have 62. They are inter-fertile; and when they mate, they produce a mule—or a "hinny" should the male parent be a horse—with 63 chromosomes (32 from one parent, 31 from the other). The breeding unites the unequal numbers of parental chromosomes, leading to a creature different from either parent, but sharing many characteristics of both. Mules or hinnies, of course, are only rarely able to bear their own offspring.

Most new species of any importance are not sterile like the mule. They have even numbers of chromosomes, but the length or the composition of their chromosomes differs from those of the parents. There are at least two million living species now on earth, and uncounted millions have perished and become extinct. Each of those species, past and present, has had a unique chromosomal makeup. Each new species was defined when an offspring was in some way produced with a genetic composition different from that of its parents.

Dr. Morrow and his team gave the most intensive attention and care to these four infants. None like them had ever appeared on Earth, so far as was known. Theirs was a most remarkable scientific achievement.

The infants were named Dawn, Starr, Thor, and Adam.

Primates—the monkeys and the apes—have 48 chromosomes. Scientists have identified two pairs of primate chromosomes which, in ancient times, evidently fused end to end like two garden hoses being hooked together. One human chromosome (number 2, our second-longest, which indicates that it carries the second-largest amount of genetic information) exactly matches the end-to-end joining of two primate chromosomes. That discovery produced a Nobel Prize.

No one knows why or how the conjoining occurred, nor how it propagated from a lone individual into his or her offspring and eventually became stable through the generations. All human males and females possess that merged chromosome. Each parent now contributes 23 chromosomes to the child, instead of the 24 which primates contribute. That is the major way in which humans are chromosomally different from primates. Those species, of course, are not inter-fertile.

The children were orphans, in the most complete sense possible. The genetic material from which they were made came from no living human. The original sperm and ovum from which they developed had been physically and chemically manipulated, modified with temperature and radiation, and assembled as a composite from contributions of many anonymous donors. Their genes could be matched with those of no other living beings. They were unique; humanoid, yet almost—or perhaps—a new species.

Chromosomal breakdown produces a genetically altered individual. When a single human chromosome (number 22, generally) breaks in half during gestation, for reasons not well understood, the result is a 47-chromosome Down's Syndrome child. They are equally human, but have facial, bodily, and mental characteristics somewhat different from those of normal 46-chromosome people. (A clinically similar condition occasionally occurs in primates, such as chimpanzees, as well.)

Chromosomal fusion evidently occurs as well. It also produces a genetically altered individual. It is apparently the source of many new species.

The unmistakable chromosomal fusion that eventually produced humans almost certainly occurred first in a single individual. His or her offspring would have been 47-chromosome beings; yet it is clear that at least some of those must have been fertile. The inevitable interbreeding with siblings, as occurs in the natural world, would have led to some 46-chromosome offspring—the origin of humanity.

Yet some offspring of those fertile 47-chromosome individuals would also have had 47 chromosomes, perpetuating the anomaly. They may have been fertile, with a stable genetic structure. There is good evidence of the existence of the Yeti (also called the Abominable Snowman), the Sasquatch, and other ape-like yet humanoid wild creatures. None has been captured, no remains have been found, so there is no concrete information about any of them. Is it possible that those creatures represent the continuing blood-lines of our 47-chromosome ancestors, the fertile link between modern man and the great apes? Such speculation must be tabled, until physical evidence proves or disproves the hypothesis.

There is little scientific appeal in attempting to create a viable, 47-chromosome being by splitting the number-2 chromosome of one parent, except to find out what such a retrograde, semi-human being would be like. Such births may occur rarely, for natural reasons not yet understood. There are records and even photographs of offspring whom human women brought forth: exceptionally hairy, physically deformed, and mentally limited children, bearing a strong resemblance to apes. A very few recorded cases exist of such mutations surviving to adulthood. All of those occurred before modern understanding of genetic makeup. There is no way to know now whether such births did produce 47-chromosome "people" or were simply the fault of some other genetic accident.

The advent of molecular biology and the success in altering specific DNA components—a science commonly called "genetic engineering"—led Dr. Morrow and his associates to a bold concept: if two pairs of primate genes had in some unknown way fused, producing the human, with such spectacularly advanced qualities relative to those of the primate, might not certain other human genes be fused to produce a yet more capable successor?

Dr. Morrow had no idea whether any chromosomes could be fused artificially. If they could, the normal replication process would perpetuate the new configuration. The real questions were: which chromosomes should be joined? What would the results be? More than a thousand chromosomal-fusion possibilities had to be investigated.

A governmentally funded program had been commissioned. The first 253 attempts at chromosomal fusion were failures. Though certain elements had been conjoined, either gestation proved impossible or the fetuses were severely malformed and miscarried. On the 254th effort, with a previously untried pairing, Morrow and his brave scientists had succeeded, at least in producing viable human children from genetically altered fertilized ova.

Prior to Morrow's work, molecular biologists had concentrated on identifying the individual regions and components of human genes that were responsible for genetically transmitted deficits, inherited susceptibilities, and unusual strengths passed from parent to child. The hope was to transplant more desirable genetic material to specific sites, either to produce healthier offspring or to enhance certain favorable qualities.

Such work had been done for generations in animals and plants, by selective breeding, which accomplishes the same ends, but in a clumsier manner. The molecular biologists hoped to achieve their purposes in an exquisitely focused, controlled procedure.

Those were not trivial challenges. Altogether there are more than 100,000 locations on the chromosomes that control human characteristics. They encode everything from the number of legs to one's predisposition to pimples. By the last decade of the twentieth century, less than 3 percent of those genetic sites had been mapped and defined.

Once the scientists found the location that controlled a certain characteristic, such as inherited muscular dystrophy, they then had to discover how modify it to correct the flaw. Then they had to make that change, test the results, and introduce it into a host human body.

As daring as those experiments were, many succeeded. Unlocking the secrets of the DNA spiral permitted people to influence and improve the characteristics of their children. Major, crippling diseases and deformities were eliminated from humanity. Genetically altered humans were healthier and performed better, just as when breedlines were improved in animals or cultivars were improved in plants.

Dr. Morrow and his team were drunk with elation at the births. They extended that to a lengthy celebration, at which party they all became jubilantly drunk with alcohol. "My God, we did it! Can you imagine? We did it!!" was the most common discussion that evening. It was most unaccustomed behavior for the ordinarily austere and dedicated scientists.

The four babies, in their nursery two stories above, slept through the entire party.

As with much other government-sponsored scientific work, Dr. Morrow's project and his achievements were kept Top Secret—Priority Access Required. Until the outcomes were known, the political risks from failure were too large for ordinary citizens to be advised of the actions of their legally elected representatives.

Further, if these children proved to have some sort of superiority—then of course that knowledge could not be willy-nilly released to a world still suffering international tensions. Best to stay under wraps, even if it took years. Hence the work was being conducted in a specially constructed and isolated hospital-laboratory, located at a remote weapons-storage site in the Nevada desert. Few places in the world had such tight security.

The first goal of the project had been to find out if chromosomes could be joined by biochemical manipulation, as sometimes apparently had occurred spontaneously in nature. That had been shown. The next goal was to find out if a chromosomally altered ovum could produce viable infants. That too was demonstrated. The next goal was to find out how these infants would differ from typical humans.

A highlight of Morrow's report was the section titled "Abnormalities and Super-Normalities." Another interesting fact emerged there. He wrote "X-ray and NMR examinations of the infants reveal normal organs, in conventional positions; but 212 bones exist instead of the ordinary 206. There is a deformity of the scapulae, with the emergence of vestigial or apparently incomplete auxiliary upper limbs."

What he meant was that all the babies seemed to have extra, but incomplete, right and left arms. Their shoulder bones, or scapulae, each contained a ball and-socket joint similar to that in the normal shoulder, but positioned a bit lower than the shoulder. Into each of these unexpected joints was articulated a single bone, somewhat similar to the humerus, or upper arm bone. Attached to that were a pair of bones, mimicking the radius and the ulna of the normal forearm. There were no wrist or hand bones, however. It was the only evident deformity, and all the infants shared it.

These "extra arms," as the nurses began to call them, laid down across the babies' backs, more or less parallel to the spine. They were rarely moved, unlike the vigorous arm and leg gestures which the babies otherwise exhibited during nearly every waking moment. The children were able to lie on them, and to sleep, without apparent discomfort.

The report continued, "These appendages have little musculature or fat, and no apparent function. Their greatest peculiarity is that they are fastened to the back by a web of flesh. The limbs can be raised more than 90 degrees from the back, with the fleshy web flattening to accommodate the movement. It is a region well-supplied with nerves and blood vessels, but these limbs seem otherwise as useless as one's appendix or toenails."

The chromosomal-pairing work resumed with expanded intensity and, of course, with enlarged funding. Secrecy was redoubled. However, after that success Dr. Morrow's group were unable to find other combinable genetic pairs. Except for the single spectacular success, the project ran into a complete dead end.

The children grew, as children do. They were all somewhat precocious, but that was tentatively attributed to the extensive attention they received from the adults about them. Their only deprivation was that they did not mingle with other children, but they had plenty of stimulation and entertainment otherwise, and appeared to be socially well-adjusted. They were uncommonly attached to one another, rarely squabbling, and generally exceptionally considerate of each other. That too was tentatively ascribed to their close association as playmates and schoolmates, and to the absence of other children in their environment

Beyond these, the only other notable characteristics of the children were their unusual good health, and their conspicuously large stature. They had no illnesses—no colic, no colds, no flu, and none of the typical childhood diseases. Of course, they were vaccinated against most diseases, they were somewhat sheltered, and they were exceptionally well-nourished. Dr. Morrow privately felt that "his" children's health and size probably represented the potential for all children, if parents would properly tend to nutrition, exercise, and disease prevention.

They were wonderful kids. Dawn was pale blond and intensely blue-eyed, with very fair skin. Starr was dark, almost swarthy, with deep black eyes, ebony hair, and flesh the color of walnut shells. Thor was middle-European in appearance—medium skin, medium-brown hair, medium-hazel eyes, and medium in stature between Adam and the girls. Adam, the largest, had curly dark hair yet pale blue eyes. Of all the children, Adam suntanned the most readily. Together, they were a beautiful group, with their natural appearances always enhanced by bright smiles and enthusiastic laughter.

These were hardly abnormalities; they were exactly the way all parents hope their children will develop. Other than the peculiar "extra arms," no exceptional characteristics appeared as the children grew through childhood. Dr. Morrow and his staff were hard-pressed to find enough to say in their monthly reports to justify sustaining the project funding each year after the subsequent work proved unsuccessful. There was some talk among the bureaucrats of amputating the odd limbs, returning the children to the everyday world, and terminating the study. It seemed that little was being learned, except for the benefits of careful and attentive nurturing.

Dr. Morrow cajoled and pleaded. "Too soon, too soon," was his frequently repeated advice to the skeptics. "We need to wait until they are past puberty and adolescence, so that we can know the genetic impact in the adults." The skeptics remained skeptical. However, the interest in discovering their potential fertility, their interfertility with ordinary humans, and their ultimate growth patterns overwhelmed the budget-cutters. The project was continued.

About their tenth year, all the children became moody and withdrawn. Ordinary parents, themselves having experienced that pattern as children, are yet unable to understand it and rarely can cope well with it. So it was with the four quasi-orphans and their caretakers. As new hormones began to circulate, they became private, silent, and unsocial. They spent virtually every free moment together, unenthusiastic about consorting with their adult friends and teachers. They were responsive to instruction in the little school which had been built for them, but showed little initiative or sincere interest. All four of the children had become, in a word, normal young pre-teenagers.

As is typical, they experienced spurts of growth, with the girls slightly ahead of the boys. All became leggy and gangly, as they became more muscular simultaneously. None could wear their clothes in a natural or well-fitting manner. They all insisted on wearing baggy smocks, in preference to their previous carefully fitted custom-made shirts and blouses.

The major change happened almost overnight. Within weeks, all four suddenly grew sets of wings! The strange, useless "extra arms" expanded, cartilage was added, and the fleshy webs sprouted feathers. In a matter of weeks, the wings grew above the childrens' heads, cresting in a graceful arc of feathers that grew downward nearly to the ground.

Dr. Morrow and the staff were astonished, and he reported the unexpected development with great caution; yet however he tried to word it, the apparent conclusion was unavoidable. The children were growing into beings that looked like what folklore and some religious teachings called angels.

By their twelfth birthdays, the four appeared fully developed. Each was larger than most normal adults. They were extravagantly beautiful, with a rich golden shimmer to their wings, and an almost radiant appearance to their faces. The characteristic smiles and laughter had returned. The few observers privileged to see the children felt that there was an unusual quality to their appearances, some describing it as a sort of glow or a halo effect.

The Congressional overseers were rather uneasy about it. News of this new human-form would be decidedly unsettling to many voters. The military observers were even more uneasy. Most of them anxiously suspected that these angel-children might have qualities that could make them formidable enemies, if they could not be harnessed as fighters for The Right and The Good—meaning, of course, Our Nation.

The unsettled feelings were reinforced as the children increasingly began to communicate among themselves in a language they had invented on their own. Although there were attempts to record and to interpret it, the finest linguists could make nothing of the peculiar sounds and hummings. When asked, the children would only say "Just murmuring . . . no real meaning."

The suspicious feelings intensified as the children learned to fly. They could rise at least a hundred feet with a single beat of their beautiful golden wings. Despite repeated requests and warnings, they frequently took off on steadily longer, unscheduled journeys as a group. Worse yet, they could not be located or tracked with radar. Neither were helicopters or aircraft able to follow them. As they flew away, they simply disappeared into the direction of the Sun.

Ordinarily the children returned by nightfall, but they would never discuss where they had been or what they had done. They were not obstinate nor argumentative; they just smiled. Adam, who was generally the spokesman, simply said "out for exercise." Dr. Morrow became distinctly uneasy at that. His funding sources, and their military advisors, became downright paranoid about it.

"They must be controlled," came the order; "for who knows what they are doing, or plotting, when they have vanished? How can we know how dangerous they might be, when they will tell us nothing of their expeditions?" As the angel-children would not discuss any form of control over flights, and would not report their whereabouts or their doings while away, the lack of information became a confirmation of people's worst fears. They must be doing something wrong, something dangerous. They had to be controlled.

Various proposals were offered: clip the wings; amputate the wings; imprison the children in windowless buildings; tether them to the ground with long cords or chains; interrogate them under drugs if necessary; affix cameras to their backs, to record their travels. Some approaches were more far-fetched, such as asking the children to take an ordinary mortal along on their voyages.

The times away from the secret base became more frequent, and more protracted. The lid of secrecy became yet tighter. Unknown to Dr. Morrow and his aides, reports began to filter in to the nation's data-monitoring networks. UFO sightings declined, as people around the world reported visitations of extraterrestrials, strange winged beings who would appear unexpectedly and could evidently disappear at will, beings who spoke with foreign citizens, and on occasion with foreign officials and even military personnel. Yet, although the visitors could be seen, touched, and heard, their images could not be captured on photographs; only a strange smear or blur appeared on the films.

It became clear to the policymakers that a threat to national security existed. This was a special threat, because the source could not be combated nor controlled. Dr. Morrow was advised, then instructed, and finally ordered to restrain the chromosomally altered children. He either could not, or would not, comply. Finally, certain Primary Top Secret orders were issued. In response, one summer evening a report was beamed to a satellite by a member of the child-care staff, who had from the beginning carried dual loyalty. She advised as requested that the winged children had returned from one of their voyages, and were sleeping.

Operation Wingclip was activated.

From a remote North Dakota airbase, a B-5 Protector defensive bomber was ordered to make an unscheduled training run. At a certain point in the course, the pilot was to launch a dummy Black Widow thermonuclear air-to-ground missile, to test retaliatory accuracy under simulated emergency conditions.

The missile's target coordinates had been programmed into its inertial navigation system prior to the flight by ground crews. Those target vectors were relative, not absolute; where the dummy missile would explode depended on the point from which it was launched. Where it was to be launched was recorded only on the secret flight instructions exhibited on the B-5's flight-control computer screen after the aircraft was well into its mission.

Long before, in anticipation of such need, a fully armed Black Widow missile had been included among the training stocks, without notification of its character. The orders issued that night specifically called for that particular pseudo-dummy missile to be loaded aboard the Protector. A Security Flamer chamber then consumed the only record indicating that the missile was at all different from any other in the warehouse.

The programming was exquisitely accurate. The Black Widow, launched at 50,000 feet above the Earth, traveled 340 miles on its own propulsion system, moving at nearly Mach 3. It detonated precisely above the Nevada experimental station, 7,000 feet into the atmosphere. A section of desert eight miles in diameter was fused into radioactive glass. The shock wave was felt in Denver, Los Angeles, and Albuquerque.

Almost immediately, the military released news stories about the accidental explosion of a major thermonuclear device in the Nevada storage facility. They described in elaborate detail how the multiple safety and control systems must have simultaneously failed or been sabotaged.

The four angel-children, Dr. Morrow, and 657 other humans perished in the fireball. The land would bear no further life of any sort for more than ten thousand years henceforward. There was no possibility of entering the site to investigate the disaster, nor (as was later revealed by spy satellite photographs) was there anything material remaining to examine.

It was a beastly action, but of course the pilot of the B-5 Protector knew nothing of the explosion. He had, as instructed, launched; then immediately headed his aircraft east at a velocity almost equal to the westward velocity of the presumed dummy missile.

Shortly before the Nevada explosion, a Python strategic response fighter was scrambled from an Illinois base, on a performance demonstration mission. The purpose was to indicate the ability of the aircraft to detect and track a high-speed drone, and destroy it using the newly developed Ferret laser-guided air-to-air missile. The Python's radar spotted the drone as intended. Both of its Ferrets were launched, and the drone was blown to fragments.

Scratch one B-5 Protector and crew. Upon returning to base, the Python suffered an unfortunate collapse of its landing gear. That can have severe consequences in a 200-knot contact with the runway. The Python disappeared in a ball of flame that hurtled for more than a mile along the concrete strip.

Dead men file no debriefing reports. They are also unable to talk with congressional investigators, or with the news media. Such is the military mind.

Dr. Morrow passed through his own Birthing, and became a neophyte angel. It was, of course, a marvelous process, filled with wonder and astonishment. He was humbled and immensely grateful for his own redemption, as newly made angels always are.

After the Awakening and the Rebirth, after the Welcoming and the Investiture, and after all the other Ceremonies of Renewal and the Triumphal Homecoming, Dr. Morrow still carried some residual curiosity about his now unimportant earthly life and its untimely end. He waited until after the Investiture, the Regarbing, The Serenade of the Mixed Choirs, and The Adoration of Deity to express his inquiry.

The officiating Archangel was only too happy to fill in the details and the necessary explanation. "We were most fascinated by your experiments," he said. "The last time we saw angels like that was when Lucifer and his bunch of mutants occurred. That too was part of The Greater Plan, even though naturally we had to throw them out of Heaven." The Archangel continued, "Your four, of course, we have simply redeemed and rebirthed. They have become full-fledged real angels just like you. And just as have the other, um, 661 souls I believe. You will be together with them all, shortly."

Dr. Morrow, still dazed by his unexpected elevation to angelhood, was genuinely confused. "Other angels like that? Mutants? What does that mean?" he inquired.

"Well, you were on the right track," replied the Archangel. "You created what we call Mule Angels. Real angels have only 42 chromosomes."